Educating Tiger

My spiritual

and

intellectual journey

Jacob A. Loewen

ISBN 1-877941-08-5

Tabor College, Hillsboro, KS 67063

Contact Peggy Goertzen
Center for Brethren Studies
Hillsboro, Kansas
for the information
E-mail address: peggyg@tcnet.tabor.edu

Sales Representative, Mennonite Books
844-K McLeod Avenue
Winnipeg, Manitoba R2G 2T7

DEDICATION

This book is dedicated to all my grandchildren:

By birth: Andrew, Nicolas, Karissa, Kimberly, Jason and Adam

By marriage: Allison and Jennifer

By immigration: Trung, Ngon, Trang, Trinh and Huong

By honorary appointment: Shanti and Sarah Justine

THANKS!

I want to thank:

1. The Center for Mennonite Brethren Studies, Hillisboro.
2. Wally Kroeker and Lori Matties for their capable editing.
3. Carole Springthorpe for producing the printable manuscript.
4. Delbert Wiens for his creative foreword.
5. The many who were willing to educate Tiger.

Note to all readers:

The experiences here described and the opinions here expressed are entirely my own and many aren't even final. Other people who participated in some of the experiences may have very different recollections—a fact amply borne out by our own children's recollections. The experiences here recounted are retold from my personal perspective. All conclusions, not only the tentative ones, are my very own. They do not necessarily reflect the opinions of either the MB Church, or Tabor College, or the Center for MB Studies which has graciously agreed to publish this volume.

FOREWORD

Upon Reading the autobiography of Jacob A. Loewen

Tiger, tiger, burning bright
In the forests of the night,
What immortal hand or eye
Could frame thy fearful symmetry?
from "The Tiger" by William Blake.

"Stop, Tiger! I have to let my soul catch up with me." Jake chuckled as he told the story. "You see," he explained, "they identify their soul with their breath, and there is danger that a demon could snatch it away from them when they become winded." Jake was telling us about other worldviews. I have become more impressed with what it told me about Jake.

The indigenous Indians of the eastern Colombian jungle recognized that something about his character called for the nickname Tiger. And it seems entirely fitting to me that Jake was out-pacing his native guide along a forest trail.

Jake's "tigerish" qualities have enabled him to explore many trails. He has helped missionary translators to publish the Scriptures in dozens of languages. He has contributed much to the contemporary theology and theory of missions. He has helped non-Western peoples to fit the truths and virtues of their older ethos into Christian patterns. He has mediated many quarrels. He has helped to transform our thinking about other cultures and religions. And he has helped those of us who share his heritage to understand ourselves better. Those historians to come who track our Mennonite Brethren passage into and beyond modernity will honor this prophet.

But these same qualities help to explain why some of us wished that he would sometimes have stopped, at least for awhile, to let our souls catch up with us. Those who would most profit from this book may also need to pause to let their souls catch up with them.

> *When the stars threw down their spears,*
> *And water'd heaven with their tears,*
> *Did He smile His work to see?*
> *Did He who made the lamb make thee?*
> from "The Tiger" (verse 5)

William Blake also wrote "The Lamb," in which he asks the lamb if it knows its maker, and answers:

> *Little Lamb, I'll tell thee,*
> *Little Lamb, I'll tell thee:*
> *He is called by thy name,*
> *For He calls Himself a Lamb.*
> *He is meek, and He is mild;*
> *He became a little child.*
> *I a child, and thou a lamb,*
> *We are called by His name.*
> *Little Lamb, God bless thee!*
> *Little Lamb, God bless thee!*

In telling his life story, Jake tells us that the massive stroke he suffered has become his opportunity to stop and to let his soul catch up with him. This last October (1997) he responded to my comments in a letter to him about my own not very damaging heart attack.

> The account of your experience with your ticker is sobering. I find it interesting that God has to resort to some pretty drastic methods to get our attention. The stroke certainly got mine and I am deeply grateful....I am sure your experience has given you pause. I am glad that God could get your attention with a much lighter call. I needed a big jolt.

And so Jake, confined to an apartment now, is walking down another kind of trail, the trail of suffering that leads to Christ-likeness. And this book is his gift to us. He allows us to look in on the travail of his soul. The final trail he walks, while sitting still, is a trail that we all must someday walk. Some of his thoughts may not be our thoughts, but he, and then we, have to be responsible for them before God.

But is it possible for a tiger to become a lamb? Could we even want a tiger to become a lamb? No, that cannot be what God wants! Perhaps that is why Jake, and others of us, have to halt so long. So how can the tiger join with the lamb? Surely it must be possible. This book is itself a testimony to the tigerish qualities of ruthless persistence that it takes to be honest with oneself. It is also an example of lamblike vulnerability that we are permitted to observe and to learn from his baring of himself.

How ironic! Back in the early 60's when Jake was urging us to become completely honest and transparent, I demurred. I still hope that there is something to say for "my" truth that, ever since Eden, it is appropriate for us to preserve at least an apron around our psyches, except before God. But I now gladly admit my appreciation for the tigerish stubbornness with which Jake has made himself as vulnerable as a lamb for our edification. And I am the grateful recipient of letters which reveal that the qualities of the tiger and the lamb can be joined without losing the real virtues of either.

And that joining, of course, is exactly what one would expect for those who are walking the way of Christlikeness. Ancient Palestinians knew very little about tigers, but they did have lions in their wilderness in the old days. And when the disciples reflected about the Jesus who had made himself known to them, they also came up with nicknames: the Lamb of God was one; the Lion of Judah was another. And they cherished the promise that the lion would one day lie down with the lamb. And so, Jake, we are privileged to paraphrase the conclusion of Blake's poem:

Tiger-Lamb, God bless thee!
Tiger-Lamb, God bless thee!

Delbert Wiens, October 1997 (September 1998)

PREFACE

Autobiography by its very nature is intensely personal. It is a genre so private as to make the readers at times uncomfortable, as he is permitted glimpses into the travail of a person's soul, attempting to sort out situations and observations, circumstances and reflections, seeking truth. The process is at once refreshing and disturbing.

Consider the young couple on the ridge. "Look, isn't the moon beautiful?" "Where, where, I can't see it." "Look, look over there, isn't the moon beautiful?" "Oh, there it is, I finally see it." The two came together. It is not so much that the young lady is looking for the moon in the wrong place but that she is looking at the moon from a different angle.

Truth is truth. Truth cannot be altered by viewing it from a different angle. Jake Loewen's autobiographical account allows us an opportunity to peer at truth from a different angle.

Peggy Goertzen, Director
Center for Mennonite Brethren Studies
Tabor College, Hillsboro, Kansas

CONTENTS

INTRODUCTION

On June 4, 1993, between 10:00 and 10:30 p.m., my life was jolted to an entirely new plane. I had a stroke! This stroke has become my great divide, separating my life forever into BTS—before the stroke, and ATS—after the stroke.

Up till then I had regarded my retirement in 1984 as the definitive break with my active past. Returning to Canada from abroad, staying home and letting go of my traveling consultant and missionary roles had meant a total change of purpose and lifestyle. But after the stroke I realized that the effects of this momentary event were even more fundamental and far-reaching. Now my retirement joys of fishing, traveling to new countries, and helping to solve cultural problems in crisis situations had in one quick moment become mere memories. Now only the left side of a completely right-handed person still functioned relatively normally. There was a slight possibility that extensive and hard exercise might restore at least some function on my right side, but from now on my basic reality was that my left half plus a little was all the function I would ever muster.

The stroke has been a traumatic blow, regardless of how one might cut it. But, thank God, even that sinister cloud has had at least a partial silver lining. Being strongly right-handed meant that now, ATS, only the motor function of the nervous system on my right side was out of commission. My speech and my mental faculties had come through the ordeal largely unscathed. One side of my mouth might be dry. The right side of my face might not function as smoothly as before. But I could think. I could remember. I could reason. I could dictate. I could still produce something worthwhile.

Urgent questions called for resolution: What, now, was my reason-to-be? What of God's will for my life was still left undone? Were there still lessons to learn? The stroke had obviously made many of my BTS perspectives and possibilities totally obsolete. Up to now life had been an expanding continuum, but now that had all changed abruptly. There would be new experiences, but never again from the previous perspective. Most of my BTS activities had in one fell swoop become events that I would never replicate. My rich life of learning wasn't ended, but it had been irrevocably altered. The burning questions now were: Was there still a niche that I could fill? What new lessons were there to learn? Was there unfinished business that I still needed to complete?

The answer I gleaned from my Lord was that I needed to write three testimonies:

One directed to the Church that produced me.

Another directed to my fellow missionaries and Christians.

A third directed to my grandchildren and their generation.

The first resulted in *Only the Sword of the Spirit,* the second in *The Bible in Cross-Cultural Perspective,* and the final testimony in *Educating Tiger.*

This book represents my testimony about my personal BTS pilgrimage as a human being trying to find and to do God's will for my life. It proposes to share a wide variety of experiences which I was privileged to have as I increased in knowledge, obedience and spiritual maturity. It tells how I tried to bring to fruition that with which God has endowed me. The very title calls attention to the fact that the people, to whom I thought I was being sent to bring God's *truth,* had a lot of God's truth to teach me. *Jaco*—pronounced 'haco'—was my name among the Waunana; *Tiger (Imama)* was my nickname among both the Colombian and Panamanian Empera. These two tribes began my cross-cultural education. Over the next thirty years several hundred other language groups added their cultural knowhow to this education.

I hope and pray this candid personal testimony about my learning pilgrimage will encourage others to press on to clarify the burning questions in their lives. Life's wealth of experience has helped me reach some significant conclusions—some of them even ATS. But I know that not all the answers are in and that not all my personal conclusions and decisions are eternally or universally valid. They may have been completely valid for me at one time, but that does not mean they are valid for all times even for me or that they have any validity whatsoever for anyone else. At best they represent an interim report on my progress in my life to develop God's image in me. It is with a deep consciousness of my own finiteness, now greatly sharpened by the stroke, that I share some of the intimate lessons of my life with you—my grandchildren.

This testimony is not intended to be a biography. I merely want to highlight *some* of the lessons I have learned and *some* of the interim conclusions I have reached. I am really interested in tracing my intellectual and spiritual development, and that not necessarily in chronological sequence. In some cases an experience retold may have happened in the innocence of my childhood but was then developed further over the years. In other cases a critical event later in life helped unearth a long-forgotten childhood experience which was now being expanded, reinforced or given a very different value tag.

To compensate for the lack of chronology, this introduction includes a brief sketch of my life's story. Perhaps this summary will provide enough of a framework for the reader to locate specific events in their proper chronological period. There is one notable exception. Chapter 1 does actually begin with chronology, since the health problems of my infancy and my mother's cradle dedication were fundamental to setting the tone and direction for my life.

The chronology of my life

I was born in 1922 in Orenburg, near the Ural Mountains in European Russia. My parents were of Germanic peasant stock and lived in a German-speaking Mennonite colony. I spent the first seven years of my life in that isolated and sheltered setting. In 1929, because of the Bolshevik Revolution that had swept the country, my family decided to leave Russia. We traveled to Moscow. After more than six months of hassles with government authorities, we finally obtained that coveted exit permit. We arrived in Germany at the height of the depression. Most of the 1,500 Mennonite refugees that left Russia in November of 1929 had to find a new home in the Chaco of Paraguay, but my family, together with twenty-nine others, was fortunate to be permitted to emigrate to Canada.

I entered elementary school in rural Manitoba after my eighth birthday. My teacher, a conscientious Mennonite, worked hard to bring me up to par with my age-mates. By the time my family moved to British Columbia in April, 1934, I had been with my age-mates in Grade 5 for just two weeks. The change of residence came at a most inopportune point in my mathematical development. In Manitoba we had just begun to learn about fractions, but in British Columbia they were finishing with decimals. This gap in my mathematical education led to a traumatic demotion from Grade 5 to Grade 4 shortly after our arrival in Yarrow, British Columbia.

When I completed Grade 8 in 1936, there was no high school in the local community. My parents had no money to send me to a boarding school, so I was unable to continue my basic education. At first I worked with my father making cordwood in areas where people were clearing land for farming. During the winters, however, my parents chose to send me to a Bible school which the local church was then operating.

When World War II erupted, I was just turning seventeen. After completing five winters at Bible school, I was able to attend high school in Chilliwack for a year, for by then school bus transportation was available in Yarrow.

In 1942-43 I attended the Missionary Medical Institute in Toronto in order to learn the rudiments of missionary medicine. At the same time I served as a conscientious objector doing alternative service at Toronto Western Hospital. I was ordained as a minister in 1943.

During the summer of 1944 I enjoyed my first taste of linguistics with the Summer Institute of Linguistics in Briercrest, Saskatchewan. I then served for one year in my church's home missions program under the banner of the West Coast Children's Mission in British Columbia. In August 1945 Anne Enns and I were married and within a month left for Tabor College, Hillsboro, Kansas, where we both earned a bachelor's degree in humanities (foreign languages).

The Board of Missions sent us to Colombia, South America as Mennonite Brethren missionaries in December of 1947. Our assignment there was to reduce the Waunana tribal language to writing, to study the various dialects of the Chocó language family to which the Waunana language belonged, and to translate the Scriptures into them. We served in that country until 1957 with a furlough during the years 1953-55. While on furlough, I attended graduate school at the University of Washington.

Because of intense religious persecution in Colombia at that time, the Board of Missions recalled us to North America in 1957. I then finished my Ph.D. at the University of Washington, where I also taught anthropology (1953-55) and modern languages (1957-58). I was then appointed Professor of Anthropology and Modern Languages at Tabor College in Hillsboro, Kansas in the fall of 1958.

During the years at Tabor College I continued to be involved in the Chocó church program, now in Panama. We were dealing with some of the same people—the Waunana and Empera—that we had originally contacted in Colombia. In 1959 we and the David Wirsches made a twenty-five-year commitment to help develop a church among these tribespeople. This commitment matured in 1984. It represented an attempt at a full generation of cultural change within a Christian framework—a kind of religious replication of an earlier secular cultural change experiment carried out in Vicos, Peru.

While at Tabor College, I also completed a six-month study assignment with the Mennonite Central Committee to assess how best to help several aboriginal tribes, who were neighbors of the Mennonites settled in the Paraguayan Chaco, to solve some of their livelihood and cultural change problems.

In 1964, the United Bible Societies appointed me translation consultant with the responsibility for training mother-tongue speakers as translators of the Scriptures in third-world languages. In my first assignment in this capacity I was responsible for all of South America (1964-70). I taught at the Moslem University of Mashad, Iran during the summer of 1970. In September of 1970 I became responsible for Bible translation in Central East Africa, including the countries of Angola, Zambia, Malawi, Rhodesia-Zimbabwe and Mozambique. I also had some advisory responsibility for the Bible translation program in South Africa.

In 1978-79 I enjoyed a sabbatical at Emory University in Atlanta, Georgia. My next assignment was in West Africa, where I served as translation consultant for the countries of Ghana, Benin-Dahomey, Niger, Upper Volta-Burkina Faso and Togo. I retired in 1984 to do research and writing.

Since my retirement I have completed a number of short-term overseas assignments, such as helping in the reconciliation of a church split in India, aiding Mennonite Central Committee workers among the Kekchi Indians in Guatemala to solve some cultural problems there, and doing an assessment of the Mennonite mission situation among the Hopi Indians in Arizona.

Then came the stroke.

CHILDHOOD

PART I

CHAPTER 1

WHERE AND HOW IT ALL BEGAN

By the time I was born in 1922, Russia was already in the throes of the Bolshevik Revolution after World War I. My family lived in a secluded and rather closed Mennonite colony near the Ural Mountains. Up to that time this colony had had its own local government and German schools, and had taken care of all its own affairs as a self-contained little theocratic state. But now everything was changing. A rapid succession of revolutionary governments had turned everything upside down. The latest crisis had even put an atheist teacher, teaching in the Russian language, into the local Mennonite school. That was the last straw for my parents. They kept me out of school and began preparing to leave Russia. That was not easy. They were poor and had few possessions, but even those were hard to sell because almost everyone else was also emigrating.

My mother, Katherina Quiring, came from a very large family, as there had been four successive mothers. Two of the mothers had already come into the family as widows, bringing along children from a previous marriage. When my grandfather, Heinrich Quiring, passed away at the age of fifty-four, the oldest son from the first marriage, according to Russian law, gained control of the family property. My mother, who came from one of the later marriages and had no blood brother to fend for her, readily became a family pawn.

I never got to know my biological father, Jacob Isaak. He had just returned from forestry service at the end of the war and had fallen in love with my mother. They had married in spite of the fact that she was penniless and had no dowry. Within a month of the marriage Mother was expecting, but by the time I was born, my father was already ailing. They said it was typhus (probably typhoid fever because the Low German language, which my parents habitually spoke, does not distinguish between the two). He was dead before I reached my third month.

I was born allergic to milk, even mother's milk. As a result, I was an eczematous child almost from the start. Soon the allergy spread to wheat products and eggs. I became a mass of oozing ulcerations. When my mother would pick me up from my cradle, pieces of my scalp often tore off because my hair had dried to the bedding.

Since mother was penniless and medical help in the colony was almost nonexistent, there was no medical recourse. The only remedy my mother recalls was that of a visiting doctor who prescribed generous doses of cod liver oil, which at the time came only in two-and-a-half liter bottles. With no refrigeration, the oil soon became rancid. Its administration became a constant and bitter struggle. Even today the smell of cod liver oil makes me fit-to-be-tied.

My mother soon became aware that pious people in the community were praying for my demise. They were asking God to relieve this pathetic widow of her hopeless festering burden. However, for the young mother, for whom the baby was all she had, these prayers were daggers in the heart. One night, in desperation, she threw herself across my wooden cradle and harangued with my Maker in prayer, "If you cannot heal him, then take him and take him right now! But if you can heal him, I will take care of him as long as you see fit to afflict him. God! I dedicate him to your service!"

It wasn't until I was about seventeen that I learned of this secret dedication. I came home from Bible school one day full of enthusiasm and reported to my mother that I had just made a momentous decision—I was dedicating my life to God for missionary service. Instantly she broke into a flood of tears. I was embarrassed, thinking I had somehow hurt her. When she realized that, she cried, "No, son, I am not crying because I am angry or hurt! I am crying because I am so happy!" Then she told me how she had thrown herself down before God and dedicated me to his service.

The double-decker buns

One day when I was three or four my mother was baking *zwieback*, the famous Mennonite "double-decker buns." She had set out her buns to rise, but when she came to put them into the oven, she found they all had been punched flat on the pan. Since I was playing with several other children in the house at the time, she enquired as to who had done this dastardly deed. One of the boys, a cousin of mine about two years my senior, pointed to me, but I vehemently denied it. When my denials persisted, my mother decided to also teach me not to tell lies and so she spanked me. In fact, she spanked me until I admitted falsely that I was guilty. A couple of days later the cousin who had first blamed me admitted to her that he was the culprit. By now, however, the discipline had been administered and could not be undone.

This event resurfaced more than three decades later. I served as a guinea pig at a Mennonite mental hospital for a group of psychiatrists who were trying to teach ministers about counseling and mental health. In the course of these sessions it became apparent that whenever somebody accused me of something falsely, I overreacted, sometimes to the point of violent anger. When I asked the psychiatrists what might cause these furious responses, they ventured a guess that it must be a forgotten childhood event. Despite my virulent reaction, I had no memory of any such triggering incident.

On the next visit to British Columbia, I told my mother about these experiences and asked her, "Do you recall anything that may have happened to me in my childhood that might explain this reaction?" In tears she then told me about the unwarranted spanking for the punched-down buns. Interestingly, even though I now know the origin of these strong emotions, I still find it hard to contain them whenever I am falsely accused.

In 1992, almost 70 years after the event, I visited a cousin who had just immigrated to Germany from Siberia. No sooner had we greeted each other then he broke down in tears and asked for my forgiveness. He had carried the guilt of the false accusation through all these decades.

The leeches did it

My eczema continued unabated. The only untried recourse was a Russian healer who reputedly could cure eczema by leeching. When I was five, my mother prevailed upon one of her half-brothers to take us by horse and buggy on a ten-hour drive to the village where this healer lived. They did not intend to stay overnight in the Russian village and wanted to return home immediately after the treatment.

When they arrived, however, the healer wasn't home. So under pressure from my family, the healer's assistant finally agreed to leech me. By the time the real healer appeared, the assistant had already put more than thirty leeches on me. When the healer realized that, she was frantic. Thirty, to her mind, was the absolute maximum for an adult, but far too many for a five-year-old. She gravely warned my mother to not let me fall asleep for twelve hours or I would wake up a moron. So for the next twelve hours, including the ten-hour drive home, my mother worked frantically to keep me awake. But once the buggy ride was over, it didn't matter what she did—I just couldn't stay awake. I slept like dead for forty-eight hours straight.

In desperation, mother finally picked me up and carried me outside and set me down in full sunshine. In the heat of the sun I began to stir and finally awoke. By this time my mother noticed that the eczematous ulcerations all over my body were beginning to dry up. Some were even starting to flake off. I was cured!

I remained free of allergic symptoms for the next thirty or so years. Only when I worked under very wet conditions did I notice that my hands cracked very easily. At age thirty-five, however, I developed severe hay fever. My childhood allergies returned with a vengeance.

A stepfather whose name I bear

Since my widowed mother, with her sore-afflicted child, was such an embarrassment to the rest of the family, they all looked for a way to get her off their hands through remarriage. They finally succeeded. A well-meaning but not overly bright young man, who up to that time had been unable to find a wife, was willing to marry her. It was a convenient marriage for the relatives, but one fraught with difficulties for my mother. Two additional girls were born into this union, but both died in their infancy while the family was in Germany en route from Russia to Canada.

This stepfather is the only father I have known. Basically he was a gentle person. Because I was a stepson, he never disciplined me physically; that always was my mother's job. Other than being severely frustrated by his lack of imagination and his unadventurous spirit, I have no unpleasant memories of my stepfather.

I inherited my stepfather's name quite by accident when we immigrated to Canada. Being unable to speak English to the immigration officer in Quebec, I was unknowingly registered in his name. My own father's name got lost in the shuffle. Even though I began grade school as an Isaak, I have chosen to be a Loewen ever since I became aware of what had happened in Quebec in 1930.

The trauma of Moscow

When my family arrived in Moscow, the city was clogged with some 25,000 Mennonite refugees wanting to leave the country. At the time the government wasn't issuing any exit permits. Housing was at a premium. Poor families like mine had to find shelter in some of the rural summer homes of wealthier Muscovites. My family stayed in such a summer home some twelve kilometers beyond the city limits.

Meanwhile the German and Russian governments were negotiating about the refugees. The German government finally extracted a promise from the Russians that any German-speaking person who would be in Moscow on November 25, 1929 would be given an exit permit. But secretly the Russians anticipated that by this date all these refugees would already have been sent to Siberian concentration camps as *kulaks* (prosperous farmers). So the Russians systematically continued to fill up freight trains of cattle cars with human beings as they shipped the Mennonites to the Siberian Arctic.

The house in which my family found refuge near Moscow had eight rooms. A Russian caretaker lived in one of the rooms and each of the other rooms contained a Mennonite family. Each family had to pay rent for the whole house and that for six months in advance. During the five months that my family was there, most nights meant a visit from the secret police who were rounding up *kulaks* to send to concentration camps.

The owner of the house must have been adept at bribing the officials, because as long as a family had enough money to pay the exorbitant rent, it was not taken by the police. Only those families whose money ran out were picked up.

I still remember those tension-filled moments at night when the secret police came. Gun butts banging on the door or on the floor! Angry stentorian commands piercing the air! The mothers would rouse all the children and we'd fall to our knees crying to God to spare us. Meanwhile the fathers, as the heads of families, had to present all their papers to the investigators.

Eventually in September the fall rains came. The dirt roads in our area now became a mass of giant mud holes as the large lorries of the secret police plowed them up night after night hauling out their human cargo. Finally, only the six families in our house were left in the area; everyone else had been carted off. Thus on the 25th of November, 1929, my family was still in Moscow. Together with some 1,500 other Mennonites who had escaped the forced exodus to Siberia, they received the promised permission to emigrate.

Looking back now I wonder how formative these childhood experiences were. My mother's dedication was certainly determinative, but did her defiance of the prayers of a pious community also rub off on me? Could that be why I seldom hesitated to look straight into the mouths of even the most sacred of cows? Did Russia's revolutionary concern with social injustice also leave its impression? Did the childhood struggles with illness, poverty and adversity leave me permanently empathetic with the underdog? Did the unjustified early childhood punishment leave an indelible mark on my psyche? I cannot help but wonder. . . .

CONVERSION

It is fitting that the story of my life of learning and growth should begin with conversion. This experience represents one of the first clear memories of my life and one of my first personal covenants with God. The centrality of conversion is further supported by the fact that it is a cornerstone of Mennonite Brethren theology and in the 1950s and 1960s it was the most favored topic of Mennonite Brethren preaching, as studies by G. D. Huebert and others have shown.

It also represents my first conscious experience with doubts about the faith as I inherited it from the ancestors. Conversion was touted to be a once-and-for-all event that changes a "fallen sinner into a child of God." My own experience, however, showed that my early spiritual changes were far from complete. The result, of course, was perpetual and intense self-doubt as I became painfully aware of the unrenewed areas of my inner life. At this stage of my life, however, I still did not permit myself to doubt the teaching of my church openly.

When our own children underwent childhood conversion experiences, we quickly realized that our inherited theology did not work for them either. Our children needed process conversion. This conviction about conversion was greatly strengthened when our efforts among the Chocó in Colombia-Panama resulted in a people's movement in which the tribespeople were converted by the hundreds. As one of the stories dramatically shows, the tribespeople intuitively treated conversion as an unfinished process. By 1969, I had picked up courage to modify my theology of conversion. (See Bibliography 1969a in the Appendix.)

As you will see throughout this book, even today, after seventy, I consider my own conversion as not yet finished. I am deeply aware of large areas of my life that still need to undergo radical change. There is no question that I need to continue to learn, to grow, and to be converted into the image of Him who created me.

CHAPTER 2
CONVERSION: A FAMILY STORY

Kronsgart, Manitoba

As already said, I grew up in a church in which conversion was defined as the once-and-for-all transaction that transformed a lost sinner into a child of God. A favorite Scripture text for preachers was: "Therefore if any man be in Christ, he is a new creature: old things have passed away; behold all things are become new." (2 Cor. 5:17). In this conversion-charged atmosphere, I, too, underwent a crisis conversion at the age of ten. I then experienced a period of years of intense conflict between my actual experience and the ideal proclaimed from the pulpit.

Here's how it happened:

I was about eight or nine years old when I entered what my mother called "a terrible phase of telling lies."

After our arrival in Canada in 1930, my parents—following several not-so-successful starts at work on some Mennonite farms in Southern Manitoba—found a congenial workplace with a Mennonite widower-farmer in the village of Kronsgart. My parents both worked in the barn and in the fields with the widower-owner. In addition, Mother did the housework and the cooking. We all ate together as a family.

During the day I either had to tag along to the fields or play alone in the house or yard. I got desperately lonesome. I craved playmates. I hated my solitary existence. Whenever I got permission to visit some neighbor children, I always overstayed the allotted time and then came home with the most "creative" explanations of why it had been impossible to be home on time. My mother considered these fanciful explanations as unadulterated lies. She did not understand my intense craving for other children's company. So she did what she felt was her bitter but God-given duty—she began to wean me from "my terrible lying habit."

I still remember how bitterly Mother wept and prayed every time before giving me my due with a doubled-up canvas hose from an old gas pump. When my lying persisted, Mother began the "escalator" approach, adding five lashes for each new infraction. We must have been at about twenty or twenty-five lashes when I became convinced I needed a fundamental change of heart—I needed to be converted—to become a new creature!

A tent meeting was in progress in a nearby town that summer. A missionary evangelist was preaching and many people were "being saved." At the conclusion of one of these emotion-charged revival meetings, I asked my parents for permission to go forward to the altar to be saved! Now I was a new creature! No more lies! But before I knew it, I was back in the old rut again—facing thirty lashes, then thirty-five lashes. I became convinced that my conversion had not been genuine. So I underwent "conversion" again and again in an effort to achieve the real thing.

Yarrow, B.C.

When my family moved away from the farm in Manitoba and came to British Columbia, I eventually got over the "lying" syndrome. But by that time I was already deeply involved in other things which also made me doubt the validity of my latest conversion.

I had another major conversion just before my fifteenth birthday. This more or less coincided with my sexual maturity. The sexual dreams and the accompanying nocturnal emissions (which I thought were Onanism, because I had heard preachers making veiled references to this "terrible sin") convinced me that this latest conversion experience had not reached the mark either.

I spent two more years of terrible agony until I was able to find help with an elderly minister to whom I confessed my plight. Under his encouragement and counsel I found "victory" and peace of mind. I was baptized shortly thereafter.

Interestingly, however, conversion represents the first area where I felt I had to challenge my church's teaching. That came in 1969 when my wife and I published the story of our family members' conversion experiences (Appendix 1969a).

Noanama, Colombia

"If I am converted will God expect me to speak to family X—to whom our family hasn't spoken for at least two generations?"

"No one but God can answer that question! But we are sure that if God should want you to talk to them, he would also give you whatever it takes to do it. Furthermore, if you do turn over your life to God, maybe even your attitude toward those people will be changed."

"I will never change my attitude towards those d——- people. They. . . . the more I think of it, the more I am convinced that God *does* expect me to talk to those low-down scoundrels. But I won't do it! I won't defile our family record! I just won't do it! May God be d——-." The door slammed.

This exchange took place in our living room on a steaming hot Sunday afternoon in the Colombian jungle village of Noanama. The lady, a mestizo, never came to church, but if she stood by her garden gate she could hear everything through the open church window. And that's where she had been standing all Sunday morning during the lesson.

She came to our home under deep conviction. God had definitely spoken to her about "being born anew." She asked for help to undergo such a fundamental change of heart and life. We had just finished answering all her questions and were now kneeling to seal the agreement with God in prayer when the convert-to-be suddenly stood up and excitedly launched into the foregoing tirade. As she spoke, she grew angrier and angrier, and her voice continued to rise with emotion until she finally stormed out of the house with an oath on her lips.

Anne and I continued on our knees, deeply moved by the pathos of the situation and completely oblivious to the fact that we had an unexpected observer. Our daughter, aged five, was standing in the doorway leading from the bedroom to the living room with tears streaming down her face. She had been napping when the conversation began but had awakened, and when we became aware of her, she was standing in the doorway crying softly. When Anne took her up into her arms, she sobbed: "Mommy, if Señora Y dies, will she go to be with Jesus?"

"We can't know that, honey, only God knows what will happen. But if she doesn't change her attitude and her heart, it sure doesn't look very likely."

"But Mommy, will I go to be with Jesus when I die? I have never let Jesus change my heart either. . . . Mommy, I want to give my heart to Jesus. I don't want to be like Señora Y." And so—wanted or not—we had a child conversion on our hands.

Cali, Colombia

Nor was this the only one. All four of our children made conversion decisions for Christ before they reached the age of seven. The next two daughters were six and five respectively when they underwent the experience.

The children and Anne had been reading a series of children's Bible studies. No one recalls that there was any special provocation either in the lessons or in the ensuing discussions, but as a result of the readings, one day at "siesta" time, our second daughter came to our bedroom and asked how she could be converted. After Anne explained the new birth in as simple terms as possible, the child insisted that she wanted to "do it" right now. There was nothing left but to pray with her and to let her make her commitment to God. She was beaming with happiness when Anne sent her off for her nap into the room she shared with her younger sister, who was already sleeping.

But the new convert didn't go to sleep. She awoke her younger sister and told her that she had given her heart to Jesus. Then with a tone of superiority she added: "I am going to heaven now, but you won't go to heaven when you die, because you haven't given your heart to Jesus." Before long our own "siesta" was interrupted, this time by our five-year-old daughter who burst into our bedroom, eyes red from crying, insisting: "But I don't want to go to hell; I want to go to heaven too!"

"But honey, who says you aren't going to heaven?"

"My sister says that since I haven't given my heart to Jesus, I can't go to heaven. She says I have to go to hell."

"You love Jesus, don't you, honey, and when you are a little older you also will give your heart to him."

"But I don't want to wait. I want to give my heart to him right now." So right now it was.

Hillsboro, Kansas

Several years later, during a rather informal Sunday evening service, the minister asked for a show of hands from all those who considered themselves as having made a total commitment to God. Our son, then six, was among those who enthusiastically and unashamedly raised his hand. This precipitated a minor family crisis right there in the pews, for his sisters "knew" that he had not undergone a conversion experience, and they were determined to make him understand that. It took some stern parental hushing to postpone the confrontation until we got home.

At first our son insisted that he loved God and Jesus and that he was totally committed, but when his sisters faced him with their dated decisions and asked when he had made his decision, he was nonplussed.

Anne and I tried to explain that not all people undergo a crisis decision experience. Some merely continue believing and growing in their commitment without any major moment of decision. On the other hand, if he was already committed, he could confirm that on the spot by telling the Lord so in prayer.

Faced with a conscious decision, our son hesitated and did not make a confirmation on the spot. But two days later at a family devotional he asked for help to make a conscious commitment to God.

That is how we came to have four unsolicited child conversions on our hands. Only later did we realize how "conversion-charged" the mission field and our home atmosphere really had been and how much unspoken pressure it had created for our children.

Noanama, Cali and Hillsboro

When our oldest daughter made her decision that Sunday afternoon in Noanama, Anne and I were convinced it was as genuine as a child of that age could make it, and we were determined not to let it "die." We did not want our child to have to experience the struggles and the repeated conversions that we as parents had had to undergo. We had special sessions with her in which we encouraged her to share the experience with us. Of course, we as parents also shared our conversion and growth experiences with her, and in the process we became aware of several important lessons.

One early discovery was that if more than four months passed without our daughter talking at length about that Sunday afternoon experience, the details of it became dim and the whole experience became remote. So we tried to have special "conversion" discussion sessions at least once every three months. In addition we as parents tried to relate and discuss answers to prayer and other current spiritual experiences during our regular family devotions. After the next two were converted, they, too, were included in the circle.

We also discovered that we needed a lot more time than what we had available for ordinary family devotional sessions. We needed time to relax, to discuss, and to answer questions. So we began to reserve Sunday evenings for this purpose. The whole family stayed home from church and met in a private family service in which we all tried to share our personal spiritual growth with its successes and failures.

Before long, however, we learned a troubling fact. These meetings were fine as long as things were sailing smoothly. But we were in deep difficulty as soon as one of the children became involved in some serious misconduct. How should that be handled? If we worked on the assumption that the children had undergone an experience of new birth and that they should now live as "new" creatures, then there was a reason to doubt that they had actually been changed. On the other hand, if we merely needed to "teach them and train them" to do what is right, what was the significance of their conversion experience?

Several times I as father decided to "raise the cost of deviance" through corporal punishment to make one or other of the children see the heinousness of his or her misconduct. But that didn't produce the desired results either; in fact, even today several of the children retain emotional scars from these misguided uses of force. We had arrived at an impasse. We knew that neither punishment nor instruction were adequate, but we didn't know what else to do. "Help" in our dilemma came from several unexpected sources. The first was my personal self-image crisis, and the second was exposure to what was going on in the lives of Christian high school and college students.

My self-image crisis. I had undertaken church college teaching with a deep desire to share my Christian outlook with students in a positive and helpful way. Before long, however, I was severely frustrated. Several of my early attempts to help students in difficulties had seriously misfired. I became convinced that I didn't know how to "listen" to the Spirit of God and that I was exceedingly insensitive to human need. I wasn't able to feel when or where others were hurting. As a result I went through a period of intense self-searching during which I discovered that I as father, preacher and long-time believer still had a rather unregenerate self-image at the very core of my personality. Instead of being open to "calls for help" from people in need and instead of hearing the impulses of guidance from the Spirit of God, my "spiritual radar" system was consumed with trying to read what my peers and superiors were thinking of me and my performance. Here was unregenerate pride at its ugliest and all under a pious mask of a recognized Christian leader. The result was another "conversion" which produced changes in my worldview that were much more far-reaching than all my previous conversions combined.

But how was I to incorporate these new experiences into my philosophy of a once-and-for-all conversion? I couldn't! I had to change my view of conversion. Rather than seeing it as a once-and-for-all comprehensive experience, I now had to accept it as involving only those areas of life of which I had been aware at the time of my decision. By extension this meant that regardless of how early a child decided to "accept Jesus," its commitment was indeed genuine; however as time went on, the convert was bound to discover new facets or new areas of life of which it had not been aware at the time of its conversion and which subsequently and consciously would have to be included in its covenant with God.

Mentoring students. My excruciating personal experience with my self-image was further reinforced in mentoring sessions with Christian college and high school students. As I came to know them more intimately, I realized that many were in deep spiritual crisis. They had been converted at the age of eight, nine or ten years, but over time had accumulated so much guilt and such a deep awareness of the absence of "newness" in large areas of their conscious lives that they doubted the reality of their childhood conversion experience.

Most of them came to the mentoring sessions asking for answers to specific questions such as: Is masturbation right or wrong? Or, how far can I go with a girl? What they really needed was not only specific answers but also help in learning how to put their accepted religious ideals into practice. In anthropological jargon, they needed support in role rehearsal[1], i.e., they needed help in learning how to break the habits which now had to be broken. It was interesting to notice that once a person achieved victory, i.e., the successful performance of a behavioral ideal, these students no longer doubted their original childhood experience, but now described it as having become enlarged.

Extending the conversion experience

These encounters showed us it was not enough to try and keep the conversion experience alive in our children—it literally had to be encouraged to grow. And this growth was of two kinds: First, there was each child's normal spiritual maturations. Then there was the need for some "major" extensions of each child's conversion experience. We discovered that in order to facilitate adequate growth, the family context had to provide the following ingredients: (1) an atmosphere conducive to growth with expectations graded according to each individual's maturity, (2) ways and means of handling the guilt that resulted when someone's actual behavior fell short of the accepted ideal, (3) help in self-discovery, self-acceptance and conversion extension, (4) support in role rehearsal wherever some "victory" needed to be achieved or when anticipatory socialization was to prepare an individual for a new Christian status-role, (5) models after which the developing individuals could pattern their ideals and by which to measure their

---

[1]In anthropology, when a person enters a new status role (such as becoming a teacher) he or she must learn how to fulfil society's expectations for someone in that role. This learning process, which also applies to religious conversion, is called role rehearsal.

achievement, and (6) guidance and support for developing greater "inner" control.

Creating an atmosphere conducive to growth

Mentoring contacts with teenagers from other Christian homes made us aware that many young people felt their parents were unable to speak about God, the Bible and Christian living in a conversational way. "Parents speak about God and the Bible only when they are mad about something or at formal settings such as family devotions," they would tell us. When our own children confirmed that this was also partly true of our home, we determined to develop an atmosphere where we could all speak comfortably and conversationally about our maturation in faith. This meant, of course, that we parents had to take the first steps in transparency and self-exposure about our successes as well as our failures in Christian living. The younger participants, meanwhile, needed to understand that expectations were graded and that each family member could share at the level of his/her development and concern.

Learning to handle guilt. Family sessions turned out to be ideal times to deal with guilt. Often, of course, guilt was dealt with promptly at the time an infraction occurred or was discovered, but the larger family gatherings provided an excellent opportunity to look at such events in terms of broader perspectives.

In cases of serious misconduct, such as stealing at a store, cheating in school, malicious deceit and falsehood, more extensive treatment was necessary. First, there were private sessions with the "culprit" in which the parents tried to serve as a mirror for self-recognition and the ultimate "owning" of the wrong behavior by the child. Where forgiveness or restitution was required, one or both of the parents would accompany the child for moral support on such occasions. Once the problem had been solved in private, the individuals were encouraged to make the victory a family affair. In this way they could experience both the group's forgiveness and its support in role reinforcement.

In this connection, another important point emerged. Both restitution and confession to the family often had to be delayed until the "guilty" party had mustered sufficient self-confidence to share the details of the event without feeling coerced.

Aiding self-discovery and the extension of the conversion commitment

As mentioned, Anne and I tried to function as mirrors to the children when they misbehaved, hoping to help them deal redemptively with negative behavior either in private or in a family session. When a child reached a "major" transition, we as parents often could point to our own similar experiences, for we too had faced decisions about extending our commitment to "new" areas of our lives. Once the child became conscious of such an "unregenerate" area of his/her life, we encouraged him/her to consciously include it in his/her conversion covenant.

Providing opportunity for role rehearsal

In cases like lying or bad temper, in which actual habits had to be broken, the family needed to provide a context for role rehearsal. First, the individual expressed the behavioral goal at a family session. Others then sought to define how they individually could be of help. This often meant that family members had to check each other's behavior to minimize the stimuli for aberrant behavior and to make it easier for the "role rehearser" to achieve the desired behavioral goal. It also meant that other family members needed to warn the role rehearser when he/she was entering a syndrome of negative behavior.

Providing models

Despite the older children's strong model influence, the younger ones still needed the parental model in several areas: (1) in personal transparency about positive and negative behavior, (2) in apologies and requests for forgiveness in the case of wrong action, (3) in an attitude of becoming, i.e., the awareness that there would be further stages of maturation in Christian experience, and (4) in the willingness to accept criticism and correction.

Keith Miller has written about a father of four children who had come to "the end of his rope" and underwent a "second touch" of God. Within two weeks of his changed behavior his oldest son, a twelve-year-old, asked him hesitantly what had happened. "I guess I was making a pretty big mess out of my life," the father told him, "and I've decided to ask God to take over and to show me how to live." The boy responded, "Dad, I think I'd like to do that too."

Developing inner control

The truly regenerate adult behaves like a Christian not because of what other people think, but because she/he has internalized what is right or wrong. The goal is to reach the stage where values, ideals and norms have been so internalized that one can follow them independently and under any circumstances.

Most people converted as adults have by then experienced a wide range of positive and negative behavior, making it easier to establish a fairly comprehensive pattern of conviction and behavior change. For children growing up in a Christian home, however, the range of experience will be largely limited to what the parents approve. Avoidance of or participation in certain types of behavior need not always emerge from personal conviction. For such children to develop an internalized set of values in an open society like ours, the socializers need to provide the possibility for some experimentation. Obviously such latitude cannot extend to all things, such as prostitution or murder.

In our home, for example, we allowed the children to read any book they found on the shelves (and the shelves were stocked with a wide range of literary classics as well as the current bestsellers), but they had to be willing to discuss the contents of the book openly with the family. The same principle applied to tobacco, liquor, movies and other forms of amusement. In order to ensure the possibility of adequate discussion, we developed a rule of thumb—if it's questionable, we'll all do it and then we'll discuss the experience to identify the good and the bad and to see whether we can extract some long-range guidelines.

This approach can be illustrated with our attempt to teach the children to evaluate movies and television programs. One Sunday afternoon shortly after we had acquired our first television set, the children found an announcement for the movie "Solomon and Sheba." Anne and I were not enthusiastic. First, it conflicted with the hour of the church service, and second, we did not think it was a picture worth watching. The children, however, protested that it was a Bible story. We countered that while it was based on a Bible story, it no longer remained one after Hollywood had gotten through with it. But the children persisted, so finally we decided to all do it together even if it meant staying home from church.

The first fifteen minutes of the film depicted the history of Israel, the building of the city of Jerusalem, and other historical facts that were truly beautiful. At several points the children said: "See, Dad and Mom, there's nothing bad about this film."

When Sheba entered, things began to change. The children didn't react during the scene where she rehearsed the sex display with which she intended to seduce Solomon. But when the actual seduction of Solomon got underway, our youngest suddenly clapped his hands over his eyes and shouted: "Turn it off. It's dirty." One of the other children ran and turned off the set. Then we all joined in a discussion to evaluate the experience.

But is this the end of the conversion story? By no means! Between thirty and forty I experienced a self-image conversion. Now in the seventies I'm trying to get my sharp tongue converted. . . but even that's not the end.

CHAPTER 3
CONVERSION OBSERVED

During our 40 years of service abroad, we have had the privilege to witness some very different types of conversion.

It takes time to convert a drunkard's stomach. In 1961, about a year after the Chocó church had been organized, one of the notorious local medicine men, a recognized drunk of the tribal community, began to come to church. Eventually he made a commitment to Christ. While there was rejoicing that a dangerous medicine man and practitioner of magic had put his life under Christ's control, many of the people took his conversion with a grain of salt. I, for one, rejoiced that the gospel had seemed powerful enough to make one of its famous enemies commit himself to become a child of God. Before long the man presented himself to the church and requested baptism. The church people rejoiced to hear his testimony and baptized him.

When David Wirsche and I came to Panama next summer to help the young church in its development, we stumbled on the new church member dead drunk in a gutter in town. He had come there to sell his bananas, and with money in hand, he had fallen into the old trap.

I mentioned this to Pastor Aureliano next time I saw him. I asked him what the church was going to do about the incident. Would they discipline the man or what?

The pastor then gently put his arm on mine and said, "Tiger, please stay out of this one. You have never been a slave of hard liquor like some of us have been, and we know how hard it is to break a life-long drinking habit. You have to recognize, Tiger, that it takes time for a conversion to reach the stomach of a drunkard. We are praying for the man, and we are telling him that one of these days his conversion is going to reach his stomach, and when that happens, he will not be able to tolerate strong drink anymore. His system will rebel against it and he will be freed from his habit. His stomach will have been converted!"

I accepted the explanation with real interest. This was my first experience of seeing that the young Chocó church regarded conversion as a process. With great patience they were working to condition this man to overcome his liquor habit. And sure enough, when David and I returned to Panama a year later, we were privileged to hear the man testify in church that his stomach had finally been converted after many defeats. Time and again he would sell his bananas, get some money in his pocket, and give in when someone offered him a drink. Once he took the first drink, he would always end up in a drunken stupor. He thanked the church members for their support and their prayers. He said, "About three months ago, for the first time in my life, my stomach rebelled when I drank liquor and I threw it all up." There had been several more attempts to drink, but each time his reaction had gotten stronger, and now he said, "The mere sight of a whiskey bottle sets my stomach in revolt and nauseates me."

The church celebrated the occasion with a thanksgiving prayer session, thanking God that the man's conversion had finally reached his stomach.

How many North American conversions have been nurtured in this way? Has our theology of instant conversion unintentionally thwarted the growth of many of our converts?

A Chulupi group conversion

One wants to become "a human being too. . . !"

The suspended intonation pattern indicated that the speaker had a lot more to say, but he didn't verbalize it! Already these words—uttered with explosive vehemence—had startled me to the core.

The speaker, a Chulupi Indian, was a member of a nomadic hunting-and-gathering tribe that in the early 1940's had decided to become "like the Mennonites" who came to the Paraguayan Chaco from Canada and Europe in 1928 and 1931 respectively. The Chulupi had abandoned their part-time work in the sugarcane fields of Argentina, where they were exposed to liquor, prostitution and venereal disease, and had migrated to the Mennonite colonies in the Chaco.

For twenty years this tribe had been content to work for the white colonists for a pittance. Then one day they exploded. Seven hundred of them rose up in armed rebellion against the colonists and demanded land, equipment, cattle and membership in the colony cooperative.

You've become rich by our sweat

"For twenty years we have worked for you. You have become rich by our sweat! Now it is time for us to get something too. We want to become 'first-class' people and have things just like you!"

When the colony leaders tried to dissuade them from violence, the rebels drowned out their words, screaming, "Our ears burn! Our ears burn!" (a vulgar Chulupi insult reserved for liars of the worst kind).

Bloodshed was narrowly averted when the government of Paraguay promised land and equipment to the tribespeople. But the promise turned out to be an empty political gesture. Months passed and no help showed up.

When a land grant was finally made, it turned out to be a sandy waste without any sweet water. Disillusioned and starving, the group broke up. Some returned to their satellite villages on the colony periphery. Others struck out for their former home on the Pilcomayo River, leaving a trail of dead in their wake.

Though the storm had passed without actual bloodshed, the colonists had been severely shaken up. They called for an anthropological investigator. Their major questions were related to the rebellion: What triggered it in the first place? Was there danger that it could break out again? Could anything be done to prevent its recurrence?

As the anthropological investigator was called in to study the situation, it became my task to visit the Chulupi camp near one of the colony villages called Sandhorst, the original source of the rebellion. Even now, more than two years later, the tribespeople were still uttering threats against white people, colonists, or missionaries, not to set foot in their camp.

I now engaged two Chulupi bilinguals (Chulupi-Spanish) to be my sponsors and sent them ahead to explain my mission to the Chulupi camp residents outside of Sandhorst village. I hoped that an invitation for me to visit them might result. My sponsors were successful, and the Chulupi villagers invited me to be their guest.

The three of us arrived in the middle of the afternoon and were overwhelmed by the welcome. Every man, woman, and child came to shake our hands. While the greetings were in progress, women scurried to get sheepskins and piled them up several layers deep so that the visitor, his Chulupi interpreters, and the village leaders could sit on them together.

Confession of the white people's sins

As soon as the greetings were finished, I began: "My two friends, your fellow tribesmen, have already told you why I have come. The Lencos (a corruption of the word 'gringo' by which the Mennonite settlers were known) have decided to help the Chulupi become 'people,' and so they asked me to come and see what things might be hindering you in your quest and what they might do so that you could become 'people' more quickly and more easily."

The effect of these few words was like pulling the cork out of a fermenting bottle. For several hours people, sometimes five and six at a time, poured forth accounts of their bitter experiences as second-class peons. Here are the kinds of things we heard:

"Six Lenco men grabbed me one night when I was returning home from work. They thought I had stolen something. They beat me bloody, but it wasn't I who had stolen."

"My whole family worked and worked, and then all farmer X gave us was old clothes. When we objected, he laughed and said, 'These clothes are plenty good enough for Indians.' "

"All my goats were killed without warning when they got into a Lenco's garden. I never got any settlement."

"Somebody had stolen at the Lenco cooperative store, and one day when six of us went there to buy something, we were grabbed without explanation and beaten mercilessly. When we protested our innocence, the whites just told us: 'Well, somebody has stolen, and we're going to show all of you that it doesn't pay to steal. You can tell the rest that the same thing will happen to anyone who steals.' "

"I was standing near a gate when a Lenco drove up with his buggy. He yelled something at me which I didn't understand, and so I didn't move. Then he jumped off the buggy and slapped my face."

The bitter words flowed like a stream swollen by a tropical cloudburst. At last the outpouring began to dwindle. Finally everyone was silent. One of the older men turned to me and said, "It is all!"

I was moved both by the lengthy recital of abuse and the intensity of the Chulupi feelings about it. Regardless of whether or not all these experiences were true, the people obviously felt keenly oppressed and abused.

Not knowing what to do next, I said, "My 'innermost' is deeply pained, for the people who did these things to you are my people. I must now go alone to think about what you have told me."

What do I do now?

Alone, I tried to bring my notes into a more legible condition. But all the while I was praying, "Lord, what do I do next?"

It was the Indians who finally forced me to act. They gathered for a meeting, and so I went and joined the crowd. No sooner had I sat down on the sand at the rear of the crowd, then the women came running with a bench and sheepskins. One of the men escorted me to the bench and told me that I was to preach. When I consulted my guides as to what I might say, they immediately responded, "Tell them what you told us in the buggy on the way here."

So I briefly repeated the story of my own struggle to become a "person." As a newly-ordained young man, I had become very frustrated when some of the older—often inactive—ministers began to "rap me on the head" because they felt I was too young to say the things I was expressing in my sermons.

In anger I turned to counterattack. Luckily, a kind, older minister drew me aside and gave me the following counsel: "Digging holes under the people who are hurting you will only hurt you more. Deal with dirt and mud and you will get your own hands dirty. God has a place for you. Go find it and go there! Don't let the words of jealous men keep you from saying what the Lord tells you to say."

I concluded my message to the Indians with a testimony of my current happiness as a missionary, for in obeying God's call, I had found my own way to first-class status.

Confession of their own sins

After my testimony had been interpreted, a man—the only confessed Christian in the village, as I learned from my interpreters—got up and said to the people, "Yes, we all want to become first-class people, too. But let's remember: even if we do get land, plows, horses and tools, we, too, have done many evil things. We can never enjoy God's blessing with dirty 'innermosts.' We have spent much time telling of all the evil things the Lencos did to us. What about all the evil we did to them?"

Then just as they had publicly declared their hurts, they now spontaneously confessed their wrongdoings. For several hours confessions poured forth:

"I killed this. . . ."

"I stole that. . . ."

"I lied like this. . . ."

"I broke that. . . ."

There were no tears, but there was seriousness—dead seriousness. Finally, the lone Christian got up again and said, "It is good and well for us to admit all the bad things we have done. But remember, all the while we were doing them, God was seeing us; and I haven't heard any of you mention God yet. What will we do about him?"

Then, following an old Chulupi custom in peacemaking, these people appointed five "talking chiefs" (the Chulupi name actually means "talkers between two"). In the silence of that Chaco night, these five talkers-between-two got up one by one and pleaded with God to forgive their personal and collective sins, and to accept all of them as his children in order to make "real people" of all of them. About 200 Chulupi underwent a group conversion that night.

As I have pondered that dramatic event over the years, I have often wondered: Does our theology allow such a group conversion? Were they really converted?

A fifth-generation Mennonite Brethren speaks about his "conversion"

"Sure, sure, I'm a church member, but what a laugh! I'm no more converted than this. . . dog," said a college student pointing to my pet. "Believe me, I've gone through all the motions. I have prayed since before I could utter actual words; I've memorized Bible verses and recited the creed. In fact, as a kid I always lived like a Christian. Of course, I had good reason to. If I didn't, my parents beat the hell out of me. Yeah! I was converted! I must have been about eight or nine when some heap-big-chief scalp hunter preached fire and brimstone in our church. He upset my tender psyche and scared me to the altar. Big deal! I've gone through the whole d----- rigmarole, but it doesn't mean a d----- thing!"

Or does it?

Catholic priests-in-training try evangelical conversion

While teaching at Tabor College, I attended an Urbana missionary conference. The first public meeting of the conference was a dedication service at which evangelist Billy Graham called 5,400 young people to voluntarily "put their lives on the altar for God." Many hundreds of them responded.

After the service I participated in one of the small-group prayer meetings that contained four or five of the newly "dedicated." They dominated the service, literally gushing dedication. "Once and for all," they testified, "We have turned our lives over to God!"

Knowing my own battles with incomplete dedication, I began to share some scenes from the mission field in which some of my co-workers' foibles had completely undone my consecration. In fact, I admitted that right at that moment my patience with students and especially with my own children was a weak spot in my consecration. It was my attempt to introduce some realism into a situation soaring high in ideals, but I failed. Instead of others joining me in confession, the group retreated behind their pious masks and prayed for the 'backslidden missionary.'

Feeling my failure rather keenly, I tried to slip out of the meeting and go to my own room, but two fellows of the group, who had not prayed, grabbed me by the arm and pulled me into their room across the hall instead. One locked the door, while the other paced the floor in great agitation. He took out a cigarette, lit it, took a few puffs, threw it down and stamped it out fiercely. "I get so fed up with all this d----- Protestant jargon!" he said. "I went to the altar in response to the appeal tonight to 'dedicate' my life. What have I actually done?"

"Nothing that you do not know about," I said quietly.

"Did I get rid of my sins?"

"Not unless you consciously turned them over to God."

Then the young man dropped into a chair and in tears cried in anguish, "Where can I finally go to deal with my sinful habits? I have already joined the church, but it didn't help a damn. So I entered the priesthood, but doing this has only made me hide my evil even more. Now I thought, 'The evangelicals know about forgiveness and peace. I'll go there and get it too.' This is what I tried to do when I got up after the preacher's appeal. But when we got into that prayer meeting and heard those 'dedicated' people spouting phony piety, I felt utterly nauseated. I don't want to be hollow like them! You seemed a little less holy, and so we thought maybe we could talk to you about our sins."

Several hours of confession followed. That night, and in several more private sessions that followed, I was able to observe some "real" sinners find a "real" Savior.

The Mennonite Brethren conversion model

The following analysis of conversion in the Mennonite Brethren Church has been largely drawn from an essay by Delbert Wiens entitled *New Wineskins for Old Wine.*

In 1860 in South Russia, a group of mature men, whose average age was in the thirties and forties, were converted. They had been living as nominal members of the Mennonite church when, through the reading of God's Word, they suddenly discovered that things were not right in their lives. As the awareness of their "lostness" grew, they developed a deep conviction of sin and an intense desire to be saved. Wiens describes a typical conversion experience as follows:

> For two weeks (three weeks, four weeks) I struggled with God. I could not eat or sleep. I felt that hell was swallowing me up. Then one day I could not stand it any longer. I stopped the horses and threw myself on the ground beside the plow and gave myself to God. Then, oh, the peace that came over me as my sins all rolled away.

Even though these men had been nominal members of the church, they suddenly saw themselves as outside God's family and as living in the "world." Their continued study of God's Word convinced them that only through a radical change in their lives could they become a part of God's family. On the basis of their own experience, they became convinced that the Body of Christ is made up only of persons who have undergone such a personal transforming encounter with God. Since the parent Mennonite church contained many who had not undergone this experience, they decided to separate from the mother church and to establish the Mennonite Brethren Church.

Even before their formal separation, these converted adults had been meeting together to study the Bible and to share their personal conversion experiences. As they compared notes, they discovered that their highly individual conversions still contained many common elements. First, they had all felt lost, empty and dissatisfied. Second, they had begun to seek for God, usually by reading the Bible, but as they read the Word, the awareness of their sin and guilt increased until they despaired of life. Third, there came a violent struggle with self which often lasted for weeks. Then fourth, they had finally submitted to God's will. This was followed by a fifth stage in which the peace of God had flooded their hearts. Having thus identified the common elements of their individual conversion experiences, they now searched the Scriptures and found corroboration for this model. As far as they were concerned, they had found *the true way* to new life in Christ. This model of conversion thus became the cornerstone of Mennonite Brethren belief and preaching at home and abroad.

A tribal medicine man proclaims a new conversion model for his people

In the mid-1970s, when Anne and I were on a two-month leave from our assignment in Zambia, we were invited to attend a conference at Three Hills, Alberta. It was a meeting of all the societies which were working with Indians and Eskimos in Canada. Our assignment was to listen during a week-long conference as these various missions and their indigenous preachers and church workers discussed their work. At the end of the session we were to share our perceptions of what we had heard.

I had to tell the assembly that we had heard two distinct message tracks. The missionaries on the whole were lamenting the fact that the gospel was having very little impact on the aboriginal community. The number of members in their churches remained constant from year to year, in fact decade to decade, but they weren't the same members. A large percentage were backsliding. There were some new converts, but no real growth in the work. There seemed to be an undertone of blame that the aborigines weren't up to becoming solid Christians.

On the other hand, from the aborigines we heard a message of hope. Indian after Indian and Eskimo after Eskimo got up to suggest that a breakthrough was just around the corner. God was working! He was preparing the soil, and one of these days a great change was going to hit the whole tribal community.

From this assignment, my wife and I started our trip back to our work in Africa. En route we stopped at the British branch of Wycliffe Bible Translators to share with their workers-in-training a number of concerns for people working overseas. After one message in which I had shared some of my deepest concerns, a man followed me. When I stopped to talk to him, I discovered that he was a second-year student who had been working for some years with the tribespeople around Great Slave Lake in Northern Canada. Now he was back doing a second-year course in linguistic analysis. He reported that a strange event had taken place just before he left Great Slave Lake to come to the sessions in England.

"One of our most famous medicine men 'died,' " he told me. "It is said that he was dead for three days, and on the third day he came to life again. He sat there totally silent for another three days. All the people who had come for his funeral sat by expectantly waiting for the 'resurrected' man to speak. When the third day of silence had passed, he suddenly opened his mouth and cryptically said, 'During the days when I was away, I walked where Jesus walks. I have now come back to tell you that in heaven where Jesus walks, there is no whiskey, no adultery, no nylons, no lipstick, no lying, no stealing.' "

That message from the "resurrected" medicine man shook me to the core. In it I had heard an emerging model for Canadian aboriginal conversion that had been predicted at Three Hills.

Richard A. King, in his book *The School at Mopass,* has severely criticized Canadian mission boarding schools for tribal people, pointing out serious mistakes made by the missionaries who ran them. Most of the aborigines, he says, had no idea what was to happen to them when they were converted because the missionaries were providing them with inoperative models. The missionary models of nurse, teacher, pastor or priest were largely inoperative for the average Indian. To my mind, the story of the native medicine man I was now hearing provided a model of conversion that would be fully operative for Canadian aborigines. (Sad to say that when I tried to sell it by letter to the missions who had invited me, they rejected it out of hand).

Conversion imitating a Western model

While in Zambia I spoke about conversion from an anthropologist's perspective at a conference made up of missionaries and African believers. I pointed out that conversion involves a fundamental restructuring of values and that a genuine conversion would make Africans better Africans. I further pointed out that conversion usually follows a model. This model can be indigenous, as in the case of the Toba of the Argentine Chaco who have restructured their traditional puberty ceremony as a model for the conversion experience; it can be imported, as in the case of many believers who have learned to be converted according to the model of the denomination of the missionary; or it can be developed indigenously.

Finally, I added that conversion in its spiritual dimension always means the ongoing presence of the Spirit of God in the converted person's life as the source of all guidance and power. As soon as the meeting was opened for discussion, a leading national believer got up and confessed:

> Sir, what you have just said about conversion moves me deeply because, I must confess, I have not been converted that way. My deeper African values have not been changed. I have merely become an imitation European on the outside. I have not learned to listen to and to follow the Spirit of God. I have only been trained to listen very carefully to what the missionary who controls the purse wants.

Have we Western missionaries really created scenes like the above on the missionfield? I'm afraid, I have to admit, I have! I am still repenting for it.

CHAPTER 4

CONVERSION: LESSONS I HAD TO LEARN

The last part of our family conversion story (Chapter 2) has already touched on some of the lessons we had to learn. Let me now summarize some of the major additional lessons on conversion that our home and professional life caused us to face.

The metaphor of the house with many rooms

Once we as parents of converted children realized we had to grapple seriously with the idea of conversion as a process, we developed the metaphor of the house with many rooms as a way to encourage ongoing renewal in each of our lives.

We showed our children that when people first invite Jesus into their lives, it is like inviting him into the front room of the house. But the house of each person's life contains many rooms, some of which the individual may not even be aware of at the time of conversion. Someday we may discover that we have a lying-room, or a cheating-room, or an anger-room. When that happens, we will have to consciously ask God to come into that newly-discovered room too.

We had to learn that such conversion extension is not always easy. Sometimes we or our children had to undergo weeks of struggle with one of the newly-discovered "unconverted" rooms before we were ready and willing to invite the Lord into it.

I have continued discovering new "unconverted" rooms in my inner house. I have already testified how I discovered my self-image room in my mid-thirties. That room contained a totally unregenerated self-protecting self-image that was calling major shots in my life. It took a real crisis for me to turn that room over to God! Now, at seventy, I have suddenly become painfully aware of my aggressive-tongue room. I am currently trying to let Christ gain control of my caustic tongue. Progress is painfully slow and very intermittent. Change this late in life is more difficult than ever.

Now, after the stroke, I have become deeply aware of how my life as a whole has been achievement-oriented. I have never learned just "to be." I have never learned to cultivate deep relationships with others. I have never allowed myself to learn to feel. Can these areas of my life still be converted? I am trying to turn them over to God's control.

Why must conversion and radical renewal be treated as processes?

There are several compelling reasons why so-called once-and-for-all renewal experiences must be understood as ongoing processes:

1. **Because any change like conversion, whether individual or group, is never complete when it happens**. Human beings are complex and many-faceted. Change, either in individuals or groups, does not penetrate all of life totally or equally. Those facets or areas of life that are in focus at the time of the crisis will be changed most. Other facets that are not in focus may be changed very little or not at all.

While one hopes that a fundamental change like conversion will spread and penetrate even those areas that were not yet in focus, the reverse is often the case. If one area of life, or one segment of the group, remains untouched by change or is very resistant to it, there will be enormous internal pressure to revert back to old conditions. Only if change is treated as a process, and active steps are taken to insure its continued growth, is there any hope that the renewal will be ongoing and increasingly comprehensive.

2. **Because life's ongoing experiences always create new situations in which new dimensions of personality or previously unrecognized culture traits come into focus.** That was the experience of our children when they discovered they could cheat in school or steal a candy bar at a store. Unless the newly-discovered "room of life" is then also consciously subjected to the change experience, the impact of the original change experience will be severely diminished.

Our children often found these additional steps far more difficult than the original decision to accept Christ as Savior. They often battled for weeks before they were able to "open another room of their lives to Jesus."

While teaching at our church colleges, I was jolted by the high percentage of Mennonite Brethren students who seriously doubted the validity of their childhood conversions. Further checking showed that the basic problem was all the "unchanged rooms" they had subsequently discovered in their lives. No one had helped or even encouraged them to bring these new areas into the light of conversion renewal.

3. **Because human behavior, like everything else in nature, is subject to the second law of thermodynamics, often called the law of entropy.** This law says: "Things in motion will slow down unless new outside momentum is applied. Hot things in cold environments or cold things in warm environments will gradually assume the temperature of the surroundings." By the same token the new convert

will find that within a few weeks or months her/his "zeal" for the new life will gradually diminish. The renewed group will discover that old problems and temptations still exert enormous pull, and their enthusiasm for the new will wane.

The history of the early church also teaches us this very lesson. No one questions that the early church of the New Testament was truly the church Jesus wanted to establish. But within three centuries that very church, which had begun as completely separated from the "world," was ready to join the "world" and become the state religion under the Roman emperor Constantine. Once this compromise had been made, the church embarked on an even more rapid road of entropy.

How much compromise are born-again Christians making to accommodate the world of today? How many "unconverted rooms" have they already recognized but have not included in their renewal experience? In what areas have they, like the Jews of Jesus' day, replaced the commandment of God with their in-group's rules? With how many recognized "unconverted" rooms of life can believers or a church live before their link to Christ is completely choked off?

The house-with-many-rooms metaphor in the experience of college students

One Sunday night a number of students were caught breaking into a college office to steal some examination papers. The sheriff took those who were caught red-handed to the county jail. When more students came to me to confess that they too had been involved, I called the sheriff and asked what to do with them. He said, "H---, if you can talk to them and help them, I don't want them. But if they turn arrogant or stubborn, call me and I'll 'soften' them up a bit."

I called these additional culprits back into my office individually, passed on the sheriff's message and asked if they were serious about solving their problems. They assured me they were! I then suggested that stealing exams likely wasn't their only unsolved problem. In order to establish an honest student/mentor relationship, I asked each of them to give me a list of all the other "unconverted rooms" of their lives of which they were aware at the time. The lists varied from eight to thirteen items. I then took each list and ceremoniously signed it in the presence of the respective student, declaring that I was now assuming responsibility for all the problems except the one on which the two of us would currently be working.

Each student's first assignment was to choose the most painful or most burning problem on his/her list. That was the problem the two of us would try to overcome. Judgment on the others would be suspended temporarily.

In several cases the problem was other thefts. As the student got the necessary money together, we would go to the store or person in question to rectify the offenses. When all debts were paid off, the students selected the next most urgent problem on their list.

Usually by the time the third or fourth problem had been solved or the bad habit had been broken, the student would suddenly burst into my office and happily report, "I've licked the whole d----- list." When I pressed for particulars, they invariably reported: "After years of failure, I had so little confidence in myself and in the power of Christianity, everything seemed so utterly hopeless. But now as I learned how to lick the problems one at a time, I found faith and self-confidence to trust that I could lick all of them with God's help."

Some additional lessons which developed out of these experiences are:

*** It usually requires considerable role rehearsal or conditioning time to break habitual behavior patterns.** My own childhood habit of concocting fanciful excuses and our children's experiences with lying, stealing and cheating all took time to overcome. The Chocó medicine man with a drinking problem needed time for his conversion to reach his stomach. Helping college students, especially in the area of sexual behavior, required extensive role rehearsal. On weekends I used to have fifteen-minute appointments with young people going on dates who wanted to review their ideals or even strengthen their commitment to new behavior patterns. They did not want to slip back into their earlier guilt-producing habits.

*** A church, a group, or an individual can develop unrealistic expectations.** This was certainly the case in my own childhood attempts at achieving newness. The church, by its emphasis on the once-and-for-all experience that would make all things new, had conditioned me to expect instant success. When this didn't happen, I doubted the reality of my experience. I wasn't alone. Most college students with whom I was privileged to work experienced the same discrepancy.

Should not Christian nurture, in the church or in the family, provide opportunity for role rehearsal? The mounting guilt of ordinary living quickly overwhelms the memory of a childhood conversion. This guilt, if not discharged properly, can negate the value of the original conversion.

I witnessed a dramatic attempt to discharge guilt in the Chulupi church in Paraguay. It occurred in connection with baptism. The Chulupi had borrowed the Mennonite pattern of asking baptismal candidates to tell about their conversion and about some of their shortcomings. The Chulupi had restructured this practice according to their own social needs. They were now providing sessions in which the church community helped individuals get rid of all their accumulated guilt. When a baptismal candidate shared some personal difficulties and shortcomings, the community would probe about other events of which they had personal knowledge. Sometimes a person might be interrogated like this for hours before being able to discharge all their accumulated guilt. On one such occasion I saw unbelievers standing outside the open church windows, tears streaming down their faces. They turned to me saying, "Oh, we wish we could also have such a session. We would like to be cleansed too."

*** Every culture and every society, probably every denomination, develops a model for conversion, either spoken or unspoken**. In the case of the

1860 Mennonite Brethren conversion, the five steps outlined earlier (lostness, guilt, struggle, submission and peace) were valid in their stable and closed society. Their closed-colony culture in Russia, where every one's life was intimately observed, provided a context in which new behavior was monitored and role rehearsal was enforced. Later, however, the church did nothing to replace these unrecognized functions when it began to move into other contexts. When Mennonite Brethren immigrated to North America, began to enter a more open society, and lost their earlier face-to-face social control mechanisms and their patterns for helping individuals in role rehearsal, they developed no substitute. The result was a sharp devaluation of their five-step conversion model.

We may now have to consider a totally new metaphor to describe conversion. I once proposed that we replace the new-birth metaphor with one of bankruptcy. As a person recognizes his or her undoneness before God and asks for forgiveness, there is release from accumulated guilt. Life then begins again at "spiritual zero." Unless the convert is helped to practice the new behavioral ideals and is encouraged to continue in narrow-road living, the conversion may die like a flower on the vine. For this reason it is essential to make our models of conversion explicit. We must review them from time to time to make sure they still are functional within our current social milieu.

* **It needs to be recognized that some conversion models may not be helpful.** I observed several examples of this fact as a missionary. In the case of the Toba of the Argentine Chaco, who have restructured their puberty ceremony as a model for conversion, the individual faints (dies) as a sinner and then "comes to" (is reborn again) as a child of God. The negative cultural linkages of this pattern to sex may produce side effects that completely negate the conversion's value.

Another society restructured its teenage counseling pattern as a model for conversion. When an individual is caught in aberrant behavior, certain relatives of the older generations are required to do the counseling. The counseling individual meets the culprit and the two of them stand back to back while the elder accuses the younger of the evil action. This provides the younger with an opportunity to air his difficulties. He or she receives forgiveness and is reinstated in the good graces of the society. This pattern, however, is also intimately linked to the first sexual experiences in puberty, giving conversion some unwholesome sexual overtones.

The book mentioned earlier, *The School at Mopass*, showed how the missionary nurses, preachers, teachers and other church workers who were the Canadian aborigines' role models actually provided models that didn't fit normal tribal Christian living. Such converts were thus hard-put to find their own culturally appropriate models for converted behavior. When the medicine man "died" and was "resurrected" and described the new model for tribal conversion, he was describing the very areas in which change had to occur in the tribal convert's life.

Sad to say, many people in foreign lands have been converted according to some alien model. The foreign missionary naively teaches his or her home church's model with no understanding of the cultural dynamics inherent in behavioral change on the local scene. This means that people from another culture are pushed to imitate a model for which they have no understanding. If they try to imitate the foreign messenger's model, they will become mere cardboard cutouts. They will not become authentically changed individuals in their own society.

*** Very often the religious concerns which the cross-cultural messenger expresses do not reflect the concerns of the people to whom he/she is ministering.** Many missionaries are so preoccupied with sin, forgiveness of guilt, and preparation for life in the beyond that many spiritual concerns of the local people are not addressed. This forces the people to resort to their old religion, producing much backsliding and syncretism. Many Africans, for example, feel that the evangelical concern with the soul and the hereafter does not meet their needs for the here and now. Of special concern for African Christians is the fact that Christianity often has so little to say about health, illness and guidance in daily life.

THE SPIRIT OF GOD

I have no doubt today that the Spirit of God was present even in the very early part of my life, but at that time I was not aware of it. My first conscious awareness of the Spirit's intervention involved green apples I had stolen as a boy (told elsewhere). After my baptism, I began teaching a Sunday School class and doing some preaching. In my Sunday School teaching and my preaching, I became increasingly conscious of the Spirit's presence, warnings and guidance. This consciousness was heightened during our first term on the mission field where I encountered the Spirit of God's presence and power especially in physical healing.

My first really conscious effort to cultivate channels for the Spirit of God's work in my life, however, came during my college teaching years. After the spiritual crisis I experienced there, I became aware of the concept of keys, of the third ear, and of clearing my channel clogged with unfinished business.

The ongoing counseling with students and others provided a ready opportunity to practice the insights I was gaining. This field of practice was greatly extended when I became translation consultant with the Bible Society and realized the Spirit's deep involvement with Scripture. The Spirit was actively trying to prevent translation errors, and could be relied on in solving seemingly insoluble translation problems.

The mission field experience and the experience with every kind of church during the Bible Society years provided me with a lot of exposure to the charismatic. But it wasn't until a West African native healer helped me to distinguish between the work of the Spirit and "beer foam" that I really felt I was grasping how the Spirit of God really worked.

Today, in my seventies, I am still learning to obey the Spirit's leading. Life's lessons still are not finished. I am glad that God's Spirit is still willing to lead me into more truth.

CHAPTER 5
EXPERIENCES WITH THE SPIRIT OF GOD

My early church experiences did not condition me to expect much from the Spirit of God. Don't get me wrong! The Holy Spirit was treated as totally positive. His name, in one form or another, appeared in most New Testament Scripture readings. He just didn't belong to the same league as conversion, although he played the key role in it.

In steps one and two of the Mennonite Brethren conversion model, it was the Spirit who brought about the awareness of lostness and the conviction of sin. My own conversion experience was prompted, however, more by the desire for newness and the hope of breaking my "habit of lying" than by any conscious guilt brought on by the Spirit of God. Nonetheless, my first clear memory of the Spirit of God's intervention in my life was in connection with strong feelings of conviction.

The green apples

I had been baptized. I was an active member of the church. I was a student at the local Bible school. On weekends I was busy with meetings in rural areas. I had recently even become a Sunday school teacher. Every week I prayed that God would help me prepare my Sunday school lesson thoroughly. I knelt beside my bed and asked God to help me present the lesson clearly and effectively to the nine-year-old boys I was teaching. I wanted to confront them decisively with the demands of God on their lives. But in the midst of my praying, I suddenly became aware of a still small voice in my interior that insistently demanded, "And what about the green apples?"

"Yes, what about the green apples. . . ?"

Many years earlier, some friends and I had been idly roaming around one Sunday afternoon. We had walked down Mountain Road out of Yarrow village and there we had come upon the orchard of an Englishman. It was still early in the season and the apples weren't really fit to eat, but we had helped ourselves liberally in his orchard. We had to throw most of the apples away because they were just too green. I had totally forgotten about the incident. But now as I was preparing for my

Sunday school lesson, the Spirit of God would time and again bring this incident to my awareness in the midst of my prayers for guidance. I resisted! After all, it was such an insignificant event. . . the apples had been grass green. . . and it had happened so long ago. But that still small voice persisted, until one Saturday afternoon I finally got on my bicycle and rode out to the old man's place and confessed our theft to him, asking for his forgiveness and offering payment.

Quaking

My next experience with the Spirit of God was not immediately recognized for what it was. In fact, it was only much later in life, when my wife and I began fellowshiping with the Quakers (Friends) while we lived in Zambia, that I became aware of this aspect of the Spirit's work. The Quakers hold that during a silent meeting one is not supposed to speak until one quakes so hard that it becomes impossible to contain the message the Spirit is inspiring. That is why they were nicknamed "Quakers."

As a young man in the Yarrow church, I sometimes felt my heart pound and my whole body ready to explode at a testimony meeting at which I felt I had to speak out, or at a prayer meeting at which I felt I was to pray. At the time I interpreted this internal pressure as feelings of inferiority—I was afraid to expose myself in public. But now I know it was the Spirit's prompting.

The Lulu Island disobedience

When I was about seventeen I spent a summer teaching daily Vacation Bible School with the West Coast Children's Mission on Lulu Island, one of the largest islands made by the spreading Fraser River delta just south of Vancouver in the area now called Richmond. The school building in which we taught our Bible classes was ten miles away from the home where we slept and ate. The lady who gave us hospitality had kindly arranged with a milk-truck driver, who came by her place at about 8:10 every morning, to let us hitch a ride as he continued on his route. This got us to school at about 8:40 a.m., giving us twenty minutes before we were to begin classes.

One morning when we got to a farm where we were to pick up forty ten-gallon cans of milk, we found that the milk had not been put out on the stand. The truck driver honked and honked. None of us dared go into the barn because that meant passing a pen in which the herd bull was confined. It was a nine-strand barbed-wire fence but the bull inside was snorting and pawing angrily. I remember saying to my fellow Bible school teacher, "I certainly wouldn't want to tangle with that beast!"

The delay continued. Finally, after more than twenty minutes, the man appeared, completely out of breath. He had been out in the field when he suddenly remembered that he had neglected to put out the milk for pick-up.

After he opened the door to the milkhouse from the inside, I went into the milkhouse with him, lifted the milk cans out of the cooling tank and put them on the platform so that they could be put up on the truck. At that very moment I received a clear message. The Spirit of God told me in no uncertain terms to speak to this man about the condition of his soul. I looked at my watch. It was already past nine o'clock. So I said, "God, it is too late today! We have ten more minutes to drive, and we are late already. I will do it tomorrow." We finished loading the milk and got to school fifteen minutes late. We taught our daily Bible classes. We did our visiting in the afternoon in the various homes of the children and their parents. Then we returned to our place of residence.

Next morning when the milk truck picked us up at 8:10 a.m., the driver asked, "Do you remember the place where we had to wait for the milk yesterday?" I began to feel a clammy hand close on my heart. "Last night," he continued, "that man was killed by the bull we saw. He heard some commotion in the pasture among his cattle at about nine or ten o'clock in the evening and went out to investigate. When he got there the bull, who had broken out of his pen, surprised him and attacked him. The bull threw him into the air and rolled him for about two miles. He broke every bone in his body."

This disobedience to the Spirit's voice has stayed with me as a lifelong reminder. I still wince when I think of it!

"The third ear"

When students began coming to me for spiritual help at the college where I taught, they often were not very articulate about what their actual needs were. Thus at first, I had no way of knowing what kind of a message to give them. It often took a number of sessions before they finally found the courage to bring up their real problem. As a result, I was severely frustrated in my early student mentoring efforts.

A lecture by the famous Quaker, Elton Trueblood, came to my rescue. He lectured on how to listen to the Spirit of God. This lecture came at about the same time that I was reading Theodor Reik's book, *Listening with the Third Ear*, which tells about his experiences as a psychiatrist. He often found it necessary "to listen with his third ear," a kind of inner radar system, to locate the actual problem of his patients. Reik describes one such incident from his professional experience in Holland.

A young woman, a member of the German Socialist party and a child of a very important family, fled Hitler's Germany. By the time she arrived in Holland, however, she was severely emotionally disturbed. Unable to work, she had to seek psychiatric help. Among the troubling aspects of her life was the memory of a love affair she had had with a married physician, also from a prominent family. Eventually the doctor broke off their relationship. Reik and this young woman had already been discussing the affair now for several months and had seemingly reached an impasse beyond which the patient seemingly could not go.

She would repeatedly lapse into long silences. After one silence she would complain of a toothache. After another she would complain that one of the books on his shelf was standing upside down. Then one day, without warning or hesitation, Reik found himself asking her, "But why didn't you tell me about your abortion?" When he began the sentence, he'd had no inkling of what was coming out of his mouth. But he realized that inside of himself, this was the truth that had suddenly come into his awareness. He was now verbalizing it. No sooner had he done so, then the patient jumped up and looked at him as if he were a ghost. Abortions were against the law in Germany, and she had been guarding that secret closely to protect the man she still loved. Reik's third ear, however, had heard her unspoken call for help.

The call girl

One day I boarded a plane traveling north in Wichita. I was actually bound for Latin America, but because of a travel agency mistake, I had to connect via New York. I took my assigned window seat. I introduced myself to the man in the aisle seat. He was a sewage engineer. We talked for a few moments. I got no special message on my inner radar, so I took up my work. I opened my briefcase and began correcting some essays I had written for *Practical Anthropology*. We made an intermediate stop in Kansas City where a pretty young woman joined us in the middle seat. I was so deeply engrossed in my correcting by then that I scarcely noticed her.

When the beverages came the man in the aisle seat interrupted my work and said, "Aren't you going to pay any attention to the young lady who is sitting next to you? She is a bunny girl in the Kansas City Playboy Club." But I was so involved in my papers that I just continued correcting. When we approached Chicago where we were to make another intermediate stop before continuing on to New York, we found we weren't able to land because of a tornado. We circled for an entire hour waiting for the tornado to pass. In the meantime I finished correcting my papers and put them back into my briefcase. As I did that, I heard the man in the aisle say, "Poor devil!" I looked at him in surprise. "Why do you say that?" I asked.

"Well," he said, "I don't know whose report you were correcting, but if anybody would put that much red ink on something that I had written, I would commit suicide."

I laughed. "I guess I'm pretty hard-shelled," I said, "I wrote these articles myself."

"What in the world do you write that takes that much precision?" the man asked. I told him I worked for the Bible Society and was writing some articles for missionaries.

The moment I uttered "Bible" I sensed a reaction in the young woman who sat between us. I felt the inner call that I was to speak to her, but I just didn't have the nerve because the inner message I'd received for her was "call girl."

We stayed stacked up for a while longer, then landed abruptly. But the weather on the ground was still so rough that the airline decided to take on no new passengers. They only discharged the local passengers and continued on directly to New York.

In the meantime I told myself, "If the young woman stays in the seat next to me until we're airborne, I will give her the message I have received." Sure enough, even though there were only nine passengers left on that whole plane, the young woman stayed right next to me in the middle seat. When the plane was airborne, I turned to her and said, "When I said that I worked for the Bible Society, I sensed a reaction in you. I then asked God whether I had a message for you, and he did give me one, but I have not delivered it because it seems so crude. The message is 'call girl.' "

The young woman then told me of the fine Catholic family in which she had been raised. I began to feel very bad and finally told her, "I'm sorry, maybe it's you who have a message from God for me. Maybe I need your reproof for a dirty mind." There was a long silence.

Suddenly the young woman opened her purse and pulled out her birth-control pills. "You're right!" she said, "I have become a call girl."

She told me how she had been drawn into this activity and how much it troubled her. She had been trying to get free. She had just taken a three-week vacation in San Francisco with the express intention of quitting. But as soon as she had returned to Kansas City, she found herself back in bed with another man. Now she was again running away to New York. She was desperate. "If I can't shake it, suicide seems to be the only way out," she said.

I listened to the rest of her story and did some preliminary counseling, but I became deeply aware that she would need daily and long-range help. I asked her whether she could talk to her priest. She could not. She did not have anybody within her Catholic background to whom she felt she could talk. But finally she recalled a Presbyterian lady in whom she had confidence, and suggested that she might perhaps be able to help.

Since I was en route to South America, I was running out of time. When we got to New York, I immediately put in a long-distance call to this lady in Kansas City. She not only agreed to help the young woman, she offered her home as a place for her to stay. I then put the young woman right back on the next plane for Kansas City, trusting that she would find a way out of her dilemma with the help the Lord was providing through the Presbyterian lady. I only had some initial keys to her life. I could only pray that the lady who received her had the rest. I do know I encouraged her to at least take the first steps on the road of obedience. Just then my plane was ready for take-off also.

"You goofed"

I was teaching at the college, and every Wednesday night that year I spoke at a church. In fact that whole day was an exceptionally busy day for me. I had classes all day till 3 p.m. and a committee meeting from 3 to 4 p.m. The time between 4 and 5 p.m. was reserved to prepare for my evening assignment. From 5 to 6 p.m. I went home, bathed, changed clothes, had a bite to eat, and then from 6 to 7 p.m. I drove as fast as I dared to get to my place of service sixty-five miles away. Once there I led the Bible study from 7 to 8 p.m. From 8 to 9 p.m. I taught next week's Sunday school lesson to all the adult Sunday school teachers. Every minute of the day was carefully scheduled.

It was shortly after 4 p.m. I had just started clearing my inner channel as part of my preparation for the evening when someone knocked at my office door. I opened the door and there was my problem student from my German class. He was a missionary's son. I had begged and threatened him time and again to come and see me because he was failing in his classes for absolutely no reason I could discern. Immediately, I was torn between my responsibility toward this problem student and my double evening assignment. Finally I said to God, "Okay God, the preparation will be your business; I am going to give this hour to the student." The student came in and sat down and I asked how I might help him. He simply said, "The German you teach is killing me." I tried to get him to be more specific, but he just kept repeating the same thing. So I began at the beginning of the textbook. Precept upon precept, I tried to review what we had covered up to that point. But I soon realized that he just wasn't listening. I became very angry inside. "Look guy," I said within myself, "I'm giving you an important hour that I really need for something else, and you aren't paying a bit of attention. I'm going to flunk you with pleasure!" Finally at five o'clock I had to shoo him out of my office so I could run home to get ready for the evening's assignment.

Next morning another student with whom I was counseling and who was learning how to use keys in witnessing to others about his Christian faith, walked into my office and simply said, "Well, you goofed yesterday." When I asked where, he asked me whether a certain German student had come to see me. When I responded affirmatively, he said, "You see, I had a key to his life, and so I used it. He responded well for a while. But then we came upon a problem with which I just couldn't help him and so I said, 'Why don't you go and see Jake?' The student then said, 'Look, it has been so difficult for me to reveal my problem to you, I just can't tell him about it.' " The counseling student then had said, "Tell Jake anything you want to, he'll be listening with his third ear and be sensitive to the real problem. I have experienced it. I didn't know how to name my problem either, and suddenly he asked me, 'Is it this?' and hit the nail right on the head!"

Obviously this time the voice of my schedule had stopped me from hearing this student's cry for help. I had let other voices drown out the still small voice of the Spirit of God.

Words bouncing off the rafters

I also had to learn that a one-time recognition of my humanity is not enough. I quickly reach for my pious mask again and so become insensitive and unapproachable. A good lesson came to me during a week of pre-Easter services. Until Wednesday night the response to my preaching had been very positive. I had been trying to be extra sensitive to the needs of others in the presentation of my messages. That evening I began my message with enthusiasm, but somehow the words all seemed to bounce back at me from the open rafters in the church. The more I struggled, the more my words rebounded back.

Finally, at the end of the service, I slipped out of the church through the side door without taking leave of anyone and began to walk toward my lodging rather than phone for the car as had been prearranged. I walked the streets for several hours, trying to search my heart to understand the why of this fiasco. Unable to discern any apparent cause, I finally headed dejectedly homeward.

As I passed a lighted window, I became aware of a "still small voice" which told me to enter and speak to the individual who lived there. The person was well-known to me as one who had been marginal to the church for many years and was often criticized publicly. I felt that I just couldn't enter there in my present state of mind. I walked another block, but then retraced my steps and went in. The individual was alone. Without any polite introduction, I said to him, "I don't know why I'm here; I just had the feeling I should come in." Then I went on to tell him what had happened in church. I told him I felt completely defeated and that maybe he was the one who could tell me what my trouble was.

I had not yet finished when he broke in, "For thirteen years I have been bearing some very bitter burdens, always wishing that somewhere I would meet someone with whom I could share these concerns, but everybody appeared so whole, so complete, so holy that I never dared reveal my imperfections." After that three-hour session I realized that God had answered my prayer. He had tried to sensitize me by making me lose my "mask of perfection."

Tiger hears a little now

At the conclusion of the first communion service at the Chocó church in Panama the leader called on the participants to share the assignments they had personally received through God's Spirit for the week to come. Various people got up and declared what they understood their assignment to be. I also rose. I said that God was asking me to teach Bible reading in the homes of various believers. (During the weeks preceding, we had been meeting in the church leader's home to read the newly mimeographed Gospel of Mark in the tribal language. As a result we had developed "an easily teachable method" of Bible reading, personal application and prayer. I felt that this was something that would help the young local church to grow.)

On Monday afternoon, therefore, I dressed in my bathing suit and set out on foot for the next Chocó believer's house, about three-quarters of an hour upriver. I walked in the water where it was shallow enough. I wallowed in the mud on the bank of the river where necessary, often in mud reaching to my waist. But finally, I got there. I bathed. Later I joined the family for supper. Afterward we all sat on the floor around the little chimney-less lamp with our Gospels of Mark. One of the newly-literate young men read a portion and we discussed its message. Each one made some comment about what God was saying to him through it. We prayed together and for each other. Without doubt, it had been a profitable evening!

After the sessions the people took me down river by canoe to where my hammock was. As we floated noiselessly downstream, I was kneeling in the canoe. I now looked up into the overcast sky, and thanked God for this wonderful experience. But suddenly it seemed as if my thank-you bounced right back and hit me on the head like a giant club. My first reaction was, "Gee, I've never had a temptation like this at the height of success before!" Before long I realized that God's Spirit was, indeed, trying to tell me something. I didn't sleep much that night as I struggled to discern what God was trying to say to me. By morning I knew the answer.

When the tribal Christians got ready to pray before breakfast, I asked if I could say a word first. I told them what had happened the previous night, and how God's Spirit had told me I had erred in saying that God was asking me to teach Bible reading. God had not asked me to do it; I had just seen it was something important to do and had assumed God wanted me to do it.

Furthermore, it seemed to me now that God had already asked some local person to do it, and I had just gotten in that person's way. And sure enough, one of the tribal men then spoke up and said, "Yes, God asked me to do it. But since you got up first, I thought that surely I must be mistaken in thinking I heard God tell me to do it." I apologized to my brother and thought this would finish the matter, but not for the Chocó church. They immediately launched out in a prayer service on my behalf. The gist of the prayers was, "God, Tiger (this is my tribal nickname) does not listen to you very often. We thought he could not hear the voice of your Spirit at all, but today we have seen that he can hear it. So we pray that you will help him to hear you better and more often." While I was grateful for the believers' prayer on my behalf, the experience itself was tremendously deflating. Here I was, the "Heap Big Missionary Chief," and the new tribal converts were fully aware that their teacher had a hearing problem when it came to God's Spirit.

The failure that wasn't

In the latter 1960s, when we were home in Canada for a year just before being transferred to Africa, teenage involvement on the drug scene exploded in our part of the country. We worried about our three unmarried teenagers. And so—following our practice that if it's questionable, we'll all do it—we as a family began spending our Sunday afternoons in the House of Daniel in Vancouver. This supposedly was a halfway house for recovering drug addicts, but there still were a lot of active users among those wanting to recover. The aroma of marijuana was heavy in the air. In fact, there were no house parents in the place at that time.

We mingled and chatted with the residents. We participated in their hymn-sings—usually the majority were mellow with grass and swayed rhythmically to the beat of the drum that accompanied the singing. We spent time in prayer with individuals and groups. We tried to understand and to befriend.

One Sunday afternoon when we were getting ready to go home, I suddenly sensed someone gently calling for me. I asked the family to wait while I looked into all the rooms in the four-storey building. Finding no one, I headed for the exit. But the call became more urgent, so I checked every room again, both on the way up and then again back down. I still found no one. Then I began looking in all the downstairs closets. In a sort of root-cellar off the back porch I found him—a young man sitting alone in semi-darkness—peeling a mountain of potatoes for the supper of the hundred or so residents. An inner click confirmed that this was the caller.

I saw an extra paring knife, so I sat down and began quietly peeling potatoes with him. After a respectable silence, I volunteered, "My 'handle' is Jake" (in the jargon of the drug culture). He gave his handle and then we continued in silence. Then I said, "You didn't sing and pray like everyone else this afternoon!"

"No," he said, "I am too discouraged—I found Jesus and quit hard drugs, but since I still occasionally have to lean on grass, I got kicked out of the school where I was trying to finish high school. Secondly, most people here are still flying (high on drugs) and don't think about what needs to be done in the kitchen. They just praise Jesus that we got a bunch of loaves of bread." (A bakery truck had just unloaded what seemed like a hundred loaves of day-old bread.) I felt that the young man was for real; but seeking confirmation I called my youngest daughter. She signaled me, "He's okay!" while the two of us helped him peel potatoes.

I then asked him, "What now?"

Sadly he poured out his heart. "I dropped out of life in Grade 10, and from then on until I found Jesus, my life is just a big black hole. I now know I was on drugs and crime almost five years. I thought I could just start over, after I found Jesus; but now the door of hope seems to have slammed in my face. It looks like I'm damned!"

My daughter was fighting back tears. I was gripped with inner pain. "What is the message of hope here, God?" I pled inwardly. Suddenly my third ear heard, "G.E.D." I immediately told the young man about this American test, first developed for young people drafted into the army, which proved a way for older dropouts to gain high school equivalency by writing five area tests. Those who passed could go directly to college. Our second daughter, who was a student at Western Washington University in Bellingham, could arrange the test for him if he would come to our home in Abbotsford to request it. (This was my test to see if he was really serious.) He came! We made the arrangements and I took him to Bellingham and paid for the exams. Our daughter took him to his exams and kept encouraging him because he seemed to lose his nerve after each test. Finally, he finished all five exams and learned that he had passed in the 54th percentile. Now he could go to college!

When I brought him back to Abbotsford, he tearfully embraced my wife and said, "Mrs. Loewen, I didn't completely blow my mind with drugs! I'm average! I'm going to make it!"

I put up the first thousand dollars. A friend put up a second thousand. I then phoned the young man's sister, a professor at Harvard, and asked if she would pay the balance of his first semester at Tabor College. She eventually agreed.

On my next trip east, I stopped at Tabor College to explain what such a venture would require, such as the continual encouragement he would need. The administrators agreed to do whatever it took to help this young man succeed. But when he enrolled, everyone was so busy that they completely forgot about checking up on him. He sat in his dorm room for a month and then took off. By the time Tabor College called me, the young man was lost in the San Francisco drug scene. We and our children all grieved deeply. We made many attempts to locate the young man, but finally gave it up as a lost cause.

Some twenty years later an acquaintance dropped by and asked, "Does the name XX mean anything to you?"

"It certainly does. We still grieve over our family failure!"

"Grieve no more! He sends you the following message: 'I eventually found my way out! The love and help of your family kept on nudging me until I finally made it. I am a member of the church your nephew pastors. I have a lovely wife and two healthy children. I own my own business. Thanks again for loving me when I wasn't worth loving'!"

For twenty years! God's Spirit had kept on working, and he wasn't finished yet. . . !

CHAPTER 6

WHAT I LEARNED ABOUT HOW GOD'S SPIRIT WORKS

Over my decades in preaching, teaching, missions and Bible translating, I've learned many valuable (and sometimes painful) lessons about how the Spirit of God works.

Here are some of them:

One cannot harness the power of God's Spirit under false pretenses

The early chapters of Acts recount the power experienced by early New Testament believers when, immediately after Jesus' resurrection, the Spirit of God manifested his power among them in a totally new way. Peter could grasp the lame man's hand and say, "Silver and gold have I none, but what I have I give you" (Acts 3:6), and then in the power of the Spirit of God upon him, he healed the man. In this power-charged atmosphere, Ananias and Sapphira were eager to acquire the same power that men like Peter, Barnabas and others were manifesting. The two sold some property, but instead of giving the entire amount of the sale to the church as Barnabas had done, they held back part of it and gave only the balance, pretending it was the total. They tried to substitute overt verbal piety for honesty, but it didn't work. The Spirit of God exacted the supreme penalty from them—they fell down dead.

I find another powerful example of this lesson in the life of my biblical namesake, Jacob. He and his mother connived to trick the blind father, Isaac, into giving Jacob the firstborn blessing that rightfully belonged to his brother, Esau. Jacob dressed up in Esau's clothes. Where his body was smooth, he put on goatskins. Then using Esau's name, he stepped into his father's presence. His father expressed surprise at how quickly his son had returned from his supposed hunt. But Jacob, his mouth dripping with false piety, lied, "Yes, God was with me, and he led the game right into my path." Still Isaac wasn't convinced, as the voice didn't sound like Esau's, so he asked him what his name was, and again Jacob claimed to be Esau (Gen. 27:17-18).

Jacob received the sought-after blessing only some twenty years later after he had faced the question of his name a second time at Peniel. This time, he answered honestly: "My name is Jacob," (and *Jacob* means 'the deceiver').

It seems to me that we, too, often seek God's blessing under false pretenses. All too often, even in the act of admitting our sin, we give it a nicer name. We want forgiveness, but we don't want to face the full ugliness of our wrongdoing.

In my early ministry I once accepted a preaching assignment but didn't really make adequate preparation. I stood behind the pulpit and piously asked God to empower me with his Spirit and help me to proclaim his truth with power, but the only thing that responded was a still, small voice inside of me that said, "Jaschke, dü best fül jewäze." (Freely translated this means, "Jake old boy, you have been downright lazy.")

There is a hierarchy of priorities in the way God's Spirit works

Many Christians make an unbiblical distinction between "spiritual" work and "ordinary" work. When asked to perform a "spiritual" task like give a testimony or lead in a prayer, they seem to think the only preparation they need is to cry earnestly to the Lord for guidance. But all too often nothing seems to happen. The reason, of course, is that they have disregarded the hierarchy of priorities in the way the Spirit of God works.

Jesus spelled out these priorities in the Gospel of John (16:7-8) when he told us, "When this counselor—the Spirit—comes from God, his first responsibility will be to convict human beings of sin, of justice and of judgment." I like to call this the channel-clearing function of the Spirit. God does not make us channels of his blessing "just any old time" we happen to call for it. He first makes sure that the channel between him and us is clear. And only after the channel has been properly cleared, can we experience the second priority in God's Spirit's work, which is expressed in verse 13, "he shall empower you and lead you into all truth."

Let me reaffirm: *you cannot be a channel of God's blessing as long as you still are the object of his channel-clearing work.*

The blocked channel may, of course, be the result of overt sin, like the green apples of my youth told about earlier. Or it can be a "sin of omission," like leaving undone something good that we knew we ought to do.

At other times, it can be ignorance or cultural prejudice as in the case of Peter in Acts 10. Peter was a good Jew who believed that salvation was for the Jews only. Thus when God called Peter to testify to Cornelius, a Gentile, the Spirit had to work overtime with the sheet full of creepy-crawlies to first remove the cultural prejudice from Peter's channel.

When I talked about third-ear hearing, I described blockage of another kind. My inner radar—the channel which the Spirit of God wants to use for speaking to us—was totally occupied with self-protection and therefore unavailable for the Spirit of God's guidance.

How do we clear the channels so the Spirit of God can work? Obviously the first step is to deal with any specific failures and wrongs of which we already are aware. We need to seek forgiveness! We have to make the necessary restitution! We have to do whatever it takes to eliminate our accumulated guilt!

My method of unblocking the channel is to pray silently. As soon as I try to focus upon God in silence, all kinds of extraneous thoughts begin popping up. I have learned it is important to write down these interrupting thoughts because they all seem to be related to unfinished business in my life. I may have forgotten to pay the telephone bill again, despite having received an overdue notice. Or I have neglected to write a note to someone who needs encouragement. Or I have failed to make an apology I knew was due.

Some items are so subtle I don't recognize them immediately. Sometimes I have had to work on them for weeks before I could discover the meaning of certain thoughts. The reason for this is that we tend to wear all kinds of masks. We try to hide our weaknesses. We try to repress our problems. We have so many inner defenses built up that frequently we don't allow even the Spirit of God to get close to certain problems. Thus a strange and seemingly unintelligible thought may be the closest that the Spirit can get to the unresolved problem spot in our lives.

I have found it necessary to keep the recorded unintelligible thoughts on my desk and to reread them several times a day. Then, lo and behold, somewhere down the line one of them suddenly will fall into place, and I will recognize what blockage it is referring to.

After the interruptions are completely taken care of, that is, after no more strange thoughts interrupt my silent prayer, I usually sign the list I have written down as a pledge to God that I will take care of the various items when the current assignment for which I am seeking guidance has been discharged.

Once the channel has been cleared, one is in a position to receive the message that God wants delivered, or one is now free to let God's power flow through oneself to heal or to help someone in need. Here is an illustration of how I have experienced it:

One day while I was teaching, a college senior came to me asking for an appointment. I knew her fairly well. She had been in my classes. I also knew that she had been seeing a psychiatrist. I wasn't sure I had any business to try and counsel her. So I put off giving her an appointment by asking her to return the following Monday. I wanted to pray to see whether God really wanted me to get involved. I talked to my wife about it, and we prayed about it together.

Early Monday morning I was leading the local Christian businessmen's prayer meeting and told them about my dilemma. First of all, I didn't have the time to spend months with her trying to identify her problem. If the psychiatrist hadn't done it, what could I do in one or two sessions? But even more important, if we did discover the problem, I didn't feel I had the spiritual resources to deal with it alone.

The business people were truly great. They asked if I would be willing to be their spokesperson with this troubled student. They asked me to name the hour when I would give her an appointment and each of them would clear his/her calendar and would get down on his knees before God in prayer, focusing their spiritual power to join mine in "healing" this troubled young woman.

Armed with the business people's assurance and support, I gave the young woman an appointment for the designated hour on Wednesday. Half an hour before she came in, I was in my office clearing my channel. After my channel was clear, and the list had been signed, I asked God what message he had for this young woman. I repeated her name and the fact that she had been in psychiatric care for some time. Then I asked God, "What is your message for her?" At once the expression *petting to climax* flashed into my mind. (This expression, no longer in use, refers to sexual foreplay.)

When the student arrived a few minutes later, I found myself wondering how serious she was about solving her problem and so I asked her, "Do you want to close the door before we begin talking?" She responded by shutting the door and triple-locking it. (Because some students had been trying to steal my examinations, I had had extra locks installed.) Then she stood by the door as if frozen. I asked her to take the chair beside my desk. She came there very hesitantly. Her eyes, sunken and cloudy, had the expression of a trapped fawn. She exuded fear.

I told her honestly why I hadn't given her an appointment the previous week. It was because I had been afraid. I told her that the Christian business people had promised to support us in prayer and that at this very moment twenty other people were praying for us as we were talking. "So you see, I am not dealing with you on my own, but in the combined spiritual strength of all these Christians," I said. "Furthermore, I don't have many weeks of time to give you. You've been seeing a psychiatrist for years already, and you seemingly haven't been able to solve your problem there. Because of this, I asked God what I shall give you as a message from him." Then I asked her: "Do you know what the expression '*petting to climax*' means?"

I was totally unprepared for what happened next. She leapt out of her chair and made for the third-floor window behind me. I managed to grab her and pull her back into her chair.

"It's dirty, it's dirty, it's dirty!" she continued gasping, foam oozing from her mouth.

Gradually as she calmed down, I said, "I did not ask you to say what it is like. I asked, 'Do you know what it means?' " She nodded hesitantly. Then I asked, "Is that your problem?" She nodded at once: "Yes, it started right after I began to date this certain boy, but I have hidden it even from the psychiatrist for all this time."

After her confession and prayer for forgiveness the frightened-fawn look vanished. Her eyes became clear again and the vibrant, alive look of a healthy young woman was back.

I don't claim to have ever cast out an evil spirit, but as I look back on this incident, it is probably the closest I have ever gotten to it. Of course, it wasn't me alone—twenty other people were praying with me. I was merely their voice.

Human beings cannot escape the principle of entropy

The second law of thermodynamics, referred to earlier, tells us that hot things cool off, and moving things tend to slow down. It is the same way in human life. At conversion or some special dedicatory experience we feel truly in touch with God. We feel spiritually alive and strong. Then as we move along in our daily lives, the awareness of God's indwelling Spirit and his power in our lives diminishes. If we once heard the voice of God speaking to us clearly, it now seems to grow fainter and fainter. In fact, we may even hear a multiplicity of voices inside of us drowning out the 'still small voice of the Spirit.' Then there are concerns about our own ego, our schedule and our responsibilities—all of which can individually or collectively block out the voice of the Spirit. Thus amid this cacophony of voices, the still small voice of the Spirit of God is often very hard to hear. It simply gets drowned out!

The Book of Acts records an illustration of multiple voices. After the apostles had been arrested for the first time, they were interrogated by the Sanhedrin, then thoroughly beaten and released. The apostles were definitely shaken by the experience. They feared that the threats of the Jewish leadership would dull their hearing of the Spirit of God, and so they prayed, "Oh Lord, listen to their threats and grant us that we may..." (Acts 4:29-31). They were afraid that the threats of their enemies would become louder and clearer than the still small voice of God's Spirit within them.

I have to confess that I have experienced entropy time and again. The incident with the student from my German class, told in the previous chapter, is a case in point. Luckily, that time I had a second chance.

The Spirit of God sometimes works in what to us seems as arbitrary ways

In his introduction to his translation of the Book of Acts, J. B. Phillips makes some interesting comments about how the Spirit of God works. He says he found translating this book to be most exciting because it was like working on the wiring of an old house in which he could not turn off the mains. The house seemed to have been rewired several times, and many of the wires were dead, but every now and then he would unexpectedly touch a live wire and get the shock of his life. He goes on to say that the most outstanding truth he learned from this book was that the Spirit of God refuses to be channeled by human design. There is a seeming arbitrariness about the way in which the Spirit works. In fact, Phillips concludes that the moment a church group or an individual establishes the exact channel in which the Spirit of God is to work, one can be sure he isn't in it. The Spirit refuses to be confined to the channels that individuals or churches may construct.

We have some beautiful examples of this arbitrariness in the Book of Acts. With the outbreak of the big persecution in Jerusalem, many believers sought safety in the surrounding areas. As a result, the deacon Philip came to Samaria where

Jesus had earlier contacted the Samaritan woman. Philip preached the good news about Jesus' death and resurrection and found that there were multitudes of people who were ready to accept Jesus as their Messiah. In fact, the group was so large that he called for the "big wheels" from Jerusalem to come and help. The apostles came, and the Spirit of God was poured out upon these people just as it had been poured out upon the Jewish disciples in the first place (Acts 2). With this, God demonstrated that the half-Jew-half-Gentile syncretistic Samaritans were also included in the divine plan of salvation. But in the midst of this ongoing revival, the Spirit of God called to Philip and told him to go out on the desert road leading from Jerusalem to Gaza. (It is interesting to note that in the New Testament, the word *desert* often does not emphasize the absence of water nearly as much as it does the absence of people.) Here, at the height of the revival in Samaria, Philip was asked to leave the crowds who were accepting Christ and go to a place where there were no people. Luckily Philip heard the still small voice and obeyed. As a result, a discouraged Ethiopian eunuch found the Christ.

In the previous chapter I recounted in detail a personal experience in this regard. While the first building of the Chocó church was being finished, David Wirsche and I spent the evenings in the prophet's house reading the newly produced Gospel of Mark in the Empera language. As we read the Scriptures, made applications to our own lives, and prayed about what we had read, a kind of family Bible study pattern emerged. On Sunday the leader of the meeting asked what God was asking each individual to do. I was so impressed by our success in teaching these family Bible readings that when David declared that he was going down river to teach reading, I automatically assumed God wanted me to continue teaching this Bible study method in other believers' homes. I proceeded to do so, only to find that God had asked someone else to do it. At the height of success I, unlike Philip, had failed to hear the Spirit in his seeming arbitrariness.

I am happy to report that on this occasion David was a lot more sensitive. As he got into the canoe that Monday morning to head down river, an Empera believer got in with him. David was surprised because the man had not asked for permission to go along. So he casually asked him where he was going. The man told him that he was going to the same place David intended to go. When David asked what he was going to do when he got there, the man said, "I am going to teach the people to read." When David asked him why, the man simply said, "Because God asked me to do that." David, sensitive and obedient, recognized his mistake. He went to speak to the chief of the area, introduced his Empera companion, and then left him there to teach the people while he himself went farther down river to teach in another village.

It is possible to learn to hear the Spirit even after years of not listening

Dr. G. W. Peters, the late Professor of Missions at Dallas Theological Seminary, told about his wife's physical healing. Over a period of thirty-six years, Mrs. Peters gradually lost all hearing in one ear. During a social gathering one evening, Dr. Peters mentioned his wife's problem, and one of the people present, an ear specialist, said, "I'm interested; why don't you have your wife come and see me sometime."

Mrs. Peters made an appointment, and the specialist examined her ear. He took out a tiny chisel and a tiny hammer. He set the chisel against the juncture of two small bones in her inner ear, gave it one tap with the little hammer and *voila*!, as the French say, she could hear again! The little bones that should vibrate in her ear had become fused by a calcium deposit; once the specialist broke the linkage, the bones could move independently again, and she could hear.

This experience of physical healing is an example of hope in regard to hearing the voice of the Spirit of God. I spent the first two decades of my Christian life relatively unconscious of my need to listen to the Spirit of God. Only when crisis overwhelmed me did I realize what a Spirit-hearing problem I had. Once I opened my life, God also provided me with what it took to develop my spiritual and "third-ear" hearing.

I know today that this can never be achieved once and for all. We will constantly need to clear our channels! We will constantly have to be ready to hear the unexpected from the Spirit! We will constantly have to distinguish his voice from a myriad of other voices! But if we are truly serious about wanting to hear, he will not let us down. The still small voice will speak to us, and we will be able to hear it.

The listening and obeying of that still small voice is never finished. Even after decades of meaningful experiences, I have not reached perfect hearing. Yesterday's obedience is no guarantee that I'll hear the Spirit today. Obedience to God is never finished!

CHAPTER 7
THE SPIRIT OF GOD AND THE WORD OF GOD

When I became a translation consultant for the Bible Societies, I looked to God to give me the sensitivity to his Spirit so that I would not let mistakes creep into the text as I checked translations into languages which I knew only in part. I doubt that I always succeeded in heeding God's voice, but the times when I did sense his intervention to prevent error were most instructive.

Inner unease in problem situations

One of the times I experienced such intervention occurred while we were checking 1 Peter in Northern Lengua. We were about into the middle of the fourth chapter when I suddenly developed strong inner discomfort. I told the translators about it. We went back over all the verses in that section time and again, but did not locate anything wrong. However, my inner discomfort remained. Finally, I told the translators I would come back six months later, and we would then review this portion again. When we looked at it a second time, the same discomfort reappeared, but still we could not find any problem. This happened again on a third visit.

The missionary translator then told me, "Jake, I think it is time you accept that there is nothing wrong in these verses." I was surprised when the mother-tongue speaker, who was serving as co-translator, turned to the missionary and said, "Please let me try once more. Every time Jake has felt such discomfort deep down in his innermost, it has meant a problem. I think we should take his discomfort seriously." Then he turned to me and said, "Will you please explain the exegesis of these verses again." I went over the exegesis[1] in Spanish and also in Low German, which the Indian had learned from his Mennonite co-translator.

When I finished, the Lengua said, "Now I want to reread the passage once more." He read the passage and suddenly he stopped and exclaimed, "I've found it!" Four verses apart there was a second negative in a language which does not

[1]Exegesis is an explanation or critical interpretation of a text.

permit double-negatives! Four verses apart the message had been essentially negated!

The case of the imported "but." After I had been transferred to West Africa, I began checking the Gospel of John in a translation made by a Roman Catholic priest, a native speaker of the Fon language. When we had done a chapter or so, I stopped and explained to him my method of listening to every translation at several levels. At one level, I listened as a linguist who was trying to find any wrong grammatical constructions or any semantic obscurity. But at a different level, I was listening as a Christian who believed in the guidance and inspiration of the Holy Spirit. Occasionally, when there was something wrong in the text, I would feel inner discomfort, and in this translation so far I had felt that discomfort in at least two verses. I pointed them out to him but noted that I had not been able to identify the problem as yet. I said I would let him know each time the discomfort recurred.

We continued our work, and every now and then I stopped him and said, "When we were in verse so and so, I again felt the same discomfort in my gut." Eventually it got to the point where the African translator just laughed at me. He read the verse once more and said, "Obviously you do not know Fon. And since you cannot speak this language, therefore your hurt has nothing whatsoever to do with a translation problem or with the Spirit of God!" I asked him to be patient with me as I continued to try to pinpoint what was troubling me.

When we got into the middle of the Book of Acts the discomfort returned. Here I was able to pinpoint it. "I think I can now nail down my difficulty a little bit more closely for you." I pointed out that every time we met a negative statement followed by "but," I was expecting that in his language we should get a positive statement followed by "because." I illustrated the problem for him with a couple of daily life examples. He admitted that that was indeed the way his language also handled it. I then said that we were continuing to get a negative plus "but" and I didn't know that languages in this part of Africa had that kind of a "but."

This time the translator did not laugh. "You may be right," he said, "because that 'but' here is not from our language; we have borrowed it from Hausa." (Hausa is a Nigerian trade language which dominates much of West Africa. It is a trade language for many tribes and probably had at one time also been a trade language for Fon.) He then changed the construction as per the grammar of his language and my inner discomfort disappeared. When we went back and checked all the other verses, we found the same was true in all the cases where I had registered discomfort.

Experiences like these have made me deeply aware of how carefully the Spirit of God watches the translation of the Word of God. He inspired it, and he watches its translation closely. But translators also need to be open to the Spirit's leading!

The Spirit of God in problem solving

"Widow" in Patamuna. When we were checking the Patamuna New Testament in Guyana, I discovered that the translators had not found a word for "widow." This was strange, because unless it was a language in which words picked up taboos as people died, there would be no reason why it should not have a word for "widow." Obviously there were people in the village who had had the experience of widowhood. But try as I might, I was unable to locate a word. We always had to come back to "a woman whose husband has died."

This circumlocution was fine when that expression was the subject of the sentence, but when it was the object of the sentence, it often became ambiguous. I pressed hard to find a solution, but to no avail.

As was my practice, I then committed the problem to the Lord in prayer. I had a siesta right after lunch as usual. I had a wristwatch alarm which I would set for the time available, twenty minutes, half-an-hour or whatever. When the alarm would wake me, I would resume my translation checking. This day, as I lay down for my siesta, I repeated my prayer to the Lord. When I awoke, I became aware that a message had risen from my unconscious into consciousness. It told me that in this language the suffix '-pï-' in verbs was a past tense marker, but in nouns, or in other kinds of words, it served to suggest that the object was a has-been, e.g., it used to be a chair, but it is now broken. Or, it used to be a house, but it has now been abandoned and has collapsed, etc. I wondered what would happen if I added that suffix to "wife."

When we began our translation checking that afternoon, I turned to the mother-tongue speaker who was helping us on this occasion and said I wanted to check a couple of words with him. So I added '-pï-' to chair and, of course, I got "a broken chair." When I added '-pï-' to house, I got "an abandoned, collapsed house." When I added '-pï-' to cooking pot, it became "a cooking pot that no longer served." However, when I added '-pï-' to "wife," the man laughed loudly and said, "You never say that! To designate 'widow,' you say wife '-lïpï-.'" When I asked why he had not told us the word before, he shrugged his shoulders and said it just had not occurred to him.

"Life" in Trio. When we were checking the Gospel of John in the Trio language of Surinam, we came to verse four in chapter one where the text reads, "And the life was the light of men." When I listened to the back translation[2] of the Trio rendering, it sounded as if a fellow was living with a woman and that the man or the situation of the two together was very bright.

---

[2] It is a literal word-for-word translation of a native language which the translation consultant doesn't know well enough to speak. By hearing how the words follow each other and knowing the construction of the grammar in the language, the consultant is able to decide whether or not this is a natural way of expressing a given meaning.

I pointed out to the missionary that this was hardly the meaning of "the life was the light of men." But try as I would, I was unable to find a better answer. To make matters worse, a consultant from another Bible translating organization was with us. This man, who also had a Ph.D. in linguistics and who worked in a closely related language, told me in no uncertain terms, "There is no better answer in our language either. There is no word for 'life!' You can't do any better than this!"

The problem was that the verb "to live" in this language was used only of men who had a female consort, and thus the word had overtones of sexual cohabitation. The resulting idea was that there was a man who was living in cohabitation with a female in a very bright situation. This rendering seemed very misleading to me, but I was unable to suggest anything better. Somewhat embarrassed and exceedingly frustrated, we halted for lunch.

After lunch I had my traditional nap, but first I again committed the problem to the Lord in prayer. When I awoke, a message had arisen from the unconscious. It said that in the Trio language many things that we consider positive in English are expressed as a negative: fast is *unslow*, good is *unbad*, straight is *uncrooked*, etc. I quickly went to the missionary and collected from him a number of adjectival expressions in which the addition of the negative affix "un" provided a positive quality. When we had done about twenty such adjective constructions, I fabricated a construction of this affix plus "die" to make the expression "undie." The Trio just roared with laughter. "You never say that!" he said. "But you are right, this is the way to solve our problem." Then he came up with the word "undyingness." This rendered verse four as: "God's undyingness or the undyingness God gives, was like a light that showed men the way."

The Spirit that first inspired the writer of John's Gospel was still alive and active in the 1960s.

When God speaks to a church which is active in translating his Word

About a year after the young Waunana translator had developed his stride in translating the New Testament into his own language, I was privileged to visit him and his tribe again. I attended the convention of their church, the Iglesia Evangélica Unida (United Evangelical Church). True to Waunana custom, I, as one of the distinguished guests, received an impromptu invitation "to bring a message from the Word." I assumed that the church was more or less in the same state of spiritual development as I had left it the year before, and so I quoted a passage of Scripture from memory, isolated a meaningful idea from it, and then discussed it in the light of my personal experience and the Waunana culture.

When I had finished, the young translator who was leading the meeting got up and apologetically said: "We asked for a message from God's Word, but since we didn't get it, I will now ask all of you to listen to what God says to the church." Then he opened the new translation of the Epistle to the Galatians and began to read and to comment. Here are some excerpts:

3:1ff. How many people do we have in this village who began

walking the way of the gospel and who are now going astray? I can think of seven people right now whose names we all know. These people began with God. They experienced the power of God's Spirit, but they have slipped back into living in the fear of the evil spirits.

3:6. Several of you are asking: "What is there for me in the gospel?" You say "I don't have any more food to eat. I haven't had any less illness in my family." Listen! Abraham followed God for many years. He even left his people and his country because God told him to. He had troubles. He had difficulties. But because Abraham continued to obey him, God rewarded him and blessed him. God does not bless those people who only begin with him; he blesses those who steadfastly continue to follow him.

3:13. We all make contracts in life. We make contracts to chop out a canoe for someone, or to clear someone's land for planting. When we have made a contract with someone, we expect that person to keep it. Now remember, when we began to believe, we gave God our hand in a contract. If we will live up to our side of the agreement, we can be sure that God will also fulfill his side. God never lets his children down.

3:28. In this meeting there are Empera and Waunana; there are white people and there are Negroes. Even among our own people—the Waunana—our community is made up of people from different rivers. But when we become members of the family of Jesus, it doesn't matter anymore from which river we originally came; it doesn't matter from which tribe we come; it doesn't even matter if the color of our skin is different. Jesus Christ makes all people equally members of his family. Have there been quarrels between Waunana and Empera? Yes, we know there have been. In fact, we know the people who quarrel right now. What are we going to do about it? Are we going to take sides in these quarrels, or are we going to remind those of our brothers and sisters who are failing to remember that we are all members of God's family, that the people of one family—God's family—do not quarrel with each other?

4:3. The Galatians, like our people, used to be afraid of the evil spirits. In fact, they were the slaves of the evil spirits. But now through Jesus Christ they have been made free. That's why today when there is difficulty, we look only to God and his Holy Spirit. But I guess it isn't really true of all of us. Some of the people who have been baptized into this church are still sneaking off to other villages to sing *hai* (chanting to the evil spirits at the healing ceremonies). Some of you are saying there is more than one kind

> of illness. There is illness that can be cured only by *hai*. Don't believe it! Even if you should meet an evil spirit in the forest and he should try and frighten you, don't let him frighten you! Don't believe what he says! If you begin to listen to the evil spirits, you will lose the companionship of the Spirit of God who is much more powerful than all the evil spirits together.

The young translator spoke so bluntly that I was shocked. I asked myself: how does this young man dare to declare what even an elder is afraid to say? Within the next few days I learned the reason: during the previous year this young man had found that he could not make many of the translation decisions on his own, and so he had begun to take his translation problems to church meetings. Preaching had given way to the reading of portions of the new translation, and at points of concern, the translator would then explain the meaning of the passage and the translating problem. Then the whole congregation would pray: "Lord, if you had spoken this word in *Waun meu,* 'the Waunana language,' in the first place, how would you have said it?" As a result of the solutions that had been reached by group consensus following the church's prayer, the translation had become a direct and authoritative message from God. The preacher could apply it boldly because the word was not his, it was God's. The people had asked God to speak plainly in their language. Now that he had spoken, they bowed to his Word, no matter how sharp a reproach it contained.

Experiences like this caused me to begin training all translators to regularly use that prayer: "God, how would you have said this if you had spoken in our language in the first place."

When tribal grammar calls for information not specified in the text

Paul saw Jesus Christ. One of the languages in Paraguay requires that all nouns and proper names be preceded by a prefix which indicates whether the item or person is visible at the time of communication. If not visible, it must be specified whether it is only currently, or permanently invisible. In the case of the former, it must be further specified whether the item was visible only in myth age or whether it has never been seen by humans. All in all there are fifteen prefix possibilities.

When the translators faced 1 Cor. 15:8 where Paul says: "I saw Jesus Christ," the missionary translator and his tribal co-worker disagreed as to which prefix to use. The missionary explained his choice on the basis of his theology and said, "Paul saw Jesus in a vision," but the tribal translator, even after listening intently to the missionary's reasoning, said, "We, as a church, asked God how he would have said it in our language, and the answer is, 'Paul really saw Jesus!' " There is no indication in the original as to which prefix to use, because the Greek did not require the specification of this information. If the translation in this language is to be as authoritative as the original, it must make explicit this additional inspiration.

The Biza-Lala encounter the Spirit of God in translation

While I was deeply moved by the impact of the newly translated Word in the Waunana setting described earlier—in spite of the putdown of being told that I had not brought a message from the Word of God—it wasn't until I had a second similar experience in Africa in the Biza-Lala language that I recognized a further important dimension of a truly inspired translation: if the translation is to have universal authoritative status, the entire church will have to be involved in the process in order to experience the Spirit's input.

As in the Waunana case, the Biza-Lala experience developed completely unplanned. This language had a New Testament, but it was an old, very poor missionary-made translation. The church was pleading for a new translation. But because it was a language of only tertiary status in Zambia, the Bible Societies could not provide full financing, although they were able to make a small sum of money available for that language. The church met and agreed to give the Bible Societies' money to one man who would bear the responsibility for preparing a basic draft. All the other people in the church would participate voluntarily without pay. Since there wasn't enough money to duplicate the drafts, the translator made five or six copies on his typewriter and sent them out for revision. This meant there weren't even enough copies to provide one per church, so several churches had to meet together over one typescript. They, like the Waunana, began to read the Word instead of preaching. They discussed its meaning and noted the points of special concern marked by the translator, and then prayed: "God, if you had said this in Chibiza in the first place, how would you have said it?" One of the first answers to prayer was that all the many transliterations[3] from English of the previous New Testament fell away without any objections. God began to speak a normal Chibiza.

A second experience involved the whole 200,000-strong Biza-Lala tribe which prayed: "God! How would you have said this if you would have spoken in our language in the first place?"

The Biza-Lala language has twelve words for basket while the Greek has only two, which it seemingly uses interchangeably. The question for the Chibiza now was: which of our twelve words should be used for basket in the story of the feeding of the five thousand? The translators sent out a letter to all the churches. The individual churches prayed. Then there were regional church meetings at which the problem was discussed. Finally the whole tribe assembled before the paramount chief and discussed and prayed over this matter before deciding on the word which God would have used for basket in the story of the feeding of the five thousand.

---

[3]Such as when the Greek word *baptidzo* is translated 'baptize' in English, or the Hebrew word *shabath* is translated as 'sabbath.' These are transliterations from Greek or Hebrew in English. There were many similar transliterations from English in the Biza-Lala New Testament.

When I returned to the translation some months after this tribal meeting, the translator ran to meet me the moment he saw my car coming. He embraced me and said, "Doctor, it has happened!" His face beamed with joy as he told me about the meeting. "God has spoken!" he said. Then he confided that he had always suspected that the Bible was white man's God speaking to white people and that the white missionaries were saying that it was good for Africans also. "But now," he said, "that has all changed because we realize that we Africans have made decisions together with the Spirit of God which no white man could have made. It truly has become our God's Word to us."

When there is trouble, look to God's Spirit!

I remember a translation in which some forty denominations and mission societies participated because it involved a very large African language. We developed some difficulties with the Adventists on the team. Even though we were following the rules that had been established with the Adventist Church International, the local Adventists seemingly did not agree. At issue was the translation of the word "sabbath" which they had just transliterated as *nsabata* in the past. Our agreement stated that expressions like "the seventh day" or "the day of rest" were acceptable alternatives for the Adventist Church and in this case we were using the expression "day of rest."

Just before the team met for the final approval of one of the Gospels, the Adventists wrote a very angry letter to the translation consultant and called him "the devil's advocate," claiming he was trying to ruin the Adventist Church and its teaching. Even though the consultant offered to speak to the Adventist conference to clarify the issue, they refused to resolve it.

The issue came to a head when all the churches and mission societies got together. I did not lead the meeting, but as translation consultant I was present as a resource person. The Adventist representative made the issue public. The result was that a Pentecostal and the Adventist spokesman tangled, and angry words were exchanged. As their argument escalated, I dropped to my knees beside my chair and began to pray that God's Spirit would somehow intervene.

Bit by bit, other members present around the table went on their knees. Finally only the two men who were shouting at each other across the table were left standing. When the two realized they were the only ones left who weren't praying, the Pentecostal man went on his knees too. This left the Adventist standing alone. He finally went down on his knees and a period of silence ensued. Suddenly the silence was pierced as the Adventist cried out in anguish, "God forgive me! I know you would have never used the word *nsabata* if you had talked in our language in the first place. Please forgive me!" The problem was solved!

Handling problems in the text

Some discrepancies in the biblical text make accurate translation particularly difficult. One example is Mark 1:2. The Greek text plainly reads, "As Isaiah said," but verse three then continues with a quotation from Malachi and verse four is a quotation from Isaiah. When we were doing the translation into one of the African languages, I explained this difficulty to the translation team. But when all the churches got together to give final approval to the Gospel of Mark, some bright individual who had not been part of the translation team raised the question: "Say doctor, what are we going to do about Mark 1:2 where there plainly is a problem? Mark says 'As Isaiah said' and he then begins quoting Malachi." I got up and told the assembled people that many people had become conscious of this problem.

Translations like the King James Bible recognized this discrepancy and "cheated" by amending the inspired text to read, "As the (plural) prophets said," because Mark is obviously quoting both Malachi and Isaiah. I then reviewed the various explanations that have been given. One was that Isaiah also said this, but it is not in any of the Scriptures that we have extant. There may have been more pieces of Isaiah than the two we now have in the Bible. The other explanation was that Isaiah also said this, but it wasn't written down. I gave all the arguments that have been used by various people trying to deal with this particular passage. But then I added my personal opinion that Mark did not unroll the scroll and thought Isaiah said it, but began mistakenly quoting from Malachi in a verse that flows very easily together with a passage from Isaiah. "Why the Spirit of God did not check him in this instance, I don't know," I said. "But it has been my experience that God's Spirit always has a reason for doing whatever he does."

When I finished my explanation the chairman of the meeting, an African, told the assembled translators, "I think it is time that we praised God." For the next forty-five minutes the assembled people praised God that Africans could be first-class Christians. I was totally puzzled by this development. When an intermission was called, I went to the chairman and asked him privately, "What happened? I don't understand!"

The man said, "Oh! Well, you see the missionaries always told us that the prophets in God's Word had made no mistakes, but we knew that our own prophets often sneak in some of their own things! We have to watch them with hawk's eyes for places where the Word of God leaves off, and they begin to put in their own words. Since missionaries said the biblical writers made no such mistakes, we thought Africans would never be able to be first-class Christians. But if Mark made such a mistake, then obviously it shows that we Africans can be first-class Christians."

I was deeply moved. I had been chased off mission stations by fundamentalist missionaries who used the King James Version as their base text for translation and who wanted to put, "As the prophets said." When I had objected they had accused me of wanting to corrupt the Word of God, where, in fact, they were the ones who were changing the text.

CHAPTER 8
THE SPIRIT OF GOD AND THE CHARISMATIC

As said earlier, my Mennonite church experience did not prepare me to expect much from the Spirit of God. He was respected, but not considered immediately relevant. However, as I became a teenager and later when I became involved in evangelistic outreach under the West Coast Children's Mission, I experienced the Spirit of God's guidance and strength again and again in preaching, in sharing my faith, and in life in general. I became deeply desirous of experiencing the full power of the Spirit of God in my life.

The "second work of grace" and "the gift of tongues"

In 1942 I left home to attend the Missionary Medical Institute in Toronto. This was my first venture away from home. I found room and board with an elderly single lady in Toronto who was a member of the Closed Brethren. My fellow boarder was a young Free Methodist minister who was considering going to the mission field and who had also come to Toronto for missionary medical training. This young minister, a graduate of several Free Methodist schools, had experienced the full range of the gifts of the Spirit that the Free Methodist faith offers. He had been baptized with the Spirit. He spoke in tongues[1]. He had even experienced what Methodists call "the second work of grace." That is, he had undergone a cleansing experience over and beyond this conversion experience in which "the very root of sin" had been removed from his life. He was a very pleasant and likeable chap, and I found him trustworthy. I felt drawn to him immediately when I met him at my first home away from home.

When he became aware of my active work in evangelism under the West Coast Children's Mission and of my deep desire to experience the fullness of the Spirit of God in my life, he was delighted. He was sure that he could help me experience the gifts of the Spirit as his church offered them.

---

[1]Speaking in tongues is generally understood as the Holy Spirit speaking through someone's speech organs in a language the person has not previously known.

He taught me how to "pray through," which meant praying three to five hours so that God would finally answer a specific prayer. He wanted me to pray for the gifts of the Spirit. I attended the Free Methodist Church with him. There they prayed for me and over me. I experienced the Lord's guidance in school, in my contacts with people, and in my work in the Toronto Western Hospital, but I did not experience the filling of the Spirit, the gift of tongues, nor the second work of grace. This left my friend perplexed. He didn't doubt my sincerity. He didn't doubt the experiences of the Spirit's leading in my life, but he was utterly puzzled by my inability to experience these additional works of grace which the charismatics hold as precious.

A charismatic missionary colleague

The next missionary couple that came to Colombia shortly after Anne and I arrived there had, like we, been raised in the Mennonite Brethren Church. But instead of being trained in our denomination's schools, this couple had chosen to attend a Pentecostal Bible school where they had experienced the baptism of the Spirit and the gift of tongues. However, when they graduated and decided to seek employment with the Mennonite Brethren Board of Missions, they were asked to graduate from Tabor College before being accepted and being sent to the mission field. Their pastor, who had charismatic leanings, was a member of the mission board. He applied pressure on the mission to accept them, even though several other board members had severe reservations about their charismatic past and present leanings. Thus the mission board insisted that they attend the denominational college for at least two years, which they then did.

At the liberal arts college their original tongues and their filling of the Spirit experiences became somewhat remote. Somehow elementary zoology, freshman English, and introduction to psychology just didn't give them much encouragement to express these spiritual gifts. Thus, by the time they arrived on the mission field, they were severely frustrated. They were no longer able to be filled by the Spirit at will. They no longer had the tongues experience at will. Then on the mission field they ran smack into the problem of language learning. They were praying that God should "give" them the language, while the rest of their fellow missionaries were pushing them to buckle down and learn it. After they had completed their mandatory year of language training, they were released from further study, but they still were nowhere near fluent in Spanish. They were assigned to a mission station when another missionary couple unexpectedly got ill. This opportunity delighted the couple and they threw themselves into the work with enthusiasm and much prayer. They were delighted when they recovered their filling of the Spirit and the tongues experiences.

I no longer remember the reasons why I became their mentor from the mission. I encouraged them by telling them of my experience with the Free Methodists and by assuring them that I did not oppose people who spoke in tongues. They began to invite me to their speaking-in-tongues sessions. I admit that I was very puzzled by the whole situation.

So I went home and studied the Bible to find out how one could discern whether or not something was a manifestation of the Spirit of God. Was it merely an emotional/psychological experience? The passage of Scripture that spoke to me at the time was from 1 John: "Beloved, believe not every spirit, but try the spirits whether they are of God; because many false prophets are gone into the world. Hereby know ye the Spirit of God: every spirit that confesseth that Jesus Christ is come in the flesh is of God. And every spirit that confesseth not that Jesus Christ is come in the flesh is not of God...." (1 Jn. 4:1-3).

Armed with this insight, I attended the next tongues session and applied the Johannine question only to find that my colleagues' speaking in tongues was stopped dead. Thereafter this couple was not able to speak in tongues in my presence. In my simplicity, I became convinced that they weren't really experiencing the Spirit of God.

Shortly thereafter there was a countrywide meeting of all the evangelical churches in Colombia, and this charismatic missionary from the Mennonite Brethren was somehow chosen to be the conference speaker. The rest of the Mennonite Brethren missionaries were utterly upset by this and wanted to intervene because they felt that the man's lack of mastery of the Spanish language would embarrass the mission as a whole. Since I carried the responsibility as the mission's delegate to the conference, I was able to prevent such intervention. But I spoke with the missionary in question. I was deeply aware of his deficiency in Spanish. I told him that this would be an occasion to call on the Lord for the gift of tongues to speak the Word of God in Spanish in such a correct and forceful way that it would really make a dent on the people to whom he would be ministering. The missionary accepted my support in prayer. When the day came for him to deliver the message, I was in prayer behind a curtain right behind the pulpit the whole time he was speaking. I was impressed that the Lord helped him deliver an excellent sermon. I was ready to give God the credit that he had been able to speak in tongues, but the missionary balked at this and said that this had not been a true tongues experience; he had just done some honest-to-goodness preparing.

Anne and her sisters

While I was in graduate school at the University of Washington in Seattle, two of Anne's sisters and their husbands paid us a weekend visit. In the course of our conversations, I mentioned the experience with the charismatic missionaries, and we had an animated discussion about the identification of spirits, whether they are of God or not. The three women were so intrigued that they wanted to test the Johannine question on the spot. There happened to be a meeting downtown led by a charismatic evangelist who specialized in speaking-in-tongues and healing. They decided to attend.

When the people went downstairs to pray for filling with the Spirit and to speak in tongues, the three sisters followed. As far as I recall (Anne herself does not have a clear recollection), Anne actually knelt beside some of the people who were rolling on the straw and speaking in tongues and asked them the question from 1 John, only to find that their tongues-speaking dried up immediately. Was this also a second fluke or a corroboration?

Various encounters with charismatics in North America

When I became professor at a Christian college and was named the advisor of the Christian Fellowship Association on campus, I tried to help the students in all their spiritual concerns. Many of them were deeply interested in charismatic phenomena. I accompanied numbers of these students to charismatic meetings where people were being filled with the Spirit, speaking in tongues and being healed! I told the students of my own experience with testing the spirits and several of them tried the question and produced the same result.

We attended healing meetings. Afterward we talked with the people who had been healed to see how they were faring. We were disturbed by how much deception there was in the staged public healings of some of these evangelists and healers.

Charismatics in Brazil

During the years that I was responsible for all of South America for the Bible Societies, I spent considerable time in Brazil and was able to make acquaintance with an indigenous charismatic group in Rio de Janeiro. This group had a leader who was called “the archangel.” He and his followers had built a massive temple in that city. The temple held some 25,000 people, many, of course, standing. It was designed like an opera house with a high stage and at least six balconies, one on top of the other on three sides of the temple.

The ministry of this temple was definitely “whole person.” Next to the worship auditorium there were kitchens to feed the hungry and dispensaries to take care of the sick. There were mending rooms where clothes could be repaired. There were places where people could get clothing if they required it. There were shoe shops. There was counseling both in spiritual matters and in daily life matters, such as homelessness and joblessness. In short, people were taken care of, whatever their need.

I had an opportunity to spend some time with the archangel and to learn about the workings of this temple from him in person. It wasn’t yet twenty years old, but already it had a million and a half adherents and was growing daily. I was privileged to give a testimony at one of the meetings, but I asked to be excused right after so that I could mingle with the congregation on the various balcony floors.

The service was impressive. Before the archangel made his appearance, twelve golden trumpets blew to herald his coming. He marched in wearing a resplendent robe, followed by those of us who were to give testimonies. Each shift in the service order was marked by the blowing of the twelve trumpets.

The sermon was a masterpiece. The archangel spoke about Zacchaeus and his encounter with Jesus. The first point he made was that Zacchaeus wanted to see

Jesus so desperately that he climbed a sycamore tree. The minister ended this part of his sermon with the question, "How many of you here today want to meet Jesus?" Pandemonium erupted as thousands of people began crying aloud simultaneously that they wanted to meet Jesus. For about ten minutes everyone was calling on Jesus. I happened to be standing next to a policeman in one of the balconies. He was not a member of the church but was deeply moved. He was crying and praying with the rest of them, "I want to see Jesus." Suddenly the golden trumpets blew and the minister continued his sermon.

The second point was that Jesus said, "Today I want to come to your house, Zacchaeus." Then the minister asked the audience, "How many of you here are ready to invite Jesus into your lives and into your homes?" Again pandemonium broke out as people by the thousands called on Jesus to come into their homes and lives.

The third point was that when Jesus entered the house, Zacchaeus confessed his misdeeds and began to make restitution. The question now was, "How many of you have done wrong? Confess your sins and make restitution!" And again there was a time of audible audience prayer before the twelve trumpets signaled the next stage in the service.

At noon the congregation ate in the church dining room before filing out through the city and its suburbs to witness. The evening service was devoted to testimonies of people who had been successful in their witness and had brought back the "trophies of grace" they had won for the Lord. It was moving to see one after the other get up and tell how they had gone out, found someone on the highways and byways and had led that person to Jesus Christ. The newly saved people were then given an opportunity to testify of their acceptance of Jesus Christ. They were then baptized and inducted into the fellowship. Those who had needs beyond the spiritual were told that the church was there to help them.

I must confess, it was one of the most moving services I have ever attended. The group did not have much emphasis on the filling of the Spirit and of speaking in tongues, though obviously some were engaged in it.

Charismatics in Chile

Chile has an evangelical Christian majority which is largely Pentecostal in orientation. The Pentecostal groups in that country number in the hundreds, if not thousands. Christian D'Epinay has made a study of these Chilean charismatics under the title of *The Refuge of the Masses*. This book first appeared in French and later in Spanish and English. D'Epinay points out that in the Chilean charismatic movement, schism is the operative factor of growth. Every three to five years each of these churches splits and new churches are born. The departure of the dissenting group that is forming the new church creates a draft which fans the embers of the mother church. Often the mother church itself gets a new lease on life and grows beyond all expectations. Meanwhile the group that has split away also has something to prove, and so they, too, work hard to make their church a success.

D'Epinay feels that Pentecostalism, with its experience of tongues, healing and filling of the Spirit, definitely provides a tremendous lift for the poverty-stricken masses of that country.

African Independent Church healers

It has been said that seven of ten conversions in Africa these days are to African Independent Churches rather than to the traditional denominational or mission churches. One manifestation of these Independent Churches is the tremendous emphasis on healing. A number of them actually have exclusively healing branches.

We made acquaintance with one such Independent Church healer in Togo in West Africa. A mutual friend introduced us, and the healer was very willing to instruct me as I tried to understand the movement.

For a number of months, Anne and I spent every Sunday evening, from six o'clock until close to midnight, at the healer's compound. He was just celebrating his twenty-fifth anniversary in the healing ministry. There was a massive reunion of all his healer-disciples who had gone out into many West African countries. They were now returning to celebrate with him and to be renewed in their healing gifts.

In my many meetings with this healer-prophet, he spoke confidently about the presence and the power of the Spirit of God. In fact, on one specific Sunday evening, he assured me that tonight I would see the Spirit of God at work. Since events often puzzled me at these meetings, I obtained his permission to leave my seat in the pews and come to his side any time he wasn't busy. I could then ask questions about things which puzzled me.

When the service was about to begin, Anne and I took our places on one of the benches. The benches were arranged to form a large open square in the middle. The healer came into the square, inspected all the corners and discovered that two were "leaky," that is, there was evil spirit traffic through them. He then cleansed the whole area and sealed off the two corners against any further evil spirit intrusion.

By this time the place was packed. Some musicians were playing in the open square and individuals were beginning to sing, dance, and speak in tongues. In no time, the whole square was a mass of writhing figures who were dancing, being "filled" with the Spirit and speaking in tongues.

I was especially impressed by the acrobatic movements of some of these dancers supposedly under the Spirit's influence. Here were a host of voluminous market mamas. These women had stalls in the market and usually were considerably overweight, but now as they danced, they jumped into the air. From a standing position they did somersaults in the air. I noticed one woman do as many as three somersaults before she landed. I was deeply puzzled by this manifestation. Seeing that the healer was not engaged, I slipped from my seat and went and sat down beside him. "Am I seeing the Spirit of God at work?" I asked, referring to these acrobats.

The healer shook his head sadly and said emphatically, "No! No! That is not the Spirit of God, that is 'beerfoam.' "

I was nonplussed. "Beerfoam?"

"Yes," he said, "that is only beerfoam."

"Is beerfoam bad?" I asked.

"No!" he said emphatically. "Beerfoam is good! You cannot have beerfoam without beer."

I pressed him, wanting to know why this was not the Spirit of God and only beerfoam.

"To experience the power of the Spirit of God you have to be willing to pay the price of obedience," he said. Very few people are willing to pay that price, he went on. Most of them only want a weekend or a monthly "fix," and so they settle for beerfoam.

"I venture to tell you that these people have experienced beerfoam with other healers already," he said. "In fact, within a couple of weeks many will be tired of the beerfoam at this place of healing and worship and will move on to another. They will then get a different brand of beerfoam."

Every time the healer intervened in the proceedings there was deathly quiet. "That," he said, "is the Spirit of God!"

Conclusion

After Elijah had had the tremendous victory over the 400 priests of Baal, he was terrified by the threat from Queen Jezebel. He ran away. He felt desperately alone. He felt that only he was left among those still serving God. Now even God had forsaken him! Now Jezebel was free to kill him!

God then had Elijah walk for a long distance to meet with him at Mount Horeb. When Elijah reached the mountain, the Lord spoke to him. Elijah begged to see the Lord. He was told that he could not see the Lord face-to-face, but only as the Lord passed by.

The Lord was not in the strong wind that rent the mountain and broke the rocks into pieces. The Lord was not in the mighty wind that shook the trees and made the earth tremble. The Lord was not in the earthquake that rocked the earth and rent its mountains. The Lord was not in the fire that roared and consumed. The Lord was a "still small voice."

This has also been my experience of the Spirit of God. For me, too, he has been "the still small voice." I am grateful that I have been able to hear him again and again!

SHARING THE FAITH

My early church and Bible school experience certainly taught me to use the Bible, but in terms of witnessing, it taught me to use it as a club. For many years I used the Bible to club sinners over the head with its message. While I felt some discomfort with this approach, I continued to use it until well into my mission experience in Colombia.

It was on the mission field that I first learned about the difference between good news and propaganda. Through a "glass darkly," I began to see that there was a lot more propaganda than good news in my ministry. Propaganda always is in the interest of the witness, while good news is a message in the interest of the one receiving the witness. This awareness of this difference developed into a full-fledged crisis at the church college where I served as advisor to the Christian Fellowship Association. The tragic failures of my strong-arm approach precipitated the spiritual crisis described in this section. But it wasn't until Elton Trueblood came to my rescue with his concept of the keys, and Theodor Reik taught me about listening with the third ear that I became aware of how much of our current evangelical Christian witness is canned propaganda! How little of it is honest, spontaneous testimony of good news!

My work with the developing Chocó church taught me the necessity of being willing to be the first sinner as one approach to sharing the faith. But it wasn't until I had been working with the Bible Society for some time that I became aware of the value of the solicited witness. I began to look for occasions when people would ask me for help rather than barging in and trying to foist my help on them when I thought they were in trouble.

It was in the Chocó church and in the various translation projects where I learned the meaning of the sensitive witness as a catalyst. Missionaries tended to be the 'center forwards' in their work of proclaiming the gospel, but in God's design his messengers often are to be merely catalysts who set something in motion and who themselves then immediately become irrelevant to God's ongoing work.

CHAPTER 9

SHARING THE FAITH

As a young man, I went to Bible school for five winters and learned how to do *"personal work"* (the technical term for witnessing in those days). Our textbook was R. A. Torrey's *Personal Work*. It taught us how to counter every known objection to the gospel by means of Bible verses—150 of them, if I remember correctly.

I armed myself with every biblical promise, warning and threat, or, if you will, "rope" tò tie an obstinate sinner's arguments in knots. And so for the next twenty years I faithfully tried to batter my way into people's lives. Looking back today, I regret to admit that I even carried the same Bible-verses-as-clubs approach with me to the mission field. My children later testified I occasionally even used this same approach on them.

I don't know whether it was part of the instruction or whether it was some idiosyncrasy of the teacher who taught the course on witnessing, but the thing I remember most vividly was the emphasis on a passage from Ezekiel, "Son of man, I have made thee a watchman unto the house of Israel: therefore hear the word at my mouth and give them warning from me. When I say unto the wicked, thou shalt surely die; and thou givest him not warning, nor speakest to warn the wicked from his wicked way, to save his life; the same wicked man shall die in his iniquity; but his blood will I require at thine hand" (Ezek. 3:17-18). These verses were indelibly etched in my mind. I felt responsible for every person I met. I felt I had to warn all sinners of their lostness "lest their blood be demanded from my hand."

We Bible school students were taught to confront everyone we met with, "Are you saved?" or "Are you a Christian?" If the answer was "yes" we were scot-free and had nothing more to say. If the answer was "no," it was incumbent upon us to warn the sinner. If they resisted our appeal, we clobbered them with the appropriate Bible verses.

The fear of "blood guilt" was so strong that I had to talk to as many people as possible when I began to travel by train. Every morning when I went into the washroom to shave and took one of the three or four washbasins, I felt obligated to ask anyone who shared the washroom with me about the condition of his soul.

For twenty years I faithfully tackled as many sinners as I could. It never dawned on me that my responsibility really was to proclaim the gospel as "good news" to them.

The crisis at college

When I took up my new assignment as professor at a Christian college, the president took me aside and told me how excited he was about my coming. "You have a vision of Christian service which I want you to share with all our college students," he said. To this end he appointed me as the advisor to the Christian Fellowship Association (hereafter CFA), the Christian life organization on campus.

I was deeply gratified by this trust and threw myself into the task with zeal. The first school year went phenomenally well. From a 35 percent student participation in our Christian effort on campus we steadily climbed until by the beginning of the second semester, 75 to 80 percent were seriously involved in CFA activities. Of these, about half were also active in outreach programs in area churches, retirement homes, slums and jails. I was excited; it was tremendous!

Then came the crash!

Student elections for the next school year were held just before the end of the spring semester. After the elections, the newly elected CFA chairman reported to my office. He was visibly uncomfortable and just blurted out, "It has been a big mistake. I never should have allowed my name to stand as candidate. I have a problem in my life. It just won't work!" I good-naturedly countered, "But the Good Lord majors in solving problems; let's see what he can do about your problem." Instead of warming up to my appeal, the young man suddenly just got up and said, "I'm sorry, I am taking up too much of your time." Then he hurried from my office, never to darken my door again in the days to come. I wrote him notes. I called him on the telephone. But he would never talk in private to me again. All our CFA business was transacted either in formal meetings, in writing, or in college halls with hordes of students milling about.

As the new school year got underway, I began to watch over the decay of CFA. The numbers of those participating in the organization slid rapidly until by Christmas we had only 25 percent of the students attending meetings, and only a handful involved in outreach. I prayed, I struggled, I tried everything I knew, but to no avail. Finally I decided that the problem must lie with me. If I couldn't reach a person from my own culture, how in the world had I dared think I could effectively reach people in another culture as a missionary?

Sources of help

Looking back today, I can clearly see a number of sources which came to my rescue in this my hour of desperate need.

The first help came just before Christmas. Elton Trueblood, the old Quaker preacher whom I mentioned earlier, spoke in Wichita, and I was privileged to hear him. He spoke about Jesus talking to Peter and telling him, "I will give you the keys" (Mt. 16:19). Trueblood said, "I know there is much theological argument about what exactly this statement means. But to me it has a very practical meaning, namely that God gives to each individual who obeys him some keys to other people's lives." He then explained: if a person has keys to another person's life, he can relate to that other person easily. He does not have to try to get his foot into the door. He doesn't have to batter down that person's defenses. The keys give him an effortless entree into that person's life.

I found this concept truly revolutionary. I was strongly attracted to it. I vowed that in future I would check if I had keys before I reached into other people's lives.

The second source of help came between Christmas and New Year. I had committed myself to speak at a week of meetings in a church nearby. I had been asked to speak about our Christian witness and our Christian experience. I spoke on them in exactly that order. I left the experience part for the last, because the current struggle in my own life was exactly in that area. Finally on Sunday night, the last night of the series, I dropped all pretenses. I admitted publicly where I found myself in regard to my CFA responsibility. I admitted my powerlessness when it came to the Spirit of God's presence in my life. I acknowledged my oversized self-image. I assured the audience that if I stepped on anybody's toes that night, I was trampling all over my own. I acknowledged that the channels which God's Spirit needed to guide me, were completely occupied by my efforts at self-protection

As soon as my message was completed, I assured them that I was going to the altar to renew my personal vows to God. I would admit that I was incapable of influencing a total student body. I would ask God to at least entrust to me one male and one female student. I would promise that I would give them all the time they required to learn some of the lessons about Christian living in their youth—lessons which I was now learning at nearly forty.

A young man came to our home late the following Tuesday. He told me he had been on his way to commit suicide when he had suddenly thought of me. Somehow the mere thought of my name had given him hope. So here he was. Even before he shared his problem, I told him about the crisis I was experiencing and of the commitment I had just made in church. I asked him whether he was the young man whom God was sending to me. He said he was. The two of us then made a contract together to share each other's problems and to help each other find solutions.

Before we broke up that night, I told him about Elton Trueblood's concept of keys and said, "I think it might be wise if you would begin looking about you to see if you hold the key to anybody's life, because before long God will surely call upon you to share something with someone else." To my surprise, the young man said, "I have held the key to a certain person's life for a long time already, but I haven't been able to use it because of this problem in my own life." To my even greater surprise, he went on to name the person to whose life he held the key, and it was the CFA chairman whom I was unable to reach.

He truly did have that key, because three days later the two fellows began using my office every noon hour to pray together. To be honest, my young man no longer really needed help from me, because the two fellows shared a similar problem, and they were now providing the support they each needed to gain victory over it.

The third source of help was Theodor Reik's book, *Listening with the Third Ear* (mentioned in Chapter 5). This book was my first introduction to the subject, but I recognized at once some of the implications of what Reik was saying. He was talking about the inner radar system by means of which I had been protecting my self-image.

The fourth source was a group of psychiatrists at a Mennonite mental health facility located nearby. These men decided to do some community service which they defined as "enlightening the benighted ministers of the area in matters of the human psyche." They invited a number of ministers from the community and began to press some of the insights of psychiatry on them—insights which the psychiatrists felt ought to be good news to the ministers. Now, ministers may be experts at knowing what is good news for others, but they found it very difficult to swallow the force-fed good news of the psychiatrists. In fact, most of them developed severe psychic indigestion and didn't come back. As a result, the psychiatrists had to scramble for a new batch of ministers each week.

I was invited to join the group, ostensibly as a missionary-anthropologist. Even if their real purpose was to enlighten just another benighted minister, I did not mind, because I was desperate for help. When I saw their problem with their ministerial audience, I volunteered to "confess" my inner experiences to the group each week. I would tell them about the things for which I had prayed. I would tell them about how I had reached certain decisions and what I had counseled students who came to me for help.

I soon realized that listening with the third ear carried two dimensions with it. First, one needed to hear the calls for help of the person for whom one had keys. One experience that is still vivid in my memory happened on a bus in California.

I had accepted an engagement to speak at a missionary conference in California. My schedule was very tight. The connection in Los Angeles to Fresno was only half an hour. The plane from Wichita, which brought me to Los Angeles, had to buck the jetstream blowing east, and as a result it arrived twenty-five minutes late. I rushed to the other airline only to find that the plane had already closed its door, and even the ramp had been removed. It was ready to taxi to the runway. I had missed my plane!

Now I would miss the ride with the Fresno student who was going to take me to the church in central California where I was to preach that evening. If I took a later plane to Fresno and caught a bus, I would arrive half an hour after the first meeting had begun. There was no other way.

Since I had several hours to wait, I decided first of all to take care of my message for the evening. After I had finished, I walked through the airport thinking, "Maybe God has someone I need to meet here." I went through the entire terminal but heard no cue via my third ear.

I got the next plane to Fresno and took a taxi to the bus depot to catch the bus for the central California town. I walked carefully through the depot to see if there was anything that the Lord had intended for me to do there. But again I received no cue. I boarded the bus and took a window seat. A man sat down next to me in the aisle. The moment he sat down and I introduced myself, I got my cue. *Here was the reason why I had missed my plane*. I told the man I was a college teacher from Kansas. He shook my hand and let slip that he had originally come from Oklahoma. But then he began to backpedal as if he suddenly remembered the "Okie" status of the 1930s dust-bowl immigrants to California who were still looked down upon in some circles. Seemingly embarrassed, he said he had been away from Oklahoma for so long, he remembered nothing about it and had nothing to do with it anymore.

I realized at once that this man was carrying a severe hurt. I asked the Lord for a message for him and the message was, "Tell him about how you were demoted in grade school." So I turned to the man and said, "You have said some kind words about me as a college professor, but I am going to tell you that inside of me there is an eleven-year-old boy who was severely hurt."

I then told him about our move from Manitoba to British Columbia, about my loss of mathematical exposure in fractions and decimals and how as a result I had been demoted a grade. I described the shame I felt as I walked the mile from the Grade 5 school to the Grade 4 school and how, when I walked in, all the kids hissed, "Another prairie chicken got his wings clipped." "I felt like crawling under the nearest clod of dirt," I told him.

I didn't finish my story before tears began to roll down my neighbor's cheeks. Suddenly he asked, "Do you think God is still concerned about me?" Nowhere up to that point had God been mentioned. I had given no indication that I was a Christian. The man then told me about his bitter experiences in Oklahoma. When he had tried to go to Sunday school there, he had been ridiculed because he had no shoes. He finally gave up on Sunday school and church altogether.

In California he was humiliated further and so he had stayed far away from the church ever since. But now, as he was getting older, he had to think of God and religion again and was deeply concerned whether God might still be interested in him. I was able to help a man make peace with God right there on the bus. But the price of contact was a painful piece of self-exposure and a late arrival at the mission meeting.

The second dimension of third-ear hearing is knowing what is good news for a specific individual. Several years ago I was invited to address an atheists' club in Washington, D.C. The person who sponsored me asked me to share how anthropology had forced me to examine my faith in God and what I had learned in the process. (More about that later.) I spent about half an hour doing that, and then a lively discussion ensued. By the time the group broke up near midnight, many people had confessed deep hurts or shameful failures which had led them to write off God in their lives.

By midnight, all but one young man had left. He had said nothing all evening, but now he approached me shyly and said, "I have learned something tonight. There were no atheists here. Most of the people were hurt Christians. People like myself who have had no Christian experience, at best are agnostic; we just don't know whether there is a God or not." Then he added, "I was impressed that you had 'good news' for so many of the people here tonight. Do you also have some 'good news' for me, an agnostic?"

I must confess, I almost panicked at this request. Then I reached out, took hold of his hand, held it for a while and said, "I took your hand to see if your body could tell my body what would be 'good news' for you. Having felt your vibes, I feel that you have some known unfinished business in your life. God, your conscience, or whatever, has asked you to do a certain thing or certain things, but so far you have not had the courage to do it/them."

To my pleasant surprise the young man answered at once, "Very true! There are two things I've known that I should do for several years now, but I've never had the guts to do them. But how will doing them answer my question about whether or not there is a God?"

I then told him I had learned that frequently when people obey the "still small voice" within them, they are in fact obeying God, and once they have obeyed, they often feel an enormous inner release. Often the further result is that they then recognize that God was behind the inner push they were feeling. Suddenly they realize it is not a question of getting some external proof of whether or not God exists, but rather they needed to discover that they already have had internal proof: God has spoken to them and they have obeyed him.

In this connection, I have found the rabbinic instruction to rabbis-in-training very illuminating. They are told never to demand that an agnostic believe in God before asking that person to pray. Instead, they are instructed to ask the agnostic to pray for some very specific personal need. After the person has experienced the result of the praying, faith in God will often follow.

As he departed, the young man assured me he would start on the first of the two unfulfilled obedience urges the very next day. I was not privileged to "lead him to the Lord," because he wasn't ready for that step yet. But I do think I helped him get started on the way to experience God, just as the rabbinic instruction urges. Faith can then follow obedience.

Failing to listen to the third ear

In the hustle and bustle of life, where many voices impinge upon us, it is not always easy to be open to receiving third-ear messages.

While at the church college, I befriended a student who belonged to the leather-jacket-motorcycle crowd. Because he was so unconventional, he rubbed many people wrong, but the two of us actually became friends. I cannot say I actually held a key to his life, but once our talking relationship had developed, he brought in dozens of marginal characters who needed my help. He held the first key to their lives, and on the strength of his confidence in me these people also were willing to trust me. He supervised their nurture and I merely provided the input. It was almost as if he lent me his keys.

All of us at one time or another will *fail to use the keys* that have been entrusted to us. I know I have failed. Occasionally, I have had a second chance.

I remember one incident specifically. My leather-jacketed friend, who sent a person to me, later had to come and tell me, "You goofed; you failed to listen with your third ear." In this case, I had a second chance. I was able to find the person, apologize for my insensitivity to his need, and establish a relationship with him.

Whenever two people begin sharing together, someone needs to be the first to open up about himself. I have found it helpful to be on the alert and ready in case the Spirit of God should ask me to expose some unfulfilled obedience in my own life.

Flying home from a weekend of preaching one Monday morning, a man with a heavy odor of hangover took the seat next to me. As I usually do, I extended my hand and introduced myself by name saying that I taught at Tabor College. Obviously, the man recognized the name of the college. "You from Hillsboro?" he continued.

"Yes!"

"You're a Mennonite Brethren?"

"Yes!"

"Then I can well imagine what you think of a stinking drunken slob like me."

I was quiet for a moment. Then I confessed, "Yes, there was a time when I would have looked down my nose at you, but no more, friend! You see I was a missionary in Colombia and I forbade all the drunken Indians to sleep at my place. One midnight I had to haul a drunk out of the yard after he stumbled into our guestroom to spend the night. Once I had him out of our yard and on the road to the village, I dropped him on the ground. The moment I did that, the man broke down and wept, as only drunks can weep, saying, 'Jaco (my tribal name) says he is my friend, but when I am drunk and most in need of a friend, then he throws me out of his yard!' From that moment on, I've been under a commitment to God that I will truly try to be a friend to any drunk person I meet."

During the rest of the flight this formerly active Christian unloaded a pack of problems and in conclusion announced, "I know what I need to do, and with

God's help I am going to do it." That flight from Denver to Wichita was only forty-five minutes long.

CHAPTER 10
GOOD NEWS OR PROPAGANDA

The gospel—the good news of God in the Scriptures—is not a fragile commodity. It has withstood the vicissitudes of time, and every kind of attack or subversion from without. However, one cannot help but be troubled by how quickly such good news can be subverted by its friends—its most pious proclaimers. Before you know it, they have transformed the good news into propaganda. This is not a problem of the good news itself, but a problem of the motivations of its communicators. Any ulterior motive on the part of the communicator of the message—the gospel—can pervert its intrinsic value. One of the most common types of such subversion is the use of the "baited hook" in witnessing.

When Anne and I went out as missionaries to Colombia, we felt we were going in obedience to Jesus' call to be "fishers of men." Since I was experienced at fishing, it seemed natural that to "catch" men we would have to use the proper "bait." And what constitutes proper bait for "fishers of men?" We were hoping to discover something that would cause people to come to our mission station to hear the Word of God.

As it was, this happened before we even knew what was going on. No sooner had we arrived in the village of Noanama on the San Juan River in the jungle of the Chocó of Colombia, than people from far and wide came to ask for medical help. Eureka! Overnight we had become "fishers of men!" Without even trying, we had discovered just the "bait" we needed. We opened a dispensary, and when the people came for medical attention, we would first make them listen to the gospel before we dispensed our help.

Our reasoning went like this: we and our time "belong to the Lord" and the medicine we handed out, paid for by the mission, was the "Lord's medicine." We felt it just and proper to make the following rule: if you want to receive the "Lord's medicine," then you must be willing to first listen to the "Lord's message." In order not to have to be on duty all hours of the day and night, we organized a fixed dispensary schedule: 9 to 11 a.m. and 3 to 5 p.m., five days a week, and before each session all patients had to listen to half an hour of Bible instruction. Those who came too late for the Bible instruction had to wait for the next dispensary session.

It took more than a decade of missionary experience before we realized that honest-to-goodness missionary witness and the baited hook just don't go together. Ever since that truth dawned on us, we have been working on "cleaning up our witnessing act," but it hasn't been easy. The temptation for Christians to use baited hooks doesn't die easily.

Many of the churches I am acquainted with here on the home scene are very enthusiastic about what is called "friendship evangelism." Church members befriend non-churchgoing individuals with the goal of bringing them to church. While establishing friendship with people is an exceedingly positive way to develop a Christian witness, today we also realize how readily it can be subverted to become a baited hook. If witnessers are concerned about getting more members for their church, or even if they are truly interested in saving someone's soul, their friendship can be feigned and unreal.

The recent influx of non-European immigrants to our area has aided and abetted the increase of baited-hook evangelism. In many cases, these immigrants provide the church members' first contact with people who do not come from the Judeo-Christian tradition and who practice what Christians are wont to call "pagan religions." Both the great cultural and religious differences which these immigrants exhibit militate against the easy establishment of genuine friendship.

Let me create a scenario and you can see for yourself if it rings a bell in your own witnessing experience or observation.

An evangelical Christian couple arrives at a resort for a long weekend. When they go to the resort restaurant for their first meal, the only other people there are an East Asian couple. They keep bumping into the Asians, who seem to radiate friendliness, and finally they introduce themselves. Both couples, it turns out, herald from the central Fraser Valley. In fact, they live only a couple of miles from each other. Soon the couples are dining together and making plans to get together on their return home. Both men have experience in the building trade, and the Asian wants the other couple to see the "dream house" he has just built for his family. While they have not talked about religious matters, the Christian couple gathers that the Asians are not Christians.

The Christians see this chance encounter as a divine indication that they ought to befriend the other couple in order to witness about Christ to them. Thus some weeks after they get back home, they phone the Asian couple and are invited over for tea.

When the Christian couple arrives at the address, they discover a mansion. The Asian family is obviously wealthy. At the front entrance the visitors come face to face with a giant statue of a benignly smiling Buddha. As they tour the rest of the house, they see several more deity figures. Almost every room has some sort of religious shrine with images and candles. This is the Christian couple's first exposure to polytheism in practice. Needless to say, they experience both religious and culture shock. In fact, they are somewhat uncomfortable all through the lavish tea, during which their hostess deluges them with endless kinds of Asian goodies.

On returning home from this exposure to paganism, the Christian couple feel their witnessing responsibility all the more keenly. They are convinced they ought to continue to build the relationship by inviting their new friends over, but then a whole series of second thoughts begin to cloud their mental horizon. Will they thereby be implicitly condoning the Asians' idolatry and maybe even compromising their Christian testimony? Will friendship with this couple draw them into condoning polytheism? They had felt very uncomfortable visiting in the Asian home with dozens of idol shrines surrounding them.

They finally "solve" their dilemma with a compromise.

They will continue *to act like friends* toward the Asian couple at least until they have had a chance to talk to them about Jesus Christ and see if the Asians show any interest in the gospel. Should their testimony draw a totally negative response, they will then feel justified in breaking off the relationship.

Now let me now follow up this hypothetical example with an actual example of baited-hook evangelism. At first I was delighted to see how many church people were inviting non-church people into their homes or taking them out to restaurants or public events. On the surface, these seemed to be indications that church people were establishing genuine friendship relationships with unchurched people. But a closer look showed that in many cases it was nothing more than a baited hook. Well-meaning Christians were merely using their invitations as gimmicks in their efforts to convert people and to get them to join their church. *What* they were doing was excellent, but the reason *why* they were doing it was all wrong. Of course, there were others who were, indeed, doing it to be genuine friends, and that truly is witnessing (or friendship evangelism) at its best.

The solicited witness

We have already mentioned the passage in 1 Peter 3:15-16 about being ready to give a witness when one is asked for it. In Acts 10:1-40, we have the account of Peter the Jew going to Cornelius the Gentile's house. Obviously the Lord was entrusting Peter with some keys to Cornelius' heart and life, but Peter wasn't ready to use them because he was so steeped in his Jewish culture which forbade him to have contact with a Gentile. He had to undergo the strange vision experience before he was ready to use the keys that God was giving him. But when he did, Cornelius and his whole household accepted the Lord.

Occasionally, such a solicited-witness experience can be triggered by some relevant encounter. When the Spirit of God whisked Philip away to communicate with the Ethiopian eunuch in Acts 8:29-39, the relevant point of contact was the question which Philip asked while running beside the man's carriage, "Do you understand what you are reading?" The man did not, so he invited Philip up into the carriage to explain the passage to him.

Some months ago I visited a recent acquaintance. I did not know much about him except that his health was not good and that someone had said he was not a Christian. During my visit I discovered that he was a serious thinker. We had a meaningful exchange about some research I was doing, and he showed me some beautiful artwork of which he was very proud. All in all, we had a very pleasant visit together.

As I was about to leave, the host suddenly stopped me and asked if he could pose a serious personal question. When I responded affirmatively, he said, "There are several Christians who frequently come to visit me. They ask me to go out for coffee with them, but I am afraid of them, because I feel that the reason for their friendliness is that they want to convert me. I know that you are a Christian, too, but I have never felt any kind of pressure from you, so I hope you don't mind, if I ask you some religious questions: what is 'being saved?' I don't think I am saved, but neither do I want to be pigheaded about it. If I really ought to be saved, I am willing to do what it takes. Can you help me sort this out?"

The conversation that followed was serious and to the point. It was not propaganda, since it was a solicited witness (1 Peter 3:15). Nor was it station-to-station type witnessing (that is, a "saved" person talking to an unsaved one). It was person-to-person communication (that is, two people, neither of whom had as yet achieved complete obedience to God, sharing deeply with each other). We discovered that both of us wanted to grow in our obedience to God. As we bared our inner lives to each other, we discovered that we had a lot in common; in fact, we discovered we were friends.

Sometimes the privilege of solicited witness is earned by doing something for someone else, especially when that "something" requires going well out of one's way. Consider the following example from Ecuador.

A Protestant missionary to a group of Quechua found that the latter had absolutely no interest in his evangelical message. However, the people did tell him that they desperately needed a priest or a catechist (a novice who is being prepared for church work) to teach their children the precepts of the Roman Catholic religion to which they professed at least nominal adherence. They were very sad that their children were growing up in almost total ignorance of their adopted faith.

The missionary volunteered to meet their need by teaching the Catholic catechism to their children. He used an official catechism and a Bible with the Catholic Archbishop's imprimatur as his textbooks. He was a good teacher, and the children really learned something. Often almost the entire village sat in the back of the schoolroom watching and listening as he taught the children in front. After several months of this teaching, the village elders took him aside and asked, "You seem to know Catholic teaching very well. Why then aren't you yourself a Catholic?" This gave the missionary the opportunity to "explain why he believed as he did." This eventually led to a major conversion movement in that part of the country.

Knowing the right steps to take in a witnessing situation is not always easy. I remember a rather strange experience on a plane. I was on a flight from

Vancouver to Lima, Peru with an intermediate stop in Calgary. No sooner were we airborne then the young woman in the next seat turned and asked me whether I was saved.

I was intrigued, but my gut reaction to her question was that the young woman was not asking an authentic question. It sounded mechanical, like someone playing a recording. So I decided to play dumb.

"Saved? When? Where? Just what do you mean 'saved'?" I queried.

Frustrated (or maybe encouraged) by my ignorant response, the young woman produced a pamphlet entitled *Four Spiritual Laws*. I took it, read it aloud and then excitedly exclaimed, "This is most fascinating. Do you mean to tell me that you have actually discovered four equally valid laws without any hierarchical arrangement between them? I just can't believe my ears. I am sure you are aware that the famous French scientist, Claude Lévi-Strauss, has conclusively demonstrated that all truth in our universe is arranged in binary sets, like good/bad, up/down, raw/cooked, etc., so the four laws could really be two sets of two." I continued musing aloud trying to fit the four laws into binary sets, and finally concluded in disappointment that they just didn't want to fall neatly into pairs. With mock innocence, I then asked her, "My dear, if these 'spiritual laws,' don't conform to Levi-Strauss' universal principle, to form binary sets, are you really sure they have validity?"

Giving up on the four spiritual laws, the young woman whipped out a sheet called *The Van Dusen Letter*. I read that silently for a while, and then began reading sections of it aloud and questioning its meaning in minute detail. By that time she was frustrated to the point of tears.

I then switched roles and told her I was a Christian, and that whenever I am in a witnessing situation, I try to read other people's covert body language. When I had tried to read hers, however, I got a very confused response.

Without any further fencing the young woman broke out in tears and began to tell me about her difficulties. She was an only child of a wealthy family from Southern California. She felt smothered by her Jewish parents' concern for her. Finally she had rebelled against them and had run away. She had recently gotten "saved" at an evangelical youth rally and had just completed a Campus Crusade retreat, where she had been trained as a volunteer witness to spend her summer vacation leading Peruvian young people to Christ.

About that time, the pilot interrupted our conversation to announce that one of the plane's warning lights was inexplicably flashing. Since Calgary was not equipped for that kind of repair, we were returning to Vancouver.

On our way back I shared some of my own experiences of rebellion with the young woman. Then and there she decided that her first step to achieve an effective Christian witness should be to make peace with her parents. After we landed at Vancouver and had arrived at the hotel in which the airline put us up for the night, I joined her in a phone call to her parents. They were overjoyed and urged her to come home with obvious accepting love. Our next step was to cancel her flight to South America and book a new flight for California.

It was only when the young woman suddenly embraced me and thanked me for "helping her take another step in obedience" that I realized under what intense internal pressure she had been. I had been privileged to help her along her personal "good news" journey.

CHAPTER 11

SHARING WITH COLLEGE STUDENTS

One day a college junior came to see me. She casually told me that she had just ditched her faith in God. Luckily I had faced issues like this a number of times before, and so I just as casually asked her, "What in the world have you done that is so wicked that it outweighs your faith in God?" Or, "What in the world are you contemplating on doing that is so outrageous that your conversion seems picayune in comparison?"

The girl seemed severely shaken by these two questions. She remained silent for quite a while. Then she suddenly seemed to reach an inward decision and said, "I guess you're right! I have just made a date with two soldiers from a nearby military base to spend a weekend in sex with them. I have never done anything like this before. I did it on a dare, but I guess now that it is getting closer, I am pretty scared."

We discussed the developments and I tried to help her analyze why she had agreed to the tryst. Then we also tried to ascertain what her childhood conversion really meant.

Even though we had only a few sessions together, it was interesting to observe how, once she had weighed her options, this student resolutely canceled her weekend plans and decided to look at some of the problems in her life. Eventually she decided to cultivate her seemingly meaningless childhood conversion and make it relevant in her life again.

The lesson that stood out loud and clear to me was that for many Christian young people the guilt they accumulate in daily living quickly outweighs the value of their childhood conversion. Unless that conversion experience is somehow nurtured, and the person is helped to understand what is happening to him/her in the temptations of life, the conversion experience can be totally crushed by the accumulated guilt.

I, too, am vulnerable

Very early in my teaching career a quiet young coed came to me one day.

She shyly told me about certain difficulties she had with her parents. She griped at length about the problems her younger sister was creating for her. Eventually she admitted that she was not finding a boyfriend.

I met with this young woman over a period of weeks, an hour each week. I realized quickly that her burning problem was the lack of a boyfriend. All the other host of problems she was bringing up were part of the camouflage or guilt that she was feeling. She was trying to atone for her strained relationship with her parents and sibling in an effort to win God's favor to find a boyfriend.

One day, in the course of our conversations, I absentmindedly put my hand on the typing board, only to realize that the student had her hand on that board too. The moment our hands touched I saw her face redden, and she began to shiver as if sexually excited. I also felt a current go through my body. I jerked my hand away! I realized that I, too, had been turned on sexually. I am grateful that this experience came early in my conversations with students, because it made me aware of how vulnerable I could be to the charms of the opposite sex. Not only did it put me on the alert, but it also made me a lot more sympathetic toward people who have failed in this regard. I realized how easy it was to fall and how close I myself had come to a slip.

Did I really have keys for her life?

You will remember that in Chapter 9 I talked about the spiritual crisis in my life during which I asked the Lord for a young man and a young woman whom I could help. I was willing to give these young people as much time as it took to help them learn how to use keys and how to listen to the Spirit of God. I wanted to help them avoid the kind of crisis in later life that I had been going through.

Well, the young woman came to me about two-and-a-half weeks after my rededication. Ostensibly her problem was her college roommate. She spent the first session detailing all her roommate's nasty foibles. She told me how her roommate seemed to hog everything. She wanted the best drawers in the chest, the best space in the closet, the best study table, the best light. It was an endless litany of selfishness on the part of her roommate.

When the student came for a second session, I asked her whether I had keys for her life and whether she was willing for me to help her so she could learn to discover if she had keys for other people's lives. I wanted her to learn how to listen to the Spirit for meaningful messages. She readily agreed. The second session was spent discussing her latest boyfriend whom she had just dropped. He, too, was a bundle of selfishness. It was tempting to sigh with relief and say, "I'm sure glad you were able to recognize this in time and get rid of the guy before you got seriously hurt." But as the sessions went on week after week, we went through dozens of boyfriends and a succession of roommates, but the story always remained the same.

About six or seven months into our sessions I asked about life with her newest roommate. Suddenly she stopped and asked, "Do you mean to say that I am projecting my selfishness on my roommates? That it is I who has the best space in the closet? That it is I who has the best desk? That it is I who has the top drawers in the chest?"

In the course of three-and-a-half years of weekly one-hour sessions we went through endless boyfriends, numbers of roommates and continual difficulties with her parents. By the time she graduated we had made virtually no progress. There had been occasional glimpses of self-recognition, but we had gotten nowhere with the keys, nowhere with sensitivity to the Spirit of God! It seemed to have been a total waste of time. Perhaps this time I did not have the right keys after all.

Freudian slips

One day I established a friendship with a young man who was a college junior. He had served overseas for a period of years as a volunteer in a mission program. He was serious and sensitive. We spent the first few sessions talking about his overseas service and some of the problems he had encountered there.

All at once he abruptly shifted gears and said, "I need to do some serious confessing!" For the next several weeks, this young man went over his life with a fine-tooth comb and confessed sin after sin. We asked God for forgiveness and tried to bury all the confessed items, but he said he still felt as guilty as ever. He had found no forgiveness! No relief! I struggled with this situation for a while myself. Then I decided to tell him that if he had been honest in his confession and had not found forgiveness, then it was up to me to find the real problem in his life.

At our next appointment, I explained the situation to him and said, "From now on I want you to just talk about whatever comes to your mind. I will listen carefully with my third ear to what you say. Occasionally I will ask you a question. I want to see whether I can locate your real problem."

This approach seemed to throw the young man off stride. "But I don't know what to talk about," he protested.

"Just talk about the first thing that comes to your mind," I said.

After a lengthy silence he began talking. In his second or third sentence he stumbled over an English word. This immediately caused a click in my innermost, and so I asked him, "How significant is this word in your life? I saw no reason for you to stumble over the word, and yet you did stumble. I wonder whether there is a message for you in this!"

The young man was quiet for a while again and then said, "Well, I guess maybe there is. I am in love with a coed in my English class, but she is engaged to another student. I don't feel that it is right for me to ask her for a date, because she is already engaged. On the other hand, I am deeply in love with her, and I can't shake my feelings for her. Just before I came to see you, I had to make a presentation in that English class. In the course of the presentation I stumbled over this word. Everybody in the class laughed, and I felt I had made a fool of myself in front of the very person I wanted to impress."

Psychiatrists had drawn the significance of such Freudian slips to my attention during the time I served as their guinea pig. Here I learned firsthand what a significant role these slips can play. Very often when we are unable to admit our problem, then our tongue trips us up and calls attention to the very thing we are trying to hide.

The overweight "wallflower"

One day the dean of women students sent a coed to me who had a weight problem. At first the young woman was a bit embarrassed, but gradually we established some rapport and she seemed to relax in my presence.

She told me that among her bad habits was that every evening she took her girlfriends out for pie and ice cream at a local restaurant or gorged on some other heavy-duty snacks. As I listened to her expound on her weight problem and her seeming obsession with food, I got a completely different paramessage from her and that was: "Why can't I get a reasonable boyfriend?"

One day I confronted her about this. I said my third-ear listening had convinced me that her real problem was still hidden and unmentioned. "Isn't that problem the fact that you do not have a boyfriend?" I asked.

She looked at me in wide-eyed amazement. "How did you know that?" she asked.

"I didn't know it," I said, "but the paramessage I heard over and above the words you were uttering was this tremendous desire for you to strike up a meaningful relationship with some worthwhile fellow."

When we began to focus on her feelings of insecurity, it became apparent that her extra weight was part of her insulation against exposure to meaningful male company. Once we had identified her true concern, she began to shed pounds quickly. Before many months had passed, she was an attractive looking young woman.

The lesson for me was that it is easy to be misled by overtly stated problems. She claimed her problem was overweight, but that was merely a decoy for the fundamental issue which she wasn't able to face.

A "false" confession

One day a woman student came to see me. When I asked how I could be of help, she said she had a number of sins that she needed to deal with in her life. I assured her that Christ had died for all our sins so that any sins we might have committed had already been atoned for. "The problem," I said, "was that often we human beings weren't willing to let go of our sins. We hang on to our guilt for one reason or other." She assured me that that was not her problem. So I permitted her to begin her confession.

For the next four or five sessions this woman confessed illicit relationships with a number of men. After she had made a clean breast of all the affairs, I had to tell her that I had some doubts about her story. Would she permit me to follow up certain things that troubled me? She expressed readiness.

So I asked for details of where the incidents had taken place—in the bedroom? On the bed? In the living room? On the couch? On the rug? She could provide no specific information about any of the events she had confessed.

Gradually it became apparent that she had been secretly in love with different men at different times, and had really only indulged in sexual fantasies. But to her these fantasies had become as real as actual events. Once we established that we were dealing with fantasies rather than actual acts, the woman made rapid progress. After her graduation from college she served overseas in several very meaningful capacities.

The experience impressed me with how easy it is for people to mistake their fantasies for actual actions. It has always made me listen to confessions with the third ear in order to detect whether the confession was real or only based on fantasy.

Do not allow too much time for confession

One day I established contact with a young man who confessed he was a few weeks away from his marriage, but had accumulated a lot of guilt because of considerable premarital sex in his past. He dealt with his guilt. But he asked me to contact his fiancée, who worked in a café close to where I was teaching. He said both of them wanted to enter into their marriage with a clean slate.

I contacted the young woman at her place of work. I told her I had spent some time with her boyfriend and was wondering whether he had written to her about it. She said he had. I then offered to give her some time if she wanted to talk about these matters. Since only a few weeks remained before the wedding, we would have to hurry if we wanted to deal adequately with the situation.

She agreed to come to my office within a couple of days for her first session. From experience I knew there were a number of phases through which one needs to take the penitent. First, the person needs to have opportunity to get all past guilt settled. Second, there needs to be analysis as to what triggered the individual's involvement in these things so that future incidents could be avoided. Third, the person needs to develop a relevant behavioral ideal: how do I want to deal with temptations of this kind in the future?

Since I might have only three sessions with the young woman, I allowed her to disclose her entire past during the first session. She confessed for almost two-and-a-half hours. We ended the session with prayer, committing the things she had confessed to God and speaking her free from her sin before God.

When the next week's appointment came due, the girl called it off. I persuaded her to come in a day later. She showed up in high heels, a fancy dress, and wearing plenty of makeup. When she strutted into my office belligerently, I was just standing by the bookshelf in front of my desk. I turned my face away from her to face the bookshelf and said quietly, "I wonder whether I am helping you any longer. Maybe you would rather drop the whole thing." Without a word she wheeled around and strode out of my office and my life for good.

I learned a lesson here: never allow more confession than can be lived with the next day. The individual has to be able to face you a week later, otherwise you will no longer be in a position to help the person.

Overcoming courtship guilt

One day a young woman came to see me, followed by her boyfriend a few weeks later. She confessed that they had gotten involved in heavy foreplay and that she had accumulated considerable guilt. She feared that if they got married this guilt, like a canker, would eventually destroy their relationship. I listened to her confession, prayed with her and later with him. Then we began working on how to live together during the rest of their courtship to avoid more guilt of this kind. The school year ended, the young couple got married, and I lost track of them.

A number of years later I preached in a church. I greeted the audience at the church door after my message. Finally only one person was left—a young woman carrying a child in a papoose. She approached me hesitantly, but with a broad smile on her face. I extended my hand to greet her but she threw her arms around me and whispered in my ear, "I want to thank you for helping me get into marriage clean. We are enjoying a good marriage!" Experiences like this have provided me with enough encouragement to always be willing to spend a few hours with someone who needed a listening ear.

Young people look for honesty

Probably the thing that impressed me most in conversing with college students was the scrupulous honesty they required of their mentors, especially when talking about sex. After we were well on the way to solving their problem, the students frequently asked to talk to my wife. They would say to her, "Your husband said that in your courtship you and he did this, is that true?" When she would answer in the affirmative, they would specifically ask, "You're sure you didn't also do this? You're sure you didn't also do that?" They wanted to make doubly sure that I had been honest with them about my own past.

This quest for honesty had another implication. Occasionally when someone shared a problem with me, I would realize that their problem was also an issue in my own life that I hadn't yet dealt with. At first I did not interrupt the students and acknowledge that I, too, needed to deal with this problem. Then I realized that such a silence automatically made me a phony. I was acting as if I had the matter solved, when I hadn't. It behooved me to join the student as just another sinner, and the two of us would draw grace from God simultaneously to gain our victory together. Talking with people as a learner, is something I have had to do time and again.

CHAPTER 12

LENDING A LISTENING EAR TO MISSIONARIES

"Should I destroy the idols?"

One night, well after 11 o'clock, while I was home alone in Togo, the bell at the front gate rang. My wife had already left for our North American furlough, and I was going to join her after completing another assignment. At the gate was a white man I had never seen before. He introduced himself as a third-generation missionary from Ethiopia who was currently working in Northern Ghana. He told me he would like to discuss a problem with me. I invited him in.

"I have been a missionary in this area of Ghana for three years now," he told me. "At the beginning we saw very few results from our preaching of the gospel. But lately a number of young people have been accepting the Lord. However, there are problems. One of them is that there are some Christians in the community who I doubt are really born again. I think they are mere syncretists[1]! All of them have some small white stones in their houses to which they seem to pray."

I immediately recognized the typical West African pattern whereby a family will add a new white stone each time a meaningful elderly relative dies. The stones are then known by the names of the deceased. When problems in the family arise, these ancestors are consulted for guidance.

He went on to say that the other problem involved the deity shrines (God-living-in-things). There are two kinds of these shrines. Each home had a family shrine. This is where the white stones were kept. They frequently burned candles in this shrine, just like Catholics. Then there was the village shrine, which housed the deity responsible for the whole village. It supposedly was a peacekeeping deity.

---

[1]The term syncretist often refers to new Christians who mix some of their pre-Christian religion together with Christianity.

Both kinds of shrines are typically West African. The *Ifa* or *Afa* are family or clan deities. Since a village is made up of more than one clan, they also need a deity that is going to relate to several clans, because family deities are responsible only for extended families.

"I consider these stones and shrines as so much idolatry," the missionary now continued. "I recently challenged the young people to tear them down. They were very hesitant at first, so I helped them. Together we tore down the village shrine. Now a delegation of the elders has come to my house and told me in no uncertain terms that I have a choice to make. I will either recognize that I am a guest in their village and will not tear down what the people are worshiping, or if I persist in my attack, they will find ways to eliminate the problem. They are happy if I preach and help the young people, but they do not want me to teach them to destroy all the things that God has already taught the people."

This missionary was convinced that the people were ready to kill him, and he probably was absolutely right.

He asked, "What is my responsibility? You see, my grandfather was a missionary in Ethiopia, and he and the early believers there tore down the village shrines and that became a major turning point for the gospel there. When nothing bad happened to the Christians, the local people believed the missionary's God was more powerful than all the village gods. I feel I should do the same! But now it seems as if that will destroy my entree to the village and maybe even cost me my life. What should I do?"

I gave him a short description of West African belief. The people feel they already believe in the God whom the missionary preaches. But they also believe that this God has manifested himself in a number of forms. One of these is *Afa*—the family deity. I told him that in biblical times such gods were called the *teraphim*. Abraham and Jacob also had teraphim.

The West Africans further believe that there is another manifestation of God at the village level for all the clans who live together in the same village. This is a peacekeeping manifestation of God which adjudicates difficulties that develop between clans living together.

I went on to tell him about the West African belief that the living are responsible for the salvation of the dead. Those white stones reminded the living that the dead were watching over their moral and physical behavior and their spiritual well-being. If someone should do evil to some other person, there could be far-reaching consequences. It was the ancestors' responsibility to warn the living whenever one of the latter has done something wrong that will have far-reaching consequences.

Meanwhile the living had a responsibility to remember the deceased ancestors in funerals and other remembrances. The living were to consult the ancestors about life's problems and be open to receive any messages from beyond that the ancestors were duty-bound to convey to them.

When the missionary insisted that he couldn't accept local manifestations of God, I pointed out that Christianity believes in at least three separate manifestations of God: Father, Son and Holy Spirit. Furthermore, messages like Hebrews 12:1 tell us that our deceased ancestors surround us like a cloud of witnesses watching our spiritual race. Whether the Africans are right when they take this one step further, I don't know, but it doesn't seem out of keeping with the message contained in the Bible that was written in a totally different cultural context from our own.

Deep wells and dysentery

A retreat at which I was the resource person was attended by missionaries and short-term workers who worked in a region similar to the one described in the previous account. The Canadian government through its development arm, CIDA, had been drilling deep wells in an area where water was scarce. In the past, many people had to walk for five or ten miles to get water for drinking and cooking. The foreign engineers had discovered water 200-300 meters down and were putting in boreholes so that each village now had its own source of good water.

The first year or so after the wells were drilled, things went fine. But now in the third year, a serious health problem had developed. All of the foreign workers recognized the cause of the problems. Because water was now so readily available, people had begun keeping it in their houses. It would be left in an open pot into which people could dip, thus infecting it with germs. Since the water was warm from standing in a hot climate, the germs multiplied quickly and were now causing dysentery. Hundreds of children were becoming sick, and many were dying.

The nurses described their efforts to teach the villagers about germs and hygiene. In spite of all their teaching, they seemingly had been unable to change the people's behavior. They asked me whether anthropology had any answer for them. I suggested that anthropology might be able to help, provided they would be willing to explain the problem in terms of the worldview of the local people.

In the missionary worldview, I said, the illness is caused by germs. The missionary could demonstrate that the drinking water contained these germs. When these germs infected small children who did not have the necessary resistance, the latter would get sick and die. The Africans however, believed that the real cause of illness was spirits sent either by ancestors as a warning for people who had done some wrong, or by unknown malevolent sources out to do them harm, if not kill them.

I suggested that if they wanted to explain this to the local people in terms that the latter would understand, they should use the spirit approach. They might, for example, tell the villagers that in the biblical worldview, especially that of the New Testament, evil spirits are stacked in the atmosphere above us. They are listed in different categories, such as principalities and powers, suggesting that some of the higher ones are the more dangerous. Perhaps they could suggest that the same might be true of the earth below. They might say that there were evil spirits stacked below us and that the lower or deeper one went, the more virulent they became. Thus when people brought up too much water from 300 meters underground and stored it in their houses, the spirits from down below became mixed with spirits at earth level, and the resulting cross-breeding produced virulent new spirits which were causing the children to die.

When I asked them whether they could use this type of explanation, the missionaries were horrified. "But it isn't true!" they protested. I countered that no worldviews are "true." I don't think our Western worldview which sees the world only in terms of the material is entirely true. We can demonstrate that it contains a lot of truth, but it is not entirely true. There is also a spirit dimension. Likewise, the African explanation entirely in spirit terms is not really true. But if the Africans have such a worldview, there is nothing wrong in using it to explain something in terms that make sense to them. But the missionaries said, "No thank you!"

Soul "adultery"

While I was still working in South America, a missionary asked me to come to their mission station to deal with a very promising young tribal man whom their Bible school was grooming for the ministry. This young man had recently become totally distraught and had tried to commit suicide. They had prayed with and for him, but they weren't finding any meaningful way to help him in his depression.

When I first met with the missionary and the native, the latter was remote, and I couldn't reach him. I asked the missionary whether I might have some time alone with the man.

I tried a number of different approaches. I suspected his distress might be related to sex. I thought the native might have gotten involved in masturbation which is relatively unknown in tribal societies because they engage in coitus so early in their lives. I suggested something of this nature to him, but he did not respond in the slightest.

I then tried various other approaches, but he continued to remain totally remote. Somewhere in the discussion, however, I had begun to speak about my own youth and began telling him about my experience with nocturnal emissions, the so-called "wet dreams" of youth. I was still continuing this story when the man suddenly interrupted me and excitedly asked, "So your soul commits adultery, too?"

Suddenly I realized what the problem was. While at Bible school this tribesperson was away from his people and his wife. He was now experiencing nocturnal emissions. He was interpreting the "wet dreams" as "soul adultery."

When I asked with whom his soul had been committing adultery, he said, "With the chief's youngest wife." Then I understood the source of his fear. He feared that the chief would find out about his "soul adultery" and kill him. That is why the young man had attempted suicide.

The missionary who bought a whole tribe

At a large missionary conference, a missionary asked me to spend the evening after the service with him and his wife because they were facing a serious problem. They told me about the people with whom they worked, a small jungle tribe in the Amazon basin where a white man had set up a sawmill. This white man had begun advancing credit to the people, and the whole tribe had become permanently indebted to him. Now they were his debt-servants, forced to work in his sawmill to pay off their debt.

What had happened was that each time someone made a purchase, say a dollar's worth of goods in the sawmill store, a stroke was made in the book saying that the person owed so much. Each day the people worked, a stroke was to be erased from the debt they owed. However, this man was conveniently forgetting to erase the strokes when they worked but kept on adding the strokes when they bought goods. The result was that these people were by now hopelessly indebted not only in this generation, but for generations to come.

When the missionary realized this, he went to the sawmill owner and asked him to calculate the total debt of the tribe. It totaled about US$6,500. On his next furlough in the United States the missionary told the people at home about the plight of these indebted slaves. He raised enough money to pay off the entire tribe's debt. And when he returned to the field that is exactly what he did. He then told the people they no longer were slaves of this white man who was exploiting them.

As soon as the tribe was free, they all moved away from the sawmill to live near the mission station. When they ran out of food, however, they asked the missionary to provide it. When he told them to work and plant gardens, the people just shrugged their shoulders and went away sullenly. Eventually the whole thing got out of hand. The people became belligerent and angry. They blamed the missionary that he had taken them away from their steady source of food at the sawmill and "was now going to let them die of starvation because he had no compassion."

I had to tell this missionary that in paying their debt and ending their relationship with the sawmill owner, he had obligated himself to help these people develop a livelihood that they could sustain. They had been slaves for so long, they now had to relearn independence and personal responsibility. Not an easy task!

The Christian who killed himself

While I was serving in Africa with the Bible Society, a missionary friend came over one day and told me the following: "We have been having difficulty in our mission churches with church treasurers. One after the other absconds with the church's money." He asked me to explain this cultural phenomenon.

In this part of Africa uncles are generally responsible for their nephews' education. Most of the men have nephews who want to study or who are already studying. They are supposed to provide the money for their education, but most of them are hopelessly in arrears. When they get into a position like church treasurer and get their hands on some money, they are under tremendous pressure to meet their financial obligations to their younger relatives. So they abscond with some of the entrusted money, presumably under the pretext of just borrowing it, to be paid back later. But that "later" never seems to materialize.

The missionary went on to say that their Bible school had had a very promising young student who had been studying to become a pastor. But one day this young man had said, "I think what the church really needs is people who can make money so that the church can have the wherewithal to do its work." So he left Bible school and established a rather successful farm. He raised money for the church.

But as this farmer paid the money to the church for its outreach efforts, he discovered the problem of treasurers absconding with church funds. Eventually he became severely frustrated, and now had begun to complain that he wasn't feeling well physically. I immediately recognized the symptoms.

In African society, when a person is faced with people running off with money, the solution generally is sorcery. A hex is put upon the thief and then he or some member of his family suffers the consequences. But this believer was too much of a Christian to practice sorcery. Therefore he was internalizing his anger and this anger was now avenging itself by "killing" him. I urged the missionary to go right back to the believer and to bring him to me so I could ascertain from his cultural situation whether my judgment of the situation was correct or not. The missionary, however, had other immediate pressing obligations. He said he would visit the man as soon as possible. When he finally visited him the following Tuesday, it was too late. He had died on Monday.

The missionary who replaced herself with a national

While in South America I became acquainted with a single missionary who was truly committed to establishing an indigenous church. In my many conversations with her, I was impressed by the length to which she was willing to go to make sure that the indigenous church prospered. She was the head of a thriving program to train mother-tongue speakers to write literature in their own language. This program was reaching several tribes and she was the instructor responsible for training all these people. By now she had built up a cadre of nationals who could not only write well, but who could help her in the training of others. She was even grooming one of them to replace her. She was going to phase out.

The date came to install the trained national as the head of the program. The missionary would from now on only be a resource person, holding no actual office.

As soon as the national took over, he began "stepping on the missionary" because he didn't trust her to really let go of leadership. He did not want to be dominated by her. He did unkind things which seriously hurt this well-meaning woman. For at least eighteen months, every time I visited the area I had to speak words of encouragement for her to hang in there until this man realized he had nothing to fear from her. It took three years before the national finally grasped that this missionary was no threat to him. She truly exemplified the "he must increase and I must decrease" philosophy of John the Baptist.

Missionaries and furlough dishonesty

One of the most frequent confessions I have heard from missionaries has been that while on furlough the expectations of the home constituency pushed them toward dishonesty. This manifested itself in two ways.

On the one hand, the churches were eager to have the missionaries detail the sin and the depravity which they found on the mission scene. On the other hand, they were always ready to glorify the wonders of God's grace when the missionaries could report some miraculous conversion or other success. The churches seemingly wanted sin to be made more sinful and God's grace to be more glorious. And missionary after missionary succumbed to the temptation to comply.

Missionary after missionary confessed that they had been carried away by the pressure to tell one-sided stories of depravity. They were no longer presenting a balanced picture. Repeatedly they reported that they had continued to tell exciting conversion or discipleship stories about nationals who might no longer be walking with the Lord. In other words, they were glorying in a victory when that victory no longer existed. The following experience illustrates just how serious the problem was.

In a country in South America the nationals and the missionaries developed a serious dispute. The nationals got so angry that they were asking the government to cancel all visas for foreign missionaries so that the local church could become truly indigenous. They felt the missionaries were hanging on to power, because they controlled the money. When some saner heads tried to mediate the dispute, they began looking for a person to stand in the gap. Seemingly Jake, the Mennonite, was the one in whom both sides had confidence.

I thus flew to that country, ostensibly to give a week-long series of public lectures in the capital city. Every evening I lectured to all the Christians in public sessions, but during the daytime the national leaders and the missionaries met in secret meetings in which we tried to air the problems separating them. In these discussions, both missionaries and nationals were urged to be completely honest. I then tried to interpret for the other party what a given experience meant or what was actually happening in the situation.

On one occasion, a young national who had just returned from North America where he had studied for three years on a scholarship provided by the missionaries, got up and began spouting invective. He uttered such outrages as, "We are the missionaries' manure! We are the shit from which they raise their money, while they are on furlough!" He went on and on. Soon the missionaries stopped their ears and just looked at the ground. The nationals began to hiss, the local cultural sign that a person's speaking is no longer welcome. But the young man continued unfazed.

When he finished after half an hour of insults, I asked the assembled group, especially the missionaries, whether they knew what this young man had been talking about. None of the missionaries seemed to have the faintest idea. I told them I thought he was talking about the form letters missionaries sent to their supporters. I said that many faith missionaries, in their efforts to raise money, tend to exaggerate sinful situations to tug at the hearts of believers at home so they will give more generously.

After detailing some of these scenes, I turned to the angry young man and asked, "Did you read any missionary form letters while you were in North America?" He literally spat out his answer, "In every home I visited while doing deputation work, I was shown form letters about our country that the missionaries were sending to church members. I saw the filth they were writing about our people." Eventually, some of the missionaries got up and owned the problem. They confessed their own concerns, especially these furlough failings that I mentioned earlier. They asked their national brothers and sisters to forgive them. A tremendous meeting of reconciliation resulted.

Independence for national Christians

In one of the French-speaking countries of West Africa, I became friends with a young woman, a single missionary from France. She was very capable, but as I saw it she was building her ego at the expense of the national church. She was translating the Scriptures and riding tight herd on all the nationals whom she used as paid translation helpers. She always had the final word in everything.

In the course of my work with her translation team, I gradually was able to move the nationals into a position of responsibility, side-lining the missionary in the process. She became severely depressed and began to consider me her enemy. I had to spend a lot of time with her to explain what I was doing and why. She agreed that she wanted the church to become indigenous, but she also became aware that she needed some way to build her self-image. I then spent considerable time teaching her methodologies to build her self-image without undermining that of the nationals in the church. In fact, one of the most frequent questions I learned to ask missionaries was, "How are you building your ego without doing so at the expense of the national church?" This is a crucial problem in all mission endeavors.

CHAPTER 13

THE WITNESS MAY NEED TO BECOME THE FIRST SINNER

Mrs. Woodrum, a widow of fifty-five, jumped to her death early one morning from her twelfth floor apartment on Chicago's north side. Just before she jumped, she saw the janitor working on the balcony across the court in the next wing of the building. She waved to him and smiled, and he smiled and waved back. When he turned his back, she jumped.

On her desk, Mrs. Woodrum left this note, "I can't stand one more day of this loneliness. No sound from my telephone. No mail in my box. No friends!" Mrs. Jenkins, another widow who lived on the same floor of the same large city apartment building, told reporters, "I wish I had known she was so lonely! I am very lonely, too! I could have called on her. We could have been friends."

Sociologists and psychologists studying our Western culture have noted the frightening increase of social distance that has accompanied rapid urbanization. When people move to large urban centers, they leave behind the familiarity of rural areas. They often feel lost and alone in the impersonal city, but they mask their insecurities with an aloof, conventional smile, not realizing that the one at whom they flash this smile also wears a mask that may cover the same loneliness.

In sharing with college students, I've often seen them poke their heads into my office door and ask with a broad smile, "Are you very busy?" I would then say, "No, not especially. Come on in!" Still smiling they enter. As they step in, I suggest, "Would you want to kick the door a bit?" They push the door and watch as the latch falls. The moment they see the door lock, they often drop their smiling masks. In the four steps from the door to the chair beside my desk, they may have changed from a dazzling smile to the most bitter weeping.

I've been even more startled to learn how soon children learn to use such masks. Our son was in first grade together with a boy whose father had been killed recently in a tractor accident. Our son was praying for his classmate regularly every day. About that time our family decided to learn how to be sensitive to the Spirit of God in witnessing and in sharing our lives with others. Our son also tried.

That night he could hardly wait for table prayers to finish before he shared his experience. As he'd been walking down the stairs after school with the bereaved boy, he had decided to share something with him. "How are you getting along?" he asked. The boy smiled and said, "Fine, just fine!" Bill, obviously disappointed at the response, had blurted out, "Do you know I've been praying for you every day since your Daddy got killed?" At once the other little fellow grabbed Bill's hand, took him behind the school building and said, "That was a lie when I said things are going fine; they are not fine! We are having all kinds of trouble with the cows and with the milking machines. My mother doesn't know what to do. But I didn't know that you were praying for us."

Religious distance

Christians also practice religious distance. J.B. Phillips, in the *New Testament in Modern English,* describes Pharisees as people who ordered their lives "with an eye to the effect." The famed hypocrites of Jesus' day aren't the only ones. Modern people of every theological stripe are deeply involved in social and religious distance and the calculated effect. Often this invades even our testimony meetings where instead of giving an honest, open witness of our intimate experience with God, we use cliches, pious jargon and "Protestant Latin" as we try to impress other people.

We also produce religious distance by professionalizing our witness. We witness when we are in front of a Sunday school class, a congregation, or some organized group. We read the Bible and pray at our Bible study. But outside of these formal, scheduled settings many of us are unable to talk openly and unselfconsciously about our Christian experience.

I saw this some time ago at a retreat of high school young people. We were attempting to discover our true spiritual condition by laying bare the difference between the ideal we were professing and the reality we were living. There I made a startling discovery. In the course of "knowing and becoming known to each other," we had to look at the Christian homes from which we all came. Some of these Christian teenagers asserted that their parents never spoke to them about the Word of God except during family devotions or while meting out discipline! I was convinced this was a glaring overstatement until I polled my college faculty colleagues and found that many of them could not recall when their parents had ever spoken to them about the gospel outside of formal settings. This led me to check on the use of Scripture in our own home, and to my shame I found the indictment was far more true than I dared to admit; our children, too, felt that we had used the Bible to "whip" them.

The way of the mask is the way of compartmentalization, where we have a church life and an everyday life, a life of reality at home and the way of the façade in public. The pathos of such a situation is revealed through one youngster's passionate plea to his missionary mother, "Mother, why can't you be at home the way you are among the native people?"

The mask is not a modern phenomenon. When God looked for Adam and Eve after they had disobeyed his command in the garden, he found them making aprons of fig leaves—an early man-made mask to cover human failure. Cain, their firstborn, hid behind the mask of ambiguity when God asked him, "Where is thy brother?" He countered, "Am I my brother's keeper?"

Divine example

"And the Word became flesh and dwelt among us, full of grace and truth; we have beheld his glory, glory as of the only Son from the Father" (John 1:14). In these unassuming words, John the apostle begins his witness about God's full identification with humankind. But before we reach the end of John's account of "the Christ in human flesh," we learn that this biblical incarnation is only a beginning. It is a pattern, an example of a chain of becoming flesh. "As my Father hath sent me, even so send I you" (John 10:21).

If Christ crossed the infinite-finite barrier to translate the truth of God into a form intelligible to humankind, Christ's disciples are sent to translate this truth across the cultural and social barriers that separate human beings from each other. If God had to become human in order to become intelligible to the human race, it stands to reason that finite human beings will have to "become human" in other cultures, if their experience of God is to become intelligible to people in such differing cultural settings.

The possibility of such a cross-cultural identification was demonstrated when Christ Jesus was born of a woman. It was the basis for Christ's being able to suffer and die for us. Writing to the Ephesians, Paul says, "But now, through the blood of Christ, you who were once outside the pale are with us inside the circle of God's love in Jesus Christ. For Christ is our living peace. He has made a unity of the conflicting elements of Jew and Gentile by breaking down the barrier which lay between us. By his sacrifice he removed the hostility of the Law, with all its commandments and rules, and made in himself out of the two, Jew and Gentile, one new creature, thus producing peace. For he reconciled both to God by the sacrifice of one body on the cross, and by this act made utterly irrelevant the antagonism between them" (Eph. 2:13-16).

Though humankind has persistently continued to hide itself from God, God has even more persistently continued revealing himself to us. Finally, in the incarnation God actually entered the human setting where he accepted the limitations of human flesh so that he could "feel" with us and become our sympathetic high priest.

One of the valuable features of the Bible is that it accepts humans in their weaknesses and speaks of people of God not as perfect, but as those who are being perfected. It recounts their sins as faithfully as their obediences.

Paul was so deeply aware of his past as a persecutor, blasphemer and reviler that he accepted his accomplishments entirely as the grace of God working in him. James puts forth the passionate plea that people should be open with one another, for in openness there is growing wholeness. "Confess your sins to one another, and pray for one another, that you may be healed."

Human-to-human encounter

If we really want to enter into any intimate relationship with other human beings, there is a way: the way of self-exposure—of becoming the first sinner. We will have to be willing to be known, if we want to know others. Values are always best taught in the drama of daily life, not in preaching. For as we practice self-exposure, we will also become aware of the work of God in others who are willing to be known (as is recorded in the example of Peter and Cornelius).

Finally, self-exposure will help us to operate on the principle of the "heart of flesh" rather than the "heart of stone." Like God in Christ, we can become sympathetic "priests." It will prevent us from casting the first stone at the person caught in shortcoming, because we will already be the first sinner kneeling at the cross in repentance for our own weaknesses and shortcomings.

I'm not saying that nothing is private, but I feel that Christians need to be more open than they are at present if they are to share in the experiences of other people. In each situation one must decide what God wants us to reveal and what is to remain entirely personal. God's Spirit must be in charge.

One of my most revealing experiences in self-exposure was the previously mentioned encounter with the young people in camp. There we attempted to discuss the discrepancies between the real and the ideal of our lives. In our first group meeting (nine high school students and their mentor), we just attempted to establish a communication relationship by praying for each other in a circle. In the second encounter we tried to share some of our ideals and at least one area in which we were still struggling short of our mark. The discussion was to last thirty minutes, but the first of six such groups took three times that long. As the feeling of community became more actual, not only the socially acceptable "sins" were mentioned, but again and again one would interrupt the other saying, "That's exactly my problem. I thought I was alone; you all appeared so holy."

A dramatic example of becoming the first sinner took place in a jail service near the college where I taught. I was accompanying a group of college students going to conduct the service, and en route we discussed how to approach people whom society had already branded as guilty. We decided there would be little use to speak about the sinners inside the bars, for those inside were all parading under the mask of their innocence. It might be best to speak about the experiences of the sinners outside of the bars, the ones who were performing in the service.

A college sophomore with a radiant smile had been asked to give her testimony. When she got up to speak, she grasped the bars with both hands, and with a voice choked with deep emotion, she revealed to the prisoners that her father, a prominent minister, had committed suicide and that this had caused intense inner conflicts in her life. She admitted that in her darker moments she hated her father for what he'd done to her reputation. Then again she realized in those very thoughts the depravity of her own heart, and could only say she was grateful that God still cared for her, was concerned about her, and wanted her to find peace, joy and meaning in life.

One prisoner was so deeply shaken by the girl's unmasking that after the group left, he called the jailer and confessed that he wasn't an orphan from Chicago as he had been claiming. He was a runaway from a wealthy Canadian family. He said, "I don't know why that girl had to be so honest; I'm the one who's dishonest. She had no business taking off her mask like that. She wasn't that bad; not as bad as I am." The result was that this young man was reunited with his family and even the impersonal county which had condemned him to six years in prison was moved to suspend the sentence because they witnessed the dramatic transformation in his life.

In conclusion, let me summarize:

1. Just as there is a gulf between God and humankind, so also there are barriers, gulfs and walls of separation between persons.

2. All people are culturally trained to wear a variety of masks to cover their true identity.

3. God in the incarnation of Christ has demonstrated that human beings need human sympathetic friends who themselves have experienced the pull of temptation and the limitations of their human nature and are willing to admit it.

4. Effective witness to others, especially to people in a different culture, requires honest differentiation between the reality in one's life and the ideal of one's profession.

5. The honest facing and admission of the reality in one's life can often serve as a catalyst for a redemptive response in one's neighbor.

TRUTH

The concern for truth in my life must have begun at a very young age. The early experience with the punched-down buns and the resulting spanking I received indelibly imprinted on me the dangers of false accusation.

In my youth in the church, telling the truth was not as important as the concern about upholding Christian truth. The church and Bible school taught me that we, as God's people, had the truth, the whole truth and nothing but the truth. My job as a Christian witness at home and abroad was merely to make this already revealed truth known to people. But it wasn't until I tried to teach the Waunana the *truth* that malaria is not caused by fever spirits but by malaria germs that I realized that sharing one's truth is no easy matter.

The major crisis about truth in my life, however, came at the university. Here for the first time, I became aware of the fact that the church had most of its truth "canned"—partly as a result of the closed canon of the Bible. The church as a whole had little expectation of discovering new truth. However, at the university I found hundreds of excited people who were discovering all kinds of new truth. The temptation for me at this stage in life was not, do I abandon my faith, but where do I want to throw in my lot? With those who are discovering new truth or with those who are dealing largely in canned truth?

When I got to Africa and into a cultural setting that was much more like that of the Old Testament, I began to realize the fallacy of Western thinking that all truth must be historical. I discovered that most African societies make a clear distinction between historical truth, which is only a few generations deep, and the timeless truth, which is eternal. Once this difference sank in, I realized how foolish it was to think that we can protect biblical truth. God's truth needs no protection, especially not human protection.

As my life's story shows, we all experience our truth wrapped in our own culture. I also learned that untangling some of these cultural wrappers of truth is no easy matter. It involves limitless openness and a constant willingness to look at things from the other person's point of view.

Translating Scripture made me deeply aware how truth in the Bible more often than not is clothed in metaphor and metaphors are inextricably linked to the local culture. The reason for this is that human beings cannot know or express the spiritual through literal language. They have to express it in analogy, simile or metaphor.

Once I realized how much Christian truth is expressed in metaphor, I became aware that other religions also have truth, but they usually wrap it in totally different metaphors. I must confess that I have become a lot less smug about Christians having the whole truth and nothing but the truth as I learned to appreciate the rich metaphors of other religions!

Today the discoveries in sub-nuclear physics, quantum mechanics and other fields are revealing fascinating new truths about how this universe is structured and how it functions. It is exciting to know that we can learn new truth, but at the same time it is humbling to know that there is so much more new truth to be discovered and learned. There even is energy in the universe beyond $E=MC^2$! To me it sounds like the power of the Spirit of God.

CHAPTER 14

TRUTH: CANNED OR FRESH?

My early smugness

I grew up in a church atmosphere that was convinced it was dealing only with the truth. I absorbed that attitude fully. At Bible school I became versed in manipulating that truth. All my youthful experience reinforced the conviction that I had truly found God's truth. By the time I volunteered to be a missionary, I was confident I had the truth, the whole truth and nothing but the truth. It was with this certitude that I went to Colombia eager to communicate this truth to the heathens who, as I had been led to believe, were totally devoid of the truth and were steeped in ignorance, error and sin.

My superior attitude was reinforced when I stepped into a vast array of strange practices in the Waunana culture. The result was that I developed a sense of outrage. How could these people be so misguided and so blind as to follow such gross error? My ethnocentrism convinced me that it was incumbent upon me to correct their many misconceptions and half-truths, if not untruths.

One of the things that troubled me most deeply was the Waunana's unquestioning belief that all their illnesses resulted from evil spirits. Malaria was endemic in the area with 450-plus inches of rainfall per year. When the heavy rains came and the mosquitos multiplied by the hundreds of thousands, almost everyone came down with an acute attack of malaria. Again and again these people would come to us for medical help saying they were suffering from evil spirit attacks. This totally outraged me! I knew what malaria was and what the malarial parasites looked like under the microscope! How could these people affirm such falsehood?

I finally asked the mission board for a microscope. It took some time for them to locate the quality of instrument I had ordered and even longer to find an occasion to send it Colombia. When it finally did arrive, I was overjoyed. I felt that now I was equipped to teach these people some real truth and to correct some of their most glaring errors.

The truth about malaria

Malaria can be tricky to prove. I have often had to make dozens of slides before I could demonstrate the presence of the malarial parasite. Even in my own bouts with malaria fever, the doctors had to take slides again and again before they could positively identify it. Sometimes they never found it.

After the microscope arrived, and another Waunana claiming an attack by fever spirits came to our house, I was ready. I now had my microscope, the proper glass slides and the required stain. With obvious enthusiasm, I launched my truth-teaching crusade.

I punctured the man's finger, took a drop of blood, and put it on a slide. I then took another glass slide and with its edge, drew that drop of blood across the full width of the first slide. Then I pulled out the drop of blood over about half of the slide so as to make a thin film of blood. Once that film of blood had dried, I applied the appropriate blue dye. I was fortunate! On the very first slide, right in the field of vision under the microscope, there were six or seven red blood corpuscles, each with the clear half-moon shape of the malarial parasite, now stained blue.

Once I had this slide successfully prepared, I put it under the microscope and called the man who claimed to be suffering from fever spirits and told him, "You people are dead wrong when you say you are suffering from a fever spirit attack. The many mosquitos that bite us carry little bugs or bug eggs in their saliva. When they bite us they inject these bugs into our blood. Here the bugs multiply and we get the illness that is called 'malaria.' I will now prove to you that malaria is not caused by evil spirits as you say, but that it is caused by real little bugs that I can show you. Depending on the kind of malaria you have, when the malarial parasite that has invaded a blood cell becomes fully grown, it then divides into twelve, twenty-four or forty-eight individual new parasites. These new bugs will now each invade another red blood cell. Each time another batch of these malarial germs matures and escapes into the bloodstream, our bodies react with an attack of fever, because the body tries to kill the invading organisms."

I then took the man to the microscope and showed him the germs now made visible on the slide. It took a long time before he was able to focus in on the small "blue" germs through the eyepiece of the microscope, but eventually he did see them. When that happened, he was so excited he didn't even stop to say anything to me but just raced to the edge of the river, cupped his hands over his mouth, and yelled to the people on the other side, "Come quickly because Jaco (my tribal name) has nailed the fever spirits onto the glass! Come quickly and see the miracle!" As soon as those people could make it across the river, they came. A flood of people came. They came day after day. They came from five, ten, fifteen, and twenty-five miles away. In droves they wanted to see this miraculous event—a white man having nailed fever spirits to glass!

Over and over again, I tried to explain to the Waunana that they were not seeing spirits, they were seeing the little bugs that cause malaria. But my hope of teaching them this truth was shattered completely. The people looked at the slide and then turned to me in utter amazement and exclaimed, "You know, we always knew that fever spirits had blue noses, but we didn't know that those beggars were all blue and that they were that tiny!"

When I realized how they were interpreting what they saw on the slide, I could have torn out my hair. I realized I wasn't teaching them the truth about germs after all. My microscopic demonstration was not correcting what I considered a major error in their belief system. I was actually compounding their error! They now believed that fever spirits were all blue because I couldn't get them to understand that it was I who had stained the parasites blue. They were still interpreting the parasites on the slide as evil spirits. I realized on the spot that even when you do know *the truth*, communicating it across cultural boundaries isn't going to be easy.

Which truth?

So far in this book I have used the word "truth" with a variety of shades of meaning: I began with "religious truth"—the verities my church felt it had distilled from the Scriptures. I then switched to "cultural truth"—all the things people in given cultures feel as intrinsically true and right. The microscope presumably presented "scientific truth"—the facts which science discovers about our universe. Elsewhere I have spoken of truth in contrast to a lie. Finally I want to introduce "virtual" truth (an analogy to "virtual reality" in computer jargon) such as when a face-to-face society must deal with virulent gossip in its midst. It does not ask whether this gossip is based on fact or not, but deals with the tension as if the act gossiped about actually happened. Their reasoning is: if it did happen, it must not happen again; if it hasn't yet happened, it must be prevented from ever happening.

I will continue to use "truth" in these multiple senses.

My experience with truth at the university

As my awareness of cultural diversity grew, my determination to learn what I could about culture and its working increased proportionately. I sincerely wanted to be a good missionary! Thus I enrolled in the graduate school in anthropology at the University of Washington in Seattle as soon as we came home on furlough. I had some nervous moments when I applied because Tabor College had not been accredited at the time I had graduated. Would the university accept my degree from a non-accredited school? They did! I was overjoyed!

But imagine my chagrin when I arrived on campus and the head of the department took me into her office and told me why they had accepted me. She said, "We looked over your transcript and your recommendations and found that you have some of the highest recommendations as a very bright, intelligent human being. We also saw that you come from a non-accredited school. We decided that the lack of accreditation didn't really matter. If you were as bright as your recommendations say, you should have no trouble doing graduate work. The real reason that we accepted you, however, was because you are a missionary. You see, we have never had a missionary in our department. We thought you would provide us with an excellent occasion to see how good this department really is at communicating scientific truth. If we are as good as we think we are, we should be able to get rid of your religious superstition in one year. If we are better than we think we are, we ought to be able to get rid of it in one semester."

I gulped! Obviously I hadn't expected this kind of reception. But by now I had already lost some of my smugness about having the whole truth. So I honestly told the head of the department, "If you have truth here in the university that can correct or eliminate what I believe as a Christian, I am certainly anxious to get it. In fact, I, too, would say, the sooner the better!"

One of my introductory courses was taught by the department head herself. I found it very enlightening because it dealt with the discovery and formulation of truth. One thing that stood out loud and clear in her lectures was her assertion that the truth we currently hold about something must be a simple statement that covers all the known facts. Occasionally we will have to make some subsidiary statements, but they all have to grow out of the first general statement. They may never again be fundamental premises. This made eminent sense to me, and I was anxious to pursue its implications.

I soon realized that there were hundreds of individuals on the university campus searching for truth in manifold fields of scientific endeavor. Dozens of researchers were discovering new truth or were modifying existing truth. For example, when I had been in grade school, my teacher had still been able to bang his fist on the table and emphatically say, "The atom is indivisible!" Well, by the time I entered graduate school the atom had not only been divided, it also had been exploded with the biggest bang yet. Humankind had discovered that the atom itself was a very complex structure. It had numerous parts, in fact, moving parts. It was divisible! It contained enormous power!

"Financial" truth

When our family arrived at the university we had several thousand dollars in savings in the bank. We were getting $170 a month from the mission board as furlough pay. However, our monthly outlay in university expenses was well in excess of $400 per month. Therefore, I applied to the university's scholarship and student aid fund immediately on arriving on campus. What I didn't know was that the head of the anthropology department was one of the three wise individuals who had the final word on the hundreds of thousands of dollars of scholarship and student aid money which the university had at its disposal.

About halfway through the first semester, I was walking across campus one day when I met the department head. She stopped me and said, "Jake, I have just looked over your application for financial help. Is it really true that your financial situation is that precarious?" I was forced to tell her that it was even worse now than it had been when I applied. A mission board member had since visited the mission field and had spoken to the Waunana and asked whether we had taught them about Jesus. The people told him that we had never mentioned the guy. What this board member didn't realize was that the word *Jesú* is a swear word for the tribal people. Since the pronunciation of Jesus is *Jesú* in that area of Colombia, we had avoided that name. We had rather used an indigenous expression common in their language, "the Son of God." Now the mission board, thinking we had not been preaching the gospel, had cut us off from our furlough allowance until this matter was clarified. It was!

The offer of university money

Lo and behold, toward the end of the first semester I received a letter from the scholarship office offering me a readership. I would receive free tuition, which amounted to $105 a month. I would also receive a waiver of all fees, which amounted to another $105 a month. I would also receive at least another $105 a month in cash. This was excellent news, and Anne and I were overjoyed. But when we lived with this good news for a while, it suddenly brought to mind the conversation I had had with the head of the department at the very beginning, about getting rid of my faith. I now wondered: does my acceptance of this job imply that I am on the way to losing my faith or that I have already given up my faith? The more I thought about it, the more seriously the matter loomed.

I finally decided to go and see the department head. I told her how grateful I was for the offer and how much it meant to us. Then I told her about our second thoughts. I was wondering whether accepting this offer implied that I had already lost, or was in the process of giving up my faith. I told her that the university had actually strengthened my faith, rather than weakened it. She seemed intrigued and asked me to explain.

I went on, "You see, you have taught me that the truth is the simplest statement that covers all the known facts about whatever. If you have to make multiple statements about something, you may never make more than one fundamental premise statement. All additional subsidiary statements have to grow out of your first premise. As I listened carefully to the instruction which the department of anthropology gives, however, I found that when it speaks of the universe, it does not make one fundamental premise statement followed by subsidiary statements that grow out of the first one, but rather it makes five fundamental statements, none of which grows out of the other."

"Well," she said, "that is very interesting. Tell me about them."

So I told her, "The department assumes that in the beginning of the universe matter already existed. Now that is a basic assumption, just as the Christian assumption about there being a God is a basic assumption. Then somewhere along the line, the department postulates that this matter began to percolate or interact. Now, we know from the second law of thermodynamics that matter at rest always requires an outside agent to make it interact or percolate. It needs a catalyst. Now the existence of a catalyst does not grow out of the fact that matter already existed. It is a new fundamental assumption."

The third basic assumption that the department makes, I said, is that this interaction of matter gradually crossed the boundary between the inorganic and the organic. Life began! Now the existence of inorganic matter does not postulate life. The emergence of life from percolating matter is a fundamental new assumption (interestingly, current research on amino acids may be on the verge of making this premise obsolete).

Next, I continued, the department postulates that multi-celled living creatures evolved from original one-celled ones. The problem is that most of the original one-celled creatures like the euglena, the paramecium and the amoeba are still with us. We have colonies of individual cells like sponges. We have multi-celled creatures which can be cut in half and in which both halves will then regrow the missing part of the body. But we do not have any demonstrable case in which a one-celled something became a multi-celled something.

Finally, I concluded, the department assumes that animal intelligence and human intelligence are not merely different in degree, they are different in kind. I then added, "This statement really struck me, and I underlined it in my notebook, when you emphatically made that point in class: *It is not a difference of degree, it is a difference of kind*! Now there is no reason for this new kind of intelligence to arise. This new kind of intelligence thus represents another fundamental assumption."

When I had finished describing these five points, she asked me, "And what is that simple statement which you make as your basic premise?"

"Well," I said, "my simple statement is that in the beginning there was an intelligent living First Cause. It is the source of matter. This first source is also the mover or the catalyst which began the interaction of matter. It is a *living* First Cause, therefore it reproduced itself in life. It caused many kinds of different creatures, one-celled and multi-celled, to develop. It even allowed some of them to develop and to speciate far away from their original forms. Finally, being intelligent it also shepherded intelligence into existence, be that of the animal or of the human kind."

The department head was quiet for a while and said, "Gee, that is truly fascinating! I never knew that you Christians thought like that. This is terrific!" She was quiet for a while longer and then she abruptly asked, "But does this predicate that the intelligent creature has some sort of responsibility toward the First Cause?" When I said, "Yes!" she became furious. "To hell with it!" she spat out. Our conversation ended right then and there.

To her credit, she never troubled me about religion anymore. For the rest of my graduate studies, she only spoke to me in larger groups. With respect to my financial need, however, she saw to it that I got all the money I needed to complete graduate school. In fact, I wound up with several thousand dollars in the pocket when I finally graduated with my Ph.D.

The discovery of new truth

If I had any temptation or faith difficulty at the university, it definitely was not about losing my faith in God. I must honestly say my faith was strengthened there. But I did have a temptation concerning the discovery of new or additional truth. The burning question for me was: "Where am I going to throw in my lot, with those who are discovering additional truth about God's universe, or with those who deal only in canned truth?"

It seemed to me that as I looked at the panorama of churches, each had its own truth in a can and was smugly sitting on the lid saying, "We have the truth, the whole truth and nothing but the truth. Ha! Ha! Ha!" While at the university, I found people who might be blaspheming God, and yet God was allowing them to discover more truth about his handiwork, the universe. This observation jolted me severely.

I had to learn that God in his infinite patience lets humankind discover truth whenever or wherever people are willing to obey the laws on which he has based his creation. It doesn't matter in which area of existence a person is willing to obey him, God is always ready to reveal more of his handiwork. This is a part of the mercy of God. He wants humans to recognize that they are creatures under a First Cause to which they owe allegiance. He rewards obedience whenever or wherever he finds it.

The metaphor which came to my rescue in my time of need was the piano keyboard. It seemed to me that as I looked over the religious panorama, I saw individual churches playing their single favorite key. My Mennonite church might be playing middle C feeling that it was a perfect, fully comfortable and totally complete note. The Pentecostals might be playing high C and the Presbyterians might be playing low C, but each of them was content with the perfect note they had discovered.

On the other hand, I saw that the piano keyboard contained lots of keys. To top it off, some of them even were black. Then and there I made a commitment to God to be open to discovering more of the truth he had built into this universe. I committed myself to follow his truth, come what may. I vowed that I would look every sacred cow in the mouth and would ascertain for myself whether there was truth there or not. If there was, I wanted to find out how valid it was. But I also recognized what the department head had already realized: it was imperative that the person discovering new truth also be obedient to it. This could be obedience in physics, in psychology, or whatever. Anyone who was open and obedient to the truth he/she discovered would be rewarded. God would let himself and his truth be found. His creation contained whole symphonies of truth.

CHAPTER 15

TRUTH: HISTORICAL, TIMELESS, OR MYTHOLOGICAL

The previous chapter told about my interaction with the head of the anthropology department at the university. As part of my personal commitment to be open to truth, even if that should test my faith, I committed myself to enroll in several independent study courses so I would become conversant with the dating methods in archaeology and physical anthropology and in the tenets of evolutionary theory.

A second commitment I made to the department head was to become the reader to the physical anthropologist at the university. I would sit in on all his lectures. I would deliver his lectures whenever he had to be absent from class because of illness or other engagements. I would grade his papers, administer his exams and counsel his students.

Both of these commitments provided me with invaluable lessons.

Methods of dating in anthropology

In the course of my independent research I studied even such secondary methods of dating as dendrochronology—tree-ring dating. This is a method for dating archaeological artifacts in the southwestern United States, where a master chart of tree-ring growth has been established for a period covering about three thousand years. With this method even a piece of burned timber from an old shack or a chunk of charcoal can be dated as to the time when it grew.

I studied dating by the magnetic particles in pottery. When pottery is fired at intense heat, all the metallic particles in the clay will line up in relationship to the earth's magnetic pole at the time of firing. If it can be established in what position a pot was fired, then even pottery sherds can be dated, because the earth's magnetic pole shifts gradually every year.

It was very interesting to realize, when I studied radio carbon dating, that there seemed to be a fairly marked cutoff point for dates associated with humans. When I was in graduate school in the 1950s, that date was at about 15,000 years. Now it has been extended to 20,000 or so years. Once one gets beyond that time depth, however, a million years between friends seems to make absolutely no difference. In other words, the markers of human civilization, or of human habitation on earth, do not go back very far. After that time depth, there is an abrupt shift into millions of years, for then we begin to deal with geological time.

I spent most of my time, however, in the major dating methods. The first and foremost was geological dating. This relates to the length of time it took to produce a given stratum of the earth. The different strata in the earth's crust then follow each other showing how they are related to each other chronologically, that is, in their time sequence. This whole sequence is usually referred to as geological or chronological dating. Thus if skeletal remains are found in a given stratum of the earth which has an established period date, then we know that these remains found in it can be dated relatively as not older than the stratum and possibly much younger. The material could have been buried at a much later date.

The second major method is morphological dating. This method depends on the shape of the object being dated. Thus if a physical anthropologist is studying the decrease in the thickness of the bone in the human eyebrow ridge, he will line up his skeletal material according to the degree of protrusion of the eyebrow ridge from the most prominent to the least prominent. He will assume that the most prominent is the oldest and that the one with the least protrusion is youngest, because people living today do not have prominent eyebrow ridges.

Morphological dating is the standard method wherever the principles of evolution are applied to human skeletal remains. If one is studying the receding jawbone in humans, one lines up skulls and jawbones according to their degree of protrusion. The greater the protrusion, the older the skeleton. There's nothing wrong with using this dating method, if one remembers that one is no longer bound to chronology. The reason for cutting loose from chronology is that protruding eyebrow ridges require a different lineup of skeletal material than do protruding jawbones. In morphological dating, anyone can line up the material to demonstrate any progressive change, quite apart from any chronological date which may have been established for a given skeletal find. The recognition of this fact had some interesting repercussions for me.

As I said earlier, as the reader to the professor of physical anthropology I had the responsibility to counsel all his students. I soon noticed that he spent about three weeks of class time in his physical anthropology course on chronological dating, i.e., dating in terms of time depth. Then he abruptly shifted to another kind of dating which is no longer related to chronology, namely morphological dating. He then proceeded to show how humans had evolved from certain primates on the basis of a certain feature of their anatomy which had changed as humankind gradually evolved.

By about thanksgiving of that school year I began to be swamped by students who came to talk. They all were Christians who claimed they were losing their faith. They didn't feel they could go home for thanksgiving to face their parents. I did not tell them I was a Christian, but simply asked what was causing them to lose their faith. They asserted that chronological dating had proven to them that the Bible wasn't true, thus they felt that they had to abandon their faith. Rather than tackle the issue head-on, I asked these students to bring along their anthropology notebooks.

I had them go through their notebooks from the beginning. I asked them to describe for me in their own words the implications of chronological dating. Then, when it came to the section where the professor had shifted from chronological dating to morphological dating, I checked whether they had taken down that fact in their notes. Then I asked them what the implications of this new kind of dating were. Suddenly these students would look at me wide-eyed and ask, "Do you mean that one has to abandon chronological dating if one wants to make human evolution work? Do you mean that evolution only works with morphological dating which is not related to chronology?" When I nodded in assent, they looked at me in amazement and said, "If evolution only works with morphological dating and there are different sequences in skeletal material for every feature of evolution that one wants to document, then it really is no challenge to my faith!"

An Atheist but "evangelistic" professor

The several semesters that I served as reader with the physical anthropologist produced a number of worthwhile insights.

The first was that this professor was ardently anti-Christian. He was the son of missionaries. He had rejected his parents' faith and was now a crusading anti-Christian. He gloried in destroying the faith of Christian students. I told him about my conversations with the head of the department and he never ridiculed me personally. But with the students who confessed faith, he worked feverishly to destroy it.

One day he was lecturing about the things that are beyond humans. In the course of the lecture he grew intensely emotional. His eyes misted up as he talked about "the primitive" calling out, and hearing the echo of his voice coming back to him from the forest. Suddenly the primitive realized that there must be something beyond himself.

The next illustration he used involved the primitive looking into the water and seeing his reflection in it. Again this primitive was moved to the very depth of his being. He had discovered something unknown beyond himself. The professor waxed so eloquent and evangelistic that when the two of us walked from class to have a cup of coffee together in the student union building, I said, "You know doctor, today I was a little bit puzzled about who was the missionary, you or I. You were as evangelistic as a missionary at his best."

I learned that even at universities where supposedly neutral scholars eagerly pursue unbiased truth, the search is often compromised. Human bias plays an enormous role even at a university. This son's experience with his parents' Christianity had in one way or another poisoned him. So today he was evangelistically against it.

Just as there are many Christians who are willing to bend Christian truth in order to defend it, so there are many scientists who are willing to bend scientific truth to suit their own prejudices.

The truth about evolution

As I studied the theory of evolution in depth, I became aware of a number of things:

First, there is no question that the earth has a tremendous depth in terms of its geological age. God obviously used the geological processes that have been discovered in the formation of the various strata that make up the earth as we know it today. Change and development are processes that have operated in this universe since it was first created.

Another area in which I felt there was no argument was in the adaptation of species to changing environments. Identical birds, for example, become differentiated when suddenly, due to changes in climate or other conditions, they begin to live under different circumstances. They become totally new species.

Or, a continent like Australia has highly specialized animals because they have been isolated from the ongoing development in the rest of the world. As a result, many of the more primitive features in plant and animal life have been preserved on that continent.

Another area where there was little dispute was in the adaptation taking place in the human body. About one third of North Americans are now born without wisdom teeth. As people chew less hard food, their jaws are receding because they no longer need the same amount of grinding power. In another third of the people, wisdom teeth do grow but not normally. They become impacted and have to be removed surgically.

The same is true in the case of the appendix. In college zoology, I discovered that the appendix in a rabbit, which is a vegetarian, is enormous. The rabbit's appendix plays a big role in the digestion of vegetable matter. But as humans have become more omnivorous and less herbivorous, their appendix has decreased in function and size. Today in humans it often is just a nuisance in which foreign bodies can get trapped, causing appendicitis.

Other human organs that are becoming obsolete are adenoids and tonsils. People who specialize in human anatomy point to at least a dozen such obsolescences that are currently in progress. For me the question is not: is creation true or is evolution wrong? Or if evolution is true, then creation must be wrong. Some evolutionary processes are going on right now as an active part of God's design. In fact, for me evolution in the universe shows that an intelligent First Cause has been and still is at work.

Expressing truth in human language

When I was working on Bible translation in the Lengua language in the Chaco of Paraguay, I became aware that this language has five past tenses. One of the tenses deals with the recent past, another deals with the remote memory of past generations. One tense even goes back to the very origin of the people of the kind that are still living today.

The other two past tenses deal with times even farther back. At that time I agreed with the missionaries that in the beginning of the Old Testament we should use the third past tense because it dealt with events that happened while the kind of people now alive were already living. (Today, if I had to make that decision again, I would do much more serious research on the situation because after I transferred to Africa I made some startling new discoveries.)

Africans and timeless truth

Africans in general see truth as being of at least two kinds. One is historical truth, which is usually only five generations in depth. It goes from great-grandfather, through grandfather, through father, through son, through grandson, and at best, to the great-grandson. When dealing with historical truth, one must always ask, "Did it or did it not happen?" And if it did happen, "Who was there at the time and can vouch for the fact that it really did happen?"

However, Africans distinguish a second kind of truth: mythological truth. It deals with facts that have been abstracted by the ancestors as being true. It has passed the test of time. Thus, basically all Africans recognize that there is truth that reaches beyond verifiable history. They call it timeless truth. This truth is no longer connected to any specific person's experience, e.g., I would hear one African tell of a given mythological event about one of his early ancestors, while on the very next day I would hear another African tell it about one of his ancestors. When I confronted them with this discrepancy—that they were each using the same story of their ancestors without any regard to the historicity—the Africans said that that was the beauty of timeless truth. "I can tell the story of my ancestors, and he can tell the story of his ancestors because we are both dealing with the same timeless truth."

This experience brought to mind something that has been mentioned elsewhere regarding the indicative mood. There are languages that distinguish more than one indicative mood. In three indicative-mood languages, the first mood says that something is true or is a fact because I, myself, have witnessed it. The second indicative mood says, "I have this from a reliable source." And the third says, "This is hearsay—the people say...." Some languages have six or even ten degrees of factualness.

The situation with several kinds of truth came to a head for me when translating Genesis. In some African languages, timeless truth is marked by a special past-tense marker. In others it is distinguished by particles, short adverb-like words. The Africans wanted to use the timeless past for the early part of Genesis, i.e., they wanted to mark it by these special affixes or small words. The big question for them was: "at what point do we stop using that timeless past tense and begin to use the historical past tense? Even though the time depth of people in

Bible times may be greater than the five generations which they recognize in their own tribal historical past tense, it is equal to the historicity recognized by those early biblical peoples."

Missionaries felt threatened by this approach to the Bible. They wanted to be sure to establish the historicity of the creation account. The Africans, however, insisted, "If God created mankind only on the sixth day of creation, and if the days of creation were really time periods, then there were no people around to witness most of creation." For Africans, there was thus no possibility of using the historical past tense for creation itself because there were no people present to attest to it. "Because if you use the historical tense," the African said, "and no Adam was there to watch it, then of course the creation account is not true. No person can vouch for the fact that creation actually happened that way." The truth of the Bible for the African could be safeguarded only if the early part of Genesis was rendered as timeless truth.

"Bending the truth"

We already mentioned that some evangelicals are so zealous for the truth that they often are willing to "bend" it in order to protect it. I have faced such situations a number of times when translating problematic biblical texts. Take, for instance, Genesis 4 and 5, where we have two genealogies from Adam through Noah. One is through Cain, the other is through Seth. But, as Africans pointed out to me, Cain has sneaked back into fourth position even in the Seth genealogy. If we parallel the genealogies of the two chapters we find the following: In Chapter 4 in descending order we have Adam, Cain, Enoch, Irad, Mehujael, Methusael and Lamech. In Chapter 5 the list is: Adam, Seth, Enosh or Enos, Cainan or Kenan, Mahulaleel, Jared, Enoch, Methuselah, Lamech and Noah.

When we compare these two lists, several significant things emerge. Cain occurs in both lists. In the first one he occurs in second position; in the next one he occurs in fourth position as Cainan. Enoch, who is in third position in Chapter 4, occurs two times in Chapter 5, once as Enos or Enosh and then as Enoch, the seventh in the list. This seventh position in Israel was an exceedingly important one. When I pointed out to the Africans what position seven indicated, they decided that Enoch must have been a very, very important person to occur in the same genealogy two times and especially to occupy position seven.

If we compare the other names in the two lists we can readily see the correspondence between Mahulaleel and Mehujael. We can also see the correspondence between Methuselah and Methusael, and between Jared and Irad.

When the Africans asked me what the significance of these two lists was, I was taken aback totally. I had no idea what to say, because for me it was really the first time I had realized that we had the same genealogy in two different orders and with only slightly different spellings.

The Africans then enlightened me. They said, "This is a very common occurrence in our tribes. When a tribe gets big, it develops sub-tribes and these sub-tribes often have differing loyalties. Very often you will get differing genealogies because one part of the tribe will consider someone as worthwhile, while the other sub-tribe considers that same person unimportant. As a result differences in the genealogies develop."

They also pointed out that sometimes when a person is exceedingly important, he is moved into a position of greater importance, as has happened in Chapter 5 with Enoch. Again, when a person has done some nasty things, but still is worthwhile keeping in the list, he is sometimes made a grandson rather than remaining as the grandfather, as in the case of Cain/Cainan in Chapter 5.

New inspiration to amend the text

I remember a difficult translation situation in which we had with a young woman volunteer in a translation program in a Caribbean language. She was excellent because she was so far removed from the Bible that she spotted all biblical or church jargon which the translators might want to use. She wouldn't have any of it. However, she had a very obnoxious habit. She swore like a trooper. But because of her contribution to the translation team, I felt we needed to keep her.

This issue finally came to a head. I received word from the field that the evangelical missions had decided to pull all their people out of the translation team unless this woman, whom they did not consider to be a Christian, was dismissed. With a heavy heart, I looked for an excuse to visit this team. Under the guise of producing a Scripture selection for Easter, I visited them shortly after Christmas. I informed them that we needed to check the last chapters of the Gospel of Mark to produce an Easter selection.

While checking Mark 14:71 where the text says, "Peter anathematized and cursed," I discovered that the translation team had toned down Peter's profanity to read, "Peter used some strong language and said...." I was disturbed by what the translators had done, but I knew their strong evangelical feelings against swearing. I began to pace up and down the room. Finally I said, "You all know that I believe in the inspiration of translation. But I have never yet experienced new inspiration to amend the biblical text."

Both "anathematize" and "curse" in Greek are verbs that require an object. By using them as infinitives Mark avoids the issue of an object and doesn't tell us whom Peter anathematized and whom he cursed. If Mark was a nephew of Peter as some say, we can see why he did this. He was showing deference to his uncle. I continued, "There is no question in my own mind what happened here. Peter was trapped, and the old fisherman suddenly took over and let fly a couple of the oaths he used to use before he became a disciple."

I hadn't realized that I had stopped behind the chair of the young woman who had the filthy swearing habit. She now turned around with tears streaming down her face and said, "Doctor, do you really mean that? Do you really think that Peter, even as a disciple of Jesus, had trouble with swearing?" I pointed to another instance in the Scriptures where it seems as if Peter swore. This young woman then said, "Oh, doctor, I am so happy to know this. Ever since I was a little girl, my mother has washed my mouth with soap. She has spanked me. She used every kind of punishment, but I seemingly couldn't break my swearing habit. But if Peter had a problem too, and he was a disciple of Jesus, then there is hope for me!"

After that episode, I invited all the evangelical members of the translation team to a meal. I informed them that in light of what had happened, I had realized God had not called me to deprive the young woman of further encounters with the Word of God, but that if any of them felt they had been called by God to do so, he/she should just go ahead and fire her. No one did.

Permit me to say once more, I do not know why the Spirit of God permitted some of these difficulties to stay in the biblical text, but even in my limited experience, a number of them have produced messages of hope for people in need of it.

CHAPTER 16
TRUTH AND CULTURE

Truth wrapped in culture can run out

I have often been struck by the fact that most of us experience our truth wrapped in a specific culture. The encounter with the Waunana in regard to malaria is a case in point. I, who knew germ theory, was able to isolate the germ and make it visible by means of a microscope after I had stained it blue. The Waunana, whose truth was wrapped in a different culture, still saw fever spirits, and all blue ones at that. The only new insight for them was to discover that fever spirits were terribly small and that they were all blue.

I further recognized that truth wrapped in culture is very often timed. Its meaning can run out. Here is an example:

On one occasion, I told my parents about all the fascinating experiments going on in the laboratories at the university. My mother, who also had an insatiable curiosity for truth, asked whether I would someday give her a guided tour of some of these facilities. We agreed that I would do just that the next time she came to Seattle. My stepfather had no interest, but my mother was gung ho about spending a whole day touring research laboratories.

As mother was dressing for this outing, I asked her to wear a head-covering to hide her bun. You see, my mother, as a pious Mennonite woman, still wore her hair in a bun because the church had at one time declared that that was the right way for a modest Christian woman to express her piety. But I was in a dilemma. The bun was the latest craze in hairdos on the university campus. If my mother, in her old-fashioned clothes and with her basic peasant appearance, came to the university sporting a bun, the students would shake their heads in disbelief and wonder, "What is that old woman trying to prove?" They wouldn't have any idea that she was making a religious statement. When my father heard my request he said, "Boy, what is this? Do you mean that you are becoming ashamed of your mother and her Christianity?"

I said, "No, Dad! I am not ashamed of mother nor of her lifestyle. But if the fellows at the university see her with a bun, they will say, 'And that old bag too?' She will give them a wrong message. They will see her as following the latest cultural fling in hairdos."

My father wrung his hands in disbelief. Finally he blurted out in Low German, "*Oba Jung, waut ess dan schliesslichj rachjt?*" 'Boy, what is finally right then?' Yes, in this case, the cultural wrapper, in which the truth about Mennonite Christian modesty had been wrapped, had become obsolete in the American setting. The form had lost its original meaning. It may have been a potent testimony when it originated in Russia, but it gave a totally different message now on the American university campus.

Truth wrapped in culture can lead people to very different conclusions

While our children attended the missionary children's school, they made a deal with another missionary family to look after their pet dog while the family went on furlough. We were horrified. Not because we hated animals, but because this dog had once belonged to the wife of a rich mining executive. It ate cake, boneless meat and other delicacies, none of which were available to us in the jungle where we worked. How could we keep a dog like that alive, and at what expense?

But we decided to keep faith with our children, and so we took the dog and struggled with his survival. It wasn't easy!

To top it off, this missionary family did not return in one year as planned. The board extended their furlough by another year while they attended seminary. So we had the dog for two years. But as soon as they got back I contacted them and asked how I could return their flea trap. The father of the family said, "We are so glad that our children have forgotten about that beast. It is such a nuisance. That dog is good for nothing. His eating habits are just atrocious. I thought you would have long ago put a slug in that dog's head."

I was pretty upset that we had kept the faith through two difficult years. When I got home next day from upriver, I got my .22, fired a single shot into the sleeping dog's head and threw the carcass into the river. "Now there's a good riddance of bad rubbish," I congratulated myself. I then went back into the house to read the mail, which I had brought along from upriver.

In the midst of my reading I suddenly became aware of some angry talking out in the yard. I looked out the open window and saw about fifty angry Indians in the yard talking loudly and gesticulating. They were armed with spears and poisoned arrows, ready to do harm. I dropped my mail reading and went out to defuse the problem, whatever it was. Once outside, I quickly realized that I was the cause of the commotion.

As I approached them, one of the men stepped forward from the angry crowd and asked, "Did you kill Pacho?" That was the name of the dog.

I innocently responded, "I certainly did!"

Then he said, "A man who can kill the dog, who eats the food off his table, will kill his mother and he will also kill Waunana." They were now ready to practice some preventative medicine. It took some earnest cultural explanation on my part to ward off my demise at the hands of the Waunana that day. They finally left the yard, still muttering angrily, "Your culture must be awfully stupid if it permits a person to kill the dog which has eaten the food from his table!"

Truth wrapped in culture needs to be translated for transmission to another culture

A case of cultural translation has already been referred to in the experience with malaria germs. In my culture, malaria was seen as being caused by germs. My culture had a totally materialistic explanation for the cause of this disease. But the tribal culture had a spirit interpretation of those same phenomena. Unless this is successfully translated from one culture to the other, no meaningful communication between the two can occur.

Take another example. If an African and a North American hear about an accident, say a bus going off a cliff on a mountain road and killing all its passengers, both will see the accident as an enormous tragedy. Both will ask, "What happened?"

When the missionary hears that a tie-rod on the steering apparatus broke, or that the right front tire blew out, he will say, "Ah, so that's what caused the accident!" He will be satisfied that he now understands the cause. The African at that point will still be totally nonplussed because all he has heard explained is the means of the accident. He will be asking, "Okay, okay! But who caused that tie-rod to break or that tire to explode? And why?" For Africans, every accident or illness has an interpersonal cause, a social cause.

This matter of different cultures with different explanations that need to be translated into each other's categories becomes exceedingly important when we deal with such phenomena as worldviews, e.g., demon possession and exorcism. All possession phenomena have to be interpreted within the culture in which they occur. A case of demon possession in Africa may mean something entirely different than a case of demon possession in Vietnam or North America.

Uniquely Christian truth, e.g., virgin birth

One problem that many Christians face is that they look at many of the Christian doctrines or truths as totally unique to Christianity. Take for instance the concept of virgin birth. For most Christians this is a very sacred truth indeed. If Christ wasn't born of a virgin as the Bible says, these people would insist, then the whole message of Scripture becomes unbelievable. For them, virgin birth is a uniquely Christian event, a uniquely Christian truth that must be maintained at all costs.

I was shocked to discover a virgin birth story in the very first aboriginal tribe I learned to know, the Waunana. Their mythology has a pair of culture heroes, twins, that were "virgin-born" out of the calf of a man's leg. There was no human intercourse to implant a fertilized ovum in the leg of this man. His leg just began to swell up one day and when it split open the virgin-born twins emerged.

The mythology of India, especially the myths that surround the god Rama, has another fascinating example of a virgin birth. The Hindu myth says that in the beginning God established certain fundamental laws: (1) that human beings are weaker than devils, but that gods are more powerful than devils; (2) if someone prays and gives alms to the poor and does other kinds of good deeds, he/she can accumulate merit.

As a result of the latter rule, the demons decided that they, too, would begin to accumulate merit. The demons did so many good deeds and accumulated so many merit points that God was no longer able to punish them. It looked as if the devils would take over the universe. The situation was saved when a god was virgin-born among humans as Rama. God Brahma either impregnated or in some other way caused a human virgin to give birth to a divine child, which became the god Rama. As a result there now was a new type of being which was half-god and half-man. By creating this half-god-half-man, God had established a new class of beings which was exempt from the laws that had already been laid down in the universe. Therefore when Rama grew up, he would be able to fight and subjugate all the devils. Since human beings were too weak to serve as an army to fight devils, Rama could not use them as helpers. Thus Rama, the half-god-half-man, teamed up with Hanuman, the monkey god, who had an army that is half-animal and half-human. With the army of the monkey god, virgin-born Rama was able to overcome all the devils and to turn full authority over to God again.

Resurrection

The resurrection is another such concern. Most Christians feel that the resurrection of Jesus Christ is a uniquely Christian truth; it is the foundation of salvation for all of humanity. However, to those who know world mythologies, resurrection is not uniquely Christian; in fact, it is a widespread phenomenon. Many cultures recognize it. We need not go any farther than the North American aborigines to discover that the average medicine man or native healer of repute has "died" a number of times already and has been "resurrected."

An example of this would be the account of the aborigine who walked where Jesus walks after he had "died." He was then "resurrected" on the fourth day and told the people what the new tribal conversion model would be.

The fact that certain events or truths are not as uniquely Christian as we thought does not make them any less important. It only says that God has been able to communicate the same truth to people in several ages and several different cultures.

New truth usually must first be expressed in metaphor

The early New Testament church assumed that the sun revolved around the earth and that the earth was the center of the universe. In fact, up to medieval times, the church burned people at the stake for saying otherwise. Many of us are aware of the troubles Galileo had with the church in this regard. But there came a time when advancing knowledge about the universe and the discovery of new truth about the way it functions, caused even the church to change and to accept the view that our earth revolved around the sun.

In order to explain this new insight, the physicists who proclaimed it had to develop a metaphor. They said, "The universe is like a giant machine with many moving parts. The sun is moving and many other celestial objects move in orbit around the sun or each other." They explained the insight about the operation of the universe by means of this newly-coined machine metaphor.

The reason for the use of metaphors or analogies in such situations is that most new truth invariably deals with items for which the language has no existing literal vocabulary labels. Because of that, the new truth or new insight always has to be expressed in terms of nonliteral meanings, i.e., in terms of figures of speech, metaphors, similes or analogies. The same is even more true where the subject matter is otherworldly—people just cannot use this worldly vocabulary with literal meanings to discuss or explore otherworldly phenomena.

In the case of spiritual truth, its very otherworldly nature forces human statements about it to be nonliteral—to be metaphorical. Only in the figurative sense can physical vocabulary be used to talk about the metaphysical world and things spiritual. To speak about spiritual things, human beings invariably have to employ a wide variety of analogies or metaphors.

For example, we may today feel that we are talking about something literal when we use the word "spirit." But when the Bible uses the words *ruah* and *pneuma,* the Hebrew and Greek words for 'spirit' respectively, it is not saying something literal, it is using a figure of speech. Literally, these two words mean 'wind' and by extension they mean 'breath.' In the same way all truth about God and things spiritual has to be expressed in metaphor.

To accept that all metaphysical or spiritual truth has to be expressed in metaphor is very difficult for many people. One problem of the church has been that many statements originally made as metaphors eventually hardened and were then reinterpreted as literal. The most famous example is the matter of transubstantiation in connection with the Eucharist—the conversion of bread and wine into the flesh and blood of Christ. When Jesus first used the expression in the Gospels, he was plainly using it metaphorically. But it didn't take long for the church to reinterpret it as literal only to develop some severe difficulties as a result.

Not black and white, but shades of gray

In life, human beings are called upon to make many decisions. Most Christians would maintain that the issue always is choosing between right and wrong, between black and white, or between truth and error. But in fact, most decisions in life are not between absolute right and absolute wrong, about truth or error; they are about various shades of gray. The individual who makes a choice is trying to get as close to white as possible, but usually the best choice still is only a shade of gray. So much of our experience does not deal with total blacks and whites. The reason for this relativity is easy to see when one moves cross-culturally. Different cultures will classify different things as right or wrong. But the same is true at the individual level. Every person's experience is partially unique and that leads to differences in interpretation.

For instance, we would consider burping in a polite table setting to be crude, vulgar and totally out of place. But in many societies burping is the accepted way to express appreciation for the food and for the quality of the hostess' cooking. In such cultural settings burping is positive action. In the same vein the majority of the decisions in life turn out to be choosing the lightest shade of gray.

Take, for example, the matter of educating children of missionaries. Should missionary parents do less "mission" work and educate their children at home? Or should they send them to boarding school? Several of our children have been scarred for life because we sent them to boarding school. Another option is to leave children in school at home when parents go to the mission field, as we did with our oldest when I took up work with the United Bible Societies. For our daughter, that parental decision produced much heartache. We may still feel that we chose the best alternative under the circumstances, but that doesn't mitigate the pain both the parents and the children have to live with now, after the consequences of this choice have become apparent.

A lifelong quest

I recently wrote a letter to Scott Peck, the author of the book, *The People of the Lie*, in which he speaks about demon possession and exorcism and says that 95 percent of what people call demon possession can today be explained in terms of the principles that psychologists and psychotherapists have discovered about the human psyche. I asked Dr. Peck whether that assertion wasn't a bit arrogant. Shouldn't we human beings be a bit more humble and say that there was more than five percent that we did not yet understand about demon possession? He wrote back and said, "You're a man after my heart! Keep up the good work! I am already down to two-and-a-half percent of the devil in demon possession." I think Dr. Peck is overly optimistic when he feels that we are very close to knowing the full truth about evil spirit possession. I think we still have quite a way to go. We still know only in part, "But the time shall come when we shall know as we are now known, by him who created us." He is Truth!

CHAPTER 17
TRUTH AND METAPHOR

When you are sick, do you go to the doctor or to his mother?

With this simple and innocuous-sounding question, a relatively unknown evangelist launched a religious renewal that became the foundation for the Mennonite Brethren Church in the Chocó of Colombia.

The Chocó, peopled largely by runaway slaves, was 90 percent negro. Because of its heavy rainfall (450-plus inches per year) and taxing climate, whites had generally avoided it. No mission had yet braved it. It was wide open for the Mennonite Brethren mission to occupy in the 1940s.

When the mission accepted the challenge to evangelize this area, one of their early evangelists asked the question cited above. This metaphorical analogy rocked the whole Chocó region. The area was nominally Catholic and the local Catholicism was expressed largely in the worship of Virgin Mary. The evangelist's question, however, focused the attention of the Chocóano people on the truth of Christ versus his mother in such a dramatic way that within a few weeks this metaphor had run for hundreds of miles in all directions and thousands of people had responded to the call of the gospel. Soon those who still persisted in Mary worship were ridiculed by the new convert majority with remarks like, "Oh, you're still one of those who goes to the doctor's mother rather than to the doctor himself when he is sick!"

What is a metaphor?

A metaphor is a figure of speech, a type of comparison. A typical biblical metaphor would be Jesus' remark about King Herod, "Go tell that fox" (Lk. 13:32). Specifically, a metaphor is an abbreviated comparison. A full comparison is called a simile. It has four parts: The person or object that is being compared, the marker of the comparison, usually "as" or "like" or something similar, the thing or person it is compared with, and the reason or the basis on which the two are being compared.

A full simile would be, "All we like sheep have gone astray" (Is. 53:6). What is being compared is "*all we*." The marker is "*like*." The image with which "*all we*" are being compared is "*sheep*." The reason or basis of the comparison is that "we have all *gone astray* like sheep go astray."

Another full comparison would be "his (Jesus') garments became white as light" (Mt. 17:2). In this case we are comparing "*Jesus' garments*." The marker is "*as*." The image with which the comparison is being made is "*light*." The reason or the basis for the comparison is "*white*."

As we have said, a metaphor is an abbreviated comparison. In a metaphor, the marker of the comparison, "*as*" or "*like*," has been left out. For example, "Issachar is a strong ass" (Gen. 49:14). The person being compared is "*Issachar*." He is being compared to "an *ass*." The basis of comparison is that he is "*strong*." Another example is "Your God is a devouring fire" (Deut. 4:24). In this case "*God*" is being compared with "*fire*," and the reason for the comparison is that "he *devours*, like fire devours."

The problem with metaphors in the Bible is that they often are incomplete. A metaphor may lack the reason or the basis for the comparison, or it may be incomplete in other ways, e.g., "Do not throw your pearls before the swine" (Mt. 7:6). In this case we are not told what we are talking about, but that something is being compared to "*pearls*" and "certain people" are being compared to "*swine*." But we are not given the basis for either of the comparisons. These are very incomplete metaphors indeed.

What do metaphors do?

Metaphors have a number of functions in human language. First of all, a metaphor adds "spice" to the language. Like all figures of speech, a metaphor enriches the language. But since incomplete metaphors are often very difficult to understand, especially cross-culturally, simple translations like the Good News Bible have converted many of the metaphors to full comparisons or to simple statements. For example in the biblical statement, "In whom we have redemption through his blood" (Eph. 1:7), the word "*blood*" is a metaphor. It refers to the fact that Christ died for us human beings. Here the Good News Bible has said, "We are saved because Christ died for us." But, in the process, it has lost the metaphor, or the figurative enrichment "*blood*." This stands in bold contrast to the Living Bible which has introduced many new figures of speech and often thus has produced overspiced food over against the Good News Bible, which because of the loss of figures of speech, is rather bland.

The second function of metaphors is that they carry an emotive load; they stir the emotions. If a metaphor is good and rings true, the person hearing it experiences a deep emotional impact. The proof of the pudding can be seen in the evangelist's question about the doctor and his mother.

A third function of metaphors is that they serve as substitutes for grammatical complexity in a sentence. For example, the Farsi language in its classical form can have up to nine dependent clauses. It is like German in which the verbs close the clauses in regressive order at the end of the sentence. This, of course, can lead to an exceedingly complex sentence structure. When we studied the primary school versions of many classical pieces of Farsi literature, we discovered that the original grammatical complexity had been greatly reduced. At most the school version had two dependent clauses. But the number of figures of speech had been stepped up by a dramatic 17 percent. This substitution of figures of speech for grammatical complexity has been tested in other languages and has been found operative there also. When we need a simplified grammar, the enrichment of the language can be achieved by introducing more figures of speech. Technically stated, we can say that semantic density is a good substitute for grammatical complexity.

The fourth usage of metaphors is to express new ideas, or new insights. When a person gains a new insight, she/he often feels at a loss for a literal way to express it. There is no literal vocabulary to express this new idea. The result is that the communicator has to reach for figures of speech; more often than not they are metaphors. Thus, new ideas often are expressed through new metaphors. This usage is based on a well-established teaching principle which says that analogy is a teaching tool par excellence. Good teachers always go from the known to the unknown. By comparing something unknown to something that is already known, the hearer can more readily grasp a totally new idea even when he has never heard it before. Both the speaker and the hearer know that when such a comparison is made, the relationship is not one of identity, but one of analogy.

The fifth function of metaphors is closely related. It deals with discussing otherworldly phenomena. The ordinary vocabulary of a language is related to life in the here and now. When it becomes necessary to talk about spiritual things—about heavenly things, about otherworldly things—the best way to do it is to create new metaphors to explain the otherworldly phenomenon in terms of a known this-world experience.

The Old Testament uses this approach in its early characterizations of God. In order to make God comprehensible, the writers of the Old Testament used extensive anthropomorphisms. They described God in terms of the psychology and behavior of human beings. Thus in the Garden of Eden God *walked* and *talked* with human beings. To express God's warm relationship to human beings, he is called "our Father in heaven." Here the word "*heaven*" clearly marks the fact that we are not talking about an earthly biological father relationship. Or in the Lord's Prayer, humankind's moral failings are referred to as "*debts*," as in "forgive us our debts." In this case we are not talking about actual monetary debts, but rather about that which humans owe God in obedience and in which they have fallen short.

The impact of new truth expressed in metaphor

David L. Turbayne in *The Myth of Metaphor* (New Haven: Yale University Press, 1962) makes the point that new truth, especially great truth which has produced radical changes in humankind's outlook and behavior, has usually first come in the form of metaphor. (Here we must hasten to explain that Turbayne uses the word *metaphor* as a cover term for all metaphors, similes, models, analogies, etc.) He cites Galileo's novel description of the universe as a giant machine with moving parts as a classic example of new truth that was expressed in metaphor and changed the world. We have to admit that Galileo's analogy, in spite of being denigrated and rejected by the church and the civil authorities at the time, nevertheless carried the day. Indeed, it has become the foundation for the all-pervasive scientific revolution of our era.

Good examples of the use of metaphor in dealing with new information are found in Leon Lederman, *The God Particle* (New York: Delta Trade Books, 1994). In this book about particle physics, Lederman makes the reader deeply conscious of our human dependence on metaphor in the discovery of new truth. In this case, it is in delving into the subatomic structure of matter.

Lederman begins with an analogy saying that once humankind had developed the telescope and could peer into the heavens, it discovered how the force of gravity held heavenly bodies (a metaphor) and caused them to orbit around each other. This astronomer's view of the universe became the metaphor for describing the subatomic structure. The macrocosm had now become an analogy by which human beings could begin to describe the microcosm inside the atom.

The word for *atom* (Greek *atomos)* means "it is uncuttable," that is, it is the smallest unit of matter. However, the atom proved "cuttable" (a metaphor). For this reason, Lederman talks about the atom as the *a-tom*, suggesting that that which was traditionally seen as indivisible was, and is in fact, still divisible.

Lederman first discusses the molecule, which is the smallest unit of the various specific kinds of matter, for example, a molecule of hydrogen, or a molecule of some other matter. As people studied the a-tom, they discovered that it contains moving parts. There were "things" orbiting around each other just like the heavenly bodies were orbiting around each other. Thus the physicists came to discover the nucleus of the a-tom.

Now the nucleus of the a-tom turned out not to be a solid unit either. It was itself made up of still smaller particles. There were the protons which were positive in their charge, the electrons which had a negative charge, and neutrons which did not respond to either of the two charges. In the ongoing discovery it was found that protons and neutrons basically belonged to a category of particles called *hadrons*, and the electron turned out to be a *lepton*. Thus the nucleus of an atom of hydrogen contained one proton or hadron and one lepton, but the nucleus of an atom of oxygen contained eight protons and eight leptons and eight neutrinos (a metaphor designating a smaller version of a neutron).

Then the physicists discovered that the proton, the electron and the neutron themselves were divisible. As a result a second generation (a metaphor) of even smaller particles was postulated: the pions, the baryons and the mesons.

After that physicists discovered a third generation (a metaphor) of particles which they called quarks, leptons and bosons; the latter are the force carriers. With this, physicists felt they were probably approaching the underlying structure of matter in the universe. They said, for example, that there were six quarks (a metaphor based on the word "quirk") which occur in three colors: red, blue and green. To speak of different colors when no physical color is involved is, of course, metaphorical.

Quarks and leptons are particles and the gauge bosons are the carriers of the various forces like gravity, the electromagnetic force, the strong force and the weak force. These particles and the forces, physicists feel, make up basic matter. Lederman philosophizes that possibly with these particles we may finally have reached indivisible *units*, that is, units that are not divisible any further. But Lederman cautions that we may find that these particles will divide even more. There may be a fourth generation (a metaphor) of even smaller particles.

When we consider gauge bosons or the particles that carry the forces, we notice that quarks are held together by gluons (a metaphor) while a-toms are held together by the electromagnetic force.

Later, Lederman suggests that physicists often wonder whether there actually are six different quarks. Maybe the six quarks are really only one quark in six different flavors (a metaphor). The word "flavor" is also used when talking about neutrinos. In our current state of knowledge physicists postulate six neutrinos. If they turn out to be one neutrino in six different flavors (a metaphor), Lederman says, then probably the electron neutrino is the ordinary vanilla flavor (a metaphor) of neutrinos. Quarks are spoken of as *up* and *down*, as *charm* and *strange* and as *bottom* and *top* (all metaphors). Lederman suggests that the last two, *top* and *bottom*, maybe should be called *truth* and *beauty* respectively (also metaphors).

The question has been asked: "Can you see a quark?" The answer is "yes," but "*see*" now is a metaphor. What we can discern are the effects that quarks have. Quarks never occur in isolation and are always bound together in units. Thus baryons are made up of three quarks and mesons are made up of two quarks. Quarks have no mass, no circumference, and no dimensions, and they are held together by gluons. If the unleashing of the electromagnetic force that holds a-toms together gives us an atomic explosion, we have to realize that when we explode the gluons that hold quarks together, we are unleashing a force many thousands of times greater.

Lederman focuses attention on the power of metaphors when he "resurrects" Democritus who first postulated the atom 2000 years ago. Thus, he has the "resurrected" (a metaphor) Democritus innocently ask, "So you say that you've perfected a knife that is able to cut the atom into its constituent parts?" To this author Lederman, thinking of cyclotrons, bevatrons and tevatrons, answers 'tongue-in-cheek,' "Yes, sir, we have!" The "knife" and "cutting," of course, are metaphors.

In conclusion, Lederman says, "Once you get a 'clear' understanding of how the subatomic universe is structured of various generations of particles, then you realize how much you are 'seeing through a glass darkly!' " In other words, when describing the subatomic structure and function, physicists have to rely on multiple levels of metaphor.

The problems of truth expressed in metaphor

Turbayne already has pointed out that once a new concept expressed in a metaphor has become generally accepted, a new danger arises: people forget that they are dealing with an analogy and they begin to treat yesterday's metaphor as something literal. This is especially true of religion which deals with the supernatural and so-called "spiritual truth." Statements that obviously were metaphors when they were first coined or used, are later taken to be literal. This focuses attention on the fact that few Christians, especially preachers, take seriously enough religion's dependence on metaphors to explain spiritual phenomena.

Since dialogue with biblical writers is no longer possible, it sometimes is difficult to establish exactly the line between a metaphor and a literal statement of fact. I recently tried to demonstrate this in a congregation where the majority of the members had university education. I gave them the following list of statements about God and asked them to say whether we were dealing with a metaphor or a literal statement. Their responses are given in the right-hand column:

God is my shield (Gen. 15:1)	Metaphor
Our God is a rock (2 Sam. 22:2)	Metaphor
Our God is a consuming fire (Heb. 12:29)	Metaphor
God is my light (Ps. 27:1)	Metaphor
God is our father (Isa. 64:8)	Metaphor, but only after some hesitation
God is spirit (Jn. 4:24)	Literal, but with later second thoughts

Why the eventual doubt about the literalness of the last proposition? I think the dilemma comes from the very word *spirit* (in Greek *pneuma* and in Hebrew *ruach*), which literally means *wind*.

Is there a supernatural nonmaterial entity which can be likened to *wind* or *breath* which in English we call *spirit* (borrowed from Latin)? There is no question that in cultures with a worldview that postulates spirits—good or bad—people undoubtedly feel they are dealing with real entities. But even that is really not incontrovertible evidence that *pneuma* and *ruach* when denoting *spirit*, did not begin as analogies which later came to be seen as literal. (Cf English *stock* as cattle, supplies in a store and shares in a business, are all considered literal meanings today.)

We also need to remember that when we talk about God and describe the beyond, we are dealing with something we say is infinite. However, to talk about it we are forced to use finite language. When one recognizes the finite-infinite dichotomy, it is easy to see that maybe many or even most of our expressions describing the supernatural originally were analogies or comparisons based on natural entities people knew and experienced. Just consider how much of our vocabulary about God, for example, is anthropomorphic, i.e., we describe God by analogy to human beings. Examples: the right hand of God (Ps. 18:35), the feet of God (Ps. 18:9), God sits on his throne (Ps. 47:8), God works and rests (Gen. 2:2), God repents (Jonah 3:10), God is jealous (Deut. 4:24). Obviously in the effort to describe God and his activities, humans have had to fall back again and again on analogies to human beings, their feelings and activities.

Another example of truth coming by analogy can be illustrated with the biblical concept *hell*. Here we must begin with the Hebrew word *Sheol*, "the place of the dead," described as "a cold, dark place deep underneath the earth, in the heart of the ocean, the home of the souls of all the deceased." The Greek equivalent of *Sheol* was Hades (cf Ps. 16:10, Acts 2:27). By New Testament times *Sheol* was already seen as divided into a place for the good, called *Abraham's bosom* and a place for the wicked called *Gehenna*.

The Greek word *Gehenna* in fact is a transliterated form of the Hebrew expression *ge hinnom* meaning *the valley of Hinnom*. This valley lay at the foot of the southeast corner of the wall around Jerusalem. It was the dumping ground for Jerusalem's garbage. People threw their refuse over the wall onto the continually burning fires in the Valley of Hinnom below. The perpetual fires and the idea of the refuse heap outside of the city thus were at the basis of what was obviously an analogical extension when *Gehenna* became the label for *hell*. Of course, the Bible actually uses a number of analogies based on the individual elements of the burning garbage dump, not just the place name. For example: the eternal fire (Mt. 5:22, 18:8), darkness outside (the wall) (Mt. 8:12, Jude 6), cast away, refuse (Lk. 3:9, 2 Pet 2:4, John 15:6). The fact that it may have begun as a figurative extension of a literal meaning or as an analogy to a well-known observable place beside Jerusalem does not in any way negate the reality of hell. It merely says that when the concept was first expressed, it was based on an analogy to something all the residents of Jerusalem knew. A new concept about the supernatural was being expressed in terms of concrete human experience.

An important implication of the above is that different cultures, different circumstances, or different times may make it necessary for us to change to new analogies if we want to preserve the identical message. It is not the word or the expression itself that counts; it is the reality which the word designates (cf German *Bezeichnung*). In fact, even the word *book* is not the object which I literally see in the library; it is merely a word that denotes the entity. When spoken it is just a series of sounds (written, it is a series of letters) which in one language stimulates people to conceptualize this specific kind of object.

If we now apply this principle to the expression "book of *life*" (Phil. 4:3), we have to be aware that first of all, we may not be talking about a literal book of paper pages bound together, but of a spiritual reality which we can conceptualize on the analogy of the books we know. We can see this in the English Bible itself which uses the word for *scroll* or *book* more or less interchangeably (because the scroll is indeed the earlier form of our bound book). But in the society that knows only clay tablets and not scrolls or books, one may have to render the above expressions as the *clay tablets of life*. In our post-literate society one can imagine a time when we may have to speak of the *disc of life* or *memory chip of life*. (Life itself is here a metaphor which really means *the existence in the beyond.*)

By this time many readers will have realized that my deeper purpose is to show that in the so-called "battle for the Bible," the issue is not really whether a word spelled b-l-o-o-d does or does not appear in certain verses of the Bible, but whether the real meaning referred to by the word "blood" has been truly and clearly expressed. In fact, if a literal translation of the word "blood" conveys only a reference to a kind of liquid or possibly suggests a wrong figurative analogy, keeping the word itself may in fact make us guilty of the actions so strongly condemned in Rev. 22:18-19. The Bible is God's message to humankind, and as such it is not bound to any specific language or some special words. Infinite truth can never be fully captured by the words of finite language.

CHAPTER 18
DO OTHER RELIGIONS ALSO HAVE TRUTH?

In a previous chapter, I said that when I first went out as a missionary, I was convinced I had the truth and was being sent to a people who didn't have it. In fact, I believed that they had never before even heard it. The idea in the minds of many of my compatriots was that the missionary would have to create a tabula rasa—construct a completely new foundation for the knowledge of the biblical God. People in missionfields, it was assumed, knew only idols. As it turned out, our forty years of mission experience didn't support either of those assertions.

We had gone to Colombia with the express assignment of learning the Waunana language, reducing that language to writing, and translating the Scriptures into it. It was with this intent that David Wirsche and I went to the Chocó area of Colombia as soon as I had finished preliminary Spanish studies.

We intended to establish a base in Noanama village, near the Waunana community. Since this tribe lived in isolated houses along various streams and rivers, there was no tribal center in which we could locate. The negro village of Noanama on the San Juan River was the closest we could get.

Once established there, David and I bravely tried to learn the Waunana language from tribes people passing through the village. But before we got very far, we both came down with severe bouts of malaria. We had to take the next opportunity to get out of the Chocó rainforest and back into the mountains where the mission had a station at La Cumbre. There we could be nursed back to health.

A long and painful detour

Once recovered, David Wirsche went home on furlough. Our family then decided to move to Noanama to continue the work that had been started. When we got there, we quickly realized how easy it would be for us to become involved in Spanish evangelism and other kinds of mission work that would keep us from our primary Waunana assignment. We were determined just to build a house for our family to live in and then to major in our language-learning and Scripture-translating principal duties. But circumstances led otherwise.

In the chapter on medical experiences I have detailed how my wife Anne came to develop a dispensary. Individuals showed up bleeding and in desperate need of immediate help. There was no alternative but to help them that very moment. Before we knew it we had a large dispensary on our hands. This meant we had to get a nurse to take over this work. The coming of a nurse, however, meant building living quarters for her. She also needed a building in which to tend the sick, as well as places where the sick could be housed while they were being treated.

When we began to build our own house, we imported a few Christian men from the mission church upriver in Istmina to help us. As a family, we met every Sunday night for a devotional service. We closed the door to our rented house and just had a family worship service. We wanted to be sure not to become involved in Spanish work. But before we knew it we had.

First, the Christians we had imported from upriver realized what we were doing and asked, "Why can't we attend the service with you on Sunday evenings?" We couldn't refuse, so we invited these four or five men to join us in the service. Naturally we switched from an English-language family service to a regular Spanish Bible study.

Soon the village people became aware of these services, and before we knew it, they too were knocking on the door on Sunday night. This meant we had to use our living room as a chapel. By the time our house was built, there was a thriving Spanish-speaking congregation in Noanama.

The mission now supplied a nurse for Noanama. She committed herself to take care of both the medical and the Spanish work. But before long she needed a chapel because there was no place large enough to house the congregation. So we purchased an old building in town, and I renovated it as a chapel.

Then missionaries on the neighboring station took ill and had to be sent home on emergency medical leave. They were in the midst of a large building project, and since I could manage with Colombian builders, the mission instructed us to take their place for a few months. It turned out to be half a year.

Meanwhile, time was slipping by. Three-and-a-half years had elapsed since Anne and I had first come to Noanama. We were speaking less of the Waunana language now than during the first few weeks after we arrived. Then we had learned our first expressions from the tribespeople who came to the door. It soon became very boring to say nothing more than, "How are you?" and "I am fine." But that was all the Indian language we knew. We finally stopped using even that, because it was too embarrassing to not be able to continue conversing.

The Spanish work thrived so mightily that soon another couple had to be brought to Noanama. Another nurse was brought in to work with the sick, because the dispensary now was taking care of more than two hundred people a week. It was far too much for one missionary nurse. All this meant that I had to continue building.

"You are liars"

After three-and-a-half years a Waunana delegation visited us one day and sadly told us they had decided we were liars. We had initially said we wanted to learn their language and translate God's Word into it, but years had gone by with no progress. This confrontation by the tribespeople pained us deeply. We pled with the missionaries on the field and with the mission board at home to release us from other tasks so that we could dedicate ourselves to learning the Waunana language.

Finally, as the end of our fourth year approached, the mission board agreed that our fifth year was to be dedicated to language study. To be sure, many circumstances still demanded that we interrupt our language work and help out in the Spanish work, but at least we could give the bulk of our time to the primary task. And we were grateful! In order to wind up our language study we began writing a preliminary grammar. We stayed an extra six months on the field and extended our first term to five-and-a-half years to accomplish that task.

In the meanwhile, David Wirsche, who had gone home on furlough, had found a wife. The newlyweds stayed in North America while she finished her education. A child was born to them. When they now came to join us at Noanama, a house had to be prepared where they could live.

When we approached the end of our fifth year, the November rains turned into a deluge. The San Juan River, which usually rose some thirty feet at the height of the rainy season, rose to forty-five and fifty feet. Large areas of the banks around the river were flooded. On the tributaries where the tribes people lived, everything was under water. The Waunana houses were standing in virtual lakes.

The beseeching ceremony

About that time a Waunana woman went out to her plantation to cut some green bananas, their staple food. While she was in a field, she met a little white dog. She picked up the dog, but it scratched her, and so she dropped it. It ran away. She followed the dog, and before she knew it, she met one of her deceased relatives who appeared to her with a message from *Ewandama,* the Waunana God. The message was, "I have been sent to warn you that the Waunana have become exceedingly sinful again. Just as wicked as when God first sent the flood to destroy the world. The world is in danger now of being destroyed again. God is tired of all the wickedness. I am returned from the dead to tell the people that they must revive our *rogatismo*." This is an Indian prayer service asking God not to destroy the people and to forgive their wickedness.

And, sure enough, we heard via the grapevine that on one of the distant rivers the Waunana were reviving that long-neglected ceremony. The people there were going to establish a series of such prayer services. I talked to our Indian teacher about the matter and hinted that David and I would be deeply grateful to be invited to such a service. Since the chief on that river was our teacher's uncle, we received our coveted invitation.

We traveled up a tributary into and across the mountains the first day. The second day we traveled downriver there and then continued one-and-a-half days up another tributary. Finally we came to the chief's house. The prayer service was already in progress. During such a thirty-day prayer service the Waunanas fast from sunup to sundown and dedicate the entire day to pleading. No one eats or drinks during the daytime, not even the babies at the breast. So for four days David Wirsche and I sat in the chief's house watching the people pray. Occasionally we joined them for brief periods and then returned to observing. Small children and babies cried constantly. But the *rogatismo* plodded on.

The prayer service went something like this. A special kind of canoe whose edges were turned inward was suspended in the middle of the house. The canoe was then beaten on the outside with two wooden beaters. The curved-in edges made it sound like a dull drum. The oldest woman of the house beat this canoe-drum, while all the males marched around it. The oldest ones marched at the head of the line, and then came the younger men and finally the boys. They all marched in single file behind the old men. Each one had a blowpipe or flute. Some of them had giant flutes which made a dull booming sound. Others had smaller flutes. Still others had panpipes which gave off their plaintive few notes as the person blew over their holes.

Behind the boys followed the older women, then the young women and the girls. They marched for an hour or so in one direction and then suddenly the human snake turned around and marched around the canoe in the opposite direction. When the old woman beating the canoe-drum got tired, another old woman took her place. When the old people got tired, they sat down for a while and others took their place. In this way the human snake plodded on without interruption all day.

When we asked the people what they were doing, they told us they were pleading with God to not send another flood or similar catastrophe to destroy the world, because the people were sorry for their many sins. We sat there day after day as the people marched around that canoe. The whole thing seemed so utterly hopeless. Our hearts were heavy, but there didn't seem to be much we could do since we didn't as yet have a speaking knowledge of the language. Finally I said to my partner, "David, we've got to give these people a message from God, in their own language!"

"Yes," David agreed, "but how?"

Our first message to the Waunana

So we began to piece together a message in the Waunana language. It was brief and went something like this: "Your fathers told you that in the beginning God made the world. That is correct! Your fathers told you that in their early experience the people were living in communion with God. That is correct! Then one day the devil came along and misled the people. That is correct! Your fathers told you that when the devil misled the Waunana, he did it by selling them axes, so that they could plant their own gardens and didn't need to trust God for food anymore. Here the account in God's book is somewhat different. Basically, however, when the devil tempted them, both our fathers and your fathers gave their hand to Satan and began to walk on Satan's road. But God was still deeply concerned about the people. He thought and thought about how he might save them.

Finally he decided to send his son into the world to teach people about God's way. Your fathers have told you that when a man dies his soul comes out of his body. They said that this soul must turn right immediately in order to get on the right path to God's house. God's book, however, tells us that if we give God our hand during our lifetime, then he will be holding our hand when we die, and he will guide our souls directly to his house.

So the question for the people now is: What do you want to do? Do you want to give God your hand and begin to walk on God's road, or do you want to continue on the road which the fathers started when they gave their hand to the devil?"

With the help of our teacher we tried to correct as many mistakes as possible in the message. We then delivered it one evening after the prayer session had stopped.

Next morning, the Waunana continued their prayer session. David and I decided that because of the high flood waters we should head home at once, since no one knew whether we would be able to cross the mountains safely anymore. We were correct in our concern. All the mountain streams were swollen beyond belief, and a number of times we were barely able to cross the raging torrents. Finally we arrived at Noanama. We celebrated Christmas with our families and the believers.

About six weeks later, as I was working in my office one day, I suddenly became aware that somebody was looking down my neck. I turned around and there stood the six sons of the chief in whose house the prayer service had been held. I recognized them at once. I greeted them and took them in and gave them something to eat, according to tribal custom. I asked the usual questions: How was their father? How was their family? Then I said, "Obviously you men have come with a message. I am ready to listen." They told us that all the people on that river had decided to give God the hand and to walk on God's road. I countered, "There were only thirty people in the house when we gave the message, but there are at least 400 or 500 people on that river. The rest of the people haven't heard God's message, so how can they give God the hand and walk on God's road?"

"But they do know! After you left, we talked about your message for three days. Finally the chief said we had to go from house to house to tell the people about God's message. So we went to all forty houses, and all the people decided to give their hand to God and to walk on God's road."

Almost to the day, while this was happening, the Colombian government was signing a new concordat with the Vatican, turning these people over to the Catholic Church as their exclusive mission domain. The concordat, if ratified by parliament, would have made our work illegal. When David Wirsche and I tried to make another trip into that area a few weeks later—even before the ratification—to see what was happening to these new believers, we only got part of the way. The police stopped us and told us that if we continued we would be arrested, if not shot. Evangelicals were now out of bounds in Waunana territory. (The concordat was never ratified. But our work was still closed down).

Looking back at the experience today, I note that we used the Waunana word *Ewandama*, the name of their tribal god, as the name for the God of the Bible. Later when I began working for the Bible Society, I realized that this is standard practice worldwide. Missionaries have usually used the local word for god as the name for the God of the Bible. This raised a troubling question, however. Had we then been wrong when we assumed that these people had nothing but error when we first arrived on the mission field? As we became more knowledgeable, we realized just how much truth these people actually had and how many of their beliefs concorded with the Word of God. They weren't as devoid of the truth as we had been led to believe.

Redemptive analogies

We found that many people worldwide had a lot of truth in their tribal lore. We also realized that much of what happened in the Waunana situation had already happened in the Old Testament. Yahweh was the tribal God of the Hebrews. The Hebrews had to learn to see him as the God of the whole world. To achieve this, God had to send the Jews into the Assyrian and Babylonian captivities, far away from their temple where they believed their God lived. Their temple had to be destroyed. The people could no longer be in Yahweh's land. They had to recognize that their God was the God of the entire world. He wasn't bound to any land or people.

We see the development of this insight in Isaiah. In the earlier chapters he pictures Yahweh's concern for other peoples largely in terms of his punishment for their sins. Then in Chapter 50, the prophet suddenly realizes that if people from other tribes will be circumcised and obey the law of God, they too can become acceptable believers. Finally, in the last chapter of the book, the prophet realizes that when God brings together the peoples of this world, there will be many believers among all of them. God then makes many of these Gentile believers his priests and Levites. They no longer have to obey the Jewish law first. They no longer have to follow Jewish ritual. Being in a right relationship with God is all that matters.

Many missionaries have already realized that other languages and cultures have contact points for the gospel. These have been called "redemptive analogies." Thus, for example, Don Richardson in his book *The Peace Child* takes a Papua New Guinea tribal peacemaking ritual which involves the son of the chief and turns it into a redemptive analogy to explain salvation through Jesus Christ, the son of God.

In the section on conversion I talked about the Chulupi Indians who restructured their tribal peacemaking ritual at the end of war to make peace with

God. The Chulupi appointed five talkers-between-two and in the depth of the Chaco night, these five men then made peace with God on behalf of the whole village.

Many cultures have such rituals for making peace between people. In Africa, a goat is often used as a part of peacemaking rituals. The anger of both parties in the quarrel is confessed over the head of a goat. The goat is then ritually killed, and the meat shared by the people. In this way peace is reestablished. These are very much like the Hebrew rituals of the Day of Atonement in the Old Testament. Other tribes have extensive rituals of sacrifice. They have beliefs about the afterlife and about final reward and punishment, many of which resemble what is taught in the Scriptures.

This raises a tantalizing question: are there circumstances under which an individual in such a tribe, who has not yet heard about Jesus could establish a saving relationship with God?

Before we look at examples from the world in the next chapter, we need to remind ourselves of the Old Testament people of God. They also did not know about Jesus Christ. True, they expected a Messiah, but in the Old Testament they had only God. We realize that a lot of their rituals and many of their practices and beliefs were superseded when Christ came, but God still considered them acceptable as his children.

The implications of truth in other religions

If other religions do indeed have truth, several implications need to be recognized:

1) God accepts the obedience of people in that religion to the truth which he has revealed to them.

2) The presence of some truth in another religion does not exempt those of us who know the fuller truth about God and Jesus Christ from sharing it with others. We also must encourage greater obedience in those already obedient in other religions. Furthermore, since there are wayward people in other religions as well as our own, we have a responsibility to encourage them to obey.

3) Our former arrogance must be replaced with true humility. Even the best Christian today knows only in part (1 Cor. 13:12).

4) If there is truth in other religions, we need to be alert to recognize it. (For example, while they were in captivity, the Old Testament Hebrews learned from other cultures about life after death, the reward of the just and the punishment of the sinful.)

CHAPTER 19

DID THE TRUE GOD HEAR THEM?

This chapter raises the thorny question: can people in other religions find God? I feel I have met some who have! Read about these personal experiences and then judge for yourself!

Are Catholics Christians?

There was a time in my life when I was convinced that no Roman Catholic could be a true child of God. Our early experience in Colombia certainly seemed to corroborate that. But then I was transferred to Africa and spent much time on Roman Catholic mission stations and worked with many Catholics translating the Scriptures together. I realized I had much in common with some of them. Over the years I have established a genuine brother-to-brother or brother-to-sister relationship with a number of Catholic priests and nuns.

If asked to point out the most sacrificial and Christlike missionaries I have learned to know during my years of overseas service, one of the first would be Sister Maria, a member of a small Catholic order of five nuns in Mozambique.

Her order was engaged in literature preparation, production and distribution. The individual nuns were deeply involved in literacy programs and in training catechists. I first met them during the colonial era. Two of the nuns of this order became translators-in-training.

In the course of the translator training I tried to share my personal Christian experience with all trainees. Among those who responded in kind were Sister Maria and another nun from her order.

One evening the two nuns invited me over to their place to discuss their mission problems. I was amazed to learn that the problems they faced were identical to those we had faced as missionaries. I tried to be frank about our failures as well as about the lessons these difficult experiences had taught us. The nuns responded honestly and candidly. The result was a deeply meaningful exchange among fellow missionaries. Clearly, I was dealing with fellow-believers who were genuine in their faith and who were as dedicated in their service to God as I was.

At about 9:30 in the evening, when I was ready to return to my hotel, the nuns suddenly became quiet. They looked at each other, nodded, and then asked me to stay and join them in their evening prayers. They took me to a room that was completely empty except for five kneeling benches. On the wall of the room was a large map of Africa drawn as a face of Christ distorted in agony. The countries of Angola, Mozambique and Guinea-Bissau, the three Portuguese colonies in Africa, were all aflame. I joined these five nuns in prayer for the liberation of Africa from colonial domination. I have seldom been at a prayer session as intense and as moving as that one.

At the next training session, Sister Maria wanted me to speak to a group of trainees with whom they were working in a rural village. They wanted me to share my experiences with God's Spirit. We had an excellent evening together which was suddenly interrupted when a group of people burst into the chapel, many of them wounded. They were survivors of the Wirayamu massacre in which Portuguese mercenaries wiped out an entire African village suspected of harboring freedom fighters.

When independence finally came to Mozambique, the independence movements took over. Sad to say, they turned out to be doctrinaire Marxists who were enemies not only of Christianity but also of the African religions themselves. One of their first tasks, after taking over the country, was to expel most of the missionaries and take away the registration of most religious organizations. In the process the order of sisters also lost their charter.

The new Marxist government organized all the people into collectives. By then there were almost no missionaries left in the country, either Protestant or Catholic. They had all fled or been driven out. The literature production of Maria's order had been completely shut down. Sister Maria remained in the country even though she was now just a foreign layperson. She joined one of the collectives and was put in charge of the communal laundry and clothing repair. When I last met her, her hands were rough and red from the strong cheap soap she worked with every day, but her eyes were radiant, and she exuded the presence of Christ.

There is no doubt in my mind today that many Roman Catholics are truly born again. They are as much children of God as I am. However, the question still dogs me, can this be taken any further? If so, how much further can this be taken?

"But what am I then going to do with Buddha?"

A couple of years ago, Anne and I were invited by Alberta Mental Health to help with refugee and new immigrant problems in Edmonton. The parties concerned with these projects were largely Mennonites and Catholics. They wanted a Christian anthropologist to help them deal with the cultural problems of these new immigrants. While we were there, Mennonite Central Committee wanted to give their local board some background in understanding culture, so they asked Anne and me to join them in a banquet. Beforehand they had a period of discussion in which I presented some cultural precepts that might help their committee to understand refugees from Latin America and Southeast Asia.

At this meeting there was a Vietnamese physician who had immigrated to

Canada. Unable to establish his license to practice medicine here, he had been employed in a meat packing plant. MCC had recently hired him to head their interests with these Southeast Asian immigrants. When we finished the public sessions and got ready for the banquet, this Vietnamese man came and greeted us. He asked whether he might sit with us at our table. We readily agreed but were taken aback when he sat down between us. We at once realized that he must have something very intimate to tell us.

As soon as the meal started, he came to the point and said bluntly. "I am going to fail!" When we pressed him for more specifics, he said, "I am going to fail in this job I have taken." How could he be so sure, we asked. He then explained, "I am going to fail because I am not a Christian."

"Well if that is the only problem," I said, "what stands in the way of your becoming a Christian?" The man looked at me in wide-eyed amazement, if not horror, and exclaimed, "But what am I going to do with Buddha then?"

The man then proceeded to tell us that when they were fleeing from Vietnam to Thailand, their little boat was sighted by Vietnamese gunboats. Five times the government forces had begun shooting at them. Each time they had all gotten into the bottom of the boat and prayed to Buddha. All of them had made the following vow: "If you will save us, Buddha, we will be faithful to you come what may! We will be faithful to you until death!" Two times a rain squall came between them and the attacking gunboat, and they were saved. Two more times big freighters came between them and the gunboats, and they escaped. The fifth time they were caught. But since the commanding officer was not in the boat that captured them, the soldiers brought them to shore on a small island. Then they had to wait for the captain and for their subsequent execution. While they waited the refugees made a deal with a local individual concerning another boat. They escaped again.

"Having made this commitment to Buddha," he concluded, "I cannot renege. I don't see how I can become a Christian!"

I volunteered a suggestion. "Could it be," I asked, "that what you called Buddha when you were dedicating yourself in the boat is what the Christians call God or Jesus Christ?" The man just spat out his answer, "Sure, I know it is the same. But these Christians don't believe that!"

Are such Christians wrong?

A Sikh conversion

While we were in Zambia fellowshiping with the Quakers, we were visited by a Sikh who told us about his conversion. He had grown up as a nominal Sikh. He had tried to join the local Sikhs in building a temple in Lusaka, but the group had quarreled and had finally split up. He had drifted away from the religion of his birth.

Then one day word came that a famous Sikh teacher from India would visit Kenya. A devout Sikh in Lusaka offered to finance the nominal Sikh's trip to the conference where this religious leader would speak. Not wanting to offend the fellow Sikh and not minding the paid vacation, the nominal Sikh accepted the offer.

He said, "I hung around the periphery of the group. I paid very little attention to what the Sikh leader was saying and just enjoyed my vacation. One day as I was sitting in the rear of the crowd, an ant ran up my leg and bit me. I slapped it. When I looked down I saw that I had broken the ant in two. The two halves of the ant were lying there writhing in the sand. Suddenly it hit me! 'You were irritated because that ant bit you and now you have carelessly destroyed life that God himself created.' At that moment I began to realize that there were many other things in my life that were not right. I felt very bad."

"As I thought about this, a voice from God came to me suddenly and said, 'I am the God who gives life. I can make things right!' And just then I noticed that the head and the abdomen of the ant joined together again and it ran away merrily. I was so shaken by the voice and the reassembly of the ant that I realized I needed to commit myself to God. I have done just that."

Was he really converted? Did he find the true God?

The Hindu idol

The Ramayana is a collection of stories about the Hindu god Rama. One story is about a Buddhist who lived in a village of faithful followers of Buddha. His whole village had absolutely no idols. But it was surrounded by Hindu villages which were chock-a-block with deity figures.

One day the Hindus from a neighboring village moved a giant thirty-foot statue of one of their deities and planted it right beside the path, halfway between their village and the Buddhist village. One of the men from the Buddhist village had to walk by this idol every day on his way to his field. From the very first time he saw the image, he was horrified. Then and there he made a vow to Buddha that he would spit on, kick and curse that idol twice a day: once when he went to work and once on his way home. For thirty years this man faithfully spat on, cursed and kicked the idol.

Then one day when he was returning from his field, he discovered that the whole area near his village was under water as a result of a giant monsoon rain. The area around the idol was totally submerged. Still remembering his vow, he made a desperate attempt to get to the idol to fulfill his daily ritual. He climbed into the trees and crawled along their canopies until he worked his way over the idol. Darkness fell, and it was impossible for him to continue.

He decided that he would have to spend the night up in the tree. But he promised that he would curse, spit on and kick the idol twice the following morning. He fell asleep. While sleeping he lost his hold and fell out of the tree right on top of the stone idol. He was killed the moment he hit it. The tree happened to be in season with nuts, and as the man hit various branches on the way down the tree showered the idol with a tremendous deluge of nuts.

When the devil came to claim the dead man's soul, he was surprised to find that God had beaten him to the draw. Furthermore, God told him in no uncertain terms, "Stay away! This is one of my most faithful followers!" The devil was puzzled and asked, "Why, this man cursed, spit on and kicked you every day. How can you say he was serving you?"

"Well," God said, "different people make different kinds of vows. Some vows are good, some are unwise. But often they are unwise because people don't know better. This man didn't know any better. But what he knew, he did. He thought there should be no images. He believed there was only one God. And in that he was correct! So he promised to curse, to spit on and to kick the idol every day, and that's exactly what he did! I would venture that I have very few followers anywhere near as faithful as this man!"

Then as an afterthought God added, "And don't forget the generous offering of nuts that he gave me when he fell out of the tree and died!"

Is that God the one God of the world—the God of the Bible?

The other fold

The preceding story brings to mind a saying of Jesus that many people find very troublesome. "Other sheep I have which are not of this fold. Them also I must bring that they shall hear my voice and there shall be one fold and one shepherd" (John 10:16). Is this Buddhist an example of such a person making a commitment to God? Is this an example of those who belong to Jesus' other fold? My forty years of experience in mission fields has convinced me that some of them indeed are God's children.

What about "No other name?"

Like other monotheistic religions, Christianity is exclusivist, that is, it claims to be the one and only way. A favorite verse is: "Neither is there salvation in any other: for there is none other name under heaven given among men whereby we must be saved" (Acts 4:12). The name referred to in this passage is mentioned two verses earlier, in verse 10. It, of course, is the name of *Jesus*. The result has been that Christians have developed a theology which says that unless a person believes in Jesus, she/he cannot be saved.

As I began working with people from different languages translating the Scriptures, I became aware of how many biblical names have meaning. In the beginning of Genesis, for example, the name "Adam" actually means "mankind." The word "Eve" suggests the meaning of "life" or "living." Thus Eve is considered the mother of all the living. Most of the early names of the Old Testament have such meanings. These meanings are often lost to us when biblical names are transliterated in translation. This has also happened in Acts 4:12.

We are told that the language spoken among the Jews in Jesus' day was Aramaic, a dialect of Hebrew. In this dialect the name "Jesus" would have been rendered as "Jeshua." Now Jeshua is a Hebrew or Aramaic word with meaning. It means "God (or Jehovah) saves." The question thus is: does the word "Jesus" literally mean J-e-s-u-s or is it the meaning of that word in the language in which

Jesus originally said it, in Aramaic, "God saves"? If the latter is the case, then the verse would read: There is no other name given under heaven whereby men may be saved, other than Jeshua, that is, "God saves."

In Acts 10, we have an intriguing account of Cornelius, the Gentile, who prays to God. God hears the prayers and sends his angel to the man. God instructs him through the angel to invite Peter to get the full message of God. In other words, this man stands at the testamental divide. He was praying to the Old Testament God of the Jews, and this God uses Peter to communicate a New Testament message about Jesus to him.

Meanwhile, God prepares Peter for this encounter through the vision of the sheet full of unclean animals. Peter, being a faithful Jew, believed that Jews had to avoid all contact with Gentiles. They had no business giving the good news of Jesus to the Gentiles. But God wanted to convince Peter otherwise, and thus exposed him to the vision of the sheet. The whole thing left Peter puzzled. But when his vision was interrupted by Cornelius' men asking him to come to their master, he suddenly realized what God was asking him to do. When Peter shared the message about Jesus in Cornelius' house, the people, of course, believed and were baptized. But there is an intriguing conclusion to this incident. "Of a truth, I perceive that God is no respecter of persons: but in every nation he that feareth him, and worketh righteousness, is accepted of him" (Acts 10:34-35). Peter realized that God had heard Cornelius' prayer, and even though the latter didn't know about Jesus, God accepted him as a believer.

The implications of only one God in the world

I now want to return to a thought expressed in an earlier chapter: as a missionary I was committed to the belief that there is only one God in this world. Even though he is known by thousands of names in different tribes and languages, God is only one. I had to learn that the implications of such radical monotheism are both negative and positive.

In the negative we note that monotheistic religions tend to be fiercely exclusivist. Whether one deals with the Egyptian monotheistic god Atun, Islamic Allah, or the Christian God, all tend to be exclusivist, i.e., they maintain they are the only correct way because only they worship the true God. In one sense they are entirely correct. The problem is that they consider God, by the next tribe's name, to be an idol—a false God.

On the positive side, the presence of only one God in the world actually serves as a discouragement against idolatry. However, if some of the modern definitions of idolatry are valid, then anything partial that people raise to ultimate meaning becomes an idol. This can involve even Christian icons like the Bible or the church.

The triune God

Christians on the whole feel quite comfortable with the idea that there is only one God, but they say he manifested himself in three persons or in three personalities: God the Father, God the Son or Jesus Christ, and God the Holy

Spirit. When Anne and I talked to thinking Hindus during our tour of temples in India, we found that they too insisted on only one God. They say that is Brahma. However, they maintain that because ordinary people have difficulty finding satisfaction in the one-God concept, God is willing to manifest himself in whatever aspect meets the individual's needs. They say God does not demand that people meet him where he is; God is willing to meet each person where that person is. People then fall into the trap of giving these various manifestations of God separate names, thereby, as it were, creating separate gods or idols.

One Hindu priest Anne and I talked to pointed out similarities between Christianity and Hinduism. Both believe in only one God and both believe that God manifested himself in more than one form. "Christians believe that God manifested himself in the three persons; however, we Hindus have more manifestations of God than there are people," we were told. In other words, there is a manifestation of God for every person's need, and should new ones be needed, God will manifest himself in still more forms.

When Anne and I visited one of the largest Hindu temples in southern India, we were dismayed to be forbidden entry because we weren't wearing the right clothes. As we stood dejectedly beside the gate of that temple, wondering what to do, a monk in a dirty yellow robe sidled up to us and queried, "They did not let you go into the temple, did they?" We said, "No!" Then he said, "It is wrong! God does not exclude anybody from his house. God is one and he wants to receive all people regardless of who or what they are. If you want to experience God's nearness, come with me to a chapel where I know you can enter." We followed him to one side of the temple where there was a small one-room structure with a single phallic image of Vishnu. The priest then asked us to kneel in prayer. My wife and I knelt down with him. He asked us to pray, and we did. Then he prayed. When we got up and he shook our hands, I must honestly say I felt I had met a kindred soul. I had met one of my fellow members of God's family.

PRAYER

Prayer has been an integral part of my life's journey. I am deeply conscious of how my mother's prayers when I was an eczematous infant helped save my life. My own first dramatic memory of praying was when I nearly drowned while trying to learn to swim. I still vividly remember the tremendous gratitude I felt when I found strength to get out of that precarious situation.

Typically, my early experiences with prayer were very much in the spirit of asking and receiving. I saw God as a kind of celestial bellhop who could be called upon to run errands for us.

Learning to deal with interrupting thoughts during silent prayer was part of my deeper education in prayer. I began to realize how important it is to clear the channel of unfinished business so that one can establish a clear contact with our God and Maker. Prayer also means listening to God.

The discovery of the telephone analogy—a person-to-person call, a station-to-station call, or a recorded message—was probably one of most important insights into prayer. It was then I began to realize how little person-to-person praying there really is in Christian circles. Most of public prayer is: "this is a recording."

As I developed my understanding of communication theory, and began to consider prayer as legitimate communication to be analyzed, I grasped the magnitude of the self-deceit that is often carried out under the guise of prayer. I also began to realize that prayer is not about asking and receiving, as much as getting oneself in tune with God's design and purpose—of hearing from God.

CHAPTER 20

PRAYER THAT WORKED

My mother's heartfelt prayer dedicating me to the Lord's service when I was an eczematous infant prevailed over the pious prayers of those who were praying for my demise. I became what I am by the power of a deeply concerned mother's prayer. And I am proud of it!

Prayer has played—and still plays—a vital role in my life. I still remember vividly how I learned to swim as a twelve-year-old. I had gone too deep into the swimming hole and lost my foothold. As I was going under, I desperately cried to God. I mustered all my strength and actually *swam* to shallower water. I learned to swim that very moment.

As students at Tabor College, Anne and I habitually were "at the bottom of the barrel" financially. One Sunday I was to preach in a large church. I desperately needed a haircut before that, but we didn't have even the fifty cents that a haircut cost at the time. We prayed earnestly for a solution. On Friday morning before my sermon, a friend who was the editor of a school paper in another country returned the seventy-five cent subscription fee I had sent to him. He added a note saying he was sending me a complimentary subscription because I had written something for the paper. I got my haircut and had a quarter to spare!

The verb "to be"

When trying to learn the Waunana language, we were stymied by a very complex verb "to be." Our whole living room wall was plastered with long columns of forms which all seemed to say: "I am fine." We were sitting there with our Waunana teacher, praying for insight, when he suddenly got up and pointed to one column on the wall. He could not read, but we had been over the columns so often that he knew exactly which column was where. He pointed to the column and said, "Ana (my wife) would say that!" Then he pointed to another and said, "Jaco (Jake) would say that!" It was our first break! Once we recognized that there was a difference between masculine and feminine forms of the verb "to be," we just let our imaginations run. By that afternoon we had at least some grasp of what all the various columns of forms of the verb "to be" meant.

Keeping a "soul-less" Indian alive by prayer

After our first furlough I was asked to survey the ten dialects of the Chocó language to see how many translations we would need to reach the whole language family. In the course of this survey I made a trip across the mountains from our former home in Noanama, now standing completely empty. I needed to find a speaker of the Baudó dialect of the language. Finally I found one. I tried to work in the Baudó's home, but it was terribly small and very noisy. It was next to impossible for us to do meaningful work there.

After a number of frustrating days, I decided to take my informant to our empty former residence in Noanama and to try to complete the work there. I asked the man if he would accompany me there for about ten days. He was exceedingly hesitant. Meanwhile, his wife had been asking me about the price of a cast-iron cooking pot. The pot was worth a little more than the ten days' work for which I wanted to hire her husband, but I said to her, "If you can convince your husband to go with me, I would be happy to provide you with the money to get the cooking pot." The woman succeeded, and her husband agreed to accompany me. What I didn't realize was that I was taking this Indian to an alien tribe's domain where he would be outside the jurisdiction of his local protecting spirits.

We made the trip across the mountains and established ourselves in our former residence in Noanama. The work progressed well. We worked from Wednesday until Saturday and made excellent progress. However, when five o'clock came on Saturday and I wanted to call it a day, the man said, "I want to continue working." We worked until nine o'clock. By nine o'clock I was dead tired, and I finally said, "I am going to drop dead! I can't work any longer! We've got to quit!" I prepared us something to eat and by about ten o'clock we retired, each in a separate room in the otherwise empty house.

I fell asleep immediately, but after about two hours I lurched awake to hear the man in the next room groaning as if in severe pain. I got up to find the Baudó man writhing in agony on the floor. After much questioning, I finally learned from him that the tribes people of this area, to which he was alien, had stolen his soul. Now he was dying because of soul loss. Sure enough! When I felt his extremities, his legs and arms were cold and clammy. I sat down beside the man and tried to explain that I was working for God and that God was watching over this house. I assured him that he really had nothing to fear here.

My explanation seemed to relax him somewhat, and his extremities began to warm up. After his body was completely warm, I went back to sleep, this time on the floor beside him. Soon he was writhing and groaning again. Now his extremities were deathly cold. The only warm spots on his body seemed to be his belly and his chest.

I reminded him again that I was doing God's work and that God was in charge. I asked him whether he believed that God was stronger than any evil spirits that might have been sent to steal his soul. Reluctantly the Indian agreed, but it didn't seem to change his condition. So I knelt beside him and prayed, asking God to keep the man alive. As I was praying, I noticed that his extremities began to warm up. I prayed aloud until he was totally warm again.

This happened one more time. Finally I realized that although I was dead tired, I would have to stay awake to keep him alive until daybreak. For the rest of the night I held him in my arms, audibly praying that God should keep him from dying. At daybreak I hired a man with a canoe to take the Baudó back to his country. I never was able to finish the dialect work on this language. But I realized that it was prayer that had kept the man alive until I could return him to his people.

The Sabbath incident

In an earlier chapter I told about a shouting match that erupted in Africa over translating the word *Sabbath.*

We were working on a joint translation that involved Pentecostals, Roman Catholics, Adventists and various faith missions. When the draft was sent out to the churches for reading and approval, some Adventists wrote back and accused me of being the devil's helper. They accused me of trying to destroy their church.

This surprised me. Those of us on the translation team, which included an Adventist translator, knew we had an international agreement with all Sabbathist churches on how to translate the word *Sabbath.* We had agreed to use "the seventh day" or "the day of rest." The local Adventist church, however, refused to accept the decision of the parent body. They adamantly objected to the term we had chosen.

When the translation team met for the final approval of the manuscript, the said quarrel broke out between the Adventist translator and a Pentecostal on the team. I had again explained the position of the Bible Society, and that it had been accepted by all the Seventh Day churches around the world. I assured them that we were well within the range of latitude allowed by that decision. But the quarrel continued in increasing fury. It became so violent that I dropped to my knees and began to pray silently that God would intervene and give us a solution to our impasse. One by one others followed suit. Soon all of the forty-some people present, except the Pentecostal and the Adventist, were on their knees. These two men remained standing, gesticulating and shouting at each other. Eventually they looked around and saw what had happened. Then the Pentecostal also became quiet and went down on his knees, leaving only the Adventist standing. Finally he, too, joined us and there followed a painful period of silence.

Suddenly the silence was pierced by the anguished voice of the Adventist translator as he cried out to God in repentance. He finally realized he had been wrong. Our group prayer had broken the quarrel.

The power of God versus the power of evil spirits

One day, a Waunana, whom we considered a friend, came to us with his sick daughter. She obviously had serious distress with her chest, and screamed in agony as she coughed. Those in charge of the dispensary gave her some injections of antibiotics and also some sedatives. She calmed down considerably. But during the night when the sedatives wore off, she again began screaming. When the missionaries got up in the morning, however, the Waunana family was gone. We were told that before coming to our place the family had been with a medicine man who supposedly dealt with white magic spirits. Now they had gone to a man renowned for dealing with black magic spirits. We lost track of the family and heard nothing more about them for about a month.

Meanwhile, a Waunana staying in the visitors' house in our yard, died of a lung hemorrhage. Shortly afterward the father brought his daughter back to us again. By this time, she definitely had one foot in the grave. I reminded the father, "If you had stayed with us the first time, we would have been able to give her antibiotics. I am sure that we could have done something to help. But look, now she is almost dead!" He admitted that. He also admitted that the medicine man had said the spirits that had taken this girl were so much stronger than all his helping spirits, that the shaman himself was now afraid for his own life. He had actually ejected the moribund girl and her family from his house.

I realized at once that a showdown was developing between God's help through the dispensary and the shaman's work with spirit helpers. The father stood there doggedly and insisted, "I am bringing her to you to heal!" I continued to plead that there was nothing we could do for her at this stage because she was dying. But he wouldn't budge. "I am looking to you that you and your God will heal her!" he kept on repeating.

I consulted with the rest of the staff on our mission and we finally decided we had to take up the challenge. We asked the father to stay with us so that we would begin intensive treatment, but the family refused. He said that at our place the devils that make the blood run were loose, referring to the other man's hemorrhage. Nor could they stay in the negro village next to us because, according to their reasoning, negroes and devils are both black, thus the negroes might be in cahoots with, if not offspring of, the devils. Since neither our house nor the negro village was suitable, they would have to take their daughter to his own house, which was half an hour downriver (one hour upriver) by canoe. To make matters worse, our outboard motor was out of commission. This meant that every day either the nurse or one of us had to paddle the canoe to administer the necessary injections and other treatments.

Shortly after the treatment began, the girl developed a large lump next to one of her breasts. Neither our missionary nurse nor I had the courage to lance such a large protrusion. But we continued to give her cough suppressants, injections to build up her body and, of course, heavy doses of antibiotics. The girl was too weak to sit. She either lay on the mat or sat humped over in a little pile of skin and bones. She had absolutely no strength.

About this time, we got a letter from a Sunday school class in Alberta asking if there were anything that they could do to help us. We immediately wrote back and suggested they could help pay for the antibiotics and join us in prayer. Maybe then God would heal this girl and convince the tribe of the Lord's capacity in healing. The Sunday school class agreed, and we became partners in prayer.

About two-and-a-half weeks into our treatment, the lump on the girl's side opened up from the inside and she began spewing quarts of pus out of her mouth. She became a very vile-smelling bundle. Whenever we gave her cough suppressants or any kind of oral medication, she would cough and squirt a stream of vile-smelling pus over the person helping her. It looked utterly hopeless! But we continued to hope and, of course, we continued to pray fervently.

Eventually, after six weeks, the pus let up and the young woman began gathering some strength. She was able to sit up again. About two months later, as I walked out of the house, I met the father and this girl, now well. When I greeted them, the father said, "We took our daughter to a medicine man who heals with white-magic spirits, and he failed! We took her to a medicine man who heals with black-magic spirits, and he failed! But the Spirit of God has healed her!" He then and there committed his life to God.

(Later I was able to take the daughter to a doctor and have her chest X-rayed. We found that she had had an inflammation between the two linings of her lungs. The result was that one lung had become totally collapsed as the chest cavity filled up with pus, but the two lobes of her other lung had spread out and now had largely filled her chest cavity again. Two years later this young woman gave birth to a healthy child.)

On the wings of prayer

In 1957, our missionary coworkers John and Mary Dyck were killed in a plane crash in Colombia. The relatives who came to Colombia wanted someone to go up the mountain to bury the couple. Since none of them felt up to the task, I went up the mountain to do it on their behalf. It was an enormously grueling task. The trip in and out lasted thirteen days, much of it spent cutting trails through the dense jungle. The peaks we had to cross, some thirteen of them, ranged from 5,000 to 13,000 feet. The area was rocky, covered by roots from various kinds of vegetation over which a thick layer of moss had grown. By the time half-a-dozen persons had passed over a trail, the moss had been trampled into a ditch. Those who followed after them had to walk in knee-deep water that was being retained by the dense moss. It rained almost continuously. We were totally soaked the whole time.

The jungle hammock which I had taken along turned out to be useless on the mountain. The only way to rest was to have three or four individuals sit on their haunches back-to-back in a puddle so we could at least get some warmth from each other.

When a free-lance journalist reached me near the end of the trip and asked how I had been able to survive for so many exhausting days on the mountain, I could unashamedly tell him, "I have been walking on the wings of prayer!" I knew that many people in Canada and the United States were praying for me during those difficult days. I have never in my life been more conscious of being carried on the prayers of God's people than I was during the thirteen days that I was in the mountains to bury John and Mary Dyck.

A Lengua Christian's prayer

"Our innermosts are fallen down and are wandering aimlessly. All too often they are hard and are tied up in knots, working furiously and continuously. But to this innermost comes he who gives us a new innermost. He who promised to show us how to keep it from shivering or working frantically and rather to make it soft, spread out and to cause it to be untied so that we can reach beyond ourselves. May this one always be with me and you, this day and always." (This is a back translation of a Paraguayan Lengua prayer for a Christian friend.)

CHAPTER 21

LESSONS ON PRAYER

When I attended Bible school I was very impressed by books like *Prayer is asking and receiving* (John R. Rice) and *Praying Through* (E. M. Bounds). In my early youth, I actually felt that through prayer humans could coerce God to do whatever they fervently asked. If they prayed long enough and hard enough, God simply had to answer. But the more I got to know the Lord and the more experience I gained in prayer, the more I recognized that God is neither hard-hearted nor stubbornly difficult to convince. Why then does prayer often take so much time? Most likely because the one praying is so difficult to reach. Prayer is getting the pray-er to be in tune with God's working so that he/she can fit harmoniously into God's design.

Today I would say that prayer is mostly for the pray-er's benefit. It helps him/her to wait on God and become attuned to the divine purpose. As one empties one's channel of all intervening, unfinished business and becomes inwardly open to God, one can eventually hear his still small voice speaking. This, I feel today, is the real way God answers prayer. This is how he reveals to us his solutions to our problems. This is how he directs us and prevents us from doing what is not in his design.

When the Chocó Indian Aureliano was visiting us in Hillsboro, I arranged for all the foreign students at Tabor College and other foreign friends to join us in a multi-language prayer session. All participants prayed in their own language. Only a few understood any other language in which prayers were being spoken. When the prayers were finished, however, the Chocó visitor suddenly said to me, "Tiger, I have learned something today! People who have given God the hand and who are walking on God's road together with us, even when they speak languages we don't understand, can be more brother and sister to us than our very own relatives who don't believe! I didn't understand a word of what those other people were praying, but inside I felt they were my brothers and sisters because our hearts were all beating in harmony!"

I think what is being said in prayer is often less important than the fact that we are uttering something that we feel deeply. When the dying Baudó feared that his soul had been stolen, I don't think it was the words I uttered that kept this man from dying. It was the mere fact that another human being was with him and was verbalizing something they both felt deeply. Being aware of the concern of another person praying for him was enough to sustain his tenuous hold on life.

All too often we are so distracted and so involved in our own agenda that it is difficult for us to truly listen to what God is trying to say. A classic example was the *Sabbath* experience described a few pages ago. When the Adventist man eventually became quiet with forty people around him praying, he suddenly had to listen to God. This led him to utter his anguished cry of repentance.

The telephone analogy mentioned earlier has been exceedingly helpful to my understanding of prayer. There are at least three ways for us to telephone others. We can make a person-to-person call. We can make a station-to-station call. Or we can get "this is a recording." Prayer that is truly meaningful is always person-to-person. The greater the intimacy between the pray-er and God, the less will be understood by anyone who overhears the prayer. They don't understand because they don't know all the information that the pray-er and God share.

Many people, however, seldom get beyond station-to-station. They ostensibly address God, but their real concern is other people who are listening. Thus they are really speaking for the benefit of other people.

Sad to say, many of our prayers actually fall into the category of "this is a recording." Anne and I were invited to another couple's home for a meal after I preached a message on prayer using the telephone analogy. When we sat down at the table, the host-husband looked up embarrassedly at his wife and asked, "Whose turn is it to play the recording?" Though somewhat facetious, he was highlighting the fact that many of our prayers, especially table prayers, do fall into this category.

When you pray: a biblical lesson

In Matthew 6:1-17, at the very heart of the Sermon on the Mount, Jesus says some profound things about praying, especially praying in public. He gives some rather somber warnings about the dangers which this kind of praying entails. He concludes that in general, praying is better done alone in one's own room, rather than in public.

For regular churchgoers, the very familiarity of public prayer—"this is the way we've always done it"—may allow us to think Jesus is not talking about us when he utters stern words of warning about prayer. The truth is that Jesus is talking precisely to the likes of us who pray regularly in church.

First, let's summarize some of the things about which Jesus feels he must warn us:

1. Public displays of piety, including prayer, can readily become directed at the people who witness it, rather than at God to whom the prayer is ostensibly addressed (verses 1,5 & 16).

2. Praying in public easily slips into hypocrisy (verses 2,5 & 16).

3. Public praying easily becomes a contest for the most beautiful and the most pious expressions. Jesus calls this "heaping up empty phrases" (verse 7).

4. The length of one's prayer is readily confused with the degree of sincerity (verse 7).

5. Public prayer is often an insult to an all-knowing God because it tries to tell him things as if he didn't know, was unobservant, or had just plain forgotten (verse 8).

6. It amounts to an appeal to God to review the praying person's relationship with others. For example, asking for forgiveness from God when one has failed to forgive one's fellows instantly short-circuits the person's own prayer for forgiveness (verses 12 & 14).

If we now add Luke 18:10-14 to the Matthew passage already cited, we find that Jesus gives us an example of both effective and ineffective public prayer.

The tax collector, deeply ashamed of his lifestyle, prayed: "God, be merciful to me a sinner." His prayer was short, personal, to the point and from the heart. It was effective; he went away forgiven.

On the other hand, the Pharisee, a seemingly regular and experienced prayer, was merely piling up guilt and damnation by means of his prayer. First, he was lying by pretending to address God when in fact he was addressing the people around him. In thanking God, he was really patting himself on the back. Second, he was utterly blind to his own sin before God. God did not see him as any less sinful than the other man whom the Pharisee labeled "a sinner." Third, he was insulting God's intelligence by reminding him about the Pharisee's regular acts of piety of which an all-knowing God was already fully aware.

Let me explore more fully the principles of communication that underlie this criticism of public prayer. (See H. H. Clark and T.B. Carlson, "Hearers and Speech Acts," *Language* 58:332-373, 1982.) Some of its "scientific" findings can set the problems about which Jesus is talking into everyday experience and thus may help us understand why Jesus said what he did.

People often intentionally misaddress their prayers

Such misaddressing of communication takes a variety of forms. For example, the addressee can be real but have only an incidental or instrumental function, because the speaker's real aim is to give a message to others who happen to be listening in.

Imagine the mayor of a city giving a medal for bravery to a firefighter on the evening TV news saying: "On behalf of the citizens of this community I want to thank you for your heroic effort in last Thursday's fire." These words are not really directed at the brave firefighter present but at the viewing public.

The instrumental function of the addressee is even more apparent in court proceedings when a lawyer interrogates a witness. Ostensibly the words are directed at the witness, but everyone knows the real objects of communication are the judge and jury.

People learn this kind of misaddressing very early in life. Several years ago our two-and-a-half-year-old grandson was at our home for dinner. He knew that in order to be excused from the table after eating he had to thank the hostess for the meal; so while his grandmother was in the kitchen and out of hearing range, he said, "Ta ta, gamma," and then looked expectantly at his father and mother for permission to leave the table. The communication was ostensibly directed at his grandmother, but the child was totally unconcerned about whether grandmother heard; all he wanted was to secure permission from his parents. The address to his grandmother was merely a means to achieve that end.

Sometimes the addressee is entirely fictitious. For example, a mother says to a three-month-old baby within earshot of the father: "Don't you think your daddy should change your diaper?" Clearly, the baby is a fictitious addressee because it does not understand nor is it really involved in the communication. The speech is directed at the father—it is an indirect request for him to change the baby's diaper.

Many societies prohibit direct speech between certain categories of people. They use the mechanism of the fictitious addressee when circumstances demand that such people communicate. For example, one day we watched our servant in Africa as he met his mother-in-law on our front yard. Their culture forbids the two to speak to each other directly. If they must communicate, they have to do so through a third party, often a fictitious addressee. The servant immediately went down on his knees, and since there was no third person at hand, he addressed the nearest tree and said: "Tree, greet my wife's mother." The mother-in-law responded in kind, saying: "Tree, greet the husband of my daughter." Their entire conversation was then carried out through this fictitious intermediary.

If we now apply these principles to prayer, I think Jesus is saying that many, if not most, public prayers fall into the first category where God, the actual addressee, has a merely incidental or instrumental function. The prayer is really addressed to the surrounding listeners, such as when a minister uses the opening prayer to prepare the audience for the sermon he is about to deliver. If he was actually seeking the Lord's direction in preparing his sermon, then God is already fully informed as to what he is going to preach. The minister need not tell him. It is the audience who needs the background for what he is going to say.

Or it may be the elder or deacon who in the closing prayer "preaches" the sermon he thinks the pastor should have preached instead of the one that was actually delivered.

In fact, one sometimes wonders whether many of the prayers uttered in public do not really fall into the second category where God, the addressee, has a more or less entirely fictitious function.

The fictitious addressee is probably at its most blatant in the familiar setting of table prayer. Many families have a plaque in their dining room saying,

"God is a silent guest at every meal." If God were really present at our tables, would we really use the vocative when we pray? Wouldn't we then just look up and say "Thank you?" This is what we would do if we were speaking to an actual person who was present and paying attention.

The use of the vocative

In our daily conversations we use vocative address (that is, addressing a person by name or by title) for a number of purposes: (a) to gain the attention of a person whom we want to address; (b) to direct a remark to a specific addressee when there are several potential addressees present. In a longer discourse, it may be necessary to repeat the address to make sure that everyone realizes the comments are still being directed at the same person; (c) to signal a change of addressee in the course of an ongoing conversation where there are several participants.

When we pray in public our communication is axiomatically directed at God (or at one of the other members of the Trinity). Invariably some divine name is invoked. But as Jesus indicated in Matthew 6:1-17, and as we have said earlier, we often misaddress our prayer. We perform our piety for the eyes and ears of those around us rather than actually speaking to God whom we are ostensibly addressing.

Communication specialists tell us that the vocative performs several other functions in addition to those listed above. For example, the British usually like to maintain a kind of psychological reserve and speak more formally, and so they address the person with a title like "Sir, Mr. X," or "Mr. Chairperson," while North Americans, who tend to prefer a more familiar approach, usually use the person's first name. We can see something similar in prayer in the choice one makes between the different possible names of deity, such as *God* versus *Jesus*. *Jesus* is by far the more intimate form of address.

Furthermore, since the kind of address and the tone of its delivery are used to indicate the degree of intimacy or the psychological distance between speaker and addressee, the address can be used to project intimacy even where it does not exist. For example, "dearest Jesus" rather than "dear God" is designed to create the impression of greater intimacy.

However, in truly intimate speech between two friends, vocatives are much less frequent than in ordinary conversation. Those that do occur often are special expressions limited to such intimate communications. Spouses or intimate friends often have special endearment labels which they use among themselves. When people praying in public try to project intimacy with God by adding endearment qualifiers, like "dearest Jesus," but then go on to fill in all the background and all the "shared" details (see next section) in their prayers, they are actually negating real intimacy. If this occurred in a normal, daily-life context, we would regard it as artificial and insincere.

The *frequency* of the use of the vocative is also a significant indicator, according to communication specialists. High-pressure salespeople, con artists and the like use familiar vocatives as part of their sales pitch. As a result, North Americans tend to react negatively to the over-use of the vocative and tend to assume that someone is trying to "sell them something." Some people address God with almost every statement they make, and some even say *God* or *Lord* at the beginning and at the end of each statement. Does this over-use of the vocative in prayer mean the same thing as in ordinary conversation?

Shared information in communication

The degree of common experience two people share usually determines how much background information or how much detail they will provide when they talk with each other. Usually the greater the amount of common experience or shared information, the greater the amount of information that will be left implicit. For this reason it is often impossible to make sense out of a conversation between intimate friends because an outsider does not have enough explicit information to know what they are really talking about. One hears and understands all the words, but cannot decipher the message for lack of necessary shared information.

It is said that someone once listened by the keyhole of Spurgeon's bedroom to learn how this great man of God prayed. When Spurgeon finished his sermon preparation he got up, went to the window, looked up, and said: "Between you and me things remain as usual. Good night." This is intimacy!

The converse of this also operates—the greater the feeling of psychological distance between two people in conversation, the more background information and detail they will put into their verbal exchanges. This is most significant for praying. If true intimacy rests on large amounts of shared experience remaining implicit, then truly intimate prayer would be next to impossible to understand in public. The fact that public prayer tends to be relatively complete in the information it offers is a strong indication: (a) that it is not really directed at God at all, because surely he knows all the details which he and the pray-er share. If the latter insists on making this shared information explicit, he is thereby indicating that he is speaking to someone else who does not share this detailed knowledge; or (b) if it is actually directed at God, it speaks of an enormous feeling of psychological distance between the pray-er and the God to whom the prayer is addressed. The very explicitness of the prayer contradicts the intimacy the pray-er is trying to project.

Prayer meetings

Some years ago I attended a prayer meeting in Latin America which drew both Latins and North Americans. Very few of the participants knew each other. On the whole the atmosphere was warm and friendly. Everyone introduced himself and then shared some need as a prayer request. We had been doing this for about forty-five minutes when the leader suddenly realized how our time was flying. He suggested that we rush through the remaining requests in order to "leave enough time for prayer." I suggested instead that we assume God was present and had been listening to our detailed requests, and all that was still needed was to tell God that this was the extent of our list and that we wanted him to exercise his will on it. The people of Spanish origin immediately agreed that there was no need to repeat all our requests to God in a prayer formula. However the North American leader thought we should at least summarize the requests to God in prayer. Since he was the leader, that is just what we did. He rushed through the rest of the requests and then enumerated the whole list to God in the traditional prayer formula.

I found this experience most instructive. It showed me that many of us still treat prayer as a kind of ritual, if not magical formula, rather than straightforward communication with God. The suggestion for prayer meetings thus is, let's keep our prayer groups small so that we can be informal and conversational in our approach to God. If necessary, let's set out a symbolic chair for the good Lord and assume that he is present and listening to all we say so there is no need to repeat things with a special formula. We would soon recognize that it is the people, not God, who need to hear detailed prayer requests, because often God wants to use one of us to meet someone else's request. Furthermore, by hearing about someone else's need, we can often recognize our own similar need. Then the God who looks into the heart "*will hear*" also our need, even though we may have only grudgingly admitted it to ourselves in silence.

Therefore let us pray in such a way that "while we are yet speaking, the Lord will hear us" (Isa. 65:24).

MISSION SERVICE

Early on I learned that the local people on the missionfield often were more concerned with physical healing than with the soul's-salvation message that I was concerned about. I also became aware of how far Christians have separated the concept of the soul's salvation from physical healing. As I reflected upon this, I realized that the German word *Heiland* 'Savior' really means 'healer.' Thus began my still unfinished pilgrimage toward developing concern for the whole person in missions, not just the person's soul.

Our early missionary experience at Noanama began to make me aware of how much missionary activity is actually police activity. But it wasn't until I began to work with the Bible Society and learned what it means to be a catalyst, that I realized the full abhorrence of the missionary in the policeman's role.

Many kinds of lessons I learned subtly changed my approach to missions. The awareness of reciprocity, which was generated especially through my close relationship with the prophet of the Chocó church, taught me the importance of this approach to Third World people.

Eventually I reviewed my own mission history and was able to identify my growth stages in regard to how I approached witnessing the good news to others, especially to people abroad.

At the beginning I was a dyed-in-the-wool nondenominational soulwinner. As I began to see the benefit of denominational missions, I became a church transplanter. Eventually, however, I also saw how artificial such transplanting often is and that what is really needed is an indigenous church that lives and develops within its own cultural milieu. Thus I realized that the only viable task for a missionary is that of a catalyst. But even this probably isn't the end. Missions is an ongoing process and there are still many lessons to be learned. Like all of life's business, our awareness of what the mission's task involves, too, is still not finished.

CHAPTER 22
HEALING THE SICK AND MENDING THE WOUNDED

In order to begin our outreach to the Waunana, we had to locate in a largely negro village at the mouth of one of the tributaries inhabited by the tribe. This village was situated at the junction of the San Juan (St. John) and Becordó (partridge) rivers. The San Juan is not a very long river, but at Noanama it is already almost half a mile wide. Because of the heavy rainfall in the region, it carries a massive amount of water. All travel in the area is by canoe. Overland travel, except over the mountains, is possible only in the driest part of the year.

We rented an old house from a mestizo family. The house had originally belonged to the rubber company which had collected raw rubber in the jungles of the area during World War II. It was about eighteen feet wide and forty feet long. It had a lean-to in the back that served as the kitchen. The house proper had a tin roof, but the lean-to was thatched. We fixed up a living room in the front of the house; our bedroom was in the rear, next to the kitchen.

We had located an abandoned house right next to the village and bought the property rights to the place. There we intended to build our family residence. But to build the kind of house we needed in the jungle was no easy task.

First of all, houses there have to be built on stilts because of the heavy rainfall. These stilts have to be of a special kind of wood, either of the rubber family or some other kind of wood which the termites did not eat. We couldn't get such timbers locally and had to import them from upriver.

We purchased usable building lumber from a small sawmill a couple of hours downstream from Noanama. A lot of time had to be spent getting the lumber ready before we could actually begin building. First it had to be dried, then planed and edged.

The old house that was located on the property we had acquired served as a drying-shed for the lumber and as a workplace for the men who were edging and planing the boards.

We were very conscious that we had come to Noanama to reach the

Waunana. Thus we were determined to begin no Spanish services. Nor did we intend to begin any medical work. Nonetheless, a dispensary for the sick developed almost immediately.

Jesusita's eye

It began quite innocently. One day a Waunana woman, one of our first tribal contacts, came to us for help with an ulcerated eye. The whole eye had run out and the eye cavity was a mass of pus. Because we wanted to reach the Waunana, we decided we would have to do something about the woman's eye. We prayed before we did anything else. Even though I had had a one-year course in medical training, we felt very inadequate for any kind of medical work.

I set out to clean the woman's eye. I removed as much of the infected pus as I could and cleaned out the eye cavity. I filled the empty socket with sulfa powder. Then I bandaged it. A very short time later the woman informed us, "My husband needs to go back to his farm. I have to go with him. I can't stay here any longer." I injected her with some antibiotics and dressed the eye again, but this time I covered the entire bandage with a large piece of adhesive tape so that the whole eye cavity was tightly covered. I knew she would be traveling in the rain and we didn't want the eye to get wet. We instructed the woman that we would like to see her within one week. If possible she should keep that adhesive on the eye and to keep it dry and clean.

True to their word, the family returned after one week with the adhesive relatively intact. When we removed the bandage, we found that the eye was healing fairly well. In time it healed completely, though she was now one-eyed. She was the older wife of a Waunana medicine man.

We took care of the Waunana who came to us for medical help because it was such an easy way to establish a friendly relationship with them. We had malaria medicine and would give it to all who asked for it. But one day, while Anne was in the house with our first daughter, a negro woman from the village came for help. She had a large ulcer on the calf of one leg. She had been out in her plantation when she had fallen down and a stick had punctured the ulcer and torn open the whole side of the calf. Blood and pus were streaming down the leg. Anne got out some of the first aid equipment, cleaned the leg and dressed the wound. The woman returned several times for further attention. Before we knew it, a stream of negro patients was coming for medical help. Anne finally had to establish regular hours of treatment three days a week.

Stabbed in the stomach

One day a Waunana arrived in a canoe. He had been travelling for two-and-a-half days after he accidentally stabbed himself in the abdomen. The man had been pursuing a deer with his dogs, knife in hand, when he had stubbed his foot on a root, fallen down and driven the knife into his stomach cavity. It bled profusely, and when he got home his intestine began pushing out through the wound. At first the family pushed it back, but since they didn't know how to keep it in, they finally just let the intestine come out.

By the time the man got to us, a flower of intestine about twelve inches in diameter had pushed its way out through the wound in the abdomen wall. Luckily the ensuing swelling had choked off the hole so no more intestine was coming out. Now he faced the problem of a potentially fatal gangrenous infection.

The family had covered the protruding intestine with a poultice of leaves and tree cotton. When I tried to clean that off, I realized the whole thing was a mass of pus. I carefully cleaned it off, disinfected it and applied sulfa powder. I tried to push some of it back but it was too swollen. He needed real medical attention. But how? We were two-and-a-half days down river from the nearest medical facility if we took him by canoe.

I sent someone to the sawmill several hours downriver to purchase some antibiotics. I injected the tribal man with the antibiotics as I pondered how to get him to the doctor. Luckily our missionary from upriver had hired a mining company boat to bring down the termite-proof timbers for our house and we were thus able to transport the Waunana when the motor launch returned. We brought him to our fellow missionaries in Istmina and tried to contact the local doctor.

Medical services in Colombia were supposedly free, but the white doctor in the hospital there had absolutely no interest in taking care of an Indian. He had a thousand and one excuses. When we kept insisting and offered money, he said, "But I've got a dance tonight, I can't do it. And besides, the nuns who are nurses here don't work in the evening." The fellow missionary also had had missionary medical training, and so he and I volunteered to serve as his nurses. Finally, with a bribe and our offer of help we were able to get the doctor to attend to the Waunana. But we were horrified at what he did.

He just cleaned off the wound and the protruding intestine with disinfectant and then said to the Indian, "Aguante!" (which literally means "Take it!" but would be the equivalent of "Grit your teeth and bear it.") With no anesthetic, he applied enough pressure to force the intestine back into the stomach cavity. Then he took some sutures and sewed up the outside. Even though neither of us were surgeons, we were horrified at what he was doing. No peritoneum had been sewn up! No muscles had been stitched! The result would be that this Waunana would have a permanent stomach hernia. We took the man to the mission and plied him with penicillin. In two weeks the wound showed remarkable recovery. The man's fever went down. He seemed to be without infection. Then we took him downriver to Noanama. Before long he went back to his people. We saw him quite a few times during our years in the jungle, but his stomach hernia always remained prominent.

Plastic surgery

We were already living in our new house. The old rubber company house had been renovated and fixed up as a residence for two nurses. By this time we were operating a large-scale dispensary. One day a group of Waunana brought a person who was lying in the bottom of a canoe, swimming in his own blood. The whole upper part of his face, from his eyes all the way across his cheeks, had been pulled off the facial bone and was hanging below his chin. By this time the bleeding had subsided somewhat and most of the blood was coagulating.

The man had previously blown off his left hand in a fishing accident with dynamite. Now, he and his half-brother had been drinking together and had gotten into a quarrel about the family property. In the course of the fight, the two-handed man had beaten up the one-handed one. He then beat his face with a wooden club and finally slashed him across his face with an old rusty ragged-edged knife.

His family had put the wounded man on the raised front porch of the house. Still drunk, he had fallen off the edge and struck his cut face against a rotting palm-tree stump. Now rotten palm fibers were stuck in all the flesh that had been stripped off the facial bones.

As I have already said, the nearest doctor was two-and-a-half days by canoe, and we knew that if we sent this man off in this condition he would surely die of infection en route. I contacted the local police inspector, the only government authority we had in the village, and he wrote me out an order to see whether I could patch up this Waunana's face. The registered nurse we had on the station was running around wringing her hands and saying, "We need a doctor! We need a doctor!" The practical nurse, however, was busy preparing the sutures, clamps and other paraphernalia. I scrubbed up to see what plastic surgery I could do to the man's face.

The problem was that the torn-off flesh had swollen out of proportion to the rest of the face. It was possible to match such points as the edges of the nose, but the two cheek areas bulged out grossly. It took thirty-five stitches to piece everything together. The swollen part had to be "shirred in" to the upper part of the face. When the swelling went down, it turned out that the face had been matched fairly well. The only problem was that in the process of stitching, I had sewed off the tear duct in one eye. I showed the Indian a mirror and indicated the problem to him. I volunteered to take out that one stitch and re-do the corner of his eye. But he said it hurt so much, he just couldn't stand any more. With antibiotics and the nurses' care, the man recovered.

Twenty-five years later I was in Panama one summer visiting the Chocó church when a one-armed man came forward and extended his other hand to me and pointed to his face. He had almost no scar tissue in the face as a result of that accident twenty-five years ago. He had been well ever since. Only his nose was much flatter, and there still was no functioning tear duct in his right eye.

Boils

One of the big problems in the tropical jungle is that when the body overheats it develops boils. I have had several bouts with boils, and they can be exceedingly painful. The worst was when I got two boils simultaneously, one on each buttock, and could no longer sit.

One day while there were no nurses on the station, a woman arrived who had both legs covered with boils, more than twenty on each leg. The boils were old. They had opened up but had not been cleaned out. Each one had a heavy core of solidified pus, which had to be removed before the boil could heal. Even on the shin, where there is very little flesh, she had a whole series of ulcerated boil "craters."

An older minister from North America was visiting us at the time. He watched me as one by one I popped out the cores of these old ulcers, cleaned them up and bandaged them. After about a dozen cores he got sick and had to excuse himself hurriedly. Later he asked me, "Doesn't your stomach turn when you do that?" I admitted that I often had to bite my tongue bloody because I, too, was revolted by the stench of the leg and the pus cores that I had to remove. But eventually all forty or more ulcers had been cleaned. The woman recovered completely.

The axe-cut in the knee

One day while David Wirsche and I were traveling deep in Waunana territory several days' journey away from Noanama, we were floating down river past a house. Suddenly we saw the people frantically waving for us to stop. We were surprised, since this was our first time on that river and we didn't think anyone there would know us. But word of our dispensary and of our work with the sick had spread far and wide. The Waunana had recognized us.

When we came to shore, they greeted us and said they needed help with a very sick man. At the house, we found a twenty-year-old with an axe cut right through his knee. His kneecap and the heads of the lower and upper leg bones had been split wide open. The whole wound was now covered by leaves. It was an oozing mass of infection and pus. I pled with the family to let us take the man to some medical facility, but they were afraid to move him to a territory where alien spirits would be in charge. I would have to do what I could right here. I cleaned out the wound, filled it up with sulfa powder and bandaged it. I never saw the man again, so I don't know what happened to him. I am sure he never recovered the use of his leg again.

The spirits that make the blood run are loose

As a new missionary, I knew I had a lot of things to teach the people. Not only did I know the religious truth, I also knew the right way to do many other things, including agriculture. The Waunana plant their bananas on forest land. They find a fertile-looking place that has tall trees on it. Then they clear away the underbrush and plant their banana shoots. Finally they fell the big trees on top of the newly planted bananas. By the time the bananas are ready to bear, the leaves of the felled tree have rotted and the smaller branches of the trees have all been broken off. One can now walk on the trunks of the felled trees and cut off any full grown stocks of bananas, because the tree trunks are lying pretty well at banana height. To me this was an awful messy way to farm.

One day I hired a couple of people to clear a mountain slope for me right behind our house. It had beautiful big trees on it and obviously looked fertile. We cleared all the trees and collected the wood for firewood. Then I set some workers to plant the bananas. One afternoon about 4:30, I called to the two men and told them to call it a day. I went in to join my family at supper. We had no sooner sat down, when the wife of one of the workers came running in and begged, "Come quickly, my man is spitting blood!" I was going to say, "I will quickly eat my supper," but the tone of her voice was extremely urgent. So I excused myself from my family and ran after her. As I approached the house where they stayed, I could see the man leaning over the edge of the house and vomiting a stream of blood. I ran to the dispensary to get a coagulant to inject but by the time I got there, he was dead.

He had been working out on the hillside in the hot sun all day and when I called them to stop working, he went to bathe in the river. Obviously, he had had a tubercular lesion in his lung and when he stepped into the river and cooled the surface vessels of his body, it forced the blood back into his insides. The result was the lung hemorrhage.

The wailing began almost immediately. We were very sad that the man had died, but we didn't realize how serious the situation actually was. The family immediately dispatched a messenger to a medicine man to enquire, "What happened?" The medicine man, after making the proper spirit consultation, informed them that at our guest house the spirits that make the blood run were loose, and that this man might not be the only victim! In a flash all the Waunana, including my language teacher, were gone. For weeks we waited in vain for them to return.

One day my language teacher, Alcides, was at the door. I was delighted to see him and invited him in, but he refused. I could see he was pale with fear. He begged me, "Please come out, I have a message to give you." He hurried out of our yard as quickly as possible, and together we walked toward the village. After we had crossed the pole bridge that separated us from the village, we stopped and he told me he had gone back to the medicine man to ask whether these spirits would also be dangerous to white people. When the medicine man had assured him they were, Alcides had risked his life to warn us. There was no thought of asking him to stay. He said, "My wife is so afraid, she is parked at the mouth of the river about half a mile down river from the village. She is trembling with fear that I may not come back because the spirits that make the blood run will get me too." When I asked him about coming back to work, he said, "I can't work until these spirits are penned up. I have bargained with the medicine man and he said he would pen them up if we each give him ten pesos. Then I can come back to work again."

At that stage in my mission work, I still was very much afraid of kowtowing to a pagan religion. I absolutely refused to have anything to do with it. I said I could not give him the ten pesos because that would show I did not trust my God. The man wept and begged, and finally I relented and gave him a ten-peso gift. It was months before we could resume our language work. I presume the Waunana raised the rest of the money, or the medicine man lowered his price, because eventually my teacher did come back to work.

There is a sequel to this story. The banana plantation which I had laid out on the hillside as a lesson in farming flourished beautifully. We had an enormous span of beautifully blossoming banana trees ready to produce an abundant harvest when the November rains came. As already said, this area of Colombia has some 450 inches of rainfall a year and almost half of that will fall between the first of November and the middle of December. We had enormous downpours that year and the river ran thirty to forty feet higher than normal. As a result of the heavy rains, the earth on the hillside became waterlogged and my entire banana plantation slid into the river. So much for teaching people a better way to plant bananas.

The "infected" tooth

After the signing of the new concordat, our school, dispensary and church in Noanama were all sealed with government seals on all their doors. We had just come back from our furlough, and I was engaged in a survey of the various Chocó dialects. I had come here to work with a group who spoke a different dialect and who lived several days across the mountains from Noanama. There were no other missionaries at the place because the government had effectively closed everything down.

I had no sooner arrived at the house when my former Waunana language teacher arrived with his wife who had a badly abscessed tooth. Her face was swollen grotesquely on one side, and she was suffering from intense pain and fever. She was lying on my doorstep when her husband showed her to me. I tried to explain to him that the government had sealed the dispensary and all our equipment, and that it was against the law to break the seal. But the husband just stood there wringing his hands, saying, "Jaco used to have a good spleen (the Waunana equivalent for heart), but now his spleen has gone bad. He will no longer help us even though I have helped him so much in the past."

I was torn. I finally went into the house, threw myself across a bed and wept bitterly. I harangued with God: "During the years when we had opportunity to witness to the Waunana, the mission made me build houses and build more houses. Now that we've learned the tribal language and are in a position to evangelize the people, the work is closed because of the new concordat." I was bitter against the mission. I guess I was even bitter against God who had permitted this situation to develop.

Suddenly I realized that an inner rage had taken hold of me. I got up and said to myself, "Come what may, (I actually used stronger language) I am going to open that dispensary." I strode into the village, went to the back door of the dispensary, broke the seal, unlocked the door and took out the forceps for pulling teeth. I also took sulfa powder, disinfectant and dressing. Then I came back to the house to attend to the Waunana woman's infected tooth. I pulled the tooth, cleaned out the pus, disinfected the wound, tamped it with sulfa powder and put in a cotton batting plug to make sure it didn't bleed any more. I gave the woman several injections of penicillin plus some oral antibiotics to take when she got home.

When I saw her some years later in Panama she was well. She said that after the wad of batting had come out, she had suffered no more pain and no infection. The wound had healed quickly.

Lessons I learned from the healing ministry

1. These among many other experiences showed me why Jesus healed both body and soul in his ministry on earth. When a person is in a physical or medical crisis, that need must be taken care of first; the spiritual need seems picayune in comparison at that moment. Jesus never asked desperately ill people whether or not they were right with God; he healed them first and took care of the God questions later.

2. I also learned our English vocabulary for salvation doesn't show much interest in the healing of the body. It suddenly jumped at me that the German word for "Savior" *Heiland* really means 'healer.' While it is a metaphor referring also to the healing of the soul, it certainly doesn't close the door to the healing of the body. It is very much in line with Jesus' attitude toward human beings in need.

3. Probably the most painful thing I learned was the tremendous prejudice toward tribal people worldwide. The most blatant example was the Waunana with the knife wound in his stomach. The doctor didn't think enough of the Indian to sew up his peritoneum and suture his stomach muscles, an unforgivable deed.

4. Some of what we did in Noanama seems foolhardy today. However we acted in faith and obedience to the Lord, under very primitive circumstances, and he blessed our efforts. In later years, I never would have dared to do what I did as a new missionary, nor was it necessary. In the 1990s, I guess there are really no more places like early Noanama left.

CHAPTER 23
MISSIONARIES AS POLICE

As new missionaries, we didn't recognize this problem for what it was. As we learned to know the Waunana, we soon realized the extent of their liquor problem. We were determined to help them overcome it. There was so much sugarcane in the region that the people were able to grind endless amounts of it, ferment the juice and make sugarcane wine. They were also able to distill this wine and make hard liquor. The only social gathering that we witnessed among them was the drinking festival, the *chupata*. Almost every weekend someone would arrange a drinking party on one river or another. Many people spent three and four days a week drinking. We became convinced that liquor was one of their major problems.

Once we finished building our house and could move into it, we established a no-drinking rule there. We had a screened porch on one side that was about ten feet wide and thirty feet long. We often took our evening meal there because by that time it usually was getting cooler. But gradually our Chocó friends began to ask for permission to sleep in that screened porch where they would be protected from the voracious Chocó mosquitos. So bit by bit, our porch became a guest room for tribal visitors. We said everyone was welcome to stay there, except when they were drunk. Drunks were not allowed to use the room.

I remember one Saturday night when our screened porch was again serving as the guest room. It must have been fairly full already when, at about 11:30 p.m. after we had been sleeping for some time, we heard a loud commotion. I awoke, my wife awoke and we both realized that the rumpus was being caused by a drunk Waunana stumbling in to find a place to sleep.

At first I was just going to ignore it and act as if I hadn't heard anything. But then my conscience took over. So I put on my trousers and went out to look for the drunk. The porch was chockablock with people. There must have been at least thirty people sleeping on the floor, one right next to the other. I couldn't identify the drunk, who by now was snoring along with the rest of them. So I had to go down the entire row and smell one after the other until I found him.

I shook him, but he refused to wake up. Finally I draped his one arm over my shoulder, put my other arm around his waist and literally dragged him out of the screened porch. As I was dragging him out of the yard, he awoke. I again explained to him, "Compadre (which is an intimate form of address, like brother), you know what the rule at our house is. You are welcome to sleep there as long as you are not drunk."

I took the man through the gate of our yard. I was afraid he was too drunk to get across the two poles that served as a bridge across a deep ravine, which was often water-filled. It led to the path that went to Noanama village. In what I thought was Christian charity, I dragged him across the bridge. Once we were safely to the other side, I deposited him on the road. He slumped into a drunken heap.

But no sooner had I dropped him than he began to cry pathetically and said, "Jaco always says that he is my friend. When I am sober and know what I am doing, I don't really need a friend that much. But when I am drunk and don't know what I am doing, that is when I desperately need the friend. But then Jaco chases me out of his yard!" The Waunana wept bitterly, as only a drunk can weep. At that moment I recognized my action for what it was—I was playing cop. I was not being a friend of sinners. I realized that when a man is drunk, he desperately needs a friend to prevent him from harming himself or somebody else. I have never again been able to march a drunk out of my yard.

Other police activities

I soon realized that my attitude toward drinking wasn't the only area in which I functioned as a policeman. As I said, when we wanted to build our house, we needed help. Since we couldn't find very many local people who knew about carpentry, Christians from our mission station upriver, which was older and better established, came down to Noanama to work for us. We had four or five men who stayed with us and prepared the lumber for building. But we still needed considerable unskilled help, and for that we employed local people.

Early on we realized that the morality of the negro village from which we did most of our hiring was not the highest. There was a lot of marital infidelity. I thus established a rule that employees who were caught in adultery would lose their jobs. It didn't take long for me to realize that I had opened an ugly can of worms. Now people began telling me that so and so did not sleep home last night, that he was together with such and such a woman, and could they have his job. Again I found myself trapped in the policeman's role. And I wasn't the only missionary caught in this situation.

A missionary policeman among the Lengua

When I was doing the research with the Lengua and Chulupi in Paraguay, I tried to establish a friendly relationship with the missionaries who worked among them. I tried to train the missionaries to gather the anthropological information that we needed. Many of them turned out to be excellent investigators. One man especially proved to be a natural anthropologist. As we worked together, he began to grasp the meaning of some of his earlier actions.

One day he confessed something from his earlier mission work. When he first had come to the station, he had found a number of native healers among the people who chanted to the spirits at night to heal the sick and ward off evil. So one of the first rules he had established was that nobody who engaged in healing by means of spirits would be allowed on the mission compound. Soon he was deluged by tribes people who came asking if he would help them get a new innermost from Jesus Christ. (This was the expression the Lengua used for conversion.) He had been delighted that his firm stand against witchcraft and sorcery was paying such rich dividends. Soon he had helped hundreds of Lengua to get new innermosts from Jesus Christ.

Gradually, however, he became suspicious that something was wrong. So he asked one of the Lengua men with whom he was relatively close, "How come so many people are coming to me wanting to get new innermosts from Jesus Christ?" The man was visibly embarrassed, but he finally said, "That is the only way that the people know how to protect themselves against those who are still chanting to spirits." The missionary inquired whether people were still chanting to the spirits. The man answered, "Yes, only now since you have established the rule, they sing softly." This missionary realized that the people had not been converted because they wanted Jesus Christ as Savior; they just wanted a different innermost so that evil spirits could no longer harm them.

Catholic missionaries as police

While working with the Chulupi Indians in Paraguay, I encountered one of the most tragic policing scenes I ever witnessed. A number of the local missionaries and I made a several-hundred-mile trek to the Pilcomayo River, the original home stomping ground of the Chulupi. There was a fairly large Roman Catholic mission located on the banks of the river. We visited an order of priests there. They were German, and we were able to converse with them in High German.

Since I was considered the distinguished visitor, I was lodged in the section that housed the priests. There was an empty room there which they assigned to me. The two Mennonite missionaries who accompanied me had to stay in the back where the visitors usually stayed. After we had been on the station for a little while, I noticed that each of the priests carried a giant key ring. "The people steal us blind and so we have to lock all doors behind us," they explained. And sure enough, when the priests took us on a tour of their work, we discovered that all gates, doors and windows had to be locked and unlocked as they showed us around.

Somehow word had gotten out who I was and a number of the tribal leaders tried to speak to me alone. Since we both spoke Spanish this was relatively easy to do. One day a number of the older men came to me and asked whether I would be willing to come out with them to look at something during the night. They said they would knock gently at my door about 10:30 in the evening after all the priests and nuns were asleep. Then I should slip out quietly, and they would take me to what they wanted me to see. At 10:30 the knock came, and they took me to a part of the mission compound I had not yet visited, but where I had seen a very large pen.

The priests had a crude sawmill. They sawed the outside slabs off all the logs before cutting the rest into lumber. These outside slabs, about fifteen feet long, had been used to build this giant pen. The men informed me that because of promiscuity, the priests locked all the unattached women in the pen every night. Every girl beyond eight years old, every widow, and every other unattached woman was locked up there.

But, the priests had not been very wise. The crossbars holding the upright boards of the wall were on the inside. The girls could climb up the crossbars, come out over the top and then jump out of the pen to seek out their sex partners. I watched the spectacle for an hour or so as dozens of girls and women came out of the pen. Then the old tribal men said to me, "Do you see, we are like cattle. We are being penned up like animals." I then realized that I was witnessing the policing role in the nth degree! But I also realized that missionaries make very lousy policemen.

Protestant missionary police

While doing the dialect survey among all the Chocó dialects in Colombia, I also came to Panama to visit a number of missions who had some contact with the Chocó in that country. I got these people started on the language and gave them the dictionary and grammar file that I had built up in the weeks of my research.

One of the Pentecostal missions decided to send one of their missionaries, a faith healer, to the Chocó. This person went into the tribe on one of the rivers which had about 2,000 inhabitants living along it and in short order baptized most of them. They all had come forward in healing sessions and he had healed them. He had then baptized them as believers.

However, this missionary had been praying that God should "give" him the tribal language. When God didn't give him the language without any learning on his part, he moved on to another Latin American country and abandoned the Chocó work. His mission then sent in several negro church women to take over the tribal work, not understanding the implications that negroes had for the Chocó.

When we visited this mission station about a year after the first missionary had left the country, we found a large tribal village clustered tightly around the missionary residence. There was a dispensary, a school and a church. All the Chocó had abandoned their dwellings on the river and had moved into this tightly enclosed village, producing an enormous amount of disease and also tremendous promiscuity among the young people.

Among the Chocó, a young man who becomes sexually mature looks for a wife by visiting an area where there are eligible young women. When such a dressed-up young man comes to an isolated tribal house where there is an eligible girl, the parents know exactly why he is there. They will then decide whether to give the young man access. Once the boy has slept with a given girl, the two are considered in trial marriage and sexual contact with others is supposed to be avoided. However, with all the close contact which they now had at the mission and at school, the boys and girls were engaging in frequent trysts. The parents were unable to do much about such casual sex.

Furthermore, the woman missionary in charge did not allow the tribespeople to marry off the girls at the customary young age. When I talked with the parents, they said they felt would have to leave the gospel "because it was spoiling their young people." They were especially bothered by the tremendous increase in promiscuity. Determined to find out more, I sneaked to the school during school hours and listened outside the open window. The teacher, who could speak only Spanish, was unable to understand what the boys and girls were saying to each other in their tribal language. They were arranging meetings. The girl would say, "I have to go for firewood after school. I will meet you there and there."

Within six months of our visit, this whole Christian village broke up. Their entire group had been immunized against the gospel. They refused to have any further part in it.

The missionary and the Mounties

North American missionaries to the Indians have been caught in the same policing trap. During a conference of mission agencies working with aborigines in Canada, a missionary told us about a sad experience on his mission station. A girl had been raped by an older man, and the tribe was outraged. Eventually word of this rape reached the Mounties (Canadian police) who came to investigate. They went first to the missionary who told them what he knew and whom else they might talk to.

But the Mounties could find no one who would talk to them. Everyone feigned complete ignorance. The missionary was horrified that believers of long standing who had spoken to him in confidence about the offence now denied any knowledge of it.

I then had to enlighten the missionaries that the tribal people probably now saw the missionary in a policeman's role. Since the tribe was determined to keep the Mounties out of their reservations, they would not divulge any information to them. Furthermore I told them that probably the missionaries' own sources of information would have dried up for the future because the people had now definitely established them in the role of police informers.

Look under the bed

That missionaries make poor policemen was evidenced in the experience I had on one of the larger Latin American mission establishments where I had been asked to give a series of lectures. One lecture was about the roles missionaries tend to play on mission fields, among them the policing role. I said one problem I often found was that missionary wives got daughters of some of the believers to serve as kitchen help. These parents expect the missionaries to police the morals of these girls, but the missionaries often did not understand the tribal culture well enough to provide this type of protection. I told of some missionaries who had locked up their maid when they left home in the evening, but neglected to look under the bed first, and nine months later a baby arrived. When I said this, one of the women present gasped and said, "Why, we locked up our maid before we came to this meeting, but we didn't look under the bed." Sure enough, nine months to the day, another baby arrived!

The missionary as disciplinarian

One of the greatest tragedies I witnessed was a missionary who spanked the tribal believers' children. This tribe was very respectful of its children and felt that any type of parental coercion was wrong. Therefore they themselves would never spank their own children. But for the missionaries to do it was another matter. The parents wanted their children disciplined and convinced the missionary to handle any spanking chores that were deemed necessary. So every Saturday morning this missionary would hold court, the parents would furnish a list of their children's violations, and the missionary would accordingly spank the children for them. Fortunately, this was a unique occurrence. I have never witnessed or heard about anything like it anywhere else.

What the policeman's role taught me

I had to learn the hard way that legalisms like taking drunks out of the yard, or not permitting people caught in adultery to work for the mission, majors in externals. Very often the content of the message or the intent of the gospel is vitiated in the process. The people simply learn to hide the behavior which the missionary treats as negative.

When the Chocó church was first organized, it had only a Gospel of Mark. We told the Indians that there was much more information in the Bible, but we wouldn't give it to them until they had learned to obey what they found in Mark. When we shared this approach with the mission board, the latter were dismayed. One of the mission executives decided to visit the mission field to see what he could do to remedy this situation.

We arranged for him to meet with the indigenous church leaders. He asked the tribes people about their conversions and about the progress the church had made. The people told him joyously of some of their victories with the Lord. When he asked them about Christian behavior, he was told that those people who had it in their hearts were following the things they had learned. Those who didn't were still having difficulty, but they were being prayed for and counseled.

When he asked them about specific church rules, the leaders said, "No, we haven't taught that rule yet, because that is not in the Gospel of Mark. There are quite a few rules that we want the people to learn to obey in the Gospel of Mark first before we give them any more." When the mission executive continued to press this point, the Chocó finally said, "If you know how to make people obey something that is not in their heart, we want you to teach us how to do it. Our people are odd in that respect. We have never been able to make them do something if they do not have it in their hearts." Gradually the executive realized he should back off and leave the tribal church alone.

Another lesson I learned was that many missionaries are caught in unwanted roles. This chapter has focused on the policing role, but many missionaries who have opened a little store find themselves in the merchant's role. Others find themselves in the employer's role. Many of us have found ourselves caught in roles which we did not really want, and which did not really further the cause of the gospel—our real reason for being there.

CHAPTER 24

RECIPROCITY

One day the Chocó leader Aureliano was under a heavy cloud. The banana market had dried up. His pigs had died mysteriously. His oldest two sons were in trouble. When I came to visit his house, he asked me to buy a pound of salt, since there was no salt in his house, and he had no money to buy any.

I asked God what I might tell my friend about my own recent testings to cheer him up. The only answer I received was to share with him that I had just turned down a job with a Canadian university offering three times my salary at Tabor College, a seven-month school year and plenty of research money. Aureliano knew what I earned at the college. Now he didn't even have a nickel to buy a pound of salt. To talk of thousands of dollars seemed like rubbing salt into an already painful wound.

Furthermore, our children had been deeply unhappy about my decision. I wanted to go to Panama and that took the money we had earmarked for air conditioning. After seeing their unhappiness, I had borrowed money and installed the air conditioning before I left for Panama.

Finally I told Aureliano what God had asked me to tell him. I never finished my story, because he began telling me of his dilemma. He had an offer to be foreman on a giant building project, but it involved liquor. He did not know if he was strong enough to be in the presence of hard liquor and not get drunk again. Furthermore, it meant abandoning the church. When he turned the job down, his wife had been very angry and had said, "So you don't want us to have salt?" We cried together and rededicated ourselves to God.

When Aureliano later met David Wirsche, he slapped him on the back and said, "David, I'm a real Christian! Tiger and I have the same temptations!"

Suddenly a mission principle jumped at me: reciprocity! Such reciprocity must manifest itself in a number of ways: in the exchangeability of the participants' material facilities; in a willingness on the part of both to know and be known; in bidirectional communication; and in reciprocal recognition of and respect for each other's individual worth and status.

Identification between missionary and nationals is a complex issue. Many concerned overseas workers have wrestled long and hard with this question: "What is a realistic goal in the matter of identification? For what can I realistically strive?"

I believe that reciprocity can be a realistic and practically attainable goal in any foreigner-national relationship.

False identification

It has been adequately demonstrated by both Roman Catholic and Protestant missionaries alike that "going native," the attempt to identify through standard of living or kinds of dress, by no means guarantees inner identification. This kind of identification may actually be false and may even close the doors for a reciprocal relationship with nationals who "misunderstand"—or who may actually understand too well—that such behavior is feigned. E. A. Nida has verbalized the nationals' suspicion effectively: "If these Europeans know how to live better than we do, why don't they? We would if we could." On the other hand, remaining totally aloof from what the nationals eat, have or do is equally objectionable.

Exchangeability of material facilities

While visiting Latin America, I conversed with a missionary about whether he should accept the only bed when circumstances forced him to stay with a national family. This person felt that the missionary should be humble and polite enough not to take up a bed which would normally sleep all the family. Further probing convinced both of us that this professed politeness might really be only a rationalization. A more honest reason was that we often did not really want to become that intimate with the nationals. By being "polite" when we were in their homes, we missionaries were telling the nationals that they, too, should be equally "polite" when they came to visit our missionary residences.

This principle is documented effectively in a letter from Jane and Wendell Sprague who report how an African leader told missionaries that their so-called wealth—nice homes, clothes and appliances—was not the real problem to the Africans as long as the missionary's heart was right.

And when the heart is right, staying in the missionary's guest bedroom could be a very ego-building experience for nationals who have often wondered what it might be like to sleep in a soft bed. The important point, in my estimation, is that the national's home, whatever it be, and the missionary's guest room, however good or modest, should be exchangeable.

This matter of exchangeability of facilities has become a rather interesting outgrowth of the exchange visits by Aureliano Sabugara, the Chocó who visited America, and American short-term missionaries. This reciprocity began to develop during the summer of 1959 when the missionaries were testing the Empera literacy materials at Jaqué. Both the missionaries and the tribes people came to the home of missionary F. Glenn Prunty.

To give the teachers more control over the working day, it was decided that at least the noon meal should be eaten together. Thus every noon the missionary teachers and the tribal literacy students shared in a fellowship meal which consisted of both foreign and national food. While lunch was being prepared after the morning classes, both missionaries and Empera students would go out into the ocean, where the latter tried to teach the foreigners how to ride the surf. At first the missionaries' clumsy failures became a source of great amusement for the Empera. But as the missionaries gradually gained proficiency, the nationals actually cheered, happy that they had been able to teach something to their foreign instructors.

At the end of the school day, the teachers and students again took an hour off to play volleyball, a totally new experience for the Empera. The rules had to be modified for them, but gradually they learned to play a respectable game.

It was in this setting of cooperative play that Aureliano, during one rest period, inquired about the cost of the missionary's trip to Panama. When he heard the amount he asked, "Does it cost the same amount for a person from Panama to visit your country?" When the answer was affirmative, he said, "Well, since I have given God the hand and am walking on God's road, and don't drink anymore the way I used to, I can easily save that much money from my banana cuttings to come and visit you in the United States." And that is just what he did.

When Aureliano came to stay at the missionary's home in the U.S., he occupied the guest room and participated in all the activities of a North American family. Whenever he needed to go to town to make some purchases, we took him in the family car. When his laundry needed washing, Anne looked after it. He ate the food on our table with the rest of us, even though there were some things, like raw salads, which he did not like. All in all he was a fairly congenial guest.

His parting prayer—offered at the airport while waiting for the flight back to his family in Panama—was heartwarming. He asked God for the opportunity to have the missionary come to his house in Panama so that he and his wife could share their things in reciprocal fashion. And so in 1961, when the missionaries went to Panama for the next summer's program, they were really paying a return visit to the home of Aureliano.

Their reception at Aureliano's home was almost overwhelming. He helped string their hammocks, set up substitute worktables for them and saw to it that they had water in the house to wash and shave. While the missionaries pitched in by purchasing rice and some of the other "store" items, Aureliano assumed the burden of the provisions for the whole period of their visit. He told local visitors that the foreign guests in his home were just like tribes people who belonged to the family. It is reminiscent of Stanley Soltau's statement: "They eat our food with us, and we feel close to them."

It also parallels Bill Reyburn's experience that "to empty a pan of caterpillars" is more convincing identification than many pious words and kind deeds. Certainly the highest tribute for a missionary is to be accepted by nationals as their equal: "White man Kaka is eating caterpillars. He really has a 'black heart.' " (A free translation of a Kaka man's words about Reyburn.)

One afternoon the missionary went to the river to wash his nylon shirts. When Aureliano realized this, he protested excitedly, "When I was at your house, your wife washed my shirts, and so when you are in my house, my wife will wash your shirts!"

A similar scene took place when we tried to pay him for the use of the canoe we had borrowed. He said, "You never charged me for taking me around in your car when I was in your country, and certainly you can't expect me to charge you for my canoe when you are guests at my house!"

The willingness to know and be known

One of the first qualities that a new missionary needs is an endless willingness to learn. This quest must be motivated by a genuine concern to appreciate deeply a way of life that is very different from one's own. Gushing over "native things" as if they were quaint novelties will lead to psychological distance. No one wants to be taken lightly. The missionary will have to take both the nationals and the national way of life seriously, regardless of how strange or exotic their practices may seem.

A common substitute for genuine relationships is a smug paternalism in which the missionaries speak familiarly in terms of "our people," "our Christians" and "our Indians." Such a speaker is really building his own ego and views himself or his mission as the center and the national people as a "nice flock of dependent satellites."

A missionary in West Africa made it a regular practice during his itinerant evangelism to stop in a village for several days and inquire about the local beliefs in God, before trying to deliver his message. After having explained their way to him, the elders invariably asked him to explain his faith. The missionary did this not only to elicit curiosity; but he was convinced that to effectively tell the people about God he would first have to understand their way of thinking.

Earl Stevick provides a convincing example of the value of the "learner approach" in his account of entering a store in Central Africa to hear the people talk. The proprietor's wife greeted him with a subservient but aloof, "Yes, boss?" However, when Stevick mustered his best Shona to say, "I have come to stand here and to listen to the people talk, so that I can learn to speak Shona more correctly," the woman relaxed. She showed him to the best spot in the store, no longer as a "boss-foreigner," but as a friend.

Another facet for the missionary to consider is a willingness to also be known. This requires willingness to sacrifice our obsession for privacy. Our sense of privacy keeps us from asking questions like how many suits of clothes a person has. And because the nationals may not always respect this obsession, the missionary is inclined to lock his/her barrels[1] to assure at least some privacy.

In our society, it is not polite to ask about someone's income, but revealing this may be precisely the price we pay if we want to know and be known—if we want to establish a reciprocal relationship with individuals in the different culture in which we are trying to serve. As Eileen Lageer so aptly says, "In missionary work, at least in this part of the world, the gospel is always easy to give, but it is the *imparting of our souls that counts and hurts*." (Italics mine)

When Aureliano visited us in the United States he freely asked me about my income, how much rent I paid for my house, how much it cost to operate my car, and so on. I tried to be open and honest about all these things, including how much I spent in tithes.

When David Wirsche and I visited the Chocó church in 1961, it was rather surprising to hear Aureliano use the wages of the two North American visitors as his point of departure in a public appeal for national volunteers to witness to their people in other areas. He laid our finances bare, outlining our monthly payments for house, light, car, water (here he added parenthetically, "You see, Fox [Dave's nickname] and Tiger don't have a river by their house"). He concluded, "So you see they really don't have enough loose cash left over to come here. But when they do, they come here not for fun but because they want us, their friends, to learn more about God, so that we too can walk on God's road and do what God wants us to do." As a result of this testimony one of the Indians got up and said, "If Tiger and Fox (Imama and Kuriwa, the intimate nicknames of the two visiting missionaries in this tribe) are willing to make a sacrifice to come here to give God's message to us, I, too, am ready and willing to be a missionary for other people also." To our great joy this man not only volunteered but actually left the next morning to take the gospel message to an Empera settlement several hours downriver.

Paramessage

As E.A. Nida has pointed out, the structure of communication includes not only a source, message and receptor (SMR in his model), but also a more subtle ingredient, he calls the paramessage. The paramessage involves our inner attitudes—prejudices and values—which may substantiate, detract from, or even vitiate completely the message that is being audibly transmitted. In a meeting with psychiatrists, I was struck to hear them affirm that children, schizophrenics, and so-called primitive people have not lost their sensitivity toward the paramessage transmitted by others. They are able to read a paramessage, that is, the attitude of a person, much more readily than a normally acculturated adult who has learned to block out many of the more subtle cues.

Some years ago we observed a clear example of a paramessage which contradicted a spoken message. A North American missionary woman who had

---

[1]Because of the heavy rainfall we kept our things in steel drums with detachable lids.

contradicted a spoken message. A North American missionary woman who had great difficulty accepting national believers in the private sanctum of her residence, made extra efforts to invite them over for Sunday afternoon coffee. One day several of these nationals were visiting in our home and began talking about this woman. One of them said, "You know, we have never been able to enter that woman's home." I corrected the speaker, saying, "Surely you have been at her house a number of times! Why you had coffee there with us together last Sunday!" The national then responded, "Yes, we've been in her house, but she has never opened her home to us. That is closed for all of us nationals." In this case, even the very solicitous entertaining of the missionary could not block out the destructive and contradictory paramessage of her inner attitude.

Reciprocity in communication

If we look at this willingness to know and be known from the standpoint of communication, it becomes readily apparent that what we are trying to achieve is a fully bidirectional flow of communication. Under a paternalistic relationship, the communication is unidirectional, downward from the superior to an inferior. It is next to impossible for an inferior and a superior to maintain a reciprocal communication relationship.

Since the missionary task revolves around the intelligible communication of a message, feedback from the recipient becomes an indispensable indicator for the source as to how successfully his message is getting through. In our own culture, business firms frequently sample public opinion as a kind of social feedback to determine the community's reaction to their product. Sensitive missionaries, likewise, seek feedback from their recipients so they can adjust their communication until they are sure that it is being understood and is meeting the needs of the recipients.

The value of this kind of reciprocity was highlighted in an experience of David Wirsche in the summer of 1962. In teaching some arithmetic to the Empera he tried to explain the concept of zero. He had spent a number of hours on several different occasions trying to explain this elusive mathematical necessity before Aureliano finally grasped the concept. This happened just as they were called to lunch. When they were about to have their regular prayer before the meal, Aureliano called all the people to attention and said, "God has spoken this morning. He has told us what zero is." Then he proceeded in his prayer to thank God for the insight that had now come to his people.

After he had finished the prayer, he turned to Wirsche and said, "Now, Fox, if you ever want to explain this zero thing to other Chocó people, you ought to explain it like this. . . ." Here was a good example of reciprocity in communication. It shows how exchange can sharpen the missionary communicator's focus.

The missionary who wants to communicate good news to people of another culture will have to spend time—often many hours—listening to their concerns, fears and superstitions. At first this may seem a waste of time that would be better spent delivering the important message of the love of God. But once we recognize that effective communication and, in fact, all genuine witnessing is really genuine dialogue—we will realize the importance of the listening stage in establishing reciprocity with people of other cultures.

Such bidirectional communication also must take place between believers and unbelievers. A good example is seen in the account of the medicine man attending the communion service on whom Aureliano, the pastor, called for a word of advice. The medicine man's response was, "I have watched the proceedings of this day with real interest, and I am convinced that the Word you are teaching is of God. But you know that I do not belong. You know of my involvement with the evil spirits. I would like to get free from them, but I cannot." To this Aureliano responded, "Yes, we know your involvements, and we will pray for you that you find a way to be delivered from the evil spirits. For God's Spirit is stronger than all the evil spirits." And to everyone's joy, a year later this same medicine man belonged to the church.

The recognition of individual worth and status

Another fundamental lesson I had to learn in my relationship with tribal people was to respect their approach to reality and society as valid as my own. Maybe such mutuality could be extended even to our respective body odors. I remember how Aureliano, after eating only western food for a month, asked me one day whether it would take long for him to smell like a tribal person again once he got back to his people. "Now," he said, "I stink just like the rest of you Americans."

Aureliano's United States visit enlarged his concept of people. To witness this growth of his "people concept" was a most interesting experience for us. After an interracial prayer meeting which he had enjoyed very much, he confided, "I have been thinking. If we can pray together like this, then you and I are really more Empera (i.e., members of the same tribe) with each other than with our own people who do not walk on God's road." Just as Aureliano's concept of us had to grow until we changed from "white beings" to people, so our concept must grow to where we can accept people from all tribes, nations and races as equal members of the family of God.

Many of us who come to a preliterate society with our technological gadgetry for the first time are susceptible to the delusion that our way of life is superior. This ethnocentric feeling is bolstered if we add our greater financial resources, our broader educational experience, and our deeper awareness of history. There is danger that we develop a kind of "boss" or "great white father" image of ourselves. Such an image permits us to feel justified in demanding immediate attention by the native government officials, for example.

Stanley Soltau records a painful example of self-satisfied ethnocentrism in the report of his travel with another missionary couple. While traveling on a launch from the dock to a ship anchored in mid-river, they came upon a number of Chinese people sitting on a bench enjoying the river scenery. Much to Soltau's chagrin, the senior missionary preemptively ordered these people to move so that he could sit down. Such rudeness is only possible if one's self-image is grossly and ethnocentrically inflated.

Soltau also provides a positive reciprocal example in his account of the missionary who visited a notoriously anti-Christian Confucianist who was persecuting local Christians. The Confucianist invited the missionary to come in and sit on the ground. The missionary tried to get in a few words of greeting, but the host seemingly paid him no further attention. For one-and-a-half hours the missionary was completely ignored while the Confucianist scholar discoursed only with another visitor. When the missionary finally left, he felt like an utter failure. To his amazement, the native Christians came to him next day saying, "Last night you really made a friend. The Confucianist scholar is going all about the village, saying that you are one of the most humble and polite individuals he has ever seen, because he made you sit on the floor for a long time, and you did not become angry."

In preliterate folk societies, where the chiefs may have fewer external marks of status, it is important that we be the first to recognize those who bear tribal responsibility. It is very easy for the missionary to mistakenly pay high tribute to the culturally marginal or the social outcast who readily gives attention to the missionary, while neglecting to pay respect to the leader of the community who may have remained relatively aloof.

Quest for equal status

Tremendous concern was expressed by some Americans over the abuse of white women by Congolese after the independence of the Belgian Congo. I saw these cases as evidence of the Congolese search for validation of their new status as equals. White government officials on state visits had willingly accepted the African bed partners offered by the tribes people. Now that the Congolese had become first-class citizens in this world and the Congo a country in its own right, it was their turn. It seemed only natural to them to prove this status by taking liberties that white men were still failing to extend.

During our experience at Noanama, Colombia, we found that meal invitations were an excellent way to pay tribute to people's social status. The national people were well aware that we often enjoyed the company of other missionaries. They knew that at such times we put out the best china, the prettiest tablecloth and consumed quantities of choice food. Very often we and the visitors were embarrassed by the many tribal faces that pressed against the porch screen to watch. My wife and I decided to do something about it. We started to invite local villagers to similar banquets, including white, mestizo, negro, and Indian families. The only difference was that when the guests were not used to cutlery, the setting would include only spoons. We used the same china and similar menus for all the visitors.

During our later years in Cali, where we hosted many dozens of night guests, we often ran short of beds. This pushed us into an additional way to recognize status or equality. It involved paying additional tribute to the person whose position was the most precarious. We established our own "pecking order." If there was a shortage of beds, and it involved a missionary and a national, the missionary would sleep on the floor. If it involved a white and a negro, the negro would sleep on the bed. It came to a sort of climax during our last night in Colombia when so many nationals came to our home that all the beds (and much of the floor space) were taken. This meant that all our missionary co-workers who came to see us off had to sleep on the floor in the neighboring apartment.

One of the antecedents that led to the development of this pecking order is still a painful memory for my wife. A good friend, a negro, was looking for work in the city and regularly slept at our house. But then one morning another missionary arrived to claim her room and bed. Anne offered the negro a bed on the floor, but that night she did not return and never again asked us for night lodging.

William Reyburn makes the point that the African wants to be treated as a self-respecting person. He says, "He does not want to be the only first-class citizen, but he certainly wants to also be included in this category." We do well to recognize that the need on mission fields today is not for fathers who will be "paternalistic" in their attitudes towards the members of the younger churches but for brothers who will be willing to treat as equals those who also obey the gospel message.

At one point tension developed between Aureliano and another potential leader in the tribe. As a part of this struggle for power, Aureliano was accused of having made improper advances to a woman. This report also reached our ears, but since we were far away, there was little we could do at that moment. Then F. Glenn Prunty visited El Mamey and had occasion to discuss this matter with Aureliano. Together they made a tape recording on which Aureliano relayed a message to me in Hillsboro, Kansas. Aureliano reminded me of the time we sat together on a log on the shore of the Pacific Ocean and made a commitment to serve God regardless of what the cost might be. Suddenly the voice on the recording became louder as the speaker moved closer to the microphone. Then he said, "Tiger, did you mean what you said when we sat on that log and together pledged that we would be faithful to God? Well, I want you to know I meant it just as much as you did. People may accuse me of having done things. . . . I know that I made a mistake in walking together with those women, but I know too that I did not make the approach they speak of. If you want to believe their accusation, you can go ahead and believe it. But I want to tell you as man to man that I am still just as serious in my commitment to God as you were when we sat on the log together."

Such mutuality is highly desirable. Moreover, without it many a national Christian will be seriously hurt. Oscar Lewis' account of Pedro Martinez's conversion and subsequent backsliding as a result of the discrimination and the rejection he experienced in the evangelical community is certainly a pointed warning. One of the most prevalent manifestations of inequality that I have observed in Latin American mission fields is the hesitance to turn over to nationals the authority to baptize and to administer communion—both highly essential attributes of a truly indigenous church.

CHAPTER 25

DRIVERS OR SPARE TIRES?

Bernard Joinet, a French Catholic missionary in Tanzania, has written about his training and early missionfield experiences. The following "personal testimony" has been abbreviated from his longer account:

> I grew up in the church and was trained exclusively in church schools. When I volunteered for foreign service, the church gave me the special training it thought this task required. Looking back on it after years of service in Tanzania, I have to confess that my church experience and my missionary training led me to visualize the mission enterprise as a bus—a large church bus—for which I was being trained to be the leader and bus driver.
>
> When I arrived on the field, however, I found, much to my chagrin, that the indigenous church had plenty of able people who knew how to drive the bus. In fact, the scores of potential drivers were jostling among themselves to get a chance at the wheel. Instead of welcoming me with open arms as a much needed driver, they let me feel in no uncertain terms that they viewed me as a foreign intruder. In utter unbelief and dismay, I retreated into the farthest corner of the mission bus, only to further realize that as a passenger I was taking up space badly needed by local people.
>
> The bus made a trip into the "bush" to do village evangelism. When we were almost at our destination, nearly two hundred kilometers from the nearest service station, the bus blew a tire, and our trip came to an abrupt halt—our bus had no spare tire. Then and there I discovered my niche: The national church here needed a spare tire and I was willing to be one.

This account can be seen as a parable about mission service in general. To personalize it further I propose a slightly modified ending: "—the mission bus had no spare wheel and only four badly worn tires. It desperately needed a person who could endlessly patch the tubes and mend the almost threadbare tires, and I was willing to do that."

From this parable I now propose to extract several insights about the missionary enterprise. Some relate to the sending church; others to the persons being sent to serve overseas.

In regard to the sending church:

(a) The church often has erroneous conceptions about the mission task.

(b) It prepares its candidates for leadership roles which often are totally alien to the indigenous church's needs.

(c) The sending church sees its helping and serving role as a one-way street.

(d) Finally, the home church loads a whole series of unrealistic expectations on the messengers it sends.

In regard to the candidates for overseas service:

(a) In order to be useful on the field, the individual workers will need sensitivity to discover their specific "mender-of-tires" role which the indigenous church needs.

(b) They will need an extra dose of grace and courage to fulfill that role, especially when it goes against the grain of the sending church's expectations.

The sending church has erroneous conceptions of the mission task

Most churches and mission societies see their task as reproducing themselves in the Third World. Rather than merely planting the gospel "seed" and then letting it develop indigenously, they seek to replicate themselves as closely as possible. Furthermore, they are convinced that they and their emissaries are completely free of any "colonial" attitudes toward the Third World and that western paternalism, "the blight of previous eras," is extinct in their case. The sad fact, however, is that like many "bugs" and "germs," Western ethnocentric attitudes have merely undergone mutations which have made them immune to most anti-colonial pesticides.

Third World observers also have pointed out that the Western church is not merely wealthy, it often is a prisoner of its wealthy members who feel that "having paid the piper, they now have the God-given right to call the tune." The critics who make these observations may be on to something. After all, successful business entrepreneurs often tend to be very evangelistic about their methods. So why shouldn't financially successful church members push the same "tried and true capitalistic success models" on the overseas mission enterprise that they have succeeded in pushing on home churches?

The Western church, with its resources, has the capacity to provide not only all the necessary trained personnel but also all the operating money necessary to do the job. It also feels confident it has all the necessary know-how. The prevailing attitude sounds very much like: "How rich I am! And how well I have done! I have everything I want" (Rev. 3:17 NEB).

No one can dispute that many churches are very mission-minded, but I doubt whether they or the workers they send recognize the extent to which they are like the medieval Roman Catholic evangelizers who went abroad in the same ships as the Spanish and Portuguese conquistadors. Western overseas workers today, Protestant and Catholic alike, often are cogs in the same multinational capitalist machines which are exploiting the masses of the so-called underdeveloped world.

The we-have-what-it-takes attitude invariably results in the paternalistic approach we mentioned earlier, though nowadays we prefer labels like "helping" or "being fraternal." Fraternalism may sound better from our side, but on the receiving end, big-brotherism can be just as uncomfortable as the earlier suffocating paternalism.

Church-sponsored training programs often prepare cross-cultural workers for inoperative roles

Because the sending organizations are satisfied that they have learned how to do God's work, they prepare emissaries for the functions they feel are needed abroad. For example, the workers are trained in what the Western church holds to be the full and true gospel, which, by definition, missionfield inhabitants desperately need. This automatically pushes missionaries into the role of teachers or leaders, and their converts automatically become their disciples. Teachers control, disciples follow. But is this what the mission task today really calls for?

Trevor D. Verryn has challenged the current approach to mission. He says that most missionaries, by their very training, now tend to see themselves in the model or example role. As such they not only know *the* truth but also know how this truth is to be expressed in life. In short, they know *all* the answers. Their model role tends to express itself in specific relationships such as father/son, teacher/student and artisan/apprentice.

Verryn challenges the missionary-as-model approach and points out that if we truly want to follow Jesus' example in cross-cultural communication, we must step into the victim role. A missionary-as-victim means total vulnerability—anybody can reject the messenger and his message with impunity, without fear of sanction. Verryn feels that the average missionary message carries at least an implicit, if not explicit, threat. Should the hearers refuse to accept it or submit to it, the missionary may pull out the home church's resources and then divine punishment will fall upon the rejecting populace.

When I read Verryn's analysis, I found myself on a "guilt trip" over my own early mission experience in Colombia. Some people will recall how Protestant missionaries were harassed and persecuted during the latter forties and fifties in that country. But through it all, we did not act like victims, we fought back like insulted models. We went to courts, we appealed to the police and army, and we involved foreign embassies. We may have been victimized, but we certainly weren't in the victim role. True victims pray for their persecutors rather than search for a "bigger stick."

It also seems that missionary attitude preparation leaves a lot to be desired in regard to adult-to-adult relationships with Third World churches. As one Third World leader facetiously said: "Our overseas brothers are bent on helping us to the point of being willing to make our mistakes for us." Only when Third World people are free to make their own mistakes without recrimination from older churches can we speak of having arrived at a truly adult-to-adult relationship.

We faced such a test right after the Chocó church had been organized. We had promised the church that we would help, whatever their need. When we asked them what they thought their most urgent and immediate need was, their unanimous answer was: "We need education, especially for our children." When we asked how they visualized meeting that need, they said, "We think we should select two bright children and send then to a good boarding school in Panama City."

We groaned inwardly. Even though they picked an excellent school, we did not think their approach was wise. But if they were to be equal, they were entitled to make their own decisions—even wrong ones. We agreed to try and make a go of it. Thus David and I pledged to match every dollar the church would invest in the project. (In the end David and I <u>each</u> had to shell out a dollar for every dollar the church raised.)

Two children were selected. We helped make the necessary arrangements. The joint project was launched. It failed! The children were so lonesome that they dropped out of school and returned home in less then two months.

When David and I returned next summer, we found the church despondent—maybe they would have to remain "stupid" after all! David and I commiserated with them, but then cheerfully said, "This isn't the end of the world! There are lots of alternatives to consider! Maybe we picked the wrong children. Maybe we picked the wrong school. Maybe we needed to get a missionary teacher. Maybe we needed to get the government to open a local school. Maybe we should train an adult from the tribe to become the local teacher."

Now we asked the church to explore each of these avenues farther down the road. They immediately rejected the children's alternative because the twelve years it would take to become a teacher were too long. Besides, who knew whether such a child would still want to come back to the tribe after such a long absence.

A missionary teacher? The church thought that such people were too bossy.

A government school? Only a negro who couldn't get a job in the city would come to the jungle. That would mean an inferior teacher and besides, they ethnocentrically said, who wants a "black devil" to teach their own children?

An adult tribes person? If it would only take a year. . . . Then the elders would remain in charge. . . . They could educate all their children. . . . They chose the latter alternative, and it turned out to be a godsend!

(Here an explanation is required. Panama at the time had several grades of teachers. The lowest had finished only elementary school, but they could teach grades one to three. An adult could complete this elementary education in a special two-year program. David then set out to teach three adults all the basic concepts covered in elementary school. That fall one of these persons was sent to Panama City. He spent only two weeks in grades one and two, two more weeks in grades three and four, and graduated at the top of the class in one year. He became a hero on national TV and was named as teacher to the local school at government salary.)

The tribe had made its own mistake! They recovered from the failure with some help from their North American brothers. They were equals!

The sending church still views the relationship as a one-way street

The typical Western attitude is that "God has blessed us with a knowledge of the truth and with the means to share it with others." In this confidence, the churches and their workers have a clear conception of what they have to give, but they have no equivalent conception of what they are to receive in a truly reciprocal relationship with their so-called mission field.

In recent decades Third World churches have challenged this one-way-street attitude. At the Whidby conference (1947), for example, the sending societies accepted that from then on mission was to be a "partnership in obedience." However, soon thereafter an Indonesian churchman complained: "Yes, it's partnership for the West and obedience for us."

At the Uppsala conference (1968) the slogan became, "let's practice multilateral (reciprocal) relationships." The result was a flurry of professorship and pulpit exchanges between older and younger churches and their seminaries. But was this really reciprocity? Or was it merely an illusion of reciprocity?

Then the key word became "complimentarity," but what are true reciprocity and true complimentarity? Perhaps we can illustrate the fallacy of the earlier exchange program with an example from the commercial world. Is the true goal of trading partners to exchange identical products? Of course not! In an ideal trading relationship each partner gives something that can be spared, and in exchange gets something that is wanted or needed. As we have said, the sending churches have a clear vision of what they have to give—the message of salvation, training, health ministries, help in technology, social development, training for leadership, etc. But what is it that the sending churches expect to receive in exchange?

Do younger churches have something to offer which older churches really need? Martin Kähler said that "mission is the mother of theology." With this he wanted to say that the sending church, by virtue of its age, is in danger of becoming too bound in its own culture. Younger churches in totally different cultural contexts thereby can offer the sending churches the possibility of a meaningful cross-cultural encounter in which to test the validity of Western theological models. Younger churches can be cultural mirrors to older churches.

To my mind, the areas in which Third World churches have much to say to Western theology are the following:

*Latin American Christians are challenging older churches with the development of liberation theology and the establishment of base communities for the poor.

*African Independent churches are challenging Western Christianity's theological otherworldliness by making a genuine effort to help their parishioners in all of life in the here and now, not only in the hereafter.

*South East Asian churches, by critically looking at their own culture and society in the light of the Scriptures and then identifying their idolatry (Koyama 1984), are challenging their Western brothers and sisters to do the same.

The history of the early church in Jerusalem shows the tragedy of not using cross-cultural mirrors. This was the mother church of the entire New Testament era. However, if we follow the development of that church through history, we see that the line of continuity to us is not really via Jerusalem, but via the Gentile churches. The Jerusalem church became fixated on the idea of the immediate return of Christ. As a result it fully mortgaged its future in what now seems like an unwise pattern of communally eating up all its assets. Furthermore, it persisted in its largely Jews-only attitude, and thus became a mere eddy, bypassed by the mainstream of the church which continued to flow and to grow among the Gentiles. Had the Jerusalem church continued the theological dialogue with the Gentiles which it began in Acts 15, its history might have turned out very differently.

In a sense the contrast between Peter and Paul illustrates the point. Peter had some cross-cultural encounters, but then lapsed back into the "comfort" of his Jewish cultural background. On the other hand, Paul, who was an even more fanatic upholder of Jewish culture before he encountered the Christ on the Damascus road, underwent a dramatic transformation in theological outlook. It was he who shared the gospel in Gentile settings.

The church imposes problem expectations on the personnel it sends

Several secular analysts suggest that one of the darker, unspoken reasons for sending missionaries is to help the affluent church "atone" for its luxury. Others have cast it in terms of comfortable home-church members needing someone "to suffer vicariously on their behalf."

In my judgment, by far the most difficult expectations missionaries have to face is reporting on their work both via prayer letters and deputation visits. One scene referred to earlier, is etched indelibly into my psyche. It took place in South America during an encounter between missionaries and nationals in 1965. One of the nationals accused the missionaries of making their living on their country's filth saying: "We are the manure by means of which missionaries raise their money." Here was a student who, while on a scholarship in North America, had had the occasion to read numerous missionary prayer letters from his home region. Well-meaning but ethnocentrically blind North Americans had given him copies of the letters sent home by their missionaries. These letters gaudily described degradation and filth of which the nationals themselves were ashamed. At this meeting, missionary after missionary finally confessed how they, too, had succumbed to the temptation to make overseas sin blacker so that the salvation message might shine all the more brightly.

Over the years I have frequently wept with missionaries who, while on deputation, had again sensationalized both the evil on the field and the victories of the gospel. "But if we don't do it, our funds dry up," was the invariable excuse.

A second problem expectation has to do with the "piper who calls the tune." With the sending church providing the funds both for the missionary and for a large part of the national church's operation, the missionary is often expected to ensure that money is spent wisely. Before long the missionary is cast as employer or, worse, in a policing role.

The missionary as fixer-of-worn-out-tires

During the forty years I have been abroad, my faith in missionaries has been strengthened by numerous overseas workers who had the courage to become fixers-of-tires.

Before Mozambique achieved its independence from Portugal, I made acquaintance with a small order of nuns who promoted literacy and distributed Christian literature in that country. Against the orders of the state church authorities and their own superiors, they had identified fully with the Africans seeking independence.

When independence finally did come, the nuns were not welcomed as heroes but were "invited" to step into the victim role. They now had to sell large quantities of Marxist literature in order to keep their bookstore open, but they assured me that as long as they could sell *some* Christian literature, they were willing to sell as much other literature as necessary to keep operating. But finally the government closed their bookstore anyway.

On a subsequent visit I met a sister of the order who told me she had defied the orders of her superior and had joined a commune organized by the government. She was in charge of the laundry. She hoped she would be able to teach people to read and maybe in the process also share something of her Christian faith. But for the time being, she said, she was perfectly happy to do the laundry because the people had few clothes and careful cleaning would make them last longer. A genuine fixer of worn-out tires!

Strength to go against the sending church's expectations

The number of missionaries who, like sister Maria above, are willing to risk going against the expectations of the sending body are few and far between. I suspect that if the Apostle Paul had been under an organized denomination or a mission board, he probably would not have been able to remain a member and do what he did.

David Bosch asked returning mission workers: did you return from your cross-cultural experience intact? Bosch implies that if cross-cultural workers achieve meaningful encounters with the new culture in which they serve, they will undergo value change. If they come home totally intact and can fit easily back into the home community, they probably have learned very little that is worthwhile. Bosch's question brought something into focus for Anne and me. When on retirement we returned to our home community to stay, we suddenly realized how poorly we fit into the home church setting. There seemed to be so little relationship between our concerns and those of the home church that had originally produced and sent us.

Writing this book has brought still another truth into focus: if I insist that mission is a two-way street and that I as a missionary am responsible for developing an empathetic understanding for the culture and worldview of the target audience overseas, then I also have the same responsibility towards the people in my original home community. On return I am under obligation to share with them the cultural enrichment with which Third World brothers and sisters have blessed me. But I have to do it with the same degree of respect for the people at home that I insist is necessary for the people abroad. I have to be prepared that my message will be rejected, and my concerns totally ignored.

CHAPTER 26
THREE MODELS OF MISSION

Early in my overseas career, E.A. Nida gave me the following counsel: "Jake, if you want to keep on learning and growing, always keep one eye—a critical eye—on yourself in all you do. Then eliminate what is flawed and reinforce what is helpful." In a sense this book represents a personal testimony of self-observation and learning. In the course of my overseas work, I have gone through three distinct approaches in missions.

I began my Christian witness as an ardent nondenominational soul-winner who consistently and consciously tried to hide his German Mennonite background. Next, I spent a decade-plus as a self-replicating church planter. Then followed some thirty years of learning what it means to operate as a catalyst who is striving to improve his hearing of, and his obedience to, directives from God's Spirit. As I look back, I can testify that God added individuals to his family in all of the approaches mentioned; in fact, he even used some of my major blunders to do so.

For this reason, I do not consider any of the strategies I am evaluating as errors, but rather as stepping-stones to better discharge our God-given responsibility in worldwide witness. For example, many of us have gone to university. Our experience there was utterly different from elementary school or even high school. But the earlier two school systems were not mistakes—they were essential preparation for the university experience. Nor do I consider the catalyst strategy final; it, too, is probably just another milepost in our growing obedience to God.

In trying to cover the wide panorama of mission strategies within the parameters of only three basic thrusts, it becomes necessary to lump together approaches that have distinguishable differences. Nevertheless, I hope I have been able to identify the core of each approach so that we can evaluate it in the light of Scripture, anthropology, communications and the needs of the multitudes who still need to know the message of Jesus Christ.

"Soul-winning"

This rubric includes more than just a single homogeneous approach, but I think it is correct that all the approaches discussed in this category are based on one central thrust—"to produce personal decisions for Christ."

Short-term witnessers

First in this category are the short-term witnessing approaches sponsored by various church or parachurch organizations. The sending agencies usually provide a short period of training for young people who volunteer to go to other cultures "to witness for Christ." It lasts for a period of weeks or months, usually less than a year. Much of the training involves building up enthusiasm for the task. Next there is instruction in a variety of "instant" witnessing techniques. These are usually based on some form of "canned" message like the *Four Spiritual Laws,* which are designed to quickly and systematically produce a "decision for Christ."

"Graduates" from such training programs are then sent individually or in teams to overseas destinations, usually cosmopolitan cities. There they seek out potential prospects with whom they hope to communicate. Occasionally the trainees engage in short programs to learn the local language, but seldom do they achieve sufficient fluency for effective, intimate communication. Most North American short-term witnessers expect to communicate by means of English, their own home language, because they say "so many young people all over the world have learned or are learning English and really love to practice it." Such witnessers, limited as they are to their own language, often overlook the fact that the persons to whom they witness in overseas situations seldom have more than an elementary grasp of the language being used to convert them. Since the training of such witnessers is short-term and largely "spiritual," there is little emphasis on recognizing the limitations their "home" culture imposes upon their faith. They are unaware of the many cultural presuppositions underlying both their faith and the cliches they use to express it. Their training seldom or never includes instruction in the values, worldview, and thought patterns of the people they are trying to reach.

Such short-term witnessers usually are fully convinced that they are communicating nothing but the truth. They approach the biblical message as a-cultural and, by the same token, view their message as free of the trappings of culture and language and thus applicable to any person anywhere.

They usually assume that "a decision for Christ" or a "conversion experience" will axiomatically change the new converts' values and lifestyle and that converts will instantly inherit a full-fledged model of what it means to live a Christian life. This approach sees little need for an indigenous social context or a "fellowship of believers" within which new converts will receive help to "grow in grace," or in which they can learn to obey the broader scope of dictates found in God's Word.

New converts in a different culture may require extensive resocializing in order to master biblical patterns of Christian behavior. In fact, short-term witnessers usually don't realize that before isolated converts can be resocialized as Christians, there must already exist a fairly well-defined model of what a "converted" life in that cultural setting entails.

Short-term witnessers, more often than not, operate outside of any local church context which could provide the setting for fellowship, Christian role rehearsal and continued growth in faith. Where they do operate within a church context, their witness will, of course, be of much more lasting value.

If any attempt is made to help new converts "grow in grace" it usually involves a short-term one-on-one relationship with the witnessers who "led them to Christ." Such resocialization typically is limited to teaching the converts how to pray and how to study the Bible devotionally.

Short-term witnessers tend to be unaware that one can make a premature "decision for Christ" without fully comprehending its long-term implications. Premature decisions can "immunize" against a genuine conversion. Even sincere converts who are left to their own resources without an adequate context for further growth can become disillusioned, backslide and end up "gospel-shy."

The greatest value of short-term witnessing is to the witnessers themselves. The more sensitive among them will recognize at least some of the complexity of meaningful cross-cultural witnessing. Moreover, it permits those interested in mission to make a much more intelligent assessment of whether or not God has called them to the missionary task.

Government contract missions

A second variety of the soul-winning approach includes Christian groups who work under contracts with governments or governmental agencies. Such contracts usually preclude any involvement in the growth of local churches. Certain agricultural or development-oriented groups or highly-focused mission groups like Summer Institute of Linguistics/Wycliffe Bible Translators, are examples of this subtype. If such groups work in tribes or situations where there is no existing church or where no other mission organization is working to establish a Christian church, their efforts may unintentionally immunize converts against Christianity.

In one such tribe there were no active believers left by the time the published New Testament in the tribal language arrived on the field. The mission which subsequently undertook to develop a church there found that the tribe as a whole had been thoroughly case-hardened against the gospel—"they had tried it and had found that it didn't work."

Faith missions (pseudo-denominational missions)

A third soul-winning variety involves many of the so-called "faith missions," which also seek primarily to produce individual decisions for Christ. Like the first group, they view the biblical gospel as largely culture-free, but in contrast they often view the tribal culture, especially tribal religion, as being "of the devil" and thus to be destroyed.

Unlike the earlier groups, faith missionaries usually do establish local fellowships or even churches, and in this respect their work is much more wholesome. However, as members of inter- or non-denominational faith missions, they usually come from a wide variety of church backgrounds and tend to establish fellowships resembling those of their own home experience. Even where such missions establish a common network of churches, these new churches have no overseas counterparts to whom they can relate for cross-cultural fellowship and as a source of help in times of need. Hence the sub-title "pseudo-denominational."

I remember one faith mission in which believers were strictly forbidden to attend even the church services on other mission stations of the same mission. When, as part of a translator-training program, I once took some believers from that church with me to another church of the same mission, I was severely reprimanded by the missionary founders of the first group.

Yes, these faith missions do establish churches. At worst they each develop their own individual "denomination," and at best they form a single *new* denomination for the entire mission. Thus what functions as an inter-church faith mission at home becomes a separate new denomination (or denominations) on the missionfield, thus magnifying the problem of Christian pluralism.

"Faith mission" missionaries (like many denominational missionaries) often view the believers they win to the Lord as their personal "spiritual offspring," and thus feel responsible to determine every detail of their doctrine and practice within the new church. Even where all the missionaries of a mission develop a single new denomination, they frequently try to prevent these believers from fellowshiping beyond their own group. Since Bible Society translation projects nowadays usually are inter-church efforts, this often creates serious difficulties for those who want to participate in such cooperative ventures.

Training of national leadership is another problem. Since faith missions lack an older established mother church with educational institutions and since the missionaries themselves often lack advanced studies, they tend to be somewhat education-shy. This deficiency is passed on to the national leaders. With limited opportunities for training and growth, they find it difficult to develop truly autonomous indigenous churches with a meaningful biblical theology and methodology that will equip them to cope with the problems of culture change which conversion to Christianity usually produces.

Self-replicating strategies (denominational missions)

This approach is characteristic of denominational churches who develop overseas mission programs. This includes Mennonites (in all their sub-groups), Baptists (in their infinite variety), Lutherans (in their various orthodoxies) and others who have particular doctrines and practices. Here the denomination trains some of its own members to replicate their home church in overseas cultures. Like the earlier mentioned "faith missions," denominations sometimes see themselves as the sole or at least the best example of a people following God's truth. Thus getting someone to accept their "truth package" (which usually includes large segments of the home-culture wrapper) is seen as the God-ordained task of the mission effort.

The self-replicating strategy also accepts soul-winning as primary but sees "accepting Christ" as becoming what the missionary is—a Mennonite, Presbyterian, Baptist, etc. Because the denominational package contains imported elements along with the biblical gospel, its missionaries have the formidable task of teaching new converts both an extensive doctrinal package and a large body of practices characteristic of the sending church. Such missionaries often present not only the "rightness" of their denominational views, but also often stress the "wrongness" of other denominational views. This makes the indoctrination process a very long one. And since missionaries are the only knowledgeable teachers of these models, they are usually forced into key roles in the new church to keep it functioning properly, especially in such areas as democratic elections, Western styles of dispensing justice, and church discipline.

Even a new church that has been declared "indigenous" usually still depends heavily on foreign input such as personnel, money, or Western-trained nationals who have learned the denomination's subculture.

On the plus side, the self-replicating/church planting strategy provides young churches with a supportive network of churches. Usually they also receive help to develop training institutions for local leadership on the field, and more qualified individuals also receive further training abroad. This often makes the local leadership more culturally aware and thus better equipped to develop contextualized Christianity.

During the colonial era the sword often was a powerful instrument to self-replicating evangelistic efforts. Today we have subtler forms of coercion such as baited hooks. The term "rice Christian" is just one example of converts gained by providing material benefits, education, or medical services. The soul-winning approaches described earlier normally avoided social programs beyond medicine and education because they were seen as "social gospel" and thus not part of the Great Commission. They do, however, stoop to psychological coercion, as when preachers threaten eternal hellfire during evangelistic campaigns.

In recent years there has been a growing acceptance of whole-person concerns, but as late as Lausanne (1975) the majority of faith and denominational missions still feared becoming contaminated by the so-called social gospel.

Recent church growth emphasis represents a great improvement on the basic self-replicating strategy, with greater stress on indigeneity, contextualization and whole-person involvement. However, if our North American church scene illustrates the ultimate church growth product, then we may be in for serious disappointment. Some of our fastest-growing Mennonite Brethren churches in North America now require so great a share of their resources for congregational use that both home and foreign missions, schools and seminaries, in fact, all broader outreach efforts, are in danger of being choked off.

Despite these shortcomings, both the soul-winning and self-replicating strategies have valid features: sinners must be born again, Christians must witness, new churches must be established, and established churches must send out missionaries.

The catalyst strategy

Unlike the earlier two strategies which have always assumed that the non-Christian world is "without God," a first premise of the catalyst strategy is that God and his Spirit do not show up on the mission scene when the missionary arrives. God is seen as always having been there, and his Spirit has been working there long before the first missionary arrived.

Instead of focusing exclusively on human depravity, a second premise of this strategy is that there exists "that of God" in every person and in every culture. All people everywhere were created by God in his own image, and though marred by sin, "that of God" in persons makes them redeemable, and "that of God" in culture makes it useful for building the church of Jesus Christ in their home milieu. Christian mission thus is seen as the process of developing "that of God" in individuals and in societies as a whole.

In agreement with the other two strategies, this approach sees all persons as having "that of sin" within them. For this reason, conversion is stressed. Conversion is seen as a person's conscious choice to shake off the bondage of "that of sin" and to embark on a road to develop "that of God" in his/her life. Such spiritual development, often called "growth in grace" or "sanctification" in Western church jargon, is a lifelong process. There may be dramatic crisis points when a person achieves some major breakthrough, but there also can be significant setbacks when "that of sin" gains the upper hand for periods of time. The catalyst strategy seeks to constantly address "that of God" in others, both Christian and non-Christian, to encourage them to hear and obey the voice of God's Spirit.

The catalyst strategy further expects "that of God" in the new converts' culture to enable them to depend on their own cultural mechanisms to develop truly indigenous churches which in turn will provide the resocializing and growth context for the believer's ongoing development. Thus new converts don't need to learn the operating procedures of the missionary's home church, such as how to conduct church elections, how to lead meetings according to *Robert's Rules of Order*, or how to practice church discipline, because these elements will all be supplied by the local culture.

Since culture, too, has "that of sin" in it, this approach looks to the new church to address both "that of God" and "that of sin" in the culture so the social context can be an instrument to build God's kingdom. It is in this exercise that much of the contextualization takes place.

This approach expects that the gospel will be "good news" to every recipient. In other words, the gospel will be proclaimed in a way that relates to the felt needs of persons and cultures. It need not necessarily be presented within the theological framework developed by the missionary's home church.

This assertion assumes that a people's culture embraces all of their life and that a truly functional religion, like most traditional religions, must therefore be operative in all spheres of life. It recognizes the importance of personal salvation and preparation for the hereafter, but not at the expense of a life of faith here and now. It constantly operates with a truly whole-person, all-of-life perspective.

Thus, the ideal function of a missionary is that of a catalyst. The missionary catalyst helps create an environment in which individuals and groups decide to take steps in obedience to God's design, but as soon as the action/reaction begins, the missionary becomes obsolete. In other words, foreign missionaries have only a "passing" role to play in the witnessee's personal life and in the life of the indigenous church.

New Testament catalysts

We have some powerful examples of catalysts at work in the New Testament itself:

Philip needed to help the Ethiopian eunuch understand only one Old Testament passage of Scripture, and as soon as the eunuch responded to that message, the Spirit of God "whisked" Philip away (Acts 8). (Someone pointed out that this account could also be seen as an example of the first soul-winning strategy, were it not for the fact that this catalytic event gave birth to the church in Ethiopia.)

Jesus and the Samaritan woman needed only a few minutes of talking together before "that of God" in the woman responded. Furthermore, the larger Samaritan community which responded to the woman's appeal needed Jesus' input for only a few days (John 4). Later this Samaritan community needed Philip, the evangelist, for a short period, and still later, it needed Peter and John's input for an additional couple of days (Acts 8).

Paul's evangelism, likewise, was of this type. His longest stay seems to have been two years at Ephesus (Acts 19:20) and in Rome where he was a prisoner for a couple of years (Acts 28:30-31).

Where is the catalytic approach most needed today?

This strategy is needed especially where group response is the customary way to react to new ideas. Since most of the Two Thirds World still operates by consensus at the family, clan, or even tribal level, a group response to the Christian message will be the most likely there. Such an approach will also be most likely to produce viable indigenous Christian churches because the local social context is enlisted from the very beginning. In the Mennonite Brethren experience, the church among the Chocó in Panama exemplifies this.

It is instructive to note that the Chocó church joined the Mennonite Brethren family of churches and the world Mennonite community only after it had developed the maturity to make that decision consciously and on its own. Today it probably is more faithful to cardinal Anabaptist/Mennonite beliefs[1] than many

---

[1]Traditional Anabaptist/Mennonite beliefs include: daily Christian discipleship that goes beyond mere inner experience and acceptance of Christian doctrines; limitless love, including love of enemy and avoidance of violence and coercion; and a view of the church as a "community of the redeemed" that practices sharing and mutual aid.

North American Mennonite Brethren churches.

The many independent indigenous movements springing up on the periphery of Christian missions and Christian churches in the Two Thirds World constitute the second area needing this approach. If David Barrett's statistics are correct, seven out of ten Christian conversions in Africa today are within the African Independent Church movement. Furthermore, he says we now have tens of thousands of such indigenous religious movements in Africa alone, many of which desperately need and openly welcome the help of catalysts.

One Mennonite missionary (OM) in Ghana was working with scores of prophets from dozens of Independent churches in the Accra area. Some prophets needed to become literate, others needed biblical instruction on certain topics, still others wanted to know whether the Bible had something to say about issues they were facing. This missionary always remained at "arms length" to the churches and had absolutely no control over either the leaders or the groups that sought her help, yet she stimulated dozens of prophets and numerous churches to take steps in obedience to God's Word and to the leading of God's Spirit.

A third area needing this strategy is churches that originally were established on the basis of soul-winning or self-replicating strategies and now feel a need to develop a more holistic approach. An example would be the Mennonite Brethren Church in India which has formed the Mennonite Brethren Development Organization and which is now glorying in the success of its first outreach ventures. There is real danger that social and economic concerns will now overshadow, only temporarily I hope, the church growth dimension. Genuine catalytic expatriate input could do wonders here.

CULTURE AND RELIGION

Our culture is the supreme dictator of how we live and act. The tragedy is that so few of us ever become aware of how great a role our culture plays in our behavior. We think we are making independent decisions on what is right and wrong, and are blissfully unaware that our culture is actually calling most of the shots. Recognizing just how my own culture exerts its power on me has been one of life's most important learning experiences.

Culture ranges all the way from the idiosyncrasies of our etiquette to our view of the universe and our beliefs on the afterlife. Yes, religion is an integral part of culture, and Christians are not the only ones who view their religion as above culture—as God-given. The tragedy of this view is that it obscures how much of our religion, and especially our religious practice, is culturally determined.

This section is intended to raise our awareness of culture—both our own and that of others—and help us appreciate that much of what we consider uniquely Christian is also an integral part of the religions of other cultures. My hope is that this awareness will decrease our ethnocentric smugness and help us to recognize that God also works in other cultures and their religions.

This section begins by looking at ourselves through the eyes of other cultures. Obviously this draws attention to some of our superficial foibles and mores, but occasionally it also reveals some of our deeper hidden values—especially those of which we are not proud. We are prone to see plenty of odd things among Third World people, but we often don't realize how strange our folkways seem to people of other ethnic groups. Cultural self-awareness is very important to spiritual growth.

The chapter that follows attempts to use other cultures as mirrors to reveal some of our less visible cultural flaws. Some of those revelations are painful! But all are helpful! For example, the Lengua of Paraguay unexpectedly provided me with an object lesson of what it means to lead a life of consistent abstinence from the use of force. They have been positive examples for me as I developed my current peace position.

My early missionfield experience launched my education in understanding culture. I learned how even our personal foibles and cultural quirks can become major obstacles to the gospel we missionaries proclaim.

Finally, this section focuses on forgiveness. This crucial concept sets Christianity apart from most other religions. Many of them practice expiation; an equal number push atonement; still others encourage humans to accumulate merit. But Christianity stands tall in its unqualified proclamation that forgiveness and release are freely available for all our human short-comings and failures. I am troubled that our evangelical churches often corrupt forgiveness into "cheap grace." That it certainly is not!

On the missionfield this crucial concept faces other subtle dilutions. Cultures that emphasize expiatory payment and the accumulation of merit often relegate forgiveness to a lesser status. In sub-Saharan Africa the Arabic root for 'pity' has found its way into most African languages via Islam. Several evangelical missions, not recognizing its Arabic and Islamic origin, have used that loanword to designate 'forgiveness.' This has gutted this important scriptural concept of its essential value.

The chapter on four kinds of forgiveness focuses on the significant dimensions of this fundamental Christian experience, but it does so largely with examples drawn from other cultures and their religions. The reason is two-fold: on the one hand, I want to highlight the foundation God has already laid for the concept of forgiveness in many cultures; on the other, I want to make overseas witnessers aware of cultural features that could subvert the full benefit of forgiveness. Probably in no other section do I feel more deeply inadequate. I still see culture and religion only "through a glass darkly." I still am only a beginner in my understanding of forgiveness!

By their very nature the last two chapters of this section contain much more cultural and psychological information than first-person experience—the overall hallmark of this testimony. But such technical information is essential to demonstrate just how God is even now working with all of humanity. He is no respecter of person or culture! Any person, in whatever culture, who hears his voice and obeys his will, is acceptable to him. I am overwhelmed when I see what a wise, loving and caring God we have!

CHAPTER 27
OUR CULTURE THROUGH INDIGENOUS EYES

We have all heard the expression, "See yourself as others see you." This applies not only to individuals but also to entire cultures.

When David Wirsche and I first arrived in Noanama our goal was to make contact with the Waunana. We wanted to reduce their language to writing and bring them the gospel. We rented a house in a mestizo village close by the tribe. When tribes people came to town, we would buttonhole as many of them as we could to establish more intimate contact with them. We decided that the best way to increase our contact and familiarity with them would be to travel to one of the Waunana homes up the nearby tributary. One tribesperson who came to the village frequently and often stopped to talk to us was very friendly. We asked him if he would be our guide to visit a Waunana home on the tributary.

We had no idea what such a trip would be like or how long it would take. We agreed on a per diem wage for the duration of our trip. When the appointed day came, the guide did not show up and we were deeply disappointed. He showed up next day, however, to apologize; something had gone wrong at his house and he'd had to stay home to take care of it. I was afraid that this merely was a polite excuse. As we arranged a new date for our trip, I offered to double what we had agreed to pay him previously. I was jolted when the man turned to me with sad eyes and said, "I was going to go with you because I am your friend, not because you are going to give me a pile of money." This incident brought into vivid focus our tremendous Western fixation on money. We seem to feel that money can remedy everything and persuade people to do most anything. It did not move this Waunana one iota.

The washer without the lid

One day David Wirsche and I were waiting in the port city for the boat to take us up the San Juan River to Waunana territory. To pass the time we strolled along the length of the wharf, including the various warehouses where all imported goods were stored after their arrival. We noticed that the last warehouse on the wharf housed the rejects. This enormous shed, with a fifty-foot ceiling, housed a giant pile, probably thirty feet high, of crates, boxes and miscellaneous broken items that had fallen out of other boxes or been damaged in transit. On top of this pile we noticed a crate with a washing machine. To our astonishment, the shipping label said: Mennonite Brethren Board of Missions, Hillsboro, Kansas.

We asked the guard for permission to take a closer look. Here was a Maytag washer that was totally intact, wringer and all. All that was missing was the lid. Since we still had time on our hands, we went to the customs office to scour the records of Mennonite Brethren freight movement through the port and discovered that at one time a box had gone missing. It purported to be a washing machine wringer. After talking with the customs officials, they agreed to let us bring the machine through customs on the strength of that missing box. Since none of the missionaries claimed the machine and the mission board could not recall when such a machine had been sent to Colombia, Anne and I inherited it. We now had a gas washing machine without a lid.

After our house was completed in Noanama, I built a wash house for Anne. It was a small hut, very much like the native huts on stilts. It had a wooden floor, palm walls and a palm-leaf thatched roof. On Monday mornings Anne would do her laundry there. Since the machine had no lid the soap suds would eventually foam over the top. When some tribeswomen saw this, they broke out into hilarious laughter.

Word spread up and down the river that the white people had a weird way of washing clothes. Women would come from all over to watch this spectacle every Monday morning. Some days the laundry house was so full of spectators that Anne could hardly move about to do her washing.

One day our language teacher's wife came to watch. She finally turned to my wife and asked, "Ana, why do you wash this way? Don't you know that intelligent women all take their clothes to the river, soap them and then beat them out on the rocks." Anne had already learned how to handle such cultural differences. She told the tribeswoman, "Do you know that my mother taught me to do laundry this way. She never taught me anything about beating them on the rocks."

From then on the tribeswomen recognized this as our way of doing laundry. If a new woman would break out into laughter, they would poke an elbow into her ribs and rebuke her, "Stop laughing! It is no laughing matter! That's their culture." We learned that tribal people have a tremendous respect for other people's cultural ways.

Our bathtub

When the Chocó tribesman came to visit us in Hillsboro, he had quite a time getting used to our bathtub. I had taken him to the bathroom and shown how the various fixtures functioned. I thought I explained everything well enough so that he would not have any difficulty. But right after breakfast our visitor often went into the bathroom and stayed there for three-quarters of an hour. We would hear the water run periodically. Then there would be periods of silence. Then water would run again, followed by more silence. Since there was only one bathroom in the house, his hogging it posed a problem. What should our three school girls do?

One day our guest complained that he had gotten a headache "when the tail of your whiskers-eater kicked me." I realized he was referring to the cord of my electric shaver, which I usually left dangling from the plug-in beside the sink. He had somehow hooked the dangling shaver cord over his arm as he got into the bathtub. Though the cord wasn't long enough to reach into the water, it gave him a sharp jolt when the end of it brushed against his wet hair. Now the full story of the bathtub came out.

"I was so hot this morning that I just had to cool off," he told me. "Since there is no river by your house, I have to try and do it in your bathroom. I run the tub full of cold water. Then I get in at the tap end and dive into the water but then I have splashed so much water on the floor that by the time I have wiped that up, I am all hot and sweaty again and have to start all over. By the time I have done this seven times, I am so disgusted that I just quit without being refreshed."

One afternoon, shortly thereafter, we took the visitor to Marion Lake, a man-made lake about ten miles away. Before I had a chance to explain to him that one side of the lake was for swimmers and the other side for motor boats, he dived in and proceeded to swim across it, dodging motor boats as he went. On our way back home he told my wife, "You know, Ana, I am not going to have to bathe in that pighole of yours for three days now. I have been so thoroughly refreshed in this lake!"

Later I asked him why he had called our bathtub a pighole. "Well," he said, "haven't you ever seen a pig that wants to cool off? It goes into the soft mud on the side of the river. It lies on its side and begins to wiggle. After a while it gets a hole that is shaped just like its body. As that hole fills up with water, it just lies in the water and that is just what your thing is like in the bathroom. It's a big pighole!"

Salads and tornadoes

One of the things the Chocó visitor found hard to eat was fresh salads. He did not mind eating any kind of vegetable cooked, but he was stymied by our eating of fresh vegetable salad. Anne finally stopped preparing salad for him, because it just made him angry.

One day there were tornado warnings in the region. A massive storm also hit Hillsboro, tearing off branches of the many Dutch elm trees that blanketed the town. Suddenly the town's tornado siren went off and didn't stop screaming even after the usual five-minute duration.

We all took refuge in our tiny storm cellar, an eight-by-eight foot cubicle underneath the porch floor, about seven feet deep. The siren finally quit screaming and we came out safely. Later we heard what the problem had been: A branch had broken off one of the trees and had short-circuited the wires of the siren. That's why it hadn't stopped screaming.

When the visitor heard that it had been a false alarm, he said, "That stands to reason! These people here are like rabbits. They eat rabbit food and then when the siren goes 'woo,' they all dive into their rabbit holes and hide!"

Living beyond our intelligence

While the Chocó was with us, we tried to rush some of our joint translation work into final form. Anne, who was serving as a typist, had difficulty because something went wrong with our electric typewriter. Rather than wait for the repairman to make a trip to Hillsboro, we loaded up the typewriter and took it to a repair shop in Wichita. Since the visitor was already preparing for his return home, he was disgruntled that we had to take time off our work to make this trip. While we drove to Wichita, about an hour's drive, he said, "The problem with you, Tiger, is this: You're living way beyond your intelligence! In my house there is nothing which I cannot make and of which I am not the boss. But in your house almost everything is smarter than you. When the fridge stops, you cannot repair it. When the stove breaks down, you cannot do anything about it. When the typewriter doesn't work, you can't do anything about it, because the machines are all smarter than you are."

"I need some perfume!"

After the Chocó had been with us for a few weeks, he suddenly decided he had to go to town to buy something. My wife was surprised, because he usually did not buy things. "I need to go and buy some perfume," he told her. When she asked him if he wanted to take it home for his wife, he said, "No, I need the perfume for myself. I am beginning to stink just like you do!" It was then we realized that every group of people gets a characteristic body odor from the food they eat, but since we are used to our own smell, we do not notice it on ourselves or our companions. But we often smell the different body odor of people from other cultures and find it objectionable. He found ours objectionable, too!

Chaco Indians classify Mennonites

While doing research with the Lengua in the Paraguayan Chaco, I tried to discover some of their unspoken attitudes toward the Mennonite settlers who now lived in their midst. All my attempts to get direct answers to inquiries along this line had drawn blanks. But when I was learning how to buy a horse, I stumbled on a way to get my queries answered. The Lengua told me not to buy a horse from the Mennonites. They said I would be better off to buy from the tribespeople. I asked why. They then confided that most of the Mennonites in the area weren't good people. So I began to ask what the problem was. As we went down the central street of the nearest Mennonite village, I asked how they rated the various property owners. I discovered that in the first village there were no "good" people. All the people were classified either as *yietsich* 'tight fisted,' or *bossich* 'bad tempered' or both. When I inquired of some of the other villages, I eventually found some villages that had one or two Mennonites with good innermosts, but all the others had innermosts that were either *yietsich* or *bossich* or both.

Drinking

When the Mennonites first met the Lengua and the Chulupi, all the tribespeople were nomadic. In the dry season when food became scarce, these tribespeople would depend on pods from the carob tree for sustenance. The carob pods were picked, beaten into pulp and then fermented in halves of "bottle" (baobab) trees. This tree has a soft pulpy interior that ferments quickly once it is exposed to air. Soon a fermented drink results that is somewhat intoxicating but also quite nutritious because of the beans which the pods contain. Thus, for the next six weeks to two months, while the drought was at its height, the people would celebrate and live off the fermenting carob pod mush. This left them partially inebriated and quite oblivious to the shortage of food.

The Mennonites were disgusted when they first came upon the spectacle of these partially inebriated tribespeople stumbling around the fermenting troughs of powdered carob beans. They expressed their disgust saying, "*Fuu shtinkt!*", 'Phoo, it stinks!'

As the years passed, the people's dependence on the carob in the dry season diminished greatly and so did their drinking of the fermented mush. Eventually many of the Lengua and Chulupi became Christians. As baptized believers, they were taught that drinking was sin.

Meanwhile the Mennonites in the Chaco grew more affluent, and many of them began to drink beer. Their colony cooperative trucks often brought massive loads of tall one-liter bottles of beer. One could see boxes of empties stacked up high beside the cooperative building, waiting to be returned to the brewery.

One day some aborigines asked me whether I had the courage to give a message to the largest Mennonite church, the Mennonite Brethren church in Filadelfia. I told them that if they had a message for the Mennonites I would be happy to deliver it. They then gave me the following message, "When you first came to the Chaco and saw us drinking the fermenting carob mush, you said, 'Fuu shtinkt!' Now we have become Christians and we have stopped drinking intoxicating liquor, but now we find the beer bottles by the Coop, stacked almost two stories high. Now we want to tell you, 'Fuu shtinkt!' " Two weeks later I had occasion to preach in Filadelfia on Sunday morning and I delivered the tribal message as requested.

Our concern for privacy

When Anne and I became friends with the Waunana, we quickly realized that we came across to them as being obsessed with privacy. We close our bedrooms when we go to sleep. We separate our bedroom from our children's. We close the door when we go to the bathroom. We always are private. Not so with the Waunana! They live in round thatched huts where everything is open. Morning toilet activities are public. All the people squat in the river and have friendly conversations while they go about their morning toilet. This different view of privacy was quite startling to missionaries traveling in Waunana territory who would have a problem with undressing. Since it rains so much, it is hard to stay dry. All transportation is by water. Very often it is impossible to get to shore without wading in water. As a result we often felt the need to change to dry clothes as soon as we got to a Waunana house.

When Anne made her first trip to the Waunana, I told her that if she wanted to change into dry clothes in a Waunana home she should do so in the center of the house. No one would pay any attention to her there. But she wasn't comfortable with this. She waited until we had strung up our hammocks on one side of the host's house, then began to change behind the hammocks. She hadn't realized what a stir this would cause. As soon as she began changing all the children and young people climbed on the rafters to look. What is it about her anatomy, they wondered, that was so different that it has to be kept secret. When they saw nothing different, they turned away in disgust. "She's just like us!" they said.

In missions there are lessons to be learned: The missionary needs to carefully distinguish between the gospel content and its cultural wrapper. All too often missionaries find that they are actually pushing a cultural wrapper rather than the content of the gospel.

Ethnocentrism is universal. Aborigines feel superior to white people. White people feel superior to tribespeople.

CHAPTER 28
CULTURAL INSIGHTS FROM UNEXPECTED SOURCES

Insights through a Polish anthropologist's eyes

In the early 1960s a Polish anthropologist, Alicja Iwanska, conducted an anthropological study of a midwestern American farming community. Some of her generalizations about the people of this "Bible Belt" region are very revealing. Besides being highly instructive to those of us who have lived there, her study demonstrated the important cultural insights we can gain from unexpected sources. Iwanska discovered that midwestern American Christian farmers saw the world in terms of three categories: landscape, machines and people.

Landscape for them, she wrote, included the distant mountains, the forests, the scenery, and the lakes in the environment in which the farmers operate. Landscape was never viewed as something to be manipulated or exploited. Midwesterners looked at it and enjoyed it in a disinterested sort of a way. While it had no high emotional value for them, they were very kindly disposed toward it. Interestingly enough, they saw Native Americans as belonging to the landscape category; they were part of the scenery. One took out-of-town visitors for a Sunday drive through the tribal reservation to look idly and curiously at the natives. One felt rather kindly toward them.

The second category for midwestern Christian farmers was machines. Machinery was a vital element in their lives. They cleaned, polished and took good care of their machines. Machines were highly valued because they determined the productivity and the profitability of the farmers' efforts.

Even the land itself was seen in machine terms. It was something you tilled and fertilized to produce crops. If the yield was not high enough, you fine-tuned your efforts accordingly.

Livestock also belonged to the machine category. It, too, was important for its productivity. You did not necessarily send your beef animals out to pasture; you kept them on bare ground in an enclosed pen and fed them continuously to get maximum market weight.

Chickens were not permitted to live in their natural environment, scratching and pecking for food. They were kept in wire cages, fed and watered by conveyor. They were looked after very carefully in terms of their egg production. As soon as a hen lost its egg-laying capacity, it was removed and shipped off. Like machines, they were regarded purely as producers of profit.

Good workers—Mexicans, migrants and African-Americans—also belonged to the machine category. Their value lay in their productivity. One took care of them in the same way one took care of a cow, chicken or fuel pump. When the carburetor no longer functioned properly, it was discarded. Migrant workers were likewise discarded when they no longer were useful. One felt no responsibility for them during the off-season.

The third category Iwanska discovered was people. People were the farmer's neighbors and fellow churchgoers, the folks with whom he drank coffee. He had grown up with them. He had gone to school with them. He had cooperated with them in times of emergencies. He lived and died with them. He did not expect to get any financial advantage from them. There were very few individuals in a midwestern Christian farmer's people category.

What a revealing but indicting commentary! Do midwestern Bible Belt Christians, including Mennonites, also operate on a purely mechanical view of the world? They piously serve God and faithfully support church and missions. But are they as materially oriented and as "mammon" motivated as the pagans who spout "scientific-evolution?" God help our conversions to grow!

Only a fool runs for nothing

My missionary partner and I had just finished a very exciting morning. We had begun learning Waunana—our first experience of learning a tribal language. We were excited! At that time, Waunana was an unwritten language, and we had been able to collect more than fifty nouns—names of objects that were visible in and around the house where we were doing our language study.

For the afternoon we had decided to begin learning some verbs. I was so eager to get ahead in the work that I skipped my nap and began furiously writing out verb forms: I run, you run, she runs, he runs, etc., followed by all the other tense forms. The idea was that in the afternoon all we would have to do was fill in the equivalent Waunana forms beside the English pattern already written out.

Finally our Waunana teacher arrived. We started our work. "How do you say 'I run' in your language?" I asked. The tribesman was quiet for quite a while. First he looked down; then he looked out. Then he sheepishly asked, "What did you want to know?" I repeated my question, but he continued to be puzzled.

He asked again, "What is it that you want to know?" I repeated the question a third time. Suddenly his face lit up as if struck by a flash of inspiration. He began to speak very rapidly. If I had been able to write down everything he said, it would have spread across several pages, but after a few syllables I was already hopelessly bogged down. He repeated his statement three times. Then his story began to change. I gave it up as a lost cause!

"Surely that doesn't all mean just 'I run,' " I said defensively. To this he replied, "Why, of course not. It says I was sitting here with you, then I looked out of the door and saw a deer, so I quickly grabbed my spear, and now *I am running* after it." Then, almost philosophically, he added softly as if to himself, "Only a fool would run for nothing!"

This experience brings into sharp focus one of the major problems we Westerners have with language. For us, words are something to be manipulated. They are entities in and of themselves. But for most tribal people, like the Waunana, words are a means of describing experience. They are deeply embedded in life. For this reason we often get caught on words. We check if a preacher uses certain cliches in his messages. If he does, then he is orthodox and reliable. If he doesn't, he must be a liberal or a modernist.

The gospel and its cultural wrapper

Often the missionaries' own cultural idiosyncrasies can nullify the good news they preach, because the native receives the gospel usually clothed in another people's culture—the culture of the missionary. These cultural wrappers, not the gospel message itself, are often the cause of misunderstanding and rejection.

A good example of this is the experience of two American missionaries to a Central American tribe. One day, these two women were on their knees praying in the tribal language. "Oh Lord, it's been more than seven years already, and still there are no believers! Why?"

Abruptly their prayers were interrupted by the tribal girl who was washing their breakfast dishes. She now blurted out, "Why must you drink lime juice every morning?"

To the missionary women, the answer was simple. There was no orange juice, and lime juice was the only available substitute. Doctored up with sugar and water it was a passable source of vitamin C.

In the conversation that followed, however, the missionaries learned that in this culture lime juice was considered a contraceptive. Women used it when they had been unfaithful to their husbands. For seven years the tribe had been held in suspense. The missionary women's daily consumption of lime juice meant only one thing to the people—these women were nightly entertaining men. And since no human men appeared, they must be consorting with "evil spirit men."

As soon as the two realized the implications of the lime juice, they dropped it from their diet. Before long, aloof suspicions gave way to friendship. Conversions followed.

Money is the "axle"

"Every tribe and culture uses one or more of these..." (as I spoke I pointed to the blackboard on which a simplified listing of Wissler's cultural universals[1] had been written) ". . . as the heart, the most important center or hub of their way of life. It is like the axle of a wheel, which forms the center around which the whole wheel turns. You say that you have known the missionaries for about twenty years. Can you suggest one of the items in this list which you would consider to be the axle of the missionaries' way of life?"

"Money!" the group of teachers from a South American tribe exclaimed unanimously and unhesitatingly.

"But do missionaries really teach about money?"

"No, they usually talk about God and religion, but money is still the most important thing in their way of life," the teachers—all Christians—affirmed with obvious conviction.

The missionaries present began to fidget nervously as I continued.

"How can you be so sure that money is the axle of the missionaries' way of life?"

"Because ..." and then with devastating accuracy the tribal Christians one after another recounted personal experiences that showed how money was the ultimate yardstick (value) in both the material and spiritual areas of the missionaries' life and culture.

Deeply intrigued, I probed further.

"Have you ever heard of communist Russia?"

"Yes, we have. We have received quite a few communist books here in our country already."

"Have you any idea what might be the axle in the communist way of life?"

After a moment's hesitation, one of the group pointed to *political structure* on the blackboard, and another quickly added *economics*. After a brief discussion

---

[1]Clark Wissler expounded his cultural universals in the book *Man and Culture*, New York: William Crowell, 1923. His list and the adjusted expressions used in the lecture are as follows:

Wissler	*Adjusted*
1. Language	how people talk and write
2. Art	painting, carving, dancing, etc.
3. Knowledge and education	school
4. Social organization	family and relatives
5. Economic organization	how people earn money and use it
6. Political organization	how people get their chief and how he commands
7. Religion	how people worship and pray to their god
8. Material culture	houses, canoes, weapons, and other things people make
9. War	war

the group agreed unanimously that government and money-making formed the axle of the communist way of life.

By now I was profoundly impressed and so gambled for even higher stakes. "What about your fathers and grandfathers before the missionary and the white man came; what was the axle of their way of life?"

"War," was the prompt, laconic response.

"War!" I exclaimed incredulously. "Did your grandfathers really love to fight and kill other people?"

"They had to kill because that was the only way they could get spirit power."

No sooner had the tribespeople mentioned *spirit power* then something in my own innermost clicked, and I realized we had arrived at the crucial question: "What would have been the axle in your grandfathers' way of life if they had been Christians?"

Without as much as blinking, the teachers responded: "The Spirit of God, because he. . ." Just then an audible gasp by one of the missionaries caused the speaker to hesitate for a moment, but he continued: ". . . because the Spirit of God is the most powerful of all spirits."

"And now that all of you here are Christians," I continued, "is the Spirit of God the axle of your Christian way of life, too?"

"No," they responded, obviously subdued, "our axle now is . . . is money."

"How come? Are you not children of your ancestors? If the axle of their Christian life would have been the Spirit of God, why is it not yours?"

"Money is our axle now because that is what we have learned from the missionaries."

Later I discovered the cause of the missionary's gasp. The missionaries from several missions working with the tribe had avoided the concept of the Holy Spirit in their teaching because the tribal language offered a whole series of words that could be translated as *soul* or *spirit*, and there was strong inter-mission and inter-missionary disagreement about which of these words, if any, could be used to designate the Spirit of God. So the missionaries had taught about God, God's love, God's Son, God's justice, etc., but not about his Spirit.

This encounter with the Christian Indians in the jungles of South America in 1970 aptly illustrates that human beings—whether alien missionary messengers or newly-converted receptors of the gospel message—are creatures of their own culture. Its values—spoken or unspoken—color what they see and hear, and determine what they say and do. If the gospel, brought by an alien missionary communicator, is to "scratch where it itches," the missionary not only needs to be deeply aware of the cultural matrix from which he himself comes and speaks, but must also be empathetically knowledgeable about the culture and the values of the receptors of his message. If he is not, tragedies like the watered-down Christianity of the tribespeople described above, or the Shiriana (Brazilian jungle tribe) use of the teaching of prayer in order to kill some men and to steal some women, are inevitable.

Aureliano's world

When Aureliano visited us in Hillsboro, he and I began translating portions of the Scriptures into the Empera language. Aureliano was a most dedicated worker. Whenever visitors interrupted our working schedule for too long a period, Aureliano would lean over, pull my sleeve, and suggest that I tell them we had work to do.

As Aureliano and I neared the completion of the translation of the Gospel of Mark, we came to the passage (14:27) which speaks about the uttermost parts of the earth. Aureliano translated the statement "to the uttermost part of the earth" as "to the last earth." Since I knew that the Empera view the universe as having three levels—there was the upper world which is higher and future, there was the world that is here and now, and there was an underworld that is both lower and older—I was afraid that his statement "to the last earth" might somehow be related to this three-tiered view of the world. I did my linguistic and anthropological best to explain the situation to Aureliano, but to no avail. He continued to insist that it should be translated "to the last earth."

When I saw I wasn't getting anywhere, I decided to leave the situation for the time being. The same concept would reappear in the eighth verse of the first chapter of the Book of Acts which was next on our translation schedule. When we came to Acts, I first read the statement in Spanish, then I explained the exegesis in Spanish and in his own language in order to prevent the supposed mistranslation. The whole thing amounted to a lengthy explanation about the mission's philosophy of taking the gospel to the farthest reaches of this earth. When we then proceeded to translate the eighth verse of chapter one, the translation again came back as "to the last earth." I now felt convinced that the problem was not just one of factual misunderstanding, but rather one of discrepancy in worldviews. So I began to cast around for the source of the miscommunication.

"Did you know that the world is round?"

Aureliano responded somewhat caustically, "I have always known that the world is round."

So it couldn't be the round world. . . . After many and varied attempts, I was ready to give up, when I suddenly thought of the globe. I went across the hall to the geography room and wheeled a giant globe into my office. I asked Aureliano, "Did you know that the world is round like this?"

I then located Panama and the United States. We traced his flight via Los Angeles to Portland, and his train ride from Portland to Kansas. Then we plotted the route of his return trip via Miami, Florida and Havana, Cuba to Panama.

Aureliano remembered the news about the earthquake in Chile and the tidal wave that struck the Far East in its aftermath. He wanted to know the "road" of this wave. He had heard about Russia, and now wanted to know where it was located. He was totally fascinated by the globe. He kept on turning, looking, and asking questions. Finally he turned to me and said, "So it isn't true!"

"What isn't true?"

"Well, that the earth has seven seas."

"Seven seas—why, we generally speak of five major oceans, but really you can make as many oceans as you want. You know the border between Panama and Colombia—the land is the same on both sides, but we say that on one side of the line it is called Panama and on the other side it is called Colombia. In the same way you could make lines through the water and call one side by one name and the other side by a different one."

"That is not what I mean," Aureliano retorted. "What I really mean is that the earth is one big sea and it has some islands in it."

For a moment I was stumped. Then I recovered, pointing out to Aureliano that there were different shades of blue in the water on the map. The light blue meant shallow water, the dark blue meant deeper water, and finally the very dark blue in the middle of the Pacific Ocean marked the deepest spot of all. There was a "land" bottom under the whole ocean.

Aureliano pondered that for a while, then finally went to the blackboard and drew a circle to represent his round earth. "You know," he said, "I always knew that the world was round. But I thought it was like this," pointing to the circle he had drawn. In this first circle, which represented a round but flat world, he located Panama and the United States. This makes a lot of sense since Panama, narrow as it is, has the Pacific Ocean on one side and the Atlantic Ocean on the other, giving the Indians the feeling that the "world" is surrounded by water.

Then he continued: "Since there were seven seas, I reasoned that there must also be seven 'lands'." And so around the central circle—the round but flat world—he drew a "doughnut" of water and then another of land. Then he added, "And do you know that the last two lands are frozen to the sky? There are no people living there. So what you are trying to make me translate—'to the last earth'—is really utter nonsense, but what else can I do, when you don't know any better!"

The Holy Spirit in tribal believers' lives

Most tribal people come from animistic backgrounds and see themselves as living in a world inhabited by spirits—some of them hostile. When they become Christians, they discover the amazingly powerful Spirit of God, and he radically changes their lives. Here's what one of them testified:

> One day last week, just at nightfall, a stranger asked for lodging. We agreed to let him stay the night, only to discover that he was a shaman because soon after arriving in our home, we saw him getting out his shamanistic gear. After we had eaten, we saw him trying to establish communication with his evil spirit helpers.

> Both my wife and I felt fear beginning to grab us. We retreated to our sleeping net as soon as possible. (Indian houses are one-roomed and the only privacy to be found is beneath cloth mosquito nets under which people sleep.) Once under our net we both prayed to God earnestly. We reminded him how afraid we used to be of evil spirits but how his Spirit had come into our lives and our home and had taken away all our fear. But now, faced with this strange shaman and his evil spirits in our very house, the old fear was staging a comeback. We asked God's Spirit to cool our spleens (the *spleen* is the Chocó equivalent of our *heart*) and to give us a peaceful night's sleep. Soon we were asleep.
>
> About midnight we were awakened by a loud noise. The visiting shaman was jumping up and down, shouting angrily, "Something is wrong in this house! I just can't get my spirit helpers to cooperate!" Then my wife and I realized again how much stronger the Spirit of God is than all the evil spirits. Even the shaman's spirit helpers were afraid to come into our house because God's Spirit was in charge there.

The tribal believers' obvious joy over the presence of the Holy Spirit in their lives is heartwarming. It stands in bold contrast to the distance we often feel between us and God and his Spirit.

The power of the gospel

The life-changing power of the gospel comes from God. Its power can never be generated by human efforts, no matter how dedicated, consecrated, or anthropologically sensitive a missionary might be. On the other hand, no person, no matter how determined or obstreperous, can stop the gospel. The latter was driven home to me during the height of the drug craze in North America when a well-known anthropologist went to South America to research the effects of hallucinogens in use there.

When he arrived he informed the shamans that he was going to be with them for six weeks and that he wanted to experience a full range of their drugs in order to compare what they and he experienced. The shamans bluntly informed him that his conditioning to the drugs alone would take more than six weeks. At his insistence, however, they agreed to try and compress the conditioning into three weeks so he could experience the effect of their drugs over the next three weeks.

Already with his first full dose, however, his conditioning turned out to be completely inadequate. Here are his own words.

> I took my first full dose, and no sooner had I taken it, I became aware that I was overdosed. I felt the extremities of my body—my feet, then my legs, my hands and my arms—grow cold; gradually the coldness enveloped the whole of the lower part of my torso. I felt 'death' overpowering life in my entire body until there seemed to be only a small area around my heart that was still alive. I knew

> I was dying, but I so desperately wanted to live. I struggled to hang on to my life, but it seemed futile. Just when I thought the thread of life was going to snap, the blackness of death was shattered by a brilliant light, and I saw Jesus Christ on the cross saying: 'I will save you.'
>
> And the hell of it is that I don't believe in Jesus Christ!

While the anthropologist was "dying," the shamans, realizing that something had gone wrong, were frantically giving him antidotes to counteract the effect of the drug. The anthropologist's wife and daughter, standing by helplessly, saw how all the desperate efforts of the shamans seemed to be in vain. Then suddenly and unexpectedly the anthropologist opened his eyes. When he told his family of his vision, both wife and daughter at once responded to the power of God.

A Vietnamese demon possession and exorcism

Some years ago a young Vietnamese woman immigrant to Canada became possessed by the soul-of-the-dead of her deceased Vietnamese fiancé. She had been promised in marriage to this young man, but before the marriage could take place, he had been inducted into the Vietnamese army and had been killed shortly thereafter. The young woman was devastated. When she also lost her parents in the same war, some relatives helped her emigrate to Canada with other members of the family.

Instead of getting over her grief in the new homeland, the young woman developed increasingly severe symptoms of depression and eventually became "possessed" by the soul-of-the-dead of her fiancé, whom she experienced as molesting her sexually.

She was institutionalized and treated by a variety of Canadian psychiatrists. For the next five years she was in and out of institutions as her symptoms periodically increased or abated. After years of this on-again, off-again therapy, one of the frustrated psychiatrists mentioned the case to a Vietnamese psychiatrist who had recently been licensed to practice in Canada.

The Vietnamese psychiatrist was intrigued. He contacted the young woman who had once again been discharged from a mental hospital. After meeting with her for several hours he realized he would have to depend on her Vietnamese view of the spirit world. He would also have to enlist the Buddhist religion to help him in the healing. He then arranged with the local Buddhist priest to organize a religious ceremony for curing the demon-possessed young woman.

The psychiatrist took the young woman to the Vietnamese Buddhist temple where the priest now performed an induction ceremony for the soul of her deceased fiancé into a celibate order of monks. As part of the ceremony the inductee's soul was instructed to stay away from his former fiancée forever. The young woman herself was never spoken to during the whole ceremony. But when the final blessing on the new inductee had been spoken, the young woman walked out of the temple completely free of her possession and emotional depression.

This account was first shared with me in confidence by the Vietnamese psychiatrist who arranged for the cure. It took several hours of coaxing on my part before he became willing to share the experience at a conference on refugees in Canada under Alberta Mental Health. He was afraid that his Canadian colleagues would ridicule him and maybe even cause his license to be revoked. But when he became convinced of the importance of the experience in the light of the problems for which he and I were trying to serve as resource people, he shared the experience in public. It demonstrates that one cannot heal a Vietnamese demoniac by means of Western psychiatry or even Western exorcism; he/she has to be healed in terms relevant to his/her worldview.

CHAPTER 29
THE SOCIAL CONTEXT OF GUILT AND FORGIVENESS

I now want to begin a two-chapter study of forgiveness. I consider forgiveness one of the greatest Christian insights into religion. It is sad therefore that its most ardent proponents—the evangelicals—often give it such a bad name as cheap grace: That it definitely is not!

A Nuer youth (a West African tribe from Uganda or Sudan) is badly wounded in the shoulder by a spear during a quarrel with a man from a neighboring village. The people of the two villages are normally on friendly terms with each other, and the spearer had no intention of killing the young man; for this reason his kinsmen at once sent the offending spear to the youth's home with expressions of regret and best wishes for his speedy recovery. The elders of the wounded lad's village take the spear, bend its point and then place it downward in a pot of cold water in order to "lessen the pain" and "prevent inflammation."

Next morning a delegation from the wounder's village arrives leading a goat ready for sacrifice. This is a further indication of regret and willingness to pay compensation should the young man die. They do not want a blood feud and hope the sacrifice of the goat will prevent further complications, or as the Nuer put it, "that the wound will be finished with the goat." The visiting delegation now dedicates the goat by rubbing its back with ashes and then ties it to a stake in front of the hut of the wounded youth's maternal grandmother. At this point one of the visitors delivers an invocation calling for a peaceful settlement of the dispute. His speech, addressed both to God (here called *kwoth* 'spirit') and the people, is really a detailed account of how the incident developed. It concludes with a prayer for the wounded youth's speedy recovery.

Following this speech, the people from the wounded man's village bring out a sheep and they, too, dedicate it with ashes. They pour a libation of water over the tethering peg and once more recite the events of the conflict: "Ah God! We call on you about this wound. There is no enmity between us [the party of the injured youth and the party of the spearer]. This wound came of itself [they do not attribute it to the spearer because the youth will not die, and so there will be no *thung*, 'debt of homicide']. Throw the badness away with this ox [they call a sheep or a goat an "ox" or "cow" in ritual contexts]. Let the wound heal! Ah, God, it is only a headache [it is not a wound of any importance—they speak of the most ghastly wounds in this way]. Let it be finished! Let it go right on to heal without complications. Let it be removed from the man's body. Let us be at peace!"

Another man from the home village steps forward and makes an invocation: "Friends (*maath*), God who is in this village, you are very great, so we tell you about this wound, for you are God of our home in very truth. We tell you about the fight of this lad. Let the wound heal. Let it be ransomed [with sheep]. . . ."

After a further word by the visitors, both of the animals are sacrificed, and part of the meat is prepared and then eaten in a ceremonial meal shared by the two groups. Now the offense has been confessed and atoned for. The people return home in peace.

The Nuer experience of settling an offense illustrates several important social aspects of guilt and forgiveness: (1) the development and expression of guilt, (2) the three essential steps in the process of forgiveness (confession, expiation and release), and (3) two of the most universal dimensions of forgiveness—the religious and the social. This chapter proposes to highlight each of the mentioned aspects, all of which can enhance our understanding of the cross-cultural ministry of forgiveness. One of the lessons I learned in the years of my overseas ministry was that to be truly effective, the emissary of reconciliation must be able to distinguish between those features which are universal, i.e. part and parcel of the human psyche, and those which are conditioned by the local culture.

The nature of guilt

In my personal story I have spoken about conviction, the feeling that one has done wrong. Such guilt is a universal phenomenon because people everywhere fail to live up to their moral ideals or else in selfishness infringe upon the rights of their fellows. However, not all guilt feelings can be labeled *true* guilt.

True and false guilt. There seem to be several separate usages of the true-false distinction in regard to guilt. Psychologists and psychiatrists tend to label as *true* guilt those feelings of self-indictment that accompany the violation of norms which the individual has personally internalized as right. False guilt, on the other hand, is externally imposed guilt, such as when a community develops a pattern of contempt against a person or a group of persons, and the victim or victims in time become conditioned to see themselves as inferior and guilty. This can be visibly demonstrated in the experience of known illegitimate children. As their peers are warned by their parents to avoid "these products of sin," many illegitimate children develop an acute sense of guilt about their origin.

R.D. Laing uses the label *true* or *authentic* guilt for the recognition of not having been genuine or of not having "been oneself." Like Freud, he considers all other guilt reactions as unauthentic or false, because they are the product of the person's cultural upbringing or of his society's overt reaction.

Paul Tournier, in his book *Guilt and Grace*, also makes a true-false distinction. However, he defines true guilt as estrangement from God (and therefore also from one's fellows), while false guilt is the feeling of condemnation that arises out of the violation of cultural mores.

Guilt and shame. I feel that Christians need to make another important distinction—a distinction between guilt and shame. Anthropologists have usually defined guilt as self-condemnation resulting from the violation of internalized convictions of right and wrong. (This can actually include false guilt, for in the case of the latter, the person has internalized the society's negative evaluation of his own worth.) Shame, on the other hand, is the response to disapproval by one's own peers or elders. This definition correlates with David Riesman's distinction between the inner-directed person who experiences guilt and the other-directed person who experiences shame. Both anthropologists and psychologists have pointed out that American culture is rapidly shifting from its earlier guilt sanction to the current shame sanction.

Face-to-face societies generally depend on gossip-triggered shame sanction to enforce obedience to socially accepted norms. However, one frequently finds that even in face-to-face societies these norms have been internalized to such a degree that many adult individuals experience independent guilt. This guilt is most evident in matters relating to broken taboos which are seen as supernaturally enforced. Any adverse circumstance following a taboo violation will be interpreted as supernatural intervention and will result in guilt.

The diversity of guilt reactions. First of all, I think we need to be aware of the differences as to the nature of the behavior that will produce guilt. This will vary from individual to individual within a given society, but even more from one society to another. Novelist Emile Zola highlights the individual variability in guilt reaction in the behavior of one of his characters who has committed a lust murder but feels no guilt about it. When the religious and legal communities press him to admit his guilt, he shamefacedly confesses that he once lustfully kissed the stocking of a woman.

I can illustrate cross-cultural differences of guilt reaction by responses of a North American and a Paraguayan Chulupi Christian, both of whom believe that a husband should be faithful to his wife. Traditionally the Chulupi male would feel no guilt about sleeping with unmarried girls during the time his wife was nursing their baby, but he would feel terribly guilty if he slept with his wife during lactation. Again, a Chulupi woman felt little or no compunction about strangling an infant at birth if the husband indicated that he did not accept the role of sociological father, but she would be unable to hide her intense guilt if she ate meat during her menstruation.

I see further personal and cross-cultural differences in the degree of guilt that a given violation produces. In our own society a man accidentally stumbling upon a naked woman would probably feel embarrassed, but certainly not guilty; while to a Manus Islander, looking upon the nakedness of a woman, even accidentally, would constitute a serious crime which, if unconfessed, could mean that either he or his kin would become ill and die.

Guilt and public knowledge. I also want to stress that guilt is seldom entirely intrinsic. In face-to-face societies and in the so-called other-directed societies, guilt often depends on or at least is increased by public knowledge of the infraction. This is illustrated dramatically in the following example from the North American Comanche:

An old man had a very handsome grandson of whom he was very proud and of whom he liked to boast in public. One day the young man was sitting outside his tepee in the presence of a large number of people. The grandfather, squatting beside the young man, saw a good-looking woman pass by. He at once nudged his grandson and slyly whispered: "That looks like the woman you had last night." The young man told his grandfather to go away. The old man did not move but was obviously hurt. "I didn't say anything wrong," he said. "I just said it looked like her." The grandson ignored the old man's words, but the latter still kept on repeating them. The woman's husband was there also. Pretty soon the husband spoke up and said: "Yes, she's the one." When the group broke up, the offended husband went and shot both the old man's favorite horse and the young man's pony. He had been aware of the affair but was letting it ride. But once the grandfather made it public, there was an infraction to avenge.

Bronislav Malinowski has reported a similar guilt reaction among the Trobriand Islanders. People violated the incest taboo without any apparent feeling of guilt or public censure. However, if the partner in the violation ever admitted the event publicly, the offender usually committed suicide.

Manifestations of guilt. I have also discovered that there are major differences in the manifestation of guilt. Psychiatrists point out that for the average North American blushing, turning pale, or perspiring are automatic reactions indicating that some infraction has been committed. By far the most universal reaction to guilt, however, is increased social distance. This involves not only the offender and any offended individual, but also the offender and the society at large. Guilt isolates and alienates. The Lengua demonstrate this alienation by leaving their home community as soon as their guilt is discovered.

Note the growing awareness in social psychology and psychiatry that much of mental illness, especially neurosis, is the direct result of guilt. In fact, Hobart O. Mowrer has called neurosis "a medical euphemism for a state of sin." He says:

> My own personal and professional experience and that of a small but growing number of other psychologists, psychiatrists and social workers shows that the so-called psycho-neuroses and functional psychoses can be understood only (sola!) in terms of palpable misconduct which has neither been confessed nor expiated.

Paul Tournier says something rather similar concerning somatic illness:

> I speak from my own experience as a doctor. . . . Many functional disturbances, and, in the long run, many organic lesions as well, are the direct consequence of unresolved remorse. That this is so is shown by the fact of their abrupt disappearance or reduction after confession. One has seen, for instance, cases where long-standing insomnia, palpitations, headaches, disorder of the digestive organs or of the liver had disappeared overnight after the confession of a lie or of an illicit love-affair.

He cites examples of eczema, blood deficiency and general poor health that were based entirely on repressed guilt. He then goes on to quote a physician who found at least sixty percent of his arthritic patients had developed their problems in response to some inner moral conflict.

Nor is the somatic response to guilt an exclusively Western phenomenon. A.I. Hallowell has pointed out that for the Saulteaux, interpersonal guilt almost always finds expression in serious illness.

Guilt and culture change. Finally, I want to underscore some of the problems of guilt conflict that arise when a culture is undergoing rapid and extensive culture change. In some cases there will be confusion as to when and about what to feel guilty; in others the guilt may be compounded, for the culprits will feel themselves indicted under both the old and the new standards. Notice the conflict of standards in the following episode:

An unmarried Chulupi girl, a member of the church, was seeking a husband. Under the old standard she had to take the initiative and give herself sexually to a series of young men until one of them became her husband. According to popular belief, she avoided becoming pregnant by sleeping with a different male each night. Once a young man sought her out for repeated visits, he was actually declaring that he wanted her for his wife and that he would also assume the responsibility of sociological fatherhood should she be with child. Now, however, with the new Christian standards the possibility of sexual contacts has been greatly diminished and a girl often becomes pregnant before she has found a husband. Once her pregnancy becomes visible, she usually stays away from church services until she has given birth to her child in some hospital removed from the mission station.

Now let us look at the experience of a specific girl. On the day following the delivery, her sister called for her and the baby. On the way home from the hospital the new mother strangled her new-born baby and buried it beside the trail. It was not until the hospital called to confirm the news of the baby's death that the missionary became aware of what had actually happened. He called on the girl, but she denied all guilt, saying the baby had not liked her milk, it had cried all night and then in the morning it had died. However, the date of the death was the day of her discharge from the hospital. The missionary spoke to the Chulupi church leadership asking them to investigate the facts and impressing them with the seriousness of the crime of killing one's own baby.

The church elders followed his instructions and reported that the girl herself had indeed killed her child and that the council had now decided to kill her—they were just waiting for the missionary's specific permission. The missionary refused to permit such drastic action, and a public discussion resulted. At this meeting the girl told the whole truth, but defended her action by saying the child had no (sociological) father. The girl's father, an older Chulupi, supported her, saying: "Her older sister already has two children without fathers, and I am very deeply ashamed. I could not bear to have another bastard in the family!" The church leadership, however, operating on the new standards, decided to punish the girl by announcing that nobody should marry her until she repented publicly for killing her child.

This example illustrates the conflicts between different systems of standards in a society experiencing rapid social change. Not only the young people are torn between two sets of ideals; the very tribal leadership is divided as to what values are primary (the father's counsel flatly contradicts the proposals of the church leaders) and how these values are to be enforced. If strangling an infant—which was standard pre-Christian procedure—is really as serious a crime as the missionary says, then they as leaders are responsible for applying the maximum penalty (death).

Mechanisms for disowning guilt. Even though I feel guilt is a universal social phenomenon, few people can readily "own" the fact that they have violated some of their internalized or at least professed standards or norms. The admission of guilt is not without price in terms of cost to the person's self-image and certainly often has rather severe repercussions in terms of social opinion. R.F. Fortune describes this social cost among the Manus as follows:

> Confession will make all but the patient's close friends talk of the penitent's sin as if it were the copulation of dogs. The girl penitent, whenever she has to appear in a public place, will slink through the village with all the aspect and the air of a cowed dog. The penitent will avoid all public meetings as much as possible.

Because of this cost, human beings have developed a whole series of socio-psychological mechanisms to control or reduce the pressures urging the admission of their guilt. Among the most common of these mechanisms are rationalization, repression, projection and guilt-spreading.

Pseudo-release mechanisms. Release, as I have already suggested, is the final step in the process of forgiveness. However, when individuals are unable to own their guilt and to find true forgiveness, they often will attempt to rid themselves of their guilt feelings by means of several pseudo-release mechanisms. One of these is annulling the bad deed by good works; thus a husband may bring flowers to his wife instead of apologizing to her for a wrong action, or a mother may read an extra story to her children to atone for her earlier outburst of temper. Keith Miller gives us a first-person example of this mechanism:

> For years when things went wrong around our house I would try

> to 'make things right' by bringing Mary Allen a present. But even if the surprise were a good one, it never seemed to strike a really deep chord of response. I sensed that she was somehow disappointed, though she managed to hide it well.

There is a growing feeling that the reason funeral directors are able to sell such expensive funerals is that the surviving relatives are engaged in expiating unatoned guilt which they feel toward the deceased.

Mowrer states categorically that hiding our sins by portraying our good deeds is the best road to self-destruction. Instead he calls for people to confess their sins and to hide their good works. This will give them credit and self-esteem.

Another mechanism in this category is repression. After people have deeply repressed their guilt, they often develop an atoning behavior pattern which psychologists call reaction formation. Thus, for example, a daughter represses her rancor against her mother into subconsciousness and then compensates for her hatred with anguished devotion.

A further mechanism could be called "letting off steam." This can itself take several forms. Among the Shiriana it involves chest-beating or head-clubbing between individuals in tension. In some societies it can involve the confession of a socially acceptable sin while hiding the more serious guilt; e.g. people may admit the problem of temper but hide their marital infidelities. At other times it can involve an apology in general: "I am sorry I didn't behave as I should have;" or it can involve the use of a more socially acceptable label for the transgression: "I wasn't quite honest," instead of saying: "I lied." At still other times it may involve confessing only part of the guilt so as to relieve at least some of the pressure without really coming clean. Even more common is an "accusative" confession, e.g. "I just wanted to check if any of you were hurt by my behavior yesterday; I would like to have a clear record." The "accusative" confession really tries to "pin" the onus on the other party.

Into this same category belongs "passing on the tension;" e.g. the employee who is angry with his employer, but vents his anger on the members of his own family, or Paul's mother (described by Bruno Bettelheim) who, driven by her own guilt and illusions, perpetually berated her maladjusted son as stupid and lazy.

The process of forgiveness

From personal experience, I suggest that a truly adequate process of forgiveness must include at least three steps: confession, expiation and release. These aspects are quite obvious in the case of the violated Kaka virgin reported by William D. Reyburn.

Some Kaka tribesmen living half a day's journey away have come to make a settlement in connection with a violated virgin. During the confession stage the events are examined and re-examined with microscopic realism. Shortly after dark the confession phase has been completed, and an agreement has been reached as to the amount of the expiatory payment. The money and goods are now turned over to the plaintiff as payment for the infraction. However, before the transaction is complete, the past must be "swallowed," and peace must be established. Thus as soon as the settlement has been agreed upon, the women appear in the clubhouse bringing a cooked leg of sheep. The now-forgiven culprit and his adversaries wash their hands in a special bowl of water and then pull apart the meat, exchange pieces, and eat the ritual *sataka* meal.

The same three steps to forgiveness are vividly demonstrated in the Hebrew forgiveness ritual on the Day of Atonement. First, public confession of sin is made over the heads of two goats. Then one of the goats is slain in atonement and burnt upon the altar as a sacrifice to God; and finally the other goat is led into the wilderness to show that the guilt has been removed, never to be found again.

I now want to look at each of these three aspects a little more closely.

Confession. I have treated the process of confession at length elsewhere (Appendix: 1969d & 1969i), however, several observations are in place here.

1. The necessity of it is not only based on the need for the righting of a social wrong, it is also required by the guilty person's self-image. All too often the guilty are deeply aware that they have been obtaining social belonging and respect under false pretenses; however, if they can find at least one member of the human race who will listen to them sympathetically and who, while knowing the worst, will still love and respect them, the culprits find that their own self-respect can also be restored. On the basis of this one person's acceptance, they can reasonably hope for the acceptance and respect of society at large. There is no doubt that for most people the internal conflict between self-respect and social responsibility triggered by the transgression can only be terminated by some form of honest confession.

2. Confession must be honest, open and specific. Tournier has well pointed out that the incomplete release from guilt which plagues so many people derives from the fact that their confessions have not been open and specific enough.

3. Mowrer adds that the confession must also be complete. He warns that very few people will be able to make a complete confession in one sitting. He strongly criticizes ministers who think they have done their duty after they have listened to a person for two or three hours. He insists there must be a series of sessions in which the guilty persons are allowed to "free associate," i.e., to confess anything and everything of which they are consciously aware at the moment, but that further opportunities will be necessary so that additional ramifications of the guilt can be brought to light. Because inhibitions and repressions often slow up this process, it is extremely important to allow adequate time for a full confession.

4. Mowrer continues that the confession must be public. He indicts Reformation leaders who rightfully abrogated the evils of the medieval confessional, but who in turn removed even the "one human being" who could provide a social link in forgiveness, by introducing silent prayer and secret confession to God alone. He says that Reformation leaders were so impressed with the divine aspect of forgiveness that they completely forgot the social dimension of

reconciliation. They developed powerful institutions, but in many cases have failed miserably to help the vast majority of their adherents to achieve a satisfactory release from guilt.

5. Mowrer also feels that such public confession should come at periodic intervals. Not only would such confession be healing in nature, but it would also help prevent future guilt-producing behavior. He cites a Chicago bank that gives its employees a periodic lie-detector test because "it helps them to stay honest," or as Mowrer puts it, "it increases their will-power." Lest some feel that the Catholic confessional would meet Mowrer's requirement, he specifically says it does not, for it removes the sinner too far from the essential social contact. The privacy of the confessional, the distance of the priest from ordinary life, and the average perfunctory performance totally undermine its potential positive functions.

6. To the above aspects I want to add the Christian premise that forgiveness through confession is possible only if there is genuine repentance and the serious intent to abandon the evil.

Some cautions. There is another side to confession, however, and I want to stress this fact by highlighting several cautions concerning its use:

1. Confession is not an immediate cure to all problems. If the internal pressures that were built up in order to produce the confession were very great, then the verbal catharsis may still be followed by a period of intense distress. Psychiatrist Anton Boisen has already illustrated this in the experience of the man who confessed his infidelities to his wife, but who then went into such a severe emotional crisis that he had to be institutionalized for several months. Boisen points out that because his repression had been so severe, the emotional forces required to produce the confession had grown to such intensity that once they broke through the defenses it took several months for the individual to recover his emotional equilibrium.

2. Confession can be easily abused, and any misuse can be harmful. This is true both for the confessor as well as for the person hearing the confession. For the confessor the experience may merely be a compulsive form of exhibitionism rather than a genuine experience of catharsis; for the listener, in turn, the experience may just be morbid voyeurism. For the American public which is not used to public confession, certain guidelines may be advisable.

> (a) The audience hearing the confession should include only those who are mature enough to handle its content. For example, a child in an African society might be much better equipped by its cultural experience to cope with sexual confessions than an American child of similar age.
>
> (b) The audience, at least in non-face-to-face settings, should not be indiscriminate or casual as at a Sunday morning worship service.

(c) The goal of the confession must be clearly focused on the quest of receiving forgiveness and not on exposing lurid details of the infraction.

3. A special type of misuse of confessions and forgiveness often grows out of social insecurity. In their quest for acceptance, insecure individuals may be tempted to confess wrongs they did not commit. Such confession is self-defeating, for the confessors are actually alienating themselves further because they know they are trying to gain acceptance under false pretenses.

Expiation. When the Comanche grandfather and his favorite grandson lost their best horses at the hands of the aggrieved husband, they experienced revenge rather than expiation. Expiation is a voluntary or at least expected cost which actually or ritually atones for the transgression. Mowrer says sin always impairs "the ease and the zest" with which people participate in social institutions, and undermines interpersonal "confidence and security." For this reason repayment in the sense of sacrifice, suffering and restitution (meaning replacement, restoration, putting something back) has long been widely recognized as the basic expression of human justice and the means of again making oneself acceptable after having violated some established code of conduct or social contract. As already suggested, expiation may take various forms.

1. **Restitution**. The most obvious form of repayment is, of course, restitution to repay damages inflicted. Thus when a Chulupi woman sold another woman's burros and spent the money, she had to call upon her relatives to help her assemble the full price of the animals before she could be released from her guilt. Even the violation of the Kaka virgin mentioned earlier was viewed largely as a property infraction requiring economic restitution.

2. **Expiatory payments** (payments made to atone for some grievance or offense). In cases like that of the Manus Islanders, all infractions bring about Sir Ghost[1] vengeance and only after full expiatory payments have been made to the living relatives of the offended ghosts can the culprit be assured release from spirit vengeance. With the Manus Islanders such expiatory payments carry both a social and supernatural component. Consider the following scenes described by R.F. Fortune:

> On Friday morning Pope took propitiatory payment, *kano*, to Kemwai, to expiate the offense between Noan and Pwentshiam in Kemwai's house, and another propitiatory payment to Pwiseu's house to expiate Noan's having seen Puiseu's wife naked. Standing in his canoe before Kemwai's housefront, Pope addressed the *talipolalau* (Sir Ghosts) calling them by name and saying: "Here is your payment, you ghostly ones, to expiate the

---

[1]The bleached skulls of ancestors are referred to by a respectful name equivalent to English "Sir."

> evil done under your roof." The payment, a cedar wood box with its lock and key and a European axe, he had first placed on the house platform. Kemwai did not appear. But after Pope had gone away Kemwai, as the mortal ward of the *talipolalau*, took the offering made to them unto himself.

In a similar vein Fortune continues: "Next day at dawn Paliau offered up payment to *pwanau* and to other Sir Ghosts, the relatives of *pwanau*, and divided up the payment among the wards of the Sir Ghosts."

Let me stress that such expiatory payments often are largely ritualistic or at least have greatly decreased economic utility. This can be seen in the case of the Nuer reconciliation cited at the beginning of this chapter. The goat was called an ox; even a cucumber can be called an ox in ritual contexts. This ritual aspect of expiation can also be seen in the following Ecuadorian Colorado example. A shaman was carrying on an illicit affair with a community girl. His wife, the girl's parents, and the community at large were deeply upset and came to the missionary for help. Upon his counsel, the people decided to send a delegation to speak with the offending shaman. After this public confrontation, the man at once broke off the affair. Within a few days he killed one of his choice pigs and sent pieces to all the relatives of the girl and other leading community individuals. To the missionary he sent the head. This example also raises the question of whether the missionary received a piece because he was functioning as the representative of the supernatural. If so, then we again see the social and supernatural elements linked in the forgiveness process.

Such expiatory payment, however, need not necessarily be made to the offended individuals. In fact, Mowrer (facetiously or maybe even maliciously) says that most patients of psychiatrists consider the high fees they have to pay to their counsellors as part of the "sacrifice" or "expiatory payment" needed to receive forgiveness and release from their guilt.

3. **Sacrifice.** This certainly involves a cost to the one seeking release, but it usually carries strong overtones of supernatural atonement. That it is not the actual cost but rather the sacrificial ritual which is important becomes apparent in such practices as the Nuer substitution of a cucumber for an ox; or the poor Inca's substitution of a guinea pig for a llama. It is also seen in the Hebrew sacrificial code which permitted the poor individual to substitute a pigeon for a ram.

The Hebrew atonement process, in addition to its expiatory functions, also had allusions to substitution, i.e., the sacrificial animal was dying in place of the culprit. In fact, in medieval times even the criminal who paid for his crime by his own death had to recite a special ritual formula so that his sacrifice would indeed provide release for him and for the society: "May my death be an expiation for all my wickedness." It is probably the element of equal substitution that caused the human victim to be rated as the utmost in sacrifice. For example, the Tahitians resorted to human sacrifice only in times of direst national calamity and then only after all other efforts had failed. The king then exhorted the people: "Let us offer a man as a sacrifice to atone for our unintentional offenses and to regain God's favor in this our great distress."

Sacrifice as a means of atonement has been used worldwide. It is most prevalent in societies with a pastoral economy, but even such highly agricultural societies as the Iroquois sacrificed white dogs to atone for tribal offenses.

4. **Penance**. Most major religions have placed strong emphasis upon penance. This usually involves some kind of bodily mortification. A Hindu *sadu* may sleep on a bed with projecting nails. A Roman Catholic penitent may be required to recite a certain number of Ave Marias or abstain from certain comforts or pleasures. Many Protestant groups will exclude the disciplined individual from holy communion for a period of months even after full confession has been made. Penance was also found among the Maya, Aztecs and Incas even before the advent of the Spanish conquerors. In the case of the Incas the penance prescribed by the priest often involved a night-long vigil in the cold beside the river in which the culprit washed away his sins. The Crow of the Plains spent extended periods in solitary vigils, fasting and hanging themselves up by thongs pulled through their chest and shoulder muscles.

While we Western Christians have often viewed penance as an attempt to impress the culprits with the seriousness of their infractions, the overtones of payment cannot be denied. A further dimension of penance—to evoke divine pity—seems to have played a prominent part in the religions of the Middle East. The ancient Hebrews believed that true penance always moved God to pity and that it was an ideal means of preventing divine punishment. Hebrew prophets again and again called their people to "sackcloth and ashes" to prevent the wrath of God from destroying them. Even the Gentiles of the city of Nineveh escaped divine destruction when "the great and the small" heeded Jonah's warning of impending destruction and sought forgiveness in universal penance.

Among the Plains Indians of North America, bodily mortification was probably more an attempt to buy supernatural favor than to atone for guilt, because such tortures often were essential requisites to a spirit encounter. However, E. H. Erikson interprets the Sioux sun dance, in which young braves tore their back and chest muscles, as a form of atonement for guilt accumulated during the process of growing up.

5. **Social sanction**. Especially in medieval Europe and the Middle East, penance also involved overt social sanction. The culprit was visibly marked so as to be exposed to social scorn and ostracism. Examples of this would be the famous *Sünderhemd* 'sinner's robe' which penitents were required to wear publicly, the shorn head of the "fallen girl," and the branded "scarlet letter." Also to be included in this category are exile both in its literal and figurative forms such as prohibition from participating in certain church functions for shorter periods. In the case of the Lengua in Paraguay, exile was usually self-imposed and was probably not as much the result of a penitent attitude but rather was caused by a seriously upset innermost.

Release. Once confession and expiation have been made, release is to follow. One might say that this release primarily involves the assurance that the culprit will no longer be subject to supernatural retribution. Note the expected release from the avenging Sir Ghosts in the following Manus quotation:

> ...*pwanau!* E! expiatory payment to you this. You struck them down. That was well. But they did not flee from their place. They all remained here. Later on you struck them down (again) and this time they fled.... You restore the soul stuff that you have! Send it to *topwal* who will send it to *poketa*!... The real person, the real soul stuff, is in your possession. Send this person to health. E! Expiation has come and has gone to all the ghosts who are great. All may grant your request. You made war. Expiation has come to you.

However, there is also a social dimension to release. Sin and guilt produce estrangement; confession and expiation are basically designed to re-establish fellowship. This was in evidence in both the Nuer and the Kaka examples cited earlier. The importance of such social release is very apparent in the following Lengua reconciliation scene.

A married student in the Bible school became a rather proficient singer and song director, but in characteristic Lengua fashion he shared none of his feelings or his learning with his wife. She became so outraged, partly from the slight and possibly even more because of the earlier matrilineal dominance that was now being violated, that she burned his best clothes, his song books, and even all his Scripture. When the young husband realized what she had done, he disappeared for a day. Twenty-four hours later he showed up in the Bible school quite ready to own up to his lack of communication with his wife which, according to his own words, had triggered her violent reaction. In the meanwhile, Lengua church leaders had called a public meeting for the evening. There the young man again repeated his guilt of non-communication. In the course of a lengthy discussion the wife also owned her anger. After all the participants had each said their piece and the husband and wife had agreed to mend their ways, the leader summarized the consensus and proclaimed that the evil had now been removed. Then he pointedly asked the men: "Will you now stop talking about this?" When they answered in the affirmative, he called on the women, then the young people, and finally on the children. As evidence of the full release, the young man was restored to his musical tasks at the next evening's meeting.

The release must also be personal, i.e. the guilty party must be able to accept forgiveness. In other words, she/he must be able to forgive herself/himself. This personal release restores the inner equilibrium and peace and thereby sets in motion the process of physical and psychic healing. Mowrer underscores the aspect of personal release when he says:

> But what is here generally overlooked, it seems, is that the recovery (constructive change, redemption) is most assuredly

attained, not by helping a person reject and rise above his sins, but by helping him *accept them*. This is the paradox which we have not at all understood and which is the very crux of the problem. Just so long as a person lives under the shadow of real, unacknowledged, and unexpiated guilt, he *cannot* (if he has any character at all) "accept himself;" and all *our* efforts to reassure and accept him will avail nothing. He will continue to hate himself and to suffer the inevitable consequences of self-hatred. But the moment he (with or without "assistance") begins to accept his guilt and sinfulness, the possibility of radical reformation opens up; and with this, the individual may legitimately, though not without pain and effort, pass from deep, pervasive self-rejection and self-torture to a new freedom of self-respect and peace.

CHAPTER 30

FOUR KINDS OF FORGIVENESS

In this chapter I want to discuss the four kinds of forgiveness I have experienced: supernatural (divine), social, self, and secular. The first two often combine in what I will call religious forgiveness (discussed later in this Chapter). They are all closely interrelated, and at least the first three are necessary for a full experience of forgiveness.

I. A Caribou Eskimo community is suffering intense hunger—all the game has disappeared. The members of the tribe meet with their shaman leader to ascertain the cause of their troubles. The shaman goes into a trance and "sees" that the terrible sea goddess *Takanakapsaluk* has been offended by the many broken taboos and evil thoughts of the people; in punishment she is now withholding their food supply. Acutely aware of their guilt, the people—adults and children—confess broken taboos, sins and countless wicked thoughts, but their condition continues to worsen. There is only one remedy left—they must send the shaman "in person" to propitiate the angered deity. This involves a most difficult trip to the "bottom of the sea" where the goddess lives. It is a journey fraught with extreme difficulty and terror: falling stones, fierce mythological animals and malignant spirits lurking everywhere to destroy any human who might venture this way. Only the most courageous shaman would so much as dare to try; for even if he should survive and arrive at the destination, he still would have to confront the angry goddess who, with hair disheveled and covered with filth (the product of human transgression), is seething with anger because she is suffocating from the foul emanations of human sins. She has to be cleansed and pacified if the people are to receive release from their punishment. On arriving, the shaman gently begins to wipe away the filth and to stroke and comb the hair of the fuming goddess. Bit by bit her fury subsides until finally, when she is fully pacified, he is able to turn her face to see all the animals she has been hoarding. Her wrath placated, the goddess now releases humans from their punishment and returns their food supply.

II. Looking out of the window one day, a missionary to the Chulupi of Paraguay saw two women in a violent fight beside the village well. They had grabbed each other by the hair and were hitting each other furiously. He hurried out to separate them, but succeeded only after one of the deacons from the Chulupi church came to lend a hand. On being separated, one of the women, a believer, picked up her waterpot, put it on her head and went home. Shortly thereafter the other woman, an unbeliever, passed the believer's house, where the latter again attacked her with renewed fury. Once again the deacon separated them. Next day the two accidentally met in front of the store of a nearby village and fought yet another round. By this time the believing woman was feeling very guilty, and so she and her husband came to the missionary to make confession and ask for help. Here is her story:

> A donkey buyer, offering fancy prices for burros, came to our village, and the unbelieving woman cashed in on the bonanza. However, she sold not only her own animal, but also two belonging to me. Furthermore, she not only sold them without my permission, she spent all the money before I even found out about what she had done. This made me so angry that I started to fight at the well.

The confession to the missionary was only a prelude, for the Chulupi church leadership was also moving to settle the quarrel. All the people who had sold donkeys, the relatives of the offended and the offending women, the missionary and other leading people of the village, were called together to discuss the matter. At this meeting the fighting women, along with their relatives and many others present, spoke their opinions. Finally the leader called upon several who hadn't spoken yet, and they too spoke. When all had aired their feelings, he called for a settlement. The relatives of the offending woman offered to help to raise the money necessary to pay the aggrieved woman. The latter accepted the money and promised to "let go of her anger." The leader then called on the missionary to "seal the matter" in prayer. The guilt had been aired, restitution had been made, and social forgiveness had been achieved. Finally this social transaction had been divinely validated by the missionary's prayer to God.

III. A very devout college senior had already confessed her guilt: during the last two years in high school she had yielded at least in part to the approaches of a married teacher. The affair was terminated in the early stages, nevertheless severe guilt had accumulated. She had earnestly asked God for forgiveness on many occasions. In fact, she had already confessed her guilt to one of her closest friends, but still could not find release. Finally, in a conversation with an older sympathetic female relative, she realized her problem—she needed to forgive herself. She needed to admit that she—the good girl—had fallen far short of her own Christian ideals. She also had to accept the fact that no confession could undo her deed; it could only be forgiven. After struggling for several more days, she at last was able to "own" these facts about herself, and with this honest admission she achieved a sense of peace and release—she had finally been able to forgive herself.

IV. Dear Ann (Landers):

> I am 19, a sophomore in a midwestern university and considered

good-looking and reasonably bright by my peers. I've been dating since I was 15 and, without boasting, I can truthfully say I've had more than my share of male attention.

During this summer, I met my ideal. We dated several times and I found myself saying "No" to others in the hope he would call. I loved being with him. On August 2 he was leaving for his vacation. We both hated to part and sat in the park for two hours saying good night. For some mysterious reason all my willpower and good intentions vanished and I gave in. I told myself "This is love. Why should I deny him a true expression of my feelings?"

He sent a few postcards along the way but did not telephone me as I had hoped he would. Last night he returned—a changed man. He took me to supper and informed me that it would probably be our last date. These are his words: "You are not the girl I had hoped you were. Our last night together was a nightmare. You made me ashamed of myself. I could never marry you after that. I would always wonder if there had been others. This has been the greatest disappointment of my life."

So there's my story, Ann. I am trying to keep my chin up, but it isn't easy. I tell myself no decent man would treat a girl this way, but deep down I know it was my decision, not his—and all the rationalization in the world doesn't make it right.

Yesterday's Fool

Counseling columnist Ann Landers' answer to this confession, in summary, was: We will publish your letter as a warning to others, but in the meanwhile keep your chin up. You've just learned the hard way. Remember, even the hero you've been waiting for might ask you to "go all the way." If the girl says yes, however, he may well decide that she is not the heroine he has been waiting for.

The college sophomore's guilt was confessed publicly, though anonymously. It was "atoned" by exposure and by the salutary warning it provides for others. However neither the divine nor the social aspects of forgiveness were in focus. The sophomore, using one of the modern, non-religious channels, was trying to achieve secular forgiveness.

The preceding four accounts illustrate four kinds of forgiveness —supernatural, social, self and secular. I want to further illustrate each of these types in order to show:

1. That the first three types of forgiveness (divine, social and self) are three essential aspects of a fully adequate process of guilt resolution. In a given setting and with different kinds of infractions, their relative, overt preeminence may vary, but the conspicuous absence of any one of them will leave the penitent with serious spiritual, social, psychic and often even physical problems.

2. The current popularity of secular forgiveness is in large part due to the failure of the church as a divinely ordained social institution to help humans deal adequately with their guilt.

Supernatural (divine) forgiveness

The supernatural, to which humans appeal for release from guilt, or which they try to propitiate because of their failures, assumes a variety of forms. In the Eskimo curing ceremony the appeal for the release from guilt by the penitent and the supporting community was directed impersonally to the supernatural forces that avenge broken taboos by sending illness to humans.

In the Nuer reconciliation following the wounding of the young man described in the previous chapter, the supernatural which was invoked as a witness to the social transaction was addressed as *kwoth* 'spirit.'

Among the Manus Islanders the supernatural is represented visually in the form of the bleached skulls which personify the souls of their deceased ancestors called Sir Ghosts. These supernatural forces stand in a direct kinship relationship to living persons.

Traditional Hinduism provides its adherents with a pantheon of personalized deities which is so vast that it has been said to outnumber the actual population.

The ancient Hebrews addressed their appeal for forgiveness to Yahweh, whom they considered as their own exclusive tribal God, for it was he who had chosen Israel to be his special people and had made an eternal covenant with them. In Christianity, which is essentially based on this Hebrew tradition, God has already been universalized so as to make him the God of all nations (Acts 10:34-35).

The quest for supernatural forgiveness. As I reviewed the worldwide quest for supernatural forgiveness, I realized that it almost always involves either penance (Inca, Tupinamba, medieval Catholics, etc.), expiation (North American Plains Indians, Manus Islanders, Hindu sadus, etc.), or sacrifice (animal: Nuer, ancient Hebrews, etc.; human: Maya, Aztec, Hindu, etc.). Of these ritual accompaniments, sacrifices are the most conspicuous in that they imply a substitute in life and blood to atone for guilt and to purchase the release of the culprit. Sacrifices can be personal or communal, and in their ultimate degree they require a human victim to atone for human guilt. The following two examples are merely illustrations of a wide range of sacrificial practices.

The monsoon rains had just finished destroying most of the crops when Hari Singh, a Ghaziabad street sweeper in India, returned from work and found that his two pigs had wandered away from home and had been locked up in the city pound. Since he had neither money nor prospect of getting any to redeem them, he was sure that this calamity was divine punishment for his wicked life. He was convinced that he must seek atonement, but he did not know how. That night the goddess *Kali* appeared to him in a dream and told him what he must do. The next day he did it.

While his wife and children were at work rescuing the remains of their monsoon damaged crops, he took their four-year-old son Bihram and screaming *Kali maiki jai* 'Hail, Mother Kali,' cut his throat. He sprinkled some of the blood on the back of the black image of Kali, and the rest he smeared on its forehead. Then he sat down under a tree waiting for the goddess to demonstrate her forgiveness by freeing his pigs.

The preceding is an example of spontaneous non-ritual sacrifice. It stands in bold contrast to the highly ritualized human sacrifices of the Aztecs or even the following example of African animal sacrifice.

The Tswana of Southern Africa seek supernatural release from guilt in the following sacrificial ritual. While the priests kill two animals (a black one to atone for the evil deeds and a white one to purify the culprit), the penitents kneel and make a full public confession of their misdeeds. On completing their confession they drink some of the warm blood of the sacrificed animals. Then the priest places some of the fatty entrails on the penitents' heads and calls on the angered deity to accept this sacrifice of reconciliation and to release the penitents from guilt and retribution.

Religious forgiveness

Both of the preceding examples show that supernatural forgiveness almost always involves some social dimension. (As mentioned at the beginning of this chapter, the term we are using for this combination of supernatural and social is religious forgiveness.) In the Hindu example, we see it in the human sacrificial victim. In the Tswana sacrifice, we have the officiating priests and the observing public. In fact, these two dimensions are so intertwined that it is often difficult to separate them. This supernatural-social linkage stands out boldly in the following account of reconciliation and forgiveness I witnessed among the Chulupi.

Two profligate teenage girls insulted several older church women with some very vulgar sexual language. (This is the epitome of insult and evil, since the Chulupi avoid all direct reference to sex even between husband and wife.) The women became angry and a fight resulted. As time went on more and more women on both sides became involved in the dispute, until finally even a number of men were drawn in. Before long, however, several church people began to feel guilty and asked the missionary to help them arrange for a formal reconciliation meeting.

The first part of the meeting was largely accusation and counter accusation, but gradually as more and more of the participants had spoken their mind, consensus in regard to the primary guilt of the two girls (of course, there was also clear recognition of secondary guilt of many other people) seemed to be emerging. The men, therefore, called for mutual apology and reconciliation; but the two girls, not yet ready to own their guilt, flared up in anger and stormed out of the meeting. The gathering dissolved with the matter unresolved.

Two weeks later was communion Sunday. When the group gathered, several men pointed out that before they could legitimately participate in holy communion they would first have to settle the community problem. Obviously they could not deal with the offending girls, who, not being church members, were absent from the communion service. The leader began by exhorting all the believers to get rid of their bad feelings. After some discussion, one of the men broke down and cried, admitting he had done wrong in joining the fight. Other men followed his example and confessed their part in the quarrel. After the men had set the pattern, the women followed suit and were also reconciled. Then the Chulupi leaders called on the missionary to deliver a message from God's Word. The missionary responded with a sermon on confession and forgiveness. When he finished, several of the Chulupi men rose to reinforce his words by pointing out that only as people forgive each other can they in turn receive divine forgiveness. Then, having been reconciled publicly, the group celebrated their release in holy communion.

The theology of forgiveness

I don't want to get into a full-scale discussion of the theology of forgiveness. However, I want to highlight some of the theological premises for the rituals and agencies of forgiveness which the Christian church purports to provide. The Christian practice of forgiveness, as we have suggested earlier, finds its origin in the earlier Hebrew rituals which demanded that the sinner confess transgressions to Yahweh in the presence of the priests and the people (Lev. 5:5). With his hands placed on the head of the sacrificial animal, which represented his personal substitute in the expiation for the sin committed, the penitent made his/her confession. Then the priest, as the human agent of the divine, carried out the atonement ritual and pronounced the forgiveness.

Even more dramatic was the great Day of Atonement in which the sins of the entire nation were confessed over the heads of two rams—one to be slain in sacrifice and atonement and the other to be led into the wilderness as a symbol of the removal of the guilt (Lev. 16).

The ministry of John the Baptist, as recorded for us in the Gospels, consisted of a call to confession and repentance (Mark 1:4); and on the public confession of their sins the people were baptized. Jesus went even further and stressed the mutual responsibility of the members of the believing community by assigning to them the functions of face-to-face soul nurture (Mt. 18:15-20) and "binding and loosing" of erring members of the church (Mt. 16:18-19; Jn. 20:19-23). Some of the epistles carry a similar appeal, as when James (5:13-20) calls for believers to confess their sins to one another and to pray for each other so that they may be healed.

The Anabaptist wing of the Protestant church has tried to put these functions into practice and affirms that every believer can function as priest and hear the confessions of their fellows and help them obtain divine forgiveness. They call this ministry the *priesthood of believers* since it delegates a share in the priestly function to every believer.

Retreat of the church from the priesthood of believers

As I look at the history of the Christian church, I find that already long before the Middle Ages the earlier practice of the priesthood of believers had largely given way to a professional priesthood which had the monopoly on dispensing religious forgiveness. Theologians have even raised the question whether this shift was not already well under way even in apostolic times, as signaled in the shift from the *homologeo* "to confess, to admit or declare publicly" of John the Baptist's preaching to *metanoeo* "to feel remorse, to change one's mind, to repent, to be converted" which predominates in the Pauline epistles. But whatever the cause, there is no question that the original voluntary public confession had been largely replaced by compulsory, private confession in which a professional priest assigned penance and spoke absolution. In fact, in the medieval church forgiveness had become a semi-commercial enterprise, since one could purchase indulgences, i.e. buy advance "forgiveness" for sins one intended to commit.

The Protestant Reformation proposed to sweep away these and other abuses, but—sad to say—it did not reinstate the priesthood of believers as a general practice; for with the Reformation emphasis on silent prayer and confession to God alone, even the one tenuous social link—the priest—was removed from the forgiveness process. In retrospect, one has to admit that Luther's famous Reformation slogan "the just shall live by faith" worked only as long as people lived in relatively closed communities with more or less permanent face-to-face relationships. With the advent of rapid urbanization, widespread mobility and increasing social distance, more and more people found that this "cheap grace" (as Hobart Mowrer calls the practice of confession to God alone) was no longer able to resolve their guilt.

But the church, instead of realistically facing the declining relevance of its practice and developing the necessary socio-religious contexts for meaningful forgiveness, quietly retreated from the field and relinquished its Christ-given commission to minister to sin-sick souls, and today it unprotestingly accepts the emphasis of twentieth century psychiatry that these problems are based on constitutional and biochemical factors rather than on genuine guilt. Even where the post-Reformation church did continue to involve itself in forgiveness, it largely slipped back into the medieval pattern of the minister operating as a professional rather than a "brother." However, as professionals concerned with souls, ministers often left something to be desired. Many clergymen think they have done their duty when they have listened to someone for an hour or two. When a person comes back too often, they are prone to say: "He/she is a sick person who makes mountains out of molehills." They do not grasp the deeper human problems that underlie the things such "sick" people say and do. Tournier points out that it was Freud who manifested "real love for the souls of people" for he had the patience to listen to them sympathetically for hundreds of hours.

Mowrer, in his book *The Crisis in Psychiatry and Religion,* goes even a step further and accuses clergy of "preaching beyond their experience." He asserts that many ministers have actually lost confidence in religion as an effective forgiving agent, for when they themselves have serious guilt problems, they almost invariably seek support and direction from a secular therapist rather than from within their church ranks.

Having castigated ministers, Mowrer then proceeds to indict the whole congregation, which he calls "a pious fellowship that preaches salvation" but can no longer tolerate the acknowledged sinner in its midst. In the church setting people have to conceal their sin from themselves and others because most Christians would be horrified if a *real* sinner should suddenly be discovered among the "righteous." Mowrer concludes: "So we remain alone in our sin, living in lies and hypocrisy. The fact is that we all are sinners in need of forgiveness."

Social forgiveness

Like supernatural forgiveness, I have found this "pure" social forgiveness (except in relatively superficial social-etiquette-type infractions) is relatively rare, for in major reconciliations the supernatural element, where not overtly visible, is at least implicit in the social transaction. In the previous chapter, I reported an Ecuadorian Colorado reconciliation episode in which a shaman, involved extramaritally with a girl, broke off the affair in response to community action; he then killed a pig and sent portions to members of the aggrieved family and leading individuals of the community, including the missionary. Obviously the pig was an expiatory payment, and the portions sent to the relatives and the community leaders were related to the social aspect of the atonement; however, the head sent to the missionary gives all the appearance of having supernatural implications.

The social dimension

The importance of the social dimension in the forgiveness ritual often has not been fully appreciated by religious leaders, especially those within mainstream Protestantism. On the other hand, Pentecostals in Latin America not only permit but also often encourage public confession and the accompanying social forgiveness. And it is this social dimension that seems to account in large part for their appeal to people of Catholic background who have found the secret confessional inadequate for achieving full assurance of forgiveness.

Even in those societies in which a shaman applies pressure to extract confession from a patient in the process of magic healing, the social dimension is present in at least two aspects. First, the shaman's intervention is based on the common faith of the community, and so he functions as a representative of the community as a whole. Second, the members of the community are often present in person, providing social support through singing, dancing and various types of responsive chanting.

Similarly, the Hebrew priest at the sacrifice and the Roman Catholic priest in the confessional represent both the deity and the society from which the person needs release. When the confessional becomes secret, however, the social dimension is severely weakened. It is precisely the social dimension that often makes confession to a fellow Christian so helpful, for in the involvement of this one person the whole church society is symbolically represented. We can thus generalize that when a priest or minister serves as confessor by peer group consensus rather than by profession or by bureaucratic placement, he too can function as representative of the group as a whole. However, if he is separated from the community by ecclesiastical investiture, professional expertise, or even more by celibate withdrawal from ordinary life, he compromises his function as social peer and weakens the social link in the forgiveness process.

From my point of view the social dimension is obviously related to the way in which sin and guilt function in life. Sin, as Dietrich Bonhoeffer in his book *Life Together* points out, always withdraws the culprit from the community, and the more isolated the person becomes, the more destructive the power of sin over him or her. If we add to this the Reformation emphasis on the "with God only" transaction of forgiveness (which seldom suffices to legitimately integrate the culprit into the community) and compound this with the social distance that accompanies our current secularization and urbanization (which have left people floundering with very weak or broken interpersonal relationships), we begin to understand why the social dimension of forgiveness is so essential in our day.

Thus I stress that people need a social context in which they can openly admit how far they are falling short but still be accepted and loved, and can develop the kind of group approved behavior they really desire. Mowrer feels that our dependence upon society goes far beyond mere support. He suggests that even the desire to do right depends upon the social context.

I am increasingly persuaded that willpower or self-control is not nearly as individual a matter as we sometimes think. Is it not basically a *social* phenomenon? Here in society is where the norms and values reside, and the person whose life is open to social interaction and influence has the benefit of social supports and sanctions. But the individual who practices covertness and secrecy does not have this source of strength and soon becomes the victim of uncontrolled temptation and a "weak will." Superficially, the difficulty may lie in the area of human sexual drives and practices; but more fundamentally the problem is one of social integration or the lack of it.

Group support

We all need a community—fellowship—that forgives and heals, a community that considers the sinner worth saving, and a social context that provides the penitent with the necessary support for learning new behavior. This represents the true priesthood of believers. Mowrer sees this function at its best not in the church of today, but in such organizations as the Salvation Army and Alcoholics Anonymous. He says:

> ...the most radically redemptive enterprises which we today know, notably the Salvation Army and Alcoholics Anonymous, are *lay* movements with "leaders" coming, not from our

> universities and seminaries, but from the ranks of their own converted and transformed personnel. Here the Priesthood of All Believers is more than a high-sounding Reformation slogan; it is a living reality.

Mowrer's thesis can be summarized as follows: persons overwhelmed by guilt are living in a self-created prison of duplicity and are denying their true identity. If they can be helped to overcome their unrealistic, moral fears and repudiate their old strategy of secrecy and withdrawal, and instead be encouraged to "return to the community," they can be healed. He describes such a healing community in a therapy context:

A woman whom he calls Marjorie had become so isolated by her guilt that she had to be institutionalized. But in the process of group therapy, she was finally able to own her problem publicly. One day she burst out: "This morning Dr. Mowrer said I was not a very good mother," and before either the other patients or the psychiatrist could recover from their surprise she added: "And I am not!" Then she described the specific incident which had precipitated her hospitalization. The relief she experienced from this confession was so dramatic that she could soon be discharged from the hospital. Mowrer says that because Marjorie received so much approval and support from the other patients when she made her confession, she was able to appropriate social forgiveness. Nor did the benefit stop here—Marjorie's courageous example was an inspiration to other patients, many of whom followed her example of transparency and likewise received help.

In his book *The Second Touch* Keith Miller describes such a fellowship setting in which social forgiveness can take place. Just before he left home to lead a men's retreat, Miller and his wife had a clash. It wasn't just an isolated spat; it was part of a vicious cycle of mutual harassment which they had not been able to overcome. But here he was leading a group of church men while he himself felt thoroughly unfit and dishonest.

> I realized that I really needed their prayers and that I was just protecting myself and my reputation as a Christian by my silence, since many of them had been honest about the pressing issues in their lives. So I told the group what I have just told you. After a couple of minutes silence, the man sitting next to me quietly confessed that he had had a remarkably similar weekend. Two other men then related almost identical experiences.... After we had talked a while, my whole situation was in some way different.

Why are people so ready to respond to transparency? Mowrer asserts that social forgiveness is readily available at no monetary cost to everyone, if not in a church, then in somebody else's living room or in any other assembly of close friends. He further points out, however, that confession or social forgiveness does not mean just furtively admitting sin to someone else; no, it means confessing in the sense of honestly talking with a spouse or some close friends in order to become truly known.

On the other hand, I don't think this means that the erstwhile sinners have to "tell everyone," for not everyone is that interested. But if they really want peace of mind they must carry openness to the point where they do not care who knows about them. And if sharing their life story with a stranger helps, they should be willing to do so.

In light of the above, I think it is important to point out that when a tribal society loses its social cohesiveness and traditional self-definition, social forgiveness will become increasingly more difficult to achieve. Canadian aborigines are deeply concerned about dissension on the reservation. They complain that when people are so "split up" they cannot do things cooperatively any more. Nor is it only a Canadian aborigine problem; it is a matter of universal concern. Societies undergoing rapid social change especially need a church community in which the inevitable tensions can be released.

Forgiving oneself

I have already noted that self is to a large extent defined in the social context, and when persons do not live up to their ideals, their guilt tends to alienate them from their fellows. People feel guilty not only for their original misdeed, but also because in their social interaction with others they project "a role" and begin to hate themselves for their dishonesty.

Mowrer says that when people allege that "I don't care what people think of me," they are really confessing that they are tormented by a guilty conscience and cannot honestly accept themselves. They project their non-acceptance upon others and then rationalize to cover up their ego deflation.

This leads me to the basic premise of this section. In order for persons to receive full forgiveness, they must be able to "own" their sin and "forgive" themselves. All too often, however, we attempt to help people to "rise above" their sins rather than help them to admit their failures. That is not the way to salvation. As long as people live under the shadow of real, unacknowledged and unexpiated guilt, they cannot, if they have any character at all, "accept themselves," and all our efforts to reassure them will avail nothing. They will continue to hate themselves and will suffer the inevitable consequences of this self-hatred. But the moment they begin to accept their guilt, the possibility of radical reformation opens up, and they may legitimately pass from pervasive self-rejection and self-torture to a new freedom of forgiveness and self-respect.

Secular forgiveness

The label "secular forgiveness" as I have intimated earlier, is not on par with the other three kinds of forgiveness. It stands almost as a polar opposite to supernatural forgiveness, for it represents an attempt to resolve guilt without even an implicit supernatural validation. It differs from religious forgiveness by requiring only an overt social dimension. In religious forgiveness, the social element is, in a sense, optional because it is theoretically possible for persons to make their transaction with God alone. This social element may be reduced to one person as in the case of the psychiatrist, and at other times may occur even without an actual face-to-face confrontation as in the case of the counseling columnist. In psychiatric group therapy and in Alcoholics Anonymous, it involves a more extensive social context.

The origin of secular forgiveness

When I looked for the basis of the secularization of forgiveness, I found a number of interacting factors such as (1) the general secularization that has accompanied advancing scientific education, (2) increased specialization, specifically in the area of psychic life, (3) rapid urbanization with its accompanying increase in social distance and the growing sense of isolation of the individual from the social group, (4) the Protestant emphasis on dealing personally and only with God, (5) the general retreat of the church from the priesthood of all believers and its soul-healing functions, and (6) the fact that secular counseling is often more realistically geared to human psychic needs for achieving forgiveness than the church is. Several of these factors warrant additional comment.

Increased scientific specialization has not only produced more kinds of specialists, it has also been accompanied, at least in the Western world, by an "awe of expertise." The doctor, psychologist and psychiatrist all seem to know so much more about the human psyche than the minister. One publication gives the following reasons why the "doctor" figure is replacing the "priest" and the "brother" in people's quest for forgiveness:

(1) Doctors deal with the penitent in terms of a doctor-and-patient role rather than in a person-to-person relationship. When the sessions are finished, there need be no further personal or social involvement between them.

(2) The doctor's involvement labels the problem as illness rather than as guilt or blame, so the person feels less indicted.

(3) The penitent need not fear rejection because it is the doctor's role to accept people. The doctor gets paid to accept people.

(4) Doctors solve the patient's problems through technical competence, not because they have any personal commitment to the patient.

(5) Doctors serve the patient for payment, and once they have received their due, they have no further claim on the patient.

(6) The doctors' code of ethics demands that they keep the problems confessed in strict confidence.

I think I can honestly affirm that secular counseling is often more realistic in its approach to helping people in distress. Ministers have often been taught to believe in the once-and-for-all transaction of confession and forgiveness, and as a result have often lacked the patience to help the guilty person make a complete confession, find full release and develop a new more positive behavior pattern. Psychiatry, with its emphasis on self-disclosure and authentic being, meets the long-range need for support in role rehearsal by its repeated sessions. It also prevents the counselees from overexposing themselves by rigidly limiting the amount of time allotted for each individual session.

The problems of secular forgiveness

Secular forgiveness, including psychotherapy, is not without drawbacks, however. Like the priest in the confessional, the professional counselor often does not meet the peer requirements of the guilty person for adequate social forgiveness. The counselor's acceptance may prove inadequate as a symbol of peer group acceptance, and while the guilt symptoms may be temporarily reduced, the patients actually remain bound and unforgiven in their interaction with their social peers.

In my own counseling experience as a "brother" and with considerable self-exposure, I have often been made painfully aware that my acceptance of a younger person, while helpful in the beginning stages, often fell short of the long-range need of social acceptance. For complete forgiveness, many students had to be helped to face their problems transparently with accepting peers before they were truly free. Jourard underscores this by noting that patients sometimes say, "You are the first person I have ever been completely honest with." This statement, he says, always makes him uncomfortable because it reveals that they are unable to talk with their spouse, family, or friends in a helpful way. Professional psychotherapy is but a meager substitute.

A further problem, especially for psychotherapy, is in the matter of payment. As already indicated, many patients unconsciously consider high fees as a kind of expiatory payment. But this is false expiation, and the very discovery of this fact can be harmful to the patient.

Next, Freudian psychiatry, with its assumption that guilt is basically false because it proceeds either from an abusing superego for which the person is not responsible, or it is future guilt, i.e. guilt about actions the person is afraid to perform, often works only on the reduction of the guilt *symptoms*, and leaves the actual guilt largely unresolved.

Finally, whether our science-minded generation approves of it or not, people everywhere seem to find full release from their guilt only when the process of forgiveness includes also a transcendent dimension. Since psychotherapy generally operates on a purely human plane, it denies the penitent one of the essential aspects of adequate forgiveness.

Conclusion

Even though this chapter employs many examples of guilt resolution drawn from tribal cultures and indigenous churches, it is, I think, a critique of the forgiveness practices of the organized church in Western Christendom and in Western culture in general. Since we missionaries are a product of this Western guilt-resolving milieu, there is danger that we foist our inherited and often woefully inadequate practices upon the developing indigenous church. Even where we do not actively "push" an inadequate model, we may unconsciously or even consciously discourage or stifle patterns which the indigenous church would normally develop on the basis of its cultural background. A frank look at the problem can not only help prevent harmful involvements for overseas workers, but can actually encourage them to actively help the indigenous church to develop and practice adequate guilt resolution.

Postscript

Nearly six years have passed since I began assembling this volume. As I reread the material recently I became deeply aware about several things I had learned about forgiveness since then. I now want to add these insights in this brief Postscript.

Forgiveness can occur unilaterally. I remember an old mentor of mine once using the example of a person being hurt badly by someone else. This person nursed that grudge and waited for the offender to come and apologize. It never happened. So the offended person remained in that same spot on the bank while the river of life flowed by him for 45 years. The apology never came so he did not find forgiveness. He did not realize that forgiveness could be purely in his own self-interest. It could be considered a purely selfish act. Unforgiveness binds the victim far more than it does the perpetrator of the offence. Remember the Greek *aphiemi* "forgiveness" literally means "to release." And the hurt person often needs the release more than the perpetrator.

Empathy toward the perpetrator often makes unilateral forgiveness possible. If the hurt person can find a way "to get into the offenders shoes and walk a mile in them," the hurt and the anger can be put into perspective. Often one can then release the perpetrator and in the process find release for oneself. It may take two to be reconciled, but it takes only one to achieve forgiveness.

STATUS REPORTS AFTER 70

I now want to summarize what I have learned in a few of the major areas in life.

First, my metaphors of the church and faith have profoundly changed. I no longer regard the church as a fortress where I can escape the world. Today I see it more as a hospice for sinners in need. It is a purifying context, rather than a pure one.

I cannot stress enough how the shift from faith as a walled structure to faith as a rope and an anchor in Jesus Christ has changed my life. That switch of metaphors has been most crucial in my experience.

The shift of metaphor from the church as a bounded set to the church as a centered set is still an ongoing process (see page 274 for details). I have learned that people in other faiths may also have found an anchor in God which I need to respect. I am still learning how to live out my faith as an anchoring rope and especially to respect faith in others that is different from my own.

Second, peace is a vital premise of Mennonite written theology; in practice, I feel, it probably isn't very significant anymore. As I said earlier, the great peacemakers I have learned to know were the Lengua. It has been deeply painful for me to see how the Mennonite immigrants who went to the Chaco to preserve their peace principles have been busy teaching the Lengua how to be more aggressive rather than learning from them how to be truly peaceful in daily life.

In this section I also highlight my indebtedness to Gandhi. His life has helped me really appreciate the practice of nonviolence. He has provided me with most of the rules of thumb that today guide my behavior in protest for conscience' sake.

Finally, I come full circle to face my Mennonite heritage. Life has taught me the significance of being a Mennonite. I have realized what a contribution the Anabaptists made to the Reformation. While Luther and Zwingli and other Reformers all began by realizing that the Christian faith required a separation between church and state, all of them, for reasons of convenience and protection eventually chose to compromise. Only the Anabaptist/Mennonites rejected outright the state's sword as an instrument of the church. They insisted that the sword may not be used to protect truth! It may not be used to convert people! It may not be used to enforce church discipline! Members of Christ's church are there by voluntary choice, not there to exercise violence on others. While this is still an important Mennonite principle in the statement of faith, in actual life it has lost most of its practical significance. It probably represents one of my greatest concerns for the Mennonite Brethren Church today.

I began as a young man ashamed of my heritage and my Mennonite name but my experience overseas has increasingly made me proud of this label. I am grateful that Mennonite Central Committee has taken upon itself to complete or round out the ministry of Mennonite churches. Most of the churches have fallen woefully short in regard to their responsibility toward the whole person. MCC has often taken up the slack. For those interested, I have shared my convictions in this regard in a separate book, *Only the Sword of the Spirit!*

CHAPTER 31
THE CHURCH, FAITH AND SALVATION

When I try to reconstruct my earliest mental picture of the church, I do not see anything resembling a peace church. I visualize instead a fortress with an impregnable wall, a moat and ramparts able to withstand all outside attacks, be they from the world or from the Evil One.

The walled fortress

Early on I imagined the leading individuals in the church as officers helping to equip the saints to wage the good fight of faith. The warfare, of course, was entirely spiritual, with the fiery darts or arrows of doubt and unbelief being fired by the Evil One. The saints at the ramparts carried shields of faith to deflect any darts that came their way.

Should a satanic arrow of temptation strike a saint inside the fortress, the other saints would spring to action. They would warn the brother or sister of the danger to which they were exposed and urge that individual to repent of the evil deed so as to keep Satan and his machinations out of the pure church. Failing that, the contaminated heretic would be spewed out to keep the church inside pure, free from any wrinkle, spot, or blemish.

Today I see a great resemblance between my early mental picture of the church and the Mennonite colony structure in Russia. Here were God's people organized into a separate colony with its own villages and government, running all their own affairs. They considered themselves completely separated from the world. The church and the world were seen to be two totally different spheres which had nothing to do with each other.

A big scare hit the Mennonites in Russia in 1860. A group of Bible-reading Mennonites suddenly discovered that their church had become grossly contaminated by the world, and they decided that it needed a completely new beginning. So they built a brand-new fortress. My own parents, who had been nominal members of the mother Mennonite church, were converted and joined the new Mennonite Brethren Church fortress. They spoke with anguish of their lostness within the traditional Mennonite church and of how, by God's grace, they had found refuge with Jesus through conversion in the new. Now in the new Mennonite Brethren Church they could return to the original ideal of a holy fortress which had no place for the world and the Evil One.

The move to Canada posed some problems for their church fortress. It was impossible in this new country to reconstruct the strict wall of separation between the church and the world that they had had in Russia. While Mennonites still lived in their own well-defined communities, exposure to the outside world could no longer be avoided. Many had to take jobs outside of the Mennonite islands. And these jobs required them to move into the world on a daily basis. Already as a youth in Manitoba, I began to modify my picture of the church.

The church as an enclosing wall

In this revised picture, the church was still a sheltering structure, but without the moat, the ramparts, and all the bellicose paraphernalia. Within the Mennonite community one still struggled to keep the world out. Satan was still an active enemy who shot fiery darts of temptation at the saints. The church continued its vigilance for those who might have been hit by these arrows. They still practiced mutual admonition and even occasional excommunication, but not as frequently as before.

When I examined this new structure, I saw that the wall was not made of a single solid piece. It was built of individual stones or building bricks. On the one hand, I saw this wall as being made up of the various beliefs that the church professed, and there was a long list of them. However, it was also made up of all the do's and don'ts, the internal rules for church and community life. At this stage I had no consciousness that some of these bricks might actually be culture bound. Certainly the church had no awareness that any of the world's culture might be present in its very protecting wall.

A new realization came to me about this time: the walled structure was designed not only to keep the world and the Evil One out, but also to keep the believers "penned up." This spelled trouble for the many people who had to earn their living outside of the walled community. The Russian ideal, to have a small farm on which each family could sustain itself with minimal contact with the world outside, just wasn't feasible in the new country.

Do I need all the bricks in the wall?

When I became a young man and began doing community outreach under the West Coast Children's Mission, there was already an emerging awareness that some of the bricks in the church wall were obsolete, e.g., the German language. German was of almost no value in our local outreach in Canada; once we went to Colombia as missionaries it had no place whatsoever in our daily life, except possibly to read the home church German weekly paper and to write a prayer letter to the home congregation. There, on the mission field, we generally spoke Spanish plus the tribal languages of the people we were trying to reach.

Our decade of operating abroad made us aware of the deep differences between cultures. We learned that many bricks in our home church wall were cultural and not at all biblical. Our many church biblical do's and don'ts all had a cultural wrapper. A glaring example was the traditional Mennonite view of female modesty which typically meant a certain kind of a hairdo, usually a bun for older married women, and conservative dress. Now we realized that for the Waunana, modesty was something entirely different. A Waunana woman who was properly married and was faithful to her husband would not dare to cover her breasts, because in her culture covered breasts were a signal that she was publicly available—that she was a prostitute.

So our first test came when the mission board wanted us to dress the tribal women and we found that we couldn't. The Waunana women were horrified at the very thought of covering their breasts.

Meanwhile, back home even some of our own Mennonite practices had run out of their original meaning; for example the incident with my mother's bun at the university, told earlier.

The Tabor College experience with Mennonite Brethren students who had difficulties with their childhood conversion vividly showed that even some "sacred cows" might have cultural, or even ideational flaws. The Mennonite Brethren saw conversion as a once-and-for-all experience that instantly transformed a sinner into a child of God. Yet these converted young people were not finding this complete transformation operative in their lives. What now? To top it off, the church that we had organized among the tribespeople definitely treated conversion not as a once-and-for-all event but as an ongoing process.

I also had to learn that if I removed a brick from the church wall as obsolete, I created a hole through which the world could rush in. Calvin Redekop has illustrated this well in his work with the Mennonites in Mexico. They moved from Canada to Mexico so they could retain the German language, remain isolated and would not have to go to schools where they would be contaminated by an alien language and culture. These Mennonites spoke German, but they pronounced the neuter article *Das* as *Daus*.

When Redekop was doing research among them and gained their confidence, some of the leaders asked him to help them solve a problem: certain people were telling them that they were not pronouncing German correctly. Official German was *Das* and not *Daus*. Redekop said, "I got them a German grammar which provided the official pronunciation of the 'a' sound in that word. But no sooner had I done that then I realized what a tremendous problem I had created for these people. I had introduced the world into the church, and the church didn't know how to cope with it."

The world in the church

As we continued our overseas service and came home periodically on furlough, we discovered that all the local mission work we used to do immediately around our Mennonite communities in British Columbia had now been transferred hundreds of miles north to the interior of the province. We also found the church battling furiously over retention of the German language. It abandoned its traditional multiple lay ministry for a single paid pastor. As a result, many members now realized that the walled structure of the church had included a large part of an older world's culture. In other words, many of the things that were considered "ins" spiritually in the past, were really part and parcel of Russian Mennonite culture, and not part of God's Word and his eternal design.

For us personally the next important insight was our growing awareness of the presence of tribal gods. Each tribe we worked with had a separate god and treated the god of the neighboring people as totally alien and wrong—as an idol. Gradually we realized that our home churches were no different. The Mennonites themselves were serving a tribal god. They, too, felt that others had to worship their God if they wanted to be saved.

Were we tribal in our outlook in other ways too? Of course! Our modern slavery to money, science and technology all suggested the influence of tribal deities rather than the universal God we claimed to worship. Our own proliferation of denominations, even within the Mennonite family, reflects another kind of tribalism.

As our realization of our cultural differences with the various peoples of the world grew, we realized too how ethnocentric we missionaries really were. We too viewed our culture and our way of life as God-given, and we viewed those of others as strange, if not wrong.

The depth of some of these right and wrong feelings was made clear on my first trip for the Bible Society to then British Guyana. Up to then I had never been in a country where cars drive on the left side of the road. When I got into a taxi at the Georgetown airport, and we took off in the dead of the night for the hotel, I died many deaths as we sped along the "wrong" side of the road. Whenever I saw an oncoming car on the right, I was certain I was breathing my last. Only after I arrived safely at the hotel and could reflect on the experience did I realize how deeply ingrained some of our cultural rights and wrongs really are. My way seemed intrinsically right; that which was different seemed so intrinsically wrong.

Somewhere along the line I read Dostoyevsky's novel *The Brothers Karamazov*. The author retells the story of "The Grand Inquisitor" who was burning heretics at the stake. One day the Grand Inquisitor suddenly realized that Jesus Christ had returned and that he was busily untying the victims at the stake. He ordered his soldiers to arrest Jesus Christ at once and to throw him into the deepest dungeon. There, in the dark of the night, the Grand Inquisitor visited him and said, "I recognized you at once, Jesus. What in the world are you doing back here? Why have you come back?" When Jesus did not answer, he went on, "We have worked for 1500 years to get the lid on after you made such a mess of things here on earth. We are just finishing the job of putting the church in total control and here you come to destroy all we have achieved." In the exchange that night the Grand Inquisitor tells the Christ, "If you won't leave peacefully, I am going to burn you at the stake just like all the other heretics because we have learned how to do God's work right and we aren't about to allow even you to stop us."

Dostoyevsky illustrates how a culturally bound church decides that its way is right. Should Jesus come again and suggest a different way, he would be treated as a heretic. This points out how the church can become a walled structure, blind to the world that it accepts within.

A new metaphor: An anchor and a rope

Over the years in foreign service I came to the conclusion that I desperately needed a new metaphor to describe my faith relationship with Jesus Christ. Delbert Wiens, now a professor at Fresno Pacific College, first suggested the metaphor of an anchor and a rope. Hebrews 6:19 likens our faith to an anchor that is firmly lodged with Jesus Christ behind the veil in the holy of holies of heaven. This metaphor eventually transformed my life.

Once I realized that my faith was anchored in Christ, and I was attached to him by the rope of faith, I could see why the "walled structure" metaphor of the church no longer worked for me. My faith tied me to Jesus Christ as I moved out into the world. There were no more walls to say "here you may not go" or "that you may not do." The whole world was open for me to walk in as led by the Spirit. As long as I kept a firm hold of my rope of faith, I was completely secure.

Furthermore, I discovered that the faith-rope which holds believers to Jesus Christ can be of varying thickness. Some believers, like some of the college students I learned to know, found that their early faith experience no longer gave them enough assurance or support. They desperately needed new experiences with their Lord. They needed to add new and stronger strands to their rope of faith.

I have been privileged to add many strands to my own rope. If ever, in my moving about in the world, I feel myself on slippery ground, a simple tug reminds me that my anchor with Jesus still holds secure. This new metaphor has been tremendously liberating and exhilarating in my ongoing spiritual growth.

A new, new-metaphor: The bounded versus the centered set

As I approached retirement, I became aware of yet another new metaphor to describe my faith relationship with God. This metaphor is drawn from the field of mathematics and linguistics. It involves the distinction between bounded and centered sets.

A bounded set has fixed parameters or boundaries. Thus things, events, or whatever are either inside or outside of the boundaries of a given set. Take numbers, for example. Even numbers make up one bounded set and odd numbers make up another one. There is no question into which set a given number belongs; every number is either even or odd. Likewise, all triangles, regardless of their infinite variety of shapes and sizes, are united by a single common set of boundaries, namely, all are three-sided.

In a centered set, meanwhile, the relationship between items of a set is not established on the basis of their common boundaries. In fact, boundaries are completely irrelevant, because here the defining standard is their relatedness to a common center, no matter how near or far away they are from that center. For example, the New Testament shows the church as a centered set. The center is Jesus Christ and all believers in Christ—Jews or Gentiles, educated or uneducated, male or female, barbarian or civilized, circumcised or uncircumcised, slave or master, young or old, past or present—are part of the church if they maintain a faith relationship with Jesus Christ. God's new family, the church as a centered set, cuts across all traditional boundaries, divisions and barriers.

Analyzing the church in terms of a centered set means dealing with the "spirit" and not only with the external appearance of events. For example, if the church and membership in the kingdom of God are treated as a bounded set, then all people would have to be classified as either in or out of the church. Thus a person who affirms a church's doctrines and follows its prescribed patterns of conduct must be classified as being within that bounded set. In fact, that person's heart may already be far from God or Christ, as Jesus so pointedly said of the very religious Pharisees of his day (Mt. 15:8). Thus a person may appear to be within the recognized parameters of a church, but may actually have turned away from Christ.

On the other hand, if "new life in Christ" is viewed in terms of a centered set, i.e., in terms of a person's true relationship with Christ, the center, then our faith can be compared to a sturdy rope that links us to Christ, our anchor (Heb. 6:19). Being anchored in Christ does not confine us to exist within certain specified boundaries, but rather it frees us to go wherever the Spirit moves, such as when Peter went to the house of Cornelius, the Gentile (Acts 10). This type of cross-cultural contact was strictly forbidden for even a converted Jew, but it was exactly what God called for in his new design, the church as a centered set.

An even greater advantage of the centered-set approach has to do with judging others. For example, the Mennonite Brethren Church in 1860, working in terms of its own new bounded-set church, condemned all members of the mother church as corrupt, apostate and totally outside. It could not recognize that there were many believers left inside the mother church who, like the people in Elijah's time, still had not bowed their knees to Baal. In fact, it took 126 years for the Mennonite Brethren Church to recognize its 1860 "bounded-set blindness" and apologize for its error in judgment, as it did in 1986.

Operating as a centered set permits us to speak of degrees of fidelity and degrees of compromise, giving us a much more realistic picture of any situation. This would have permitted the renewed Mennonite Brethren in 1860 to acknowledge the embers of renewal that still glowed in the mother church. They would have recognized the possibility that the mother church was still "able to strengthen" its own links to Christ (Rev. 3:2) by reviving features of Christian obedience which had already fallen into disuse for the majority. One of the tragedies of the church today is that a large segment still operates as a bounded set with walls. Its definition of who is in and who is out is very rigid. It has difficulty dealing with people who may be following God but whose approach is somewhat different from their own.

The centered-set approach permits us to be optimistic and assert that any individual, local church, or entire denomination that is still linked to Christ, the center, can at any time resolve to take new active steps to reincarnate and extend its obedience to Christ's teaching and example. It can add new strands of faith. It has been done in the past! It can be done again today at the end of the twentieth century! Herein lies the church's real hope!

In my own witnessing about my faith, I have shifted from asking people, "Are you saved?" or "Are you a Christian?" to "Has God asked you to do anything that you have not yet done?" The first two questions were clearly bounded-set queries designed to find out whether a person was in or out. The obedience question sees faith in terms of an anchor and a rope. The strands of someone else's linkage to God may be very different than my own, but if they link him to Christ, I must respect them.

For this reason, there have been a large number of cases in my life where I was not able to lead someone to the Lord in the conventional sense, but was able to help them take another step in obedience to Jesus. This is indicative of my new metaphor. The person who called Jesus Christ "Buddha" because he was unaware of the existence of Jesus Christ at the time, may have developed a strand of faith that links him to the God of all the world, the center of all. The person may have known God, the center, by a different name. God, who is not fooled by appearances but looks into the heart, is deeply aware of whether or not such a person has actually established a faith relationship with him.

To accept people from other faiths as having made contact with the true God is impossible within the metaphor of the church as a bounded set. It is only possible if one operates on the basis of a centered set. Other people's faith experiences may be totally extraneous to my own. Nevertheless, their strands may link them by faith to the same true God and Jesus Christ as much as mine do.

CHAPTER 32
MY PILGRIMAGE TOWARD PEACE

In 1984 our son Bill left the Mennonite Brethren Church because he felt it was diluting its statement of faith to the point where it was no longer able to take a clear stand on crucial Anabaptist/Mennonite peace principles. When we talked at length about these events, Bill chided me, "Dad, you have provided me with solid foundations in so many areas of life! But why in the world did you never teach me Anabaptist/Mennonite peace principles?" This poignant indictment brought me face to face with the personal unease I had experienced periodically over my own and my Mennonite Brethren Church's ambivalent loyalty to peace. Then and there I resolved to do something about it.

In 1988 I wrote a "Dear Bill" open letter (published in the *Mennonite Brethren Herald*) which gave a preliminary answer to Bill's troubling question. In response to this article, many parents telephoned, wrote, or personally told us how they, too, felt painful guilt concerning their children in regard to this issue. But like myself, their basic problem was ignorance. None of us knew enough about the basic Anabaptist/Mennonite principles involved, nor did we know how to make them relevant for life in our day. For this reason, I felt I owed it to myself and others to do an in-depth study of the issues so I could decide where to take my stand and then begin working toward a lifestyle that would reflect these convictions.

How my pilgrimage began

When World War II erupted in 1939, I was just turning seventeen. Until then, Mennonite peace principles had received only scant attention in the preaching and teaching of the Mennonite Brethren churches in which I had grown up. But as soon as war was declared and the draft became imminent in Canada, the church dusted off its doctrine of nonresistance and began to catechize its young men in it. As a dutiful son of the church, I accepted the church's position on war when my call-up came. I had been instructed to avoid arguments and theoretical discussions with the examining draft board members. I was only to affirm, again and again if necessary, "My conscience does not allow me to take up arms to kill other people!"

I had only one occasion to use this statement before the examining draft board. The chairman countered my initial statement with the question, "What will you then do if Hitler rapes your mother or your sister?" Before I could answer, he fired off a volley of similar questions, never stopping long enough for me to answer even one of them. Then, just as abruptly, he stopped. He stamped my papers disgustedly and said, "Next please!" That's how I became a conscientious objector.

The utter frivolousness of the experience stirred up a host of questions in me. I felt the need to do some serious study as to whether my professed peace position was truly a personal conviction or merely an oddity I followed because of church tradition and local social pressure.

I met my alternative service obligation by serving in a large urban hospital. Many Mennonite conscientious objectors served in forestry camps in British Columbia. Some of them came home after the war severely disillusioned. Their camp service had given them little satisfaction as a peace testimony. Many of their coworkers had been nothing more than war dodgers whose lives didn't reflect even basic Christianity, not to mention peace principles. As a result the serious conscientious objectors felt their peace witness had been seriously compromised.

When I compared my lot with theirs, I felt fortunate. By helping sick people I had been able to express my Christian faith to a degree I had never experienced before. As a service to fellow human beings, my hospital work had been exciting and deeply rewarding. But again and again, when patients asked why I was doing alternative service as a conscientious objector, it soon became clear that even though I was dead set against war, I was fuzzy about why. Worse, I did not know what I was really for. As my unease grew, I vowed to study the matter to discover what I was really "for" in my peace position.

But then the war ended and I went back to school. After my college graduation, the Mennonite Brethren Board of Missions sent my wife and me to Colombia as missionaries. As a result, the felt need to pursue the foundations of nonresistance and peace was pushed aside. After all, as a missionary I was working to reconcile "the heathen" to God, and that seemed like a very positive kind of peacemaking.

How my unease grew in Colombia

Shortly after our arrival in Colombia the state church began to persecute Protestants. I was quickly drawn into a battle royal, fighting "tooth and nail" to keep our mission's churches, schools and dispensaries open. These mission projects had all been approved by the highest authorities of the land, but now they were being disrupted, harassed and closed by provincial or local officials who were under pressure by state-church authorities to "stand up for their Catholic faith and to drive the Protestant heretics out of their communities, preferably out of their country completely."

The struggle to keep our mission institutions open meant carrying our fight to the highest levels of the capital. These officials, while conceding that our operating documents were valid (many, in fact, bore their personal signatures), still refused to reverse the lower authorities' actions because they, in turn, had the papal nuncio breathing down their necks to remind them that hell would be hot if they did not act like obedient sons of the church to defend the true faith.

To force the Colombian government to give us what we felt was elementary justice, we involved lawyers, embassies, the United States Congress, newspaper reporters and any other possible source of world opinion we could muster. In the course of this struggle, it suddenly dawned on me that I was engaged in a "war." Short of physical violence, I was using every verbal, moral, legal and diplomatic weapon available to defend our right to operate as a peace church! After some eighteen months of fighting, I became convinced that this approach didn't accord with my peace position any more than did the use of the gun or the sword in time of war. But I still had not developed an adequate rationale to explain why I felt so uneasy.

This experience, however, forcefully taught me that peace principles could never be merely a wartime issue, as my church had been teaching. To have any validity at all, such a peace stance had to involve all of life and had to guide all our interactions with people. Thus when I became convinced that I could no longer in good conscience fight with the Colombian government, I notified the mission board that I was bowing out of that battle. The mission was displeased, and saw me as a poor "soldier of the cross." But I was convinced that I could not keep on using every legal and diplomatic weapon to defend peace and truth!

Before I had fully sorted out the issues, however, a new agreement between the state church and the Colombian government made our work with the Waunana illegal. We were forced to leave Colombia and return to North America.

How my unease grew still more in North America

I finished graduate school. Then, because the mission board had no opening for a person with a Ph.D., I accepted a teaching position at Tabor College in Hillsboro, Kansas. This move coincided with the early stages of the racial protests, marches and sit-ins in the southern U.S. To put my budding peace principles into practice, I naively but enthusiastically joined the ranks of the marchers and protesters, together with some students from Tabor College. In my classes I tried to help students recognize racism in our churches and communities. As my southern involvement increased, however, I became increasingly uncomfortable with my fellow protesters. Among them I found dozens of hormonally-charged young fellows who saw these large protest gatherings as nothing more than good places to find sex. Others claimed to be anarchists. There was a wide array of leftists, and many who came just "to raise hell." Here, too, I soon realized that the nonviolent label can be very elastic. It included every use of force short of physical strangulation. As a result, I found myself withdrawing again, just like in Colombia.

The Bible Society interlude

Then the United Bible Societies offered me an overseas service opportunity to train nationals to translate the Bible into their own native languages. I was to work with all kinds of churches, missions and ethnic groups. I soon observed many conflicts in the church's overseas programs. There were tensions between the various mission societies, discord between nationals and expatriates, quarrels between various ethnic groups, and intergenerational struggles within the indigenous churches themselves. To my unexpected delight I discovered a wide variety of peacemaking opportunities, some of which are recounted in the book *Helping Resolve Conflict* by I.M. Friedmann (Herald Press 1990).

On the whole the peacemaking experience during my Bible Society service was very satisfying. However, when I tried to make it relevant for others, I found that the reconciliation processes in which I had participated involved a degree of cultural competence and peacemaking know-how which average church people might not have. Moreover, my peacemaking efforts showed no clear relationship to the Anabaptist peace concerns I espoused in theory.

The issue comes to a head

When I retired in 1984 and finally had time to pursue some of my personal interests, the peace issue unexpectedly came to a head—my son left the Mennonite Brethren Church. Now I was forced to face his haunting question: "But why in the world did you never teach me Anabaptist/Mennonite peace principles?" The answer, of course, was that I had never done the necessary homework to develop my own personal conviction. But I decided then and there to do it. The result of this multi-year effort is contained in the book ***Only the Sword of the Spirit***.

This study revealed that Menno Simons' voluminous writings had little to say about wartime abstinence from the use of the sword, but he had a lot to say about the need to develop a lifestyle which abstained from all force and coercion. He labeled such a lifestyle as "living only by the sword of the Spirit." This study not only bolstered my personal peace conviction, it also helped me develop a series of "yardsticks" or "rules of thumb" to govern my behavior when I feel I must protest for conscience' sake.

My personal yardsticks for non-violent protest

When I looked around for actual life examples to illustrate these emerging guidelines, I found, much to my chagrin, that I needed to go outside the traditional church—even outside of the Mennonite church. The best modern model turned out to be the Indian leader, Gandhi. My chagrin grew when I showed my preliminary findings to a fellow Mennonite Brethren minister; he warned me not to use them "because Gandhi, after all, was not a Christian." After some serious soul-searching, I, nevertheless have decided to use Gandhi's life and protests as an example of putting Christ's peace principles into practice. If this supposed "non-Christian" provides the best example of Christlike renunciation of force, then so be it!

Gandhi was well-versed in Christian Scriptures and gave Christianity serious consideration. But according to James W. Douglass (*The Non-violent Cross: A Theology of Revolution and Peace*, New York: The MacMillan Co., 1968) Gandhi felt that he "had to reject organized Christianity because he wanted to be true to Jesus Christ and his teaching."

Here are Gandhi's own words reported by R.K. Prabhu (*What Jesus means to me*, India: Narajuiran Publishing House, 1959):

> Today I rebel against orthodox Christianity, as I am convinced that it has distorted the message of Jesus. . . . When it had the backing of a Roman Emperor it became an imperialistic faith as it has remained to this day.

But the New Testament itself was a gold mine for Gandhi:

> The Gospels enthralled him... they seemed to confirm his earlier religious insights, bringing out clearly what hitherto he had only half believed. The Sermon on the Mount, with its teaching of nonresistance, attracted him in particular; it remained favorite reading with him for the rest of his life. On this impact he writes in his *Autobiography:*
>
> "The New Testament. . . especially the Sermon on the Mount. . . went straight to my heart. I compared it with the Gita. The verses 'But I say unto you, that ye resist not evil: but whosoever shall smite thee on thy right cheek, you turn to him the other also. And if any man take away thy coat, let him have thy cloak too,' delighted me beyond measure and put me in mind of [the Gujarati poet] Shamal Bhatt's 'For a bowl of water, give a goodly meal,' etc. My young mind tried to unify the teaching of Gita, *The Light of Asia* and the Sermon on the Mount. That the renunciation of power was the highest form of religion appealed to me greatly."

Douglass then points out that both Gandhi and Bonhoeffer correctly insisted that Jesus did not preach a new religion, he preached and lived a new life of peace and obedience to the non-use of force.

Gandhi's first protest against passbook laws

The first example of protest from Gandhi's life was his struggle against South African apartheid's infamous passbook laws. When Gandhi's fellow protestors wanted to blockade the passbook offices to make it impossible for them to function, Gandhi adamantly refused. He insisted that the protestor for conscience' sake may not harass or impede those who had legitimate reasons to enter those offices. It did not matter whether they were whites who were employed there, or whether they were blacks who felt they had no alternative but to register to get a passbook. Gandhi also insisted that the protestors had no right to block the area in front of the offices, because that would impede and inconvenience ordinary passers-by who were not involved in the protest.

Instead, Gandhi assembled his fellow-protestors in the park across the street from the passbook office where no one was impeded or inconvenienced by the protest. Gandhi believed that clear visibility was an adequate form of nonviolent protest (Hershberger 1969:197-198).

Gandhi's hunger strike

Later when Gandhi organized the strike of the textile workers in Southern India, the mill owners were led by a close friend and faithful supporter of Gandhi. Before the strike was called, Gandhi carefully ascertained what level of wage increase would be manageable for the mill owners. The workers wanted more, but Gandhi told them that exorbitant demands would make it impossible for the mill owners to remain profitable. He proposed an increase that would improve the quality of life for the mill workers but would not cripple the textile mills. In order to be just, a strike demand had to meet the essential needs of both parties, Gandhi reasoned.

During the early part of the strike Gandhi frequently dined with his mill owner friend to discuss the ramifications of the strike. Gandhi insisted that protestors or strikers may not be arrogant or hostile, nor subservient and begging. Both parties should be able to settle their differences while maintaining their dignity.

When the strike dragged on, however, and the striking mill workers began to suffer hunger, Gandhi had to learn two additional lessons:

First, he as the moral leader of the strikers also had to suffer, even though there was plenty of food at his ashram. Out of this came Gandhi's first hunger strike.

Second, some of the mill workers and their families found it impossible to survive while on strike. Some of them thus broke rank with the strikers and went back to work for their old wages. Other strikers now wanted to punish these strikebreakers, but again Gandhi opposed, saying that no one had the right to exercise violence on another. Furthermore, no one but the individual had the right to decide how much suffering he/she could bear.

Civil disobedience: the march to the sea

By the time Gandhi was on a hunger strike for his country's independence, several more issues had been clarified in his thinking.

First, civil disobedience is a valid response to laws that are patently unjust, e.g., his peaceful march to the sea to make salt.

Second, only the person whose conscience is being violated by an abuse or an injustice may be called on to suffer. The protestor may not demand nor inflict suffering or humiliation on others, whether they be perpetrators or merely uninvolved bystanders. Gandhi felt that accepting suffering without flinching empowers the sufferer. Louis Fischer (*The Life of Mahatma Gandhi*, London: Collier Books, 1962) espouses this point of view: "The British beat the Indians with batons and rifle butts. The Indians neither cringed nor retreated. That made England powerless and India invincible."

My yardsticks for protest for conscience' sake

As I worked through Gandhi's experience of nonviolent protest, I began to understand the causes of my earlier discomfort in Colombia when we had used myriad means to try and coerce the government into seeing things our way. In the same light, I can now also evaluate why I felt I had to withdraw from the racial protests in the American South. We blocked traffic, occupied seats in restaurants, tried to disrupt business, tried to embarrass people, argued fiercely with racists and tried to use courts to force our morality on others. As a result of our verbal aggression, we protestors had little or no moral authority.

Today, having examined the issues carefully and in detail, I can affirm that my personal yardstick for protest for conscience' sake involves the following rules of thumb:

(1) My peace position demands that I abstain from force and coercion at all times and in all areas of life.

(2) When I am faced with situations in which I feel I must protest, I may not insult, intimidate, or humiliate those whose behavior I oppose.

(3) I may not harass underlings who are carrying out, in the line of duty, actions I oppose, because they are not the ones who are in a position to make the changes I feel are necessary.

(4) I may not impede or inconvenience people who may be present, but who are not really involved in the situation.

(5) If there is any embarrassment or suffering involved, I may not inflict it. I as the protester should be the one suffering it.

(6) If a law is patently unjust, I may violate it peacefully, e.g., Gandhi's march to the sea to make salt, in the face of the colonial government's salt monopoly.

(7) Only the person whose conscience is violated may be called on to suffer. No one may force or coerce another person to protest or suffer.

(8) If the protest results in suffering, all the protesters must decide for themselves how much suffering they can bear. No one may ridicule a fellow protester for dropping out when the suffering becomes unbearable.

These eight guidelines have helped me evaluate and assess actions such as picketing at abortion clinics, lying down in front of vehicles carrying nuclear arms, or causing damage to nuclear facilities. They represent my studied position on Gewaltverzicht, 'abstaining from the use of force or coercion' á la Menno Simons.

I just reread this chapter and gloried in its neat and crisp guidelines. But those who know me intimately as Tiger—my informal name among the Empera—will realize how much of this I still need to convert into "the flesh of daily life." Put me in a tight spot and immediately there are "tiger hairs in my tank." The sword of the tongue still is ready with its sharp cutting edge. Like the unbelieving father of Jesus' experience, I cry, "I am peaceful, Lord; help me conquer my fighting spirit!"

CHAPTER 33
HOW I BECAME A CONVINCED ANABAPTIST/MENNONITE

This testimony involves a degree of pain. First, it passes judgment on some critical developmental phases in my life. Second, it makes an implicit indictment of the Mennonite Brethren Church and some of its leaders who played formative roles in my development. Finally, it makes painfully apparent that some of my early "church" activity was pursuing goals I now consider misguided.

My church background

The Mennonite Brethren Church did me much spiritual good as I was growing up, and for this I am deeply grateful! In its Sunday school and Bible studies, my church taught me the content of God's Word. During the many Bibelstunden, 'Bible discussions,' I learned how to exegete the Word, understand its meaning, and apply the insights to life. Later, when I had occasion to interact with trained biblical scholars, I found I could hold my own in interpreting Scripture. Furthermore, I knew where those Scripture verses were located in the Bible.

My church taught me to pray! Even as a teenager I found great strength and spiritual encouragement in weekly prayer meetings, in spite of the looming pressure that the meeting probably would not close until all present had prayed aloud. The young men's "prayer band," of which I was founding member, played a very formative role in developing my philosophy of life and service.

At the denominational Bible school I learned how to teach and preach God's Word (even though my Bible school teachers advised me to become a missionary abroad rather than a preacher back home). Yes, my church made me efficient in talking about God (teaching and preaching) and in talking to God (praying), but it wasn't until much later in life that I learned about listening to God. Here it was the Quakers who taught me about early Mennonite Gelassenheit.

Ashamed of the Mennonite name. During my youth in British Columbia, the Mennonite Brethren churches organized the West Coast Children's Mission as a nondenominational outreach arm under whose aegis many of my peers and I began our work in evangelism. At the time we young people were all deeply ashamed of being impoverished and poorly educated immigrants. We constantly ducked our Mennonite name and our Germanic origin and instead held high the nondenominational banner of the West Coast Children's Mission.

We taught Daily Vacation Bible School faithfully every summer and were able to lead many children and some of their parents to the Lord. But we were not content merely to win "souls" for Christ; we continued to visit these converts and their families and carried on various kinds of services to nurture their spiritual growth. Soon some of these new believers wanted to be baptized and join a church. We approached our home churches on their behalf. These churches, much to our embarrassment, were willing to baptize only the Friesens and the Froeses, some of whom spoke no German, and the Brauers and Kietzmanns, who spoke German. They told all the others to find a Baptist or Alliance church instead.

After serving a term on the mission field, my wife and I returned to our home in British Columbia on furlough. We were surprised, even shocked, to discover that the Daily Vacation Bible School activities that used to be carried on in the surrounding communities in the Lower Fraser Valley had now all been transferred hundreds of miles away into the interior of the province. One church leader admitted that it had been too embarrassing to win people to the Lord and then not be able to invite them into our German-speaking church services. Of course, today that language barrier no longer exists.

Mennonites do have something to offer

During our early years on the mission field I learned about other aspects of being a Mennonite. I was surprised when other mission societies invited us Mennonites to teach them how our unpaid lay ministry worked. These societies had discovered that the paid pastor model used by most missions abroad was a noose around the neck of young churches in the Third World. They were seriously looking for alternatives. Suddenly I became aware that I had grown up with something which others saw as highly desirable. When we returned home on our first furlough in 1953, however, our enthusiasm for this part of our Mennonite heritage was dampened severely because our home churches were now busily abandoning the lay ministry and rushing to hire salaried professional pastors.

"You Mennonites know something about admonishing each other"

In 1962 an ecumenical mission in the United States invited me to New York to meet with some of the upper echelons of their board. They wanted to discuss a short-term assignment with me.

They told me right up front, "We have been looking far and wide for a person to meet a request from our missionaries on the field. They have not been able to organize an indigenous church and don't seem to know why. There are severe tensions between the different missionaries, and they now want anthropological help. However, we mission executives feel that their problem is not anthropological but rather spiritual! We don't know anybody except the Mennonites who still can deal with brothers and sisters in the church in terms of a Christian admonition. We would like you to go to our mission field to see if you can reach the individual missionaries there. We would like it if you could somehow nudge them to make peace among themselves and learn to cooperate with each other in the work. We want you to recognize that officially we will be sending you to the field as per their request, as an anthropologist. But unofficially, we want you to provide them with spiritual nurture!"

I was somewhat taken aback by this frank request, but I accepted the three-week assignment. It turned out to be one of the most rewarding spiritual experiences I have ever had.

With people going on furlough and new missionaries coming to the field, the entire staff of this agency was "on the move." Everyone was moving to some other station, going home or returning to the field from furlough. So I had plenty of opportunity to either travel alone with the husband in a vehicle carrying another load of their belongings to their new mission station, or to stay with the wife to help her pack or unpack. I was able to talk at length with each of their missionaries individually.

By the time they finished moving, I had established at least some rapport with the individual missionaries. Now the head of the group on the field asked if I would lead them in a spiritual discussion. I responded that I had talked with all the individual missionaries and felt we needed a meeting at which some of the issues that were causing tension could be aired, perhaps even resolved. I suggested a setting in which we could all be honest about the conflicts that had developed. The leader assured me he would give his full backing if I could organize such a meeting. He himself had no idea how it could be done.

To begin our meeting with the entire staff, I shared some of my recent spiritual learning experiences at the college where I was teaching. I confessed that I had been totally frustrated in my effort to help a student who was in spiritual trouble. I also told them how I had learned about Elton Trueblood's concept of keys to people's lives, and of Theodor Reik's book *Listening with the Third Ear.* Both of these insights had opened the way for me to find answers to the pressing problems in my Christian life. I shared some of my recent "third-ear" hearing experiences. Finally I told the missionaries, "You have been willing to talk to me frankly and individually, and I know that you also have some severe frustrations. I wonder whether this would be an occasion for you to share some of those frustrations with each other." While the start was somewhat slow and difficult, their openness gradually picked up momentum. I soon became irrelevant, because it became an in-house sharing of problems, followed by requests for forgiveness and reconciliation. So I left. The meeting finally ended at midnight.

Next day the head of the mission asked whether I would lead another group meeting that evening. I told him of my concept of being a catalyst. I said, "You will develop new problems after I am gone, and it is my studied conviction that if what I have to offer is of any value to you, then you must be able to carry it on among yourselves."

The man then confided to me, "I think God is asking that I confess that I really have undergone a conversion experience. As a theological liberal I have always poked fun at 'converted' people." I told the man that I had found no answer other than to be honest when the Spirit of God asked me to share something. I did not go to the next meeting. The leader did share his conversion experience, and the result was a cleansing in the mission that had far-reaching effects.

When I made my final report to the mission board in person, they already had received feedback about what was happening on the field. With tears in his eyes, the chairman of the board thanked me for injecting some Mennonite "priesthood of believers" into a difficult situation. I was truly gratified. It was my Mennonite Brethren Church that had taught me about brotherly and sisterly admonition.

The social gospel

One area of learned church behavior that I today regret involves my early attitude and behavior toward the work of Mennonite Central Committee. For example, when I arrived at Tabor College as a student, I was a gung ho soul-winner. I disdained all relief work as social gospel (a movement, often suspect among evangelicals, that stressed the social and political implications of Christ's teachings). My first challenge on this score came from my American classmates in college who had recently concluded their civilian public service. When I heard the testimonies of these men and witnessed their consistent Christian lives, my condemnation of their supposed social gospel activity literally "choked in my throat."

During my years of overseas service I have witnessed firsthand the selfless Christian service which many of these MCC volunteers render. In troubled times I have seen missionaries scurry to safety while MCC volunteers continued helping, even under fire. They were worthy all-weather witnesses for Christ.

But my biggest rebuke of all has been the testimony of Third World people themselves. When I asked them to identify the best and most Christ-like foreigners they knew, people invariably picked MCC volunteers over soul-winning missionaries. Gradually I had to realize that Jesus himself had made no distinction between physical and spiritual help in his ministry.

Mennonites and Chaco Indians

When some Mennonites began emigrating to the Paraguayan Chaco in the late 1920s and early 1930s, they did not envision that they had any responsibility for the tribal people living there. After all, many of the Mennonites had moved there to escape from "the world," not interact with it. For years the tribespeople worked for the Mennonites for low wages. Then one day they rebelled! The subsequent anthropological study revealed that the Mennonites had engaged in many ethnocentric abuses. What was heartwarming, however, was that when I explained the tribal cultures to the Mennonites and pointed out what some of their behavior had done to the people, many of them not only changed their behavior for the future but also made restitution for the past.

There also were some notable failures. The revolutionary Chulupi Chief Manuel, who had led the dissident group, had just returned to the area at the time of my study. After hearing some of the background, I made a trip to the mayor of one of the foremost Mennonite colonies to share my feelings with him. I asked, "*Ohm,* (Low German polite title of address) what do you think? Do the Mennonites owe an apology to the Chulupi for some of the things they have done to the tribes people?" He wholeheartedly agreed. I then suggested, "You may be faced with this issue very shortly. I have a feeling deep down in my heart that one of these days Chief Manuel is going to come and see you. He will apologize for the rebellion which he led. The question I now have for you, 'Will you then on behalf of the colonies and all the Mennonites be able to own the colonists' part in creating the tragic events?' " The mayor said, "If it should ever come to that, certainly. But I can assure you that it will never happen!"

About three weeks later I had occasion to visit the mayor again. I was walking toward his office when his door suddenly jerked open and Chief Manuel burst out, tears streaming down his face. He didn't even recognize me as he stumbled past me. I knocked at the mayor's door, went in and found the mayor standing with his back toward me, staring out of the window. "*Ohm*," I asked, "did it happen?" There were tears in his eyes as he nodded. I then asked, "Were you able to also make apology on the settlers' behalf?" He turned to me with a deeply troubled expression and said, "It's much too hard to apologize to an Indian!"

Luckily the missionaries had the confidence of the chief and he unburdened himself with them. They were able to lead him to Christ. When the chief then asked for baptism, he was thoroughly interrogated by the believers. For three hours they grilled him about the many things in his life that needed to be forgiven. The tribal unbelievers listening outside were visibly moved. "Oh," they said, "we wish we also could have such a thorough cleansing!"

The result of the investigation in Paraguay was an extensive Indian settlement program. It is heartwarming to be able to report that today there are more tribespeople settled in their own villages with their own land, houses and gardens, than there are ethnic Mennonites in the Paraguayan Chaco. Even though the Mennonites went there to escape the world, when the chips were down they fulfilled their responsibility. They shared their farming know-how and the gospel with the tribespeople in Paraguay. I consider it one of the most successful programs I have encountered in my forty years of association with missions.

Highland Indians and the Communists

An interesting side effect of my Russian birth developed when a group of tribal leaders in the High Andes asked me to speak to a secret gathering of their tribespeople. They said I would have to be blindfolded before going. I agreed.

Late that evening a group came. They put a blindfold over my eyes and drove me to a clandestine meeting. It was a meeting organized by communist agitators trying to get the natives to rebel against the government. The Christian tribespeople, knowing of my Russian Mennonite origin, now wanted to know about communism and whether they should trust the promises the agitators were making.

When it was my turn to speak, I told the assembly that they should recognize that my family had fled Communist Russia. Our family had not liked communism, I said, but I would try to be fair and honest in my assessment of what communism would do for them. I suggested that initially communism would indeed help them get some land, but that a problem with communism was that once it was in charge, it soon became dictatorial. Then anyone who questioned the government's way of doing things was eliminated. I explained in detail what had happened to many of the Mennonites in Siberian slave labor camps, including most of my relatives who had stayed in Russia.

When I sat down an intense discussion ensued. Many people were convinced that communism was not the way for them. The agitators, however, argued that I was not telling the truth. Luckily, the Christians won the day and a revolution against the government was averted. When I grasped the seriousness of the situation, I was grateful that I, as a Russian-born Mennonite, had had their confidence and could thus be instrumental in preventing the destruction of thousands of lives and much property in a bloody rebellion.

Mennonites are esteemed abroad. Shortly after I began my first assignment with the Bible Society in South America, serious difficulties arose between the missionaries and the nationals in one country. It reached the point where the nationals were drawing up petitions to the government demanding that all missionaries be expelled and all their work privileges in the country be terminated. It was a full-blown mission crisis!

But, thank God, at the crucial moment a few saner heads, both national and missionary, got together and cast around for someone who could stand in the gap between the two factions. It needed to be a person who had the confidence of both groups and who would utilize a peaceful approach to problem solving. Both sides decided they needed an Anabaptist with a known peace orientation as a go-between. They chose Jake, the Mennonite! Suddenly I realized that I was the beneficiary of confidence that other peace-loving and peacemaking Mennonites had earned. It made me proud to be counted in their number!

During my forty years of overseas service I learned that the name Mennonite was one of the most esteemed religious names in the so-called Third World. Whether in South Africa, Thailand, Bangladesh, or Israel—everywhere I went people's faces beamed when they learned I was a Mennonite. "We know you people!" they would say. "You sent food to us during the famine and you kept us alive when we were starving. We still thank God for you Mennonites every day." Or, they said, "Oh yes, you are the peace-loving people who don't make war and rather help people in trouble. You have been an inspiration to us in our own struggle against colonial oppression."

The Lausanne Congress on evangelization in 1975 tried to bring together evangelistically-minded people from all over the world. Besides the official delegates to the conference, there were many concerned visitors from all Christian persuasions. Several Mennonites were delegates, but not necessarily as representatives of the Anabaptist point of view or of Mennonite evangelism.

In the mixed delegations from Africa with which I was associated, tensions soon arose between the white missionary and the black African delegates. The division was most apparent in the Rhodesian (now Zimbabwe) and the South African delegations. In the latter, the black delegates were more or less frozen out of all control in the country consultations that the organizers of the conference had arranged.

As a result these marginalized delegates began a separate consultation of their own among only the African representatives. But, to their credit, they did not trust themselves to be entirely objective in their deliberations, so they looked around for people off whom they could bounce ideas and get reliable feedback. So to whom did these Africans turn? To two Mennonites! Why? "Because," they said, "We have learned that you Mennonites can be trusted to be honest brokers for underdogs!"

I was deeply humbled to be one of those two Mennonites!

I wonder today whether North American Mennonites have the same credibility among their own marginalized aboriginal people that Mennonite missionaries and MCC workers have earned for Mennonites abroad.

Probably the most moving experience of this kind happened in Spain. I was attending a Bible Society conference when an evangelical church in Madrid asked for a Spanish-speaking preacher from our group. I was sent. My driver got lost and we arrived at the church late. When we finally walked in twenty-five minutes after starting time, the desperate minister rushed from the pulpit to receive me. He quickly asked me from which church I came. When I said, "Mennonite," an astonishing thing happened. The pastor cupped his hands and shouted to his wife, who was playing the organ as the congregation sang a hymn, "Querida, un Menonita!" 'Sweetheart, it's a Mennonite.' At once the organ music stopped. The organist rushed the length of the church on stockinged feet, threw her arms around my neck and gave me a resounding kiss. I was visibly embarrassed. Realizing this, she apologized. Then she explained. "During the civil war my family and I were kept alive by food that came in bags with clasped hands on them and a logo which read, 'In the name of Christ, Mennonite Central Committee'. As a family we then and there vowed that if anyone survived the war and ever met a Mennonite, that person was to kiss the Mennonite on behalf of the whole family." I happened to be that first Mennonite!

Something happened in my heart that moment. Instantly, I became very proud of my roots. For this reason it has been especially painful for me to return home to Canada for retirement and find that so many Mennonite ministers today are ashamed of the Mennonite name and the heritage it represents. I was devastated when a leading Mennonite Brethren minister told me, "The first thing I do with every church I pastor is get rid of the Mennonite name on the sign in front of the church. I consider it an impediment to evangelism." I repeat what I have said before: I think the reason why people still duck the Mennonite name is that they do not know the value it carries in the world at large. They are ignorant of the priceless heritage Anabaptism represents. It is my earnest prayer that my personal testimony may, in at least a small way, help remedy that.

For me the most convincing experience that Anabaptist peace principles are valid has come from my eight-year quest to answer my son's indicting question, "But why in the world did you never teach me Anabaptist/Mennonite peace principles?"

As I reread Menno Simons' complete works in German (seven times) and in English (two times), I realized that the highly-touted Mennonite doctrine of nonresistance suffered severe slippage. I became painfully aware that my church had failed to ground me in this non-coercive Anabaptist lifestyle and that I personally had failed to master what the founders of my church had originally proclaimed and practiced.

As I reread the trial accounts of sixteenth century Anabaptist martyrs and the defense that these simple people mounted for their faith, I recognized the depth of their obedience to Christ and their unwavering loyalty to a non-coercive lifestyle. I felt shame for the silly issues for which I had fought like a gladiator, especially during the nondenominational, soul-winning phase of my spiritual development.

In the book **Only the Sword of the Spirit** I have given a fuller testimony of why I today am a committed Anabaptist/Mennonite. My only regret is that I have spent so much of my life pursuing shallow fundamentalist sub-groupings of Christianity. I hope and pray that Mennonite churches will better expose their young believers to the rich New Testament legacy of the early Anabaptists.

"Lord, I want to be in that number!"

CHAPTER 34
MY PILGRIMAGE IN MISSION: A SUMMARY

It seems as if my journey in missions began pretty well with my birth. I was born with full-blown allergies, including an allergy towards mother's milk. So by the time father passed away when I was one month old, I was a foul-smelling, festering mess of eczematous ulcerations. Pious people everywhere were praying fervently that God might relieve this young widow of her hopeless burden.

But this afflicted child was all the young mother had left. In total anguish of soul she threw herself over my cradle and harangued with my creator—"If you cannot heal him, take him at once! But if you want to heal him, I will dedicate this child to you as a missionary! I will take care of him and nurture him until you call him!" I learned about this dedication the day I declared myself for missions at 17.

I was born in Russia in 1922 in a Mennonite family. My parents were of Germanic peasant stock and I spoke Low German and High German as my first languages. My family immigrated to Canada in 1930, and I had my first years of elementary schooling in Manitoba. In 1934, the family moved to British Columbia where I completed elementary school in 1936. Unable to attend high school due to the financial straits of my family, I nevertheless managed to attend a local Mennonite Brethren-sponsored Bible school where I was exposed to a highly legalistic Christian lifestyle rather than to the pacifist Anabaptism one would expect in a Mennonite milieu. Under that instruction I became a fervent soul-winner. The literal reading of the Bible and aggressive soul-winning became the supreme values in my religious outlook.

As World War II erupted, I was able to spend a year in highschool. Then, in 1942-43, I attended the Missionary Medical Institute in Toronto, Ontario, to learn about missionary medicine. At the same time, I served as a conscientious objector in the Toronto Western Hospital. During the summer of 1943, I had my first taste of linguistics with the Summer Institute of Linguistics (Wycliffe Bible Translators) in Briercrest, Saskatchewan. After that I began my mission endeavors as a home missionary with a children's mission in British Columbia. With hundreds of memorized Bible verses as my weapons, I conscientiously attacked sinners, large and small wherever and whenever I found them.

When I volunteered to serve as a foreign missionary, I learned that I would need to get a college education, and as a prerequisite I earned a high school equivalency certificate. In 1945 Anne Enns and I were married, and we began married life at Tabor College, Hillsboro, Kansas. Two professors in college captured my imagination—a biologist and a psychologist. The former grounded me in natural science and almost persuaded me to go into medicine; the latter began to puncture my legalistic armor by his friendly and penetrating questions. Ultimately I went into languages with the express aim of becoming a Bible translator in some tribal situation. In 1947 I received a Bachelor of Arts degree in humanities, and in December of that year Anne and I were sent to Colombia, South America, as Mennonite Brethren missionaries.

First Lessons in Colombia

We served in Colombia until 1957, with a furlough during the years 1953-55. Our initial assignment was to reduce the Waunan Indian language to writing. My first term on the field was an education in itself. I wanted to concentrate on reaching the tribal people in the region—the Waunan—with the Gospel, but the demands in the Spanish work (the chief interest of the mission) time and again kept us from our main purpose. We were involved in supervising the endless construction of schools, a dispensary, a church, teachers' and nurses' residences, and housing for longer-term sick people.

The work of the mission necessitated the training of workers in many kinds of endeavors. In keeping with my fundamentalist values, I decreed that no adulterer or drunk could be involved in any capacity in "God's work." My standard about adultery proved to be nonfunctional when I was besieged by local people on Monday morning telling me which of my workers had slept with whom over the weekend and could they now get that adulterer's job. My legalism about drinking went down the drain when a dead-drunk Indian stumbled into our guest room in the middle of the night. As I dragged the offender from the house and deposited him unceremoniously on the path to the village, he began to cry bitterly: "When I am sober and know what I am doing, Jake assures me he's my good friend; but when I am drunk and don't know what I am doing, and need a good friend to take care of me, Jake drags me out of his yard. Ai! Ai! Ai! What will become of me!" I then and there vowed to be a friend of sinners as Jesus had been.

At the four-year point in our first term, the Waunan began calling us liars—we were so busy with other things, we weren't really mastering their language, as we had promised. We pled desperately with the mission authorities, and they finally gave us permission to concentrate on learning the tribal language. But November of that year brought terrible flooding to the region, and the Waunan began to fear that God was sending another deluge to destroy the world. To prevent such a catastrophe, they revived the long-abandoned beseeching ceremony to plead with God about their sinfulness and to beg for mercy. When my partner Dave Wirsche and I were invited to a distant river to participate in such a ceremony, the pathos of their month-long fasting and beseeching almost drove us to despair. In desperation we decided that we had to give these people a message of hope from God's Word. All fundamentalist preconceptions about a pure gospel message had to be scrapped. We just did not know how to express the Gospel in the tribal language. With the help of our tribal teacher, we began to explore their tribal mythology and belief system. This gave us the necessary tribal anchor ideas to which we added a few biblical concepts in an attempt to deliver a meaningful message in their language. We had to leave shortly afterward, but to our surprise that first tentative and faltering message had so deeply moved this group of thirty tribespeople that they went from house to house and persuaded their entire river community of four hundred people "go give God their hand and to walk on God's road."

Then came the devastating news that the tribe had been signed over to the state church by a government concordat. We were declared nongrata and were expelled from the region. The whole experience shook us to the core. Much of our time had been squandered building an array of buildings that now had to be abandoned to termites.

Immersion in Anthropology

Furloughed back to the States, and convinced that I needed to be better equipped to understand the tribal culture, mythology, and belief systems, I enrolled in anthropology at the University of Washington. We stretched our furlough to two years while I furiously immersed myself in anthropology. Then we returned to South America to survey the ten Chocó dialects of Colombia and Panama (my doctoral dissertation) for Bible translating purposes. During the study I tried to convince the mission to move their tribal work across the border to Panama, since a part of the Waunan language family was native there, but the mission would not consider it.

As I made my survey, I found myself brushing up against all kinds of missionaries—different denominations, all kinds of faith missions, and many independent missionaries—all zealously defending their turf. It dawned upon me that we missionaries were not building the one body of Christ; we were simply trying to transplant our personal cultural version of it.

During the two years of my research, my nongrata status in the region was driven home with increasingly frequent police arrests. Because of the severe religious persecution in Colombia, we were recalled to the States in 1957. I finished my Ph.D. at the University of Washington and was then appointed a professor of anthropology and modern languages at Tabor College.

During the summer of 1959 I began to work with the Empera Indians in Panama, members (along with the Waunan) of the Chocó language group. One day my partner and I ran into the person responsible for tribal education in the country. When he heard our dreams for tribal literacy, he completely ridiculed them, and said, "These people are *brutos* (brute-stupid) and cannot learn to read Spanish. We have tried for decades without any success." When we contradicted his judgment, he challenged us to show him wrong. As a result, we were invited to conduct a literacy campaign among the Empera. Over the next year we prepared a set of primers in the tribal language, embedding in the primers almost the entire Spanish syllabary. We then asked the Empera, who knew a passable amount of Spanish, whether they would be able to learn to read their own language. Almost offended, they assured us, "Why, of course, we just need to learn a few letters and then we can read. We were born in our language!" In three short weeks our first batch of nine students had finished the literacy course in the Chocó dialect. Then without any explanation, we invited the local government grade school teachers to bring us all beginning readers in Spanish for a test. We gave the new tribal readers these Spanish books and asked them to begin reading aloud. Suddenly the Empera realized that they were no longer reading their own language but were reading Spanish. The tribespeople's explanation for this achievement was that since they had "given God their hand and had begun to walk on God's road, God had cleaned up their eyes," thus making it possible for them to learn to read. This idea that "God wants to clean up your life and your eyes" now became an evangelistic message that within six months auto-evangelized a large section of this tribe in Panama. Poof! went my fundamentalist ideal that the only true conversion is an individual, dated conversion—this was a group conversion very similar to what had happened with our first message to the Waunan. I thus began to appreciate the Anabaptist insight that every sinner needs to be born again into a nurturing fellowship and not stand or fall as an individual convert as my soul-winning schooling had taught me. As a result of this experience, we made a twenty-five year commitment (1959-84) to help this group of believers develop in the faith.

Meanwhile in Colombia, the state church tried to win over its new concordat charges, but it was flatly rebuffed! As a result the state church gave up the older generation as hopelessly lost and took away all the Waunan children and put them in orphanages to make Christians out of them. The tribal parents were now very angry and utterly frustrated with the situation. In desperation they stole back their own children from the orphanage and fled with them into the jungle. From time to time they sneaked back to their gardens for food, but they did not let themselves be seen or found. After two years of this jungle nomadism, rumors began to circulate that Tiger and Fox (the names the Waunan used for me and my partner Dave) had been working in Panama. In groups, these Waunan now ventured across the unmarked country border to investigate these rumors. They learned that Tiger and Fox had indeed been there and would return soon.

Mission by Professors on Summer Break

The converted Empera took in the Waunan refugees and pointed out unused land for settlement. The Waunan were then baptized by the Empera and settled into Christian villages. Out of these events came a whole series of lessons in mission. Most obvious was the fact that here we had a mission effort by two people with no formal missionary assignment and no missionfield (Dave and I were only guests of another mission). In effect, a church was being established by two college professors on summer break! Working with local legal authorities, the new church received its own legal charter under a non-denominational name—United Evangelical Church. This charter authorized the new church to strike up relationships with national and international entities in the areas of morals and religion, social concerns and services, health and medical services, and secular and religious education. It also gave the group the right to expedite birth certificates, to marry, and to bury. Before long this young church was making ample use of its legal rights and privileges.

In the development of this church we discovered what it means when a church works under the guidance of the Spirit of God. We became deeply aware of how handicapped we Western missionaries were when it came to spirit phenomena and faith healing. Because of the way this young church nurtured the conversion of alcoholics, I had to revise my theology of instantaneous, once-and-for-all conversion. I had to make room for process conversion, because the tribal believers were prepared to work patiently with a convert through counseling and prayer until his stomach refused alcohol. Then they thanked God that the person's conversion had finally reached his stomach.

When the church decided to translate the Scriptures on its own, we realized why God had kept us from doing it. He wanted to keep us missionaries from becoming enamored with our own work as Bible translators. He wanted mother-tongue speakers to do it. Furthermore, we had to learn that when the whole church is involved in the Scripture translating process and experiences its own answers to the prayer "God how would you have said this, if you had said it in our language in the first place?" then the Word achieves an authority that all too often it does not enjoy in the Western church.

We also learned that transplanting the structures and rules of the home church back in North America, like many missions seemed to be doing, did not work under the terms we short-termers had to follow. When our denominational mission insisted that we introduce the home church's behavior rules, the tribal leaders made the mission executives aware that their people did not have the whole Bible yet and that church rules could not be transmitted cross-culturally in abstract without doing damage in the receiving culture. They insisted that the believing community under the guidance of God's Spirit was the only one that could make or change all the necessary rules of behavior. Church polity, we learned, could not be transplanted; rather it must be indigenously developed.

Meanwhile at Tabor College, I was receiving all kinds of additional lessons on being a missionary: how to improve my "third-ear" hearing and how to feel with people when they are unable to verbalize their concerns and problems. I learned about the many competing inner voices derived from schedules and routines that interfere with our hearing of God's Spirit. Then came the lessons about keys. I learned that God gives each one of us the keys for lives for which we are responsible. As a result, I outgrew my earlier indiscriminate witnessing method of clobbering sinners with memorized Scripture verses. Furthermore, I had to lose my prudishness about human sexuality as I learned to help college students find solutions to their spiritual and social development problems.

Twenty Years with the Bible Societies

For five years we waited in the expectation that the mission was looking for a new assignment for us. When year after year the answer was still "no assignment," we decided to wait no longer. In 1964, when the American Bible Society offered us a possibility to train translators, solve translation problems, and supervise Bible translation quality, we jumped at the opportunity. For the next several years I was responsible for all of South America. In this new role I began to see deficiencies in many earlier missionary-made translations. Luckily my boss, Eugene A. Nida, was willing to let me experiment with the training of mother-tongue speakers as translators. When I reported on the lessons I had learned in seven languages at a workshop in Spain in 1969, the Third World representatives who were present were so enthused that they insisted that mother-tongue translation be made a worldwide Bible Society policy.

In the summer of 1970 I taught at the Muslim University of Mashad, Iran. In September of that year, the United Bible Societies (the world fellowship of national Bible societies) decided that the most mature situation ready for mother-tongue translators was in Africa, and I was therefore made responsible for East Central Africa: Angola, Zambia, Malawi, Rhodesia-Zimbabwe, and Mozambique. I also had some advisory responsibility in South Africa. In Africa I quickly realized that my earlier enthusiasm for a Bible without genealogies was totally wrong. Africans grooved on genealogies! They saw them as exceedingly important faith documents. It was in Africa that I learned the value of the Old Testament for people whose culture is so much more like earlier biblical cultures than our own or even the cultures of North and South American tribal societies. Time and again African Christians complained, "Why don't missionaries allow us to follow our Bible—the Old Testament? Why are they forcing us to walk in Western culture's ways, which are alien to our own?"

In Africa I had occasion to become acquainted with many African Independent Churches and the prophets that guide them. I noticed how often their rapid growth coincided with the arrival of the Old Testament in a major language. These churches, I saw, catered to the felt needs of their African members and did not necessarily follow a Western church's polity. From them I learned that to expedite justice in Africa it was not nearly as important to judicially establish the details of guilt and innocence in a case as it was to spread the guilt evenly over all parties concerned so that genuine peace could be established. Finally, from 1979 through 1984, I served as translation consultant in West Africa, responsible for Ghana, Benin-Dahomey, Niger, Upper Volta-Burkina Faso, and Togo.

By the time I retired in 1984, I had probably worked with several hundred different languages. In the course of this experience, I learned that there is truly only *one* God in this entire world but that this one God is known by hundreds—yes, thousands—of different names in different languages. I became convinced that this

God was at work in the various cultures of the world long before the first missionary came and would still be working after the last missionary left. I further learned that these many languages and cultures had something to teach me about God and his Word.

Since my retirement in 1984 I have served in a number of short-term overseas assignments, such as facilitating reconciliation of a church-split in India, helping Mennonite workers with the Kekchi Indians in Guatemala, and doing a survey of the Hopi mission situation in Arizona. In spite of a stroke in 1993, I am able to write with my left hand, and I employ a part-time secretary to help me continue my research.

As a missionary, I had to learn to leave my home church agenda at home. I was only truly helpful when I functioned as a catalyst. If I put my ear to the ground in the local situation and discovered where the Spirit of God was presently working and then fitted myself into the agenda, then I could be of help to set in motion indigenous efforts that truly met local felt needs and built God's kingdom there. All in all, I found that in four decades of mission I had more to learn than I had to teach! So thank you, all my Third World teachers!

And thank you, Mother, for your courageous dedication when all odds were against my survival as an infant!

CONCLUSION

CONCLUSION
LIFE'S UNFINISHED BUSINESS

While I was teaching, a student I knew committed himself to do a job for a friend. It was during exam week. He worked at the job for several hours but found it was taking much longer than expected. So half way through the job he had to leave to write another exam. He stuck this note on the door of his friend's place: "Sorry, old buddy, it's taking me longer than I thought. I've got to take another exam right now. I'll finish it later." A car struck and killed him on the way to the exam. The job was left unfinished.

Many of us find that life has a lot of unfinished business. As I said in the introduction, my stroke has become a critical watershed. It has forced me to take serious stock of my life—as no other experience heretofore has. It has forced me to ask some earnest questions: What part of God's design for my life have I been able to fulfill? What part still remains undone? This book recounts many of the things I have been privileged to experience and learn as I tried to carry out God's will for my life. But when the stroke intervened, I needed to take a completely fresh look. I needed to know specifically what parts of God's will for my life were still unfulfilled.

The stroke put most additional tasks well beyond my current capacity. The achievement chapter of my life was now more or less closed. However, the examination did reveal some significant unfinished business. It focused the spotlight on me as a person. It forced me to ask: who and what have I become? This self-scrutiny showed some major deficiencies, some areas of unfinished business, some lessons not learned or learned incompletely. I now want to draw attention to some of these character flaws that still need attention.

How big a frog am I?

Throughout my life this has been one of my most serious questions. The more honestly and accurately anyone answers this question will determine how well that person comes through life's "school of hard knocks."

There is an ancillary question—like the first and second commandment about loving God and loving one's neighbor—which is equal to the first. It is: how big a puddle do I jump into? Every person has to face these two questions repeatedly.

These are particularly pressing questions for those of us who have stepped out of our familiar home contexts to enter a totally different cultural milieu. Missionaries, Mennonite Central Committee workers, peace corps volunteers and others often have to face these questions most urgently when they return home after meaningful years of service overseas. Answering them satisfactorily will determine how effective and enriching our life's work will be.

If you underestimate your frog size and choose too small a puddle, you'll produce an enormous splash when you first jump in. But you will also splash all the water out of the puddle. A big frog jumping into a tiny puddle leaves nothing but mud.

If you overestimate your size and choose too big a pond, you won't even make a meaningful ripple. Your impact will simply dissipate.

If, however, you evaluate your frog size correctly and choose an appropriate-sized puddle, you can be assured you will cause big enough ripples to make your presence felt. Every new move will continue to affect the entire puddle.

I had to re-examine my frog size and the size of my puddle when I returned home for retirement. Now after the stroke, I've had to make yet another new assessment of the size of the puddle I can still negotiate.

Working on this book, as a testimony about my life's experience, has made me deeply aware of how many lessons I have still failed to learn. First and foremost is the control of my sharp tongue.

The tongue

As I have said elsewhere, after my son left the Mennonite Brethren Church because he felt it was no longer making a clear statement on pacifism, I launched into an intensive research project into the life, times and writings of Menno Simons who gave his name to my people—the Mennonites. One thing my research uncovered was the sharp tongue which Menno Simons manifested as a radical reformer. Time and again I found it difficult to read his lengthy polemics against other reformers. He was constantly lambasting others for their "wrong" views of Scripture.

Through this mirror I have realized that I, too, have a very sharp tongue. Time and again I, too, have cut people down with a razor sharp slash of my own verbal sword. In Chapter 33 I described the peace ideal by which I want to live. But repeatedly I find my weapon unsheathed. "Bridling my tongue," according to James, is still a major area of unfinished business in my life.

Acting versus reacting

A major ATS (after the stroke) insight has been to realize how much of my BTS (before the stroke) activity was reacting, rather than acting independently. Other people's behavior was always triggering certain reactions on my part, yet I knew that the mature self-motivated person always acts rather than merely reacts. As I reflected on this, I remembered the Quaker who bought a paper from a rude news vendor. In spite of the vendor's uncouth conduct the Quaker remained quiet and polite. As he left the newsstand, his companion exploded, "Why didn't you tell that bum off? He needed to be put in his place!" To this the Quaker firmly responded, "Why should I let that unhappy man call the shots in my life? I want to behave the way I decide to act!"

I still have much room to grow in this area. I'm still tempted to react in kind! I want to learn to act on the basis of my convictions.

Being

Some readers will recall that in the introduction I admitted that this is another massive area of unfinished business. All my adult life has been strongly achievement oriented. The poverty of my childhood and youth, and my Yarrow nickname "Squirt"—which all too accurately designated my lowly status in the community in which I grew up—created a passion to achieve. I became determined to get away from "poor row." I became determined "to show them" that I was worth something after all. But in this all-consuming drive to achieve, my learning **to be** was nipped in the bud. Now my ATS helplessness has brought me face-to-face with the deficiencies in the area of character and being.

Feeling

Two of our daughters have gone into professional counseling and have learned how important it is for human beings to handle their feelings adequately. Both the daughters and my wife can talk freely about their feelings. I cannot! When it comes to feelings, I am numb. From a young age on, I learned that we poor people couldn't afford the luxury of such indulgence. This background has left me very skittish about talking of my emotions. I shy away from them! I mistrust them! Can I still learn to become comfortable with my feelings?

I had always convinced myself that I had developed a capacity to feel with other people in difficulty—how to be empathetic, how to be sympathetic. But I now realize that I myself have never learned how to feel and how to handle my own feelings. Can I, after more than seventy years, with just over half of my body still functioning, still learn to deal with my feelings? The odds are high against it, but I still must try. I want to learn to feel! God, strengthen my weak faith in my capacity to feel!

Small talk

Early in this book I told of the gas-pump-hose therapy which my mother used to wean me from overstaying my visiting privileges when I was a young boy. That childhood experience permanently inoculated me against casual visits and small talk. One of my daughters once told me, "Dad, I think I've discovered a time when I can be with you and comfortably engage you in small talk. When you're in the garage melting lead and making sinkers and weights for ocean fishing, I can sit there with you and just chat. With your hands otherwise engaged, you don't become restless like you usually do."

Since then I have watched myself and sure enough, when we as a family sit down for casual visiting, I soon get restless. I am always ready for a serious discussion, but fifteen or twenty minutes of small talk seems to be my limit. Even now, ATS, I have little patience with extended casual conversation. Can I still overcome my childhood conditioning at this age? God's Word says that his grace is sufficient for our every need. I hope I can appropriate it!

Love

I love my wife and bask in her love for me. I love my children dearly but beyond that I must honestly confess that there have been only a few people for whom I have had great love. Some years ago I was talking with my mother's brother, my uncle Walter, shortly before he died. He asked me what single most important lesson I had had to learn in life. Unhesitatingly I said, "Obedience." He responded, "That lesson I have learned."

Then he turned to Anne, my wife, and asked her what she considered to be life's most important quest. Anne answered, "Love." To this he sheepishly responded, "That I have not learned! I know nothing about love. I haven't even learned to be *höflich*, 'to be polite.' If God insists that I have to learn to love, then he'll have to recycle me!"

A second dimension to the love issue is unconditional love. At various times in my life, one or the other of our children has cried in anguish, "But Dad, I want your unconditional love!" Again and again they sensed that my love for them depended on their successful achievement of my own ideals for them. "I can't live with that," they said. "I need to be assured of your love precisely when I fail, when I fall short of one of the ideals you have set for me." I am still struggling to love unconditionally.

The third issue is to feel loved. Can I accept love? This has become a serious issue for me ATS. My image of myself as a helper has been dealt a devastating blow, because I am now largely helpless and dependent. BTS, I always felt I could earn at least some love and respect by doing things for others. But now that I am handicapped I not only feel helpless, I also feel unlovable.

Ever since I became aware that Middle Eastern, Asian and, to a lesser degree, African cultures, regard the left hand as unclean, I have worked hard to observe this cultural taboo. I have scrupulously avoided giving or receiving anything from anyone else with my left hand so as to never offend colleagues from other cultures. But now my left hand is all I have. After three years I still have serious trouble caressing my wife with my left hand. I feel I am "defiling" her by touching her with that hand. I still feel that I am contaminating things by giving and receiving with my left hand. It is a struggle I have so far not been able to master.

A, B, C, F, or S

In college one's grade point average was a big thing. In the first two years of graduate school, grades were even more important; if your grades fell below a B, you were out on your ear! Later in graduate school, however, I noticed that I was getting an S more often than not. This grade only said that my progress was satisfactory, but in regard to grade point it was neutral.

After the stroke I pondered life's end and the completion of my course here on earth. I realized that there probably will be many courses—life's ongoing lessons—that I will never be able to complete. The more I thought about this, the more I hoped that God was grading my ongoing performance on a satisfactory (S) or unsatisfactory (U) scale. Each day he calls for some small obedience. If I comply, I achieve my S; if not, he asks me to try again. S's at this stage are all I am hoping for!

Recently someone asked me, "Can one actually be ready for death?" Now that I am no longer striving for A's and B's, I realize that I can be ready if I keep on completing each day's new obedience satisfactorily. As a result I can now wake up eagerly each day, looking to God for the day's request for obedience. No, I haven't finished learning life's lessons, but I am relaxed; for I am now only trying to keep current with any new obedience to God's design that may be revealed to me.

Conclusion

Throughout this book I have spoken of my basic commitment to learn. I know that my learning will never really be finished. My commitment to be open to new truth is firm for as long as the Lord gives me life and breath! There are three more areas in which I have unfinished long-range commitments: listening to the still small voice of God's Spirit; obeying whatever he tells me; and reducing the gap between my ideals and the real in my life. No doubt, there will be unfinished business when I breathe my last.

APPENDIX

This appendix contains a bibliography of my published writings. It is included here since many parts of this book have already been published in different form elsewhere. It also permits readers to further pursue topics of interest. This bibliography may look like a record of things that have been completed; but it, too, represents some of the unfinished business of life. I am still discovering articles of mine that have been published somewhere but which I have not been aware of until now. Again and again I am surprised when I find that an article I wrote many years ago has been reprinted in another journal or even in another language. Even now I have submitted a number of articles for publication that have not yet been printed. So the bibliography is still incomplete. In a very real sense, it represents my life as an ongoing and unfinished process.

BIBLIOGRAPHY

1948 "Äussere Mission. Colombia, Süd-Amerika. Den 7. September, 1948," *Konferenz-Jugendblatt* (hereafter *K-J*) Oct-Dec.35.

1949b "Einen Tag in der Pionierarbeit in Noanama," *K-J* Feb-Apr.8-10.

1949c "Moths, rust and white ants," *K-J* Feb-Apr.54. Also in: *Christian Leader* (hereafter *CL*) 1 Jun.4-5.

1949d "Mission in Colombia (Eine Reise und noch was)," *Mennonitische Rundschau* (hereafter *MRund*) 6 Apr.1 & 4.

1949e "Nacht in Noanama," *Zionsbote* (hereafter *Zb*) 6 Apr.3-4.

1949f *Colombian News and Views*. Hillsboro, KS.: Mennonite Brethren (hereafter MB) Board of Missions. Wrote or edited issues of Mar/49, Dec/49, Dec/50, Jan/52, Jan/53.

1949g "Aufrichtig über bitten und verstehen," *Zb* 25 May 2.

1949h "Aus der Mission in Colombia," *Der Friedensbote* Jun.4.

1949i "Schlangen in Colombia," *K-J* Oct-Dec.45-46.

1950 "Etliche Blicke ins 'Dispensario'," *Zb* 18 Jan.2-3.

1950a "Rainy season," *CL* 1 Feb.6.

1950b "Der Noanama Indianerstamm, Colombia, S.A.," *K-J* Feb-Apr.55-56.

1950c "Erstlingsfrüchte auf Noanamastation," *Zb* 17 May 3.

1951a *The Roman Catholic Church in the Chocó*. Hillsboro, KS: MB Board of Missions (pamphlet) n.p.

1951b "Die Arbeit in der 'Dispensary' (Armenapotheke) in Noanama, Colombia," *Zb* 10 Jan.6.

1951c "MB Mission in Colombia," *MRund* 21 Feb.3.

1951d "Contacting Indians for the Gospel," *CL* 15 Feb.4-5.
"The work in the dispensary in Noanama," *CL* 15 Feb.

1951e "Unauslöschbare Eindrücke," *Zb* 21Feb.5.

1951f "Indelible impressions," *K-J* Apr/50-Apr/51.42-43.

1951g "Foreign Mission: Noanama por Istmina, Chocó, Colombia, South America." March 5, 1951," *K-J* Apr/50-Apr/51.43.

1951h "Learning by Experience," *CL* 1 Jun.5.

1951i "Mission in Colombia (day school in Noanama)," *MRund* 15 Aug.9.

1951j "Mission in Colombia," *Zb* 29 Aug.5. (Co-authored with Anne Loewen.)

1951k "Day Schools in the Chocó," *K-J* Sep-Oct.9-11.

1952a "Our Mission in Colombia," *K-J* May-Jun.23.

1952b "Our Mission in Colombia," *K-J* 15 Jun.5-6.

1952c "Correspondence," *K-J* Jul-Aug.31.

1952d "Noanama por Istmina, Chocó, Colombia," *K-J* Nov-Dec.23 (with picture of three girls.)

1953 "Noanama Indians and the white dog," *CL* 1 Jan.7.

1954a *Waunana Grammar: A Descriptive Analysis*. Seattle, WA.: University of Washington. (MA thesis in microfilm.)

1954b Review of *Gramática comparada de un dialecto del Chocó*, by Nils M. Holmer. *International Journal of American Linguistics* (hereafter *IJAL*). 30: 427-430.

1956a "A Visit to the Sambu Indians," *K-J* May-Jun.21-22. Also in: *CL* 15 Sept.8-9.

1956b "Ein Besuch bei den Sambu Indianern in Panama," *Zb* 4 Jul.5-7.

1957a *Comparative Chocó Dictionary*. (Listing ten Chocó dialects) (pp. 600). Clearbrook, B.C.: MB Historical Archives, also photocopy in JAL's writings collection at Goshen College, Tabor College, Fresno MB Archives.

1957b "Kolumbien, S.A.," (A letter.) *MRund* 14 Aug.8.

1957c "The finding and burial of John A. Dycks," *CL* 1 May.8-9.

1958 *Ēmpēra Speech: Sambu Dialect.* Seattle, WA.: University of Washington. (Dissertations Microfilm Service.)

1959a *mʌa c'awaq'uĩrēabʌa.* (Ēpēra: Sambu primers, Vol. 1-7.) Hillsboro, KS: MB Board of Missions.

1959b *ēpērá nēpʌrʌta diego perrugatapa nēpʌrʌsia.* Panama City: MB Board of Missions.

1959c *c'uriwapa imamá c'ũrũcanʌmʌa* (Empera: Sambu primer, 1 vol.) Hillsboro, KS: MB Board of Missions.

1959d *talli ãc'õre pedea maharí.* (Twenty-five Bible stories explaining the way of salvation.) Hillsboro, KS.: MB Board of Missions.

1959e "The Christian and Race Relations," *CL* 22 Sep.4-5,19; 6 Oct.4-6. (Co-authored with Wesley J. Prieb.)

1959f *Race relations and the Gospel.* Chicago: Woodlawn Mennonite Church. 17-19 Apr.7-15.

1960a "A Chocó miraculous escape tale," *America Indigena* (hereafter *AI*) 20.207-215.

1960b "Dialectologia de la familia lingüística Chocó," *Revista Colombiana de Antropologia* 9.9-21.

1960c *mãr c'aug c'õchcatʌnʌm.* (Waunana primers, Vols. 1-9) Hillsboro, KS.: MB Board of Missions. (Co-authored with David & Dora Wirsche).

1960d "Spanish loanwords in Waunana," *IJAL* 26.330-344.

1960e "New trends and possibilities in missions," MB Bible College *Companion* 9.

1961a "Good News for the Waunana," *Practical Anthropology* (hereafter *PA*) 8.275-278. Also in: *Mennonite Brethren Herald* (hereafter *MBH*) 22 Jun.8-9f. Also in: *Culture and Human Values* (hereafter *C&HV*). Pasadena, CA.: Wm Carey Library. (pp.111-114.)

1961b *Los Hechos de los Apóstoles, 1-15.* (A simplified Spanish version, 3 vols.) Hillsboro, KS.: MB Board of Missions. (Co-authored with Francisco Mosquera.)

1961c *mãch hewandam hiek* (Waunana Bible Stories). Hillsboro, KS.: MB Board of Missions.

1961d *t'rʌãne zedatua* (A Spanish-Epera Hymnbook). Hillsboro, KS.: MB Board of Missions. (Co-authored with David & Dora Wirsche.)

1961e "Commissioned to redeem," *CL* 13 Jun.4-5,21; 27 Jun.4-5,17.

1961f *Lli Jarateapidap'edadarãpa Oda.* Hillsboro, KS.: MB Board of Missions. (Co-authored with Aureliano Sabugara.)

1962a "A Chocó Indian in Hillsboro, Kansas," *PA* 9.129-133. Also in: *C&HV* 27-42.

1962b *pedea pia marcopa bʌsiada* (Epẽra Gospel of Mark, Vols. 1-3.) Hillsboro, KS.: MB Board of Missions.

1962c *teapʌedada op'anãna* (Acts 1-15 in Epera-Spanish.) Hillsboro, KS.: MB Board of Missions.

1962d *Historias del camino de Dios*. Hillsboro, KS.: MB Board of Missions. (Co-authored with Francisco Mosquera.) Hermanos Menonitas de Panama.

1962e "Literacy work in Panama," *CL* 26 Jun.7. (Co-authored with David Wirsche.)

1963a "Chocó I: Introduction and bibliography," *IJAL* 29.239-263.

1963b "Nachricten von der MBG Wohlfahrts-behörde," (Paraguay Research.) *MRund* 15 May.164. (Co-authored with Wohlfahrts-behörde.)

1963c "Chocó II: phonological problems," *IJAL* 29.357-371.

1963d "Experiencia de alfabetización con los Indios Chocóes," *AI* 23.121-125. (Co-authored with Nicasio A. Vargas.)

1963e "Research in cross-cultural communication," in *Proceedings of the thirteenth conference on Mennonite education and cultural problems*. Tabor College, Hillsboro, Kansas. (pp. 101-114.)

1963f "The Church Among the Chocó of Panama," *PA* 10.97-108. Also in: *C&HV* 115-126.

1963g *Anthropologische Fragen, Eine Anleitung fuer Missionare zum Studium der Kultur der Chaco-Indianer in Paraguay*. Fernheim, Paraguay: Mennonite Central Committee. (pp.1-17.)

1963h *Marcou hevangelio hiec' Jesú Cristo den p'ãpʌatarr*. Hillsboro, Kansas: Mennonite Brethren Board of Missions.

1964a "Anthropologe berichtet ueber Paraguay-Indianer," *MRund* 12 Feb.5. (Co-authored with MCC News.)

1964b "Bible Stories: Message and Matrix," *PA* 11.49-54, 60. Also in: *C&HV* 370-376.

1964c "Culture, meaning and translation," *The Bible Translator* (hereafter *TBT*) 15.189-194.

1964d "The Chocó and their Spirit World," *PA* 11.97-104. Also in: *C&HV* 127-134.

1964e "Reciprocity in Identification," *PA* 11.145-160. Also reprinted in: *Mennonite Life* (hereafter *ML*) (pp. 600). Jan/66.10-19. Also in: *C&HV* 27-42.

1964f *Research report on the question of settling Lengua and Chulupi Indians in the Paraguayan Chaco*. Akron, PA.: Mennonite Central Committee. Also in German as: *Wissenschaftliche Untersuchung über die Frage der Ansiedlung der Lengua and Chulupi Indianer im Chaco von Paraguay*.

1964g "Sponsorship: The Difference between Good News and Propaganda," *PA* 11.193-203. Also in: *C&HV* 43-53.

1964h "The Bible On the Mission Field," *ML* 19.124-128.

1964i "The Church: Indigenous and Ecumenical," *PA* 11.241-258. Also in : *C&HV* 252-269.

1964j Review of "Estudios Chocóes: I," by S. Henry Wassen; and "Gramática comparada de un dialecto del Chocó: II," in *Etnologiska Estudier* 26, by Nils H. Holmer, *American Anthropologist* (hereafter *AA*) 66: 921-922.

1965a "A Mennonite Encounter with the 'Innermost' of the Lengua Indians," *Mennonite Quarterly Review* (hereafter *MQR*). Jan.40-67. Also reprinted in: *Evangelical Mennonite: The Messenger* 29 Oct.4-6; 12 Nov.2-4; 26 Nov.4-5. Also abridged in: *MBH* 19 Jan.4-8; 26 Jan.4-8. Also translated into German by Guenter Schulze in: *Das Mennoblatt* (hereafter *Mb*) 64/22.4,23.5,24.2; 65/1.4,2.2,3.2,4.3, 6.3,8.3,11.2,12.2. See 1965o.

1965b Field, Term and Timing in Missionary Method. *PA* 12.1- 21. Also in: *C&HV* 377-385.

1965c "Self-Exposure: Bridge to Fellowship," *PA* 12.49-62. Also as: "Key to fellowship," *MBH* 2 July 4-7. Also abridged in: *HIS* Nov/66.1-5. Also in: *The Mennonite* 12 Mar.187-189. Also in: *Gospel Herald* 21 Mar.256-257, 28 Mar.270-271. Also summarized in: *Concern* 14.61-62. Also translated into Spanish as: "Quitemos neustras máscaras," *Pensamiento Cristiano* (hereafter *PC*) Dec/68.244-254. Also in: *C&HV* 54-67.

1965d "Literacy: Bridge in Chocó Evangelism," *PA* 12.76-84. Also as: "Finding a trellis," *MBH* 19 Aug/66.4-6. Also in: *C&HV* 377-385.

1965e "Language: Vernacular, Trade or National?" *PA* 12.97-106. Also in: Wm A. Smalley, ed., *Readings in Missionary Anthropology II* (hereafter *Readings II*), enlarged edition. Pasadena, CA: Wm Carey Library, 1978, pp.663-672.

1965f "Mennonite, Chaco Indians and the Lengua Spirit World," *MQR*, Oct.280-306. Also translated into German by Guenter Schulze in: *Mb* 65/16.3,17.3, see 1965p.

1965g "Missionaries and Anthropologists Cooperate in Research," *PA* 12.158-190. Also in: *Readings II* 844-876.

1965h "Reflections of shamanism, illness and power in the church life of the Toba Indians in the Argentine Chaco," *Tabor College Research Bulletin* 2(2).1-62.

1965i "The Way to First Class: Revolution or Conversion?" *PA* 12.193-209. Also in *C&HV* 91-110.

1965j Reply to: "Is 'reciprocity' dangerous?" *PA* 12.240.

1965k "Shamanism, Illness and Power in Toba Church Life," *PA* 12.250-280. (Co-authored with Albert Buckwalter & James Kratz.) Also in: *C&HV* 178-288.

1965l Review of *Introducing Social Change: A Manual of Overseas Americans*, by Conrad M. Arensberg and Arthur H. Niehoff, *PA* 12: 287-288.

1965m "The Way to First-class: Rebellion or Conversion?" *PA* 12.193-209. Reprinted with modifications in *MBH* under "To become a man. . . ," Dec 3.4-6.

1965n *Informe del primer retiro de pastores y líderes láicos*. Quito, Ecuador: La Confraternidad Evangélica Ecuatoriana (Transcribed and mimeographed from tape recordings by Washington Padilla.)

1965o "Mennoniten begegnen dem Innern des Lengua-Indianers," Translated into German by Guenter Schulze in: *Mb* 64/22.4,23.5,24.2; 65/1.4,2.2, 3.2,4.3,6.3,8.3,11.2,12.2. (See 1965a).

1965p "Der Lengua-Christ und die Geisterwelt," *Mb* 16.3,17.3.

1966a "A Personal Reaction to 'New Wineskins for Old Wine'," by Delbert Wiens. *CL* 26 Apr.4-6.

1966b "A Personal Reaction to 'New Wineskins for Old Wine'," *MBH* 29 Apr.4-6.

1966c "An Anatomy of an Unfinished Crisis in Chulupi Culture Change," Anthropological Supplement to *Revista del Ateneo Paraguayo* 2.231-234.

1966d *Diferéncias Culturales y el desarrollo de la Iglesia: Algunos problemas de la iglesia idígena que provienen del fondo cultural.* Guatemala: Conferencia Pro-Obra Indígena. Apr/66.

1966e *Principios básicos de la traducción*. Lima, Peru: Sociedad Bíblica. Dec/66.

1966f "Aureliano: Profile of a Prophet," *PA* 13.97-114. (Co- authored with F. Glenn Prunty.) Also in: *C&HV* 73-90.

1966g "From nomadism to sedentary agriculture," *AI* 26.27-42.

1966h "How goes Scripture translation?" *Latin American Evangelist*. Feb. 8-10.

1966i "The Question in the Communication of the Gospel," *PA* 13.213-226. Also in: *Readings II* 649-662.

1966j "Lengua Indians and Their 'Innermost'," *PA* 13.252-272. Also in: *C&HV* 135-155.

1966k *Problemas de la communicación del evangelio*. Lima, Peru: Sociedades Bíblicas, Instituto Francisco Penzotti.

1966l "Reciprocity in Identification," *ML* Jan.10-18.

1966m Review of *The Life History and Anthropological Science*, by L.L. Langness, *PA* 13: 285-286.

1966n "Toward Communication That Scratches. . . Where It Itches," Students Section, *The Canadian Mennonite* 19 Apr.1-2.

1967a "Role, self-image, and missionary communication: the missionary role," *The Journal of Church and Society* (hereafter *JCS*) Spring 3-22.

1967b "Socialization, social control and the indigenous church," *JCS* Fall 37-63.

1967c "Unsere geschlossenen Türen," *Mb* 1 Sep.3-4.

1967d "Unsere geschlossnen Türen und was dahinter steckt," *Mb* 16 Aug.2-3.

1967e "Bible translating in indigenous languages in South America," *UBS Bulletin* 72.173-177.

1967f "Guidelines for Self-exposure," *HIS* Jan.30-32.

1967g *Hacia la communicación con impacto*. Huampani, Peru: Congreso de Comunicaciones Evangélicas, 16-22 Sep.

1967h "I want to be a human being too," *World Vision Magazine* (hereafter *WVM*) Dec.10-12,28.

1967i "Lengua Festivals and Functional Substitutes," *PA* 14.15-36. Also in: *C&HV* 156-177.

1967j "Matrices for eliciting translation vocabulary," *TBT* 18.184-191.

1967k "Missions and the Problems of Cultural Background," in A.J. Klassen, ed., *The Church in Mission*. Fresno, CA.: MB Board of Christian Literature. (pp.286-318.)

1967l The work of a translation consultant. "Oh boy!" *Youth's Christian Companion* (hereafter *YCC*) 48.5-6. (Co-authored with Phil Guglielmo.)

1967m "Our closed doors and what's behind them," *MBH* 9 Jun.22-25. Also translated into German by Guenter Schulze, see 1967c.

1967n "Our closed doors and how we avoid opening them," *MBH* 7 Jul.4-6. Also translated into German by Guenter Schulze, see 1967d.

1967o "Opening our closed door," *MBH* 4 Aug.4-7. Also translated into German by Guenter Schulze, see 1968t.

1967p "Religion, Drives and the Place Where It Itches," *PA* 14.49-72. Also in: *C&HV* 3-26.

1967q "Role, Self-Image and Missionary Communication," *PA* 14.145-160. (Co-authored with Anne Loewen.) Also in: *C&HV* 412-427.

1967r "The Christian encounter with culture," Part I, *WVM* Jan.13,20,28; Part II, Feb.13,26,30: Part III, Mar.11,22,30. (Also published in booklet form.)

1967s "The 'Missionary' Role," *PA* 14.193-208. (Co-authored with Anne Loewen.) Also in: *C&HV* 428-443.

1967t Review of *Manual for Kinship Analysis*, by Ernest L. Schusky, *PA* 14: 285-286.

1967u Review of *A Casebook for Social Change*, by Arthur H. Niehoff, *PA* 14: 285-286.

1967v "Toward a New Testament in Guaraní Popular," *TBT* 18.33- 39.

1968a "Why Minority Languages Persist or Die," *PA* 15.8-15.

1968b "Mission to Smaller Tribes: Challenge, Problems and Responsibility," *PA* 15.49-62. Also in: *C&HV* 386-399.

1968c "From Tribal Society to National Church," *PA* 15.97-111. Also in: *C&HV* 270-286.

1968d "Now God talks the way we speak," *Bible Society Record* (hereafter *BSR*) 113.58.

1968e "Quitemos nuestras máscaras," *PC* 15(60).244-254.

1968f "Relevant roles for overseas workers," *International Review of Missions* (hereafter *IRM*) LVII(226).233-244.

1968g Review of *The American Indian: Perspectives for the Study of Social Change*, by Fred Eggan, *PA* 15: 138-139.

1968h "Socialization and Social Control: A Resume of Processes," *PA* 15.145-156. Also in: *JCS* Fall 37-63, see 1967b. Also in: *C&HV* 211-222. Also in: *Global Civilization Foundations*, William L. Osborne & Ralph D. Winter, eds., 1994:23b-1-23b-9.

1968i Review of *How to Learn an Unwritten Language*, by Sarah C. Gudschinsky, *PA* 15: 189-191.

1968j Review of *A Workbook in Language Teaching with Special Reference to English as a Foreign Language*, by Earl W. Stevick, *PA* 15: 189-191.

1968k "The Indigenous Church and Resocialization," *PA* 15.193-204. Also in: *C&HV* 223-234.

1968l Review of *Reader in Comparative Religion: An Anthropological Approach*, by William A. Lessa and Evon Z. Vogt, eds., *PA* 15: 229-231.

1968m Review of *Field Methods in the Study of Culture*, by Thomas Rhys Williams, *PA* 15: 231-234.

1968n Review of *The Dusun: A North Borneo Society*, by Thomas Rhys Williams, *PA* 15: 231-234.

1968o Review of *A Kwakiutl Village and School*, by Harry F. Wolcott, *PA* 15: 235-238.

1968p Review of *Field Linguistics: A Guide to Linguistic Field Work*, by William J. Samarin, *PA* 15: 238-239. Also in: *IRM* LVII (225).127-129.

1968q Review of *Role Theory: Concepts and Research*, by Bruce J. Biddle and Edwin J. Thomas, *PA* 15: 283-285.

1968r "The Hazards of Contact with Unreached Tribes: A Manual for Martyrs," *WVM* Jul-Aug.11-13,17,45.

1968s “Traducciones de la Bíblia para América Latina,” *El Discípulo Cristiano* Feb.5-7.

1968t “Wie wir unsere geschlossenen Türen öffnen können,” *Mb* Feb.2-3, Mar.3-5.

1968u “Confession in the indigenous church,” *JCS* Fall 49-62.

1968v “The War of Words,” *The Youth Worker*, July-Dec.27-31.

1969a “Can Child Conversion Last?” *MBH* 17 Oct.2-6. (Co-authored with Anne Loewen.)

1969b “Socialization and Conversion in the Ongoing Church,” *PA* 16.1-17. Also in: *C&HV* 235-251.

1969c Review of *Communication and Culture: Readings in the Codes of Human Interaction*, by Alfred C. Smith, ed., *PA* 16: 44-46.

1969d “Confession, Catharsis and Healing,” *PA* 16.63-74. Also in: *C&HV* 287-298.

1969e Review of *Comparative Theories of Social Change*, by Peter W. Hollis, ed., *PA* 16: 87-89.

1969f Review of *Sociolinguistics* (Proceedings of the UCLA Sociolinguistics Conference, by William Bright, *PA* 16: 89-90.

1969g Review of *Introducing Culture*, by Ernest L. Schusky and T. Patrick Culbert, *PA* 16: 90-91.

1969h Review of *Advice from the Field: Towards a New Missiology*, by Joseph A. McCoy, *PA* 16: 91-92.

1969i “Confession in the Indigenous Church,” *PA* 16.114-127. Also in: *C&HV* 299-312.

1969j “Ingjapam’s Word: The Lengua New Testament,” *TBT* 20.24-28.

1969k Review of *Knowing the Gururumba*, by Philip L. Newman, *PA* 16: 133-134.

1969l Review of *Law and Warfare: Studies in the Anthropology of Conflict*, by Paul Bohannan, ed., *PA* 16: 134-135.

1969m “It Wasn’t in Vain,” *CL* 16 Dec.6-7.

1969n “Look behind the door,” *HIS* June.14-17.

1969o “Los Lengua y su mundo espiritual,” Anthropological Supplement to *Revista del Ateneo Paraguayo* 4.115-133.

1969p “Mythology and Missions,” *PA* 16.147-192. 1969p-v also in: *Readings II* 287-332.

1969q “I. Myth and Mission: Should a Missionary Study Tribal Myths?” *PA* 16.147-150.

1969r “II. The Structure and Content of Myths,” *PA* 16.150-159.

1969s "III. The Function of Myth in Society," *PA* 16.159-170. Also in: *Gaba Publications* 14:1-12. See 1969pp.

1969t "IV. The Dynamics of Myth-Changing and Mythmaking," *PA* 16.170-178.

1969u "V. Myth Analysis," *PA* 16.178-185.

1969v "VI. Myth As An Aid To Missions," *PA* 16.185-192.

1969w "Only a fool runs for nothing," *WVM* Jun.16-18. Also in: *MBH* 12 Jul.9,23.

1969x Review of *The Anthropologist Looks at Myth*, by Melville Jacobs and John Greenway, eds., *PA* 16: 238.

1969y Review of *Studies on Mythology*, by Robert H. Georges, ed., *PA* 16: 239.

1969z "Open Your Locked Doors of Guilt," *HIS* Oct.9-12.

1969aa *Theorie und Praxis des Übersetzens.* (Translation of: E. A. Nida and C. R. Taber, *The Theory and Practise of Translation*). Stuttgart: Weltbund der Bibelgesellschaften, 1969. (Co-translated with R. Kassuehlke.)

1969bb "God's Master Key," *HIS* Nov.26-29.

1969cc Review of *Myths of Creation*, by Philip Freund, *PA* 16: 240.

1969dd Review of *The Myths and Legends of Ancient Israel*, by Angelo S. Rappoport, *PA* 16: 240.

1969ee Review of *The Sacred and the Profane: The Nature of Religion*, by Mircea Eliade, *PA* 16: 240.

1969ff Review of *Myth and Mythmaking*, by Henry A. Murray, ed., *PA* 16: 240.

1969gg Review of *The Golden Bough*, by Sir James Fraser, *PA* 16: 240.

1969hh Review of *Magic, Science and Religion and other Essays*, by B. Malinowski, *PA* 16: 240.

1969ii Review of *Human Communication Theory: Original Essays*, by Frank E. X. Dance, *PA* 16: 276-277.

1969jj Review of *War: The Anthropology of Armed Conflict and Aggression*, by Morton Fried, Marvin Harris and Robert Murphy, eds., *PA* 16: 277-278.

1969kk Review of *Die Arahaibu-Indianer in Nordwest Brasilien*, by Franz Knobloch, *PA* 16: 287-288.

1969ll Review of *Yanomamö: The Fierce People*, by Napoleon A. Chagnon, *PA* 16: 287-288.

1969mm "The training of national translators in South America: I," *TBT* 20.131-141.

1969nn "Working As a Translation Consultant," *Focus* 1(3).1-3. The Union Church of Lima, Peru.

1969oo Review of *The Hutterites in North America*, by John A. Hostetler and

Gertrude Enders Huntington, *PA* 16: 278-279.

1969p "The function of myth in society," Gaba publications reprint 14, Kampala: Gaba Publications, Pastoral Institute of Eastern Africa. Also in: *PA* 16.4.

1970a "A Message For Missionaries From Mopass," *PA* 17.16-27. Also in: *C&HV* 400-411.

1970b "El habla Chocó 1787-1788," *Hombre y Cultura* 2(1).29-55.

1970c Review of *As Others See Us: The United States through Foreign Eyes*, by Franz M. Joseph, ed., *PA* 17: 36-37.

1970d Review of *The Swampy Cree: A Study in Acculturation*, by Leonard Mason, *PA* 17: 37-38.

1970e Review of *Contemporary Change in Traditional Societies, III: Mexican and Peruvian Communities*, by Julian H. Steward, *PA* 17: 38-39.

1970f Review of *The Savage and the Innocent*, by David Mayberry-Lewis, *PA* 17: 39.

1970g Review of *Microcosm: Structural, Psychological and Religious Evolution in Groups*, by Philip Slater, *PA* 17: 39.

1970h Review of *Magic, Witchcraft and Curing*, by John Middleton, ed., *PA* 17: 39-40.

1970i Review of *Gods and Rituals: Readings in Religious Beliefs and Practices*, by John Middleton, ed., *PA* 17: 40-41.

1970j Review of *The Antecedents of Self-esteem*, by Stanley Coopersmith, *PA* 17: 41-42.

1970k Review of *Social Work and Social Change: A Case Study in Indian Village Development*, by Sugata Dasgupta, *PA* 17: 42.

1970l Review of *The School at Mopass: A Problem of Identity*, by A. Richard King, *PA* 17: 42-43.

1970m "J.A. Loewen helps Church find their Role," *MBH* 9 Jan.16. (Co-authored with H. Friesen.)

1970n "The Social Context of Guilt and Forgiveness," *PA* 17.80-96. Also in: *C&HV* 313-329.

1970p "Four Kinds of Forgiveness," *PA* 17.153-168. Also in: *C&HV* 330-348.

1970q "The training of national translators in South America--II," *TBT* 21.10-20.

1970r Review of *Beyond the Frontier: Social Process and Cultural Change*, by Paul Bohannan and Fred Plog, eds., *PA* 17: 182-183.

1970s Review of *The Nature of Conversion: A Study of Forty-five Men and Women Who Changed Their Religion*, by Albert I. Gordon, *PA* 17: 188.

1970t Review of *When Prophecy Fails*, by Leon Festinger, Henry W. Riecken, and Stanley Schlachter, *PA* 17: 188-189.

1970u Review of *Stranger and Friend: The Way of an Anthropologist*, by Hortense Powdermaker, *PA* 17: 238-239.

1970v Review of *Anthropologists in the Field*, by D.J. Jongmans and P.C.W. Gutkind, *PA* 17: 238-239.

1970w Review of *The Craft of Social Anthropology*, by A.L. Epstein, ed., *PA* 17: 238-239.

1970x Review of *Solomon Islands Christianity: A Study in Growth and Obstruction*, by A.R. Tippett, *PA* 17: 239-240.

1970y Review of *Conflict in Culture: Problems of Developmental Change Among the Cree*, by Norman A. Chance, ed., *PA* 17: 287-288.

1971a "El cambio cultural entre los Chocó de Panama," *Patrimonio Histórico* 1.61-72. Also in: *AI* 32.159-168.

1971b "Form and meaning in translation," *TBT* 22.169-174.

1971c "Gottes Wort in der Sprache der Menschen," *Evangelische Zeitschrift* 28(3).113-122.

1971d "Paraguay: Stimmen Indianischer Christen," *Mennonitisches Jahrbuch*. Karlsruhe: Hans Schneider fuer die Konferenz der Sueddeutschen Mennonitengemeinden. (pp.76-80.)

1971e Review of *Klotzrennen Brasilianischer Indianer*, by Vera-Dagny Staehle, *AA* 73: 899.

1971f Review of *Comparative Functionalism: An Essay in Anthropological Theory*, by Walter Goldschmidt, *PA* 18: 44-45.

1971g Review of *Applied Anthropology*, by George M. Foster, *PA* 18: 45-46.

1971h Review of *Being an Anthropologist: Fieldwork in Eleven Cultures*, by George D. Spindler, *PA* 18: 185-186.

1971i Review of *Women in the Field: Anthropological Experience*, by Peggy Golde, ed., *PA* 18: 185-186.

1971j Review of *Latin American Peasant Movements*, by Henry A. Landsberger, ed., *PA* 18: 234-235.

1971k Review of *Christianity and the Shona*, by Marshall W. Murphee, *PA* 18: 239-240.

1971l Review of *Marginal Natives: Anthropologists at Work*, by Morris Freilich, ed., *PA* 18: 287-288.

1971m *Mirror for the Indians*. *CL* 29 Oct.8-9.

1972a "Anthropology," in: Robert W. Smith, ed., *Christ and the Modern Mind*. Downers Grove, IL.: Intervarsity Press. pp.135-146.

1972b "Bible translation goes mod," *Mirror* Oct.14.

1972c "Criticism can be helpful," *TBT* 23.234-240.

1972d *Drills for translator training: A workbook*. (Tentative edition prepared for the Rueschlikon Workshop.) United Bible Societies.

1972e "Language that communicates," *Evangelical Missions Quarterly* (hereafter *EMQ*) 8(3).147-152.

1972f Review of *Witchcraft, Sorcery and Social Categories among the Safwa*, by Alan Harwood, *PA* 19: 47-48.

1972g Review of *Reality and Dream: Psychotherapy of a Plains Indian*, by George Deveraux, *PA* 19: 141.

1972h Review of *Politics of Social Research: An Inquiry into the Ethics and Responsibilities of Social Scientists*, by Ralph L. Beals, *PA* 19: 141-142.

1972i Review of *Take out Hunger: Two Case Studies of Rural Development in Basutoland*, by Sandra Wallman, *PA* 19: 142.

1972j Review of *Kinship and Marriage among the Anlo Ewe*, by G. K. Nukunya, *PA* 19: 142-143.

1973a *A workbook of drills for popular language Bible translating*. (Mimeographed.) Lusaka, Zambia: United Bible Societies.

1973b *Popular language Bible translating*. A Training Course for African Bible Translators. Tapescript (of seven tapes). Lusaka, Zambia: United Bible Societies.

1973c *A handbook of diagrams for translator training*, to accompany tapescript of popular language Bible translating. Lusaka, Zambia: United Bible Societies.

1973d *Preparing meaningful literature: Some insights from cultural anthropology*. Chilema, Malawi: Malawi Literature Consulation.

1973e "'He too will eat' church says," *MBH* 21 Sep.15.

1973f "How young churches grow," *CL* 18 Sep.9.

1973g "Leadership in the Chocó Church," *Missiology* (hereafter *Mss*) 1(1).73-90.

1974a "Anthropologists and Missionaries Face to Face," *Mss* 2.161-174. (Co-authored with Donald R. Jacobs.)

1974b "Problems for export: I," *Milligan Missiogram* (hereafter *MM*) 1(4).4-11.

1974c "Problems for export II: The paid pastor," *MM* 3 (2).5-13.

1974d "Response to Dr. Ralph D. Winter's Paper," (The highest priority: Cross-cultural evangelism.) In: *Let the earth hear his voice*. Minneapolis: Worldwide Publications, pp.244-252.

1974e "The inspiration of translation: A growing personal conviction," in: Robert G. Bratcher, John J. Kijne, and William A. Smalley, eds., *Understanding and Translating the Bible*. New York: American Bible Society. pp.86-100.

1974f "Why Bantu translators use RSV and TEV as their textual base," *TBT* 25.412-416.

1974g "Raamattu jota melkien ei tehtykaan," *Raamattu-laketys* 4.12-14.

1975a "Listening with the Third Ear," *MBH* 7 Feb.2-5,7. Also reprinted in: *Moody Monthly*, Nov.44-51, see 1975i.

1975b "The Bible that almost wasn't," *UBS World Report* 64.9-10.

1975c "An Open Letter to my Mother," *MBH* 21 Mar.5.

1975d "Non-literal meanings I: How to recognize and use them effectively in translation," *TBT* 26.223-233.

1975e "Evangelización y cultura," (translated into Spanish by René Padilla). *Certeza* 58.42-46.

1975f "Non-literal meanings II: What makes them so difficult to translate," *TBT* 26.434-440.

1975g *Culture and human values: Christian intervention in anthropological perspective*. Pasadena: Wm. Carey Library.

1975h Review of *Vierhundert Jahre Araukanermission*, by Albert Noggler; *Franziskanermissionen in Brasilien 1500-1966*, by Venancio Willeke; and *Die Katolizität der Kirche und die Mission*, by Fritz Kollbrunner, *Mss* 3: 253-256.

1975i "Listening with the Third Ear," *Moody Monthly*. Nov.44,45,48,50-51.

1976a "Evangelism and Culture," in: René Padilla, ed., *The new face of evangelicalism*. London: Hodder and Stoughton. Chapter 10.175-189.

1976b "Gott spricht am liebsten in der Muttersprache," *Bibel Report* (hereafter *BR*) 4.2-3.

1976c "Roles: Relating to alien social structure," *Mss* 4.217-242.

1976d "Mission churches, independent churches, and felt need in Africa," *Mss* 4.405-425.

1976e "Non-literal meanings III: Practical suggestions for translators," *TBT* 27.201-209.

1976f "Weisst du, Bruder," *MBH* 29 Oct.7.

1976g "A Tribute to David Wirsche," *CL* 23 Nov.20.

1977a "Übersetzer bereut Kleinglauben," *BR* 10(1).2-3.

1977b "Through the New Testament termite style," *UBS World Report* 84.16-17.

1977c "Three models for missions," *The Mennonite* 92(32).13 Sep. 514-515. Also in: *CL* 11/Oct.5-6. Also as: "Missions today (2): Three models for kingdom building," *Mennonite Reporter* (hereafter *MR*) 3/Oct.5-6.

1978a "Makhua: The translation nothing could stop," *UBS World Report* 88.12-13.

1978b "'The Gospel and Culture': Five Evaluations: A new openness to anthropological concerns," *Gospel in Context* 1 Apr/1978:18-19.

1978c "Dialogue: Solicited Comments on 'A Contextualized Church: The Bali Experience'," *Gospel in Context* 1 Apr/1978:26.

1979a "Some keys or a piece of rope," *MBH* 6 Jul.11-13.

1979b "Training translators to write in their own language," *TBT* 30.224-230.

1979c "Testing your translation," *TBT* 31.229-234.

1980a "The Gospel--Its Content and Communication: An Anthropological Perspective," in: John Stott and Robert Coote, eds., *The Gospel and Culture*. Pasadena, CA.: Wm. Carey Library. pp.154-174. Also in: Robert T. Coote and John R. Stott., eds., *Down to Earth*. Grand Rapids: Wm. Eerdman's Publishing Co., pp.115-130.

1980b Review of *The Image of God among the Sotho-Tswana*, by Gabriel M. Setilone, *Mission Focus* (hereafter *MF*) 8(1).16-17.

1980c "So that's what God wanted to say!" *UBS Bulletin* 90.5

1980d "The Christian witness to new religious movements," *Lausanne Occasional Papers*. No. 11. (Co-edited with Paul Landry.)

1981a "What kind of timers does your conscience have?" *MBH* 24 Apr.2-3.

1981b *The Practice of Translating*. New York: United Bible Societies.

1981c *The Practice of Translating: Old Testament Supplement*. Lome, Togo: United Bible Societies.

1981d *The Practice of Translating: New Testament Supplement*. Lome, Togo: United Bible Societies.

1982a "Adjusting biblical names: Nzema case." *TBT* 33.229-235. (Co-authored with Gilbert Ansre.)

1982b "Some figures of speech in Hosea," *TBT* 33.238-242.

1982c Review of *La Tradition Orale comme Source d'histoire: Quatre Problemes Particuliers*, by W. J. Vansina, *Relevant Ramblings* (hereafter *RR*) BB-11.

1983a *La pratique de la Traduction*. Paris: Alliance Biblique Universelle. (Translated into French by Mme. O. Echtler.)

1983b "Can it be real if it is expressed only in metaphor?" *Direction* 12(1).10-13.

1983c Review of *Scientific creationism: An exegesis for a religious doctrine*, by R. C. Williams, *RR* EE-12.

1983d Review of *Figurative language and the definition of experience: The role of ox-songs in Atuot social theory*, by John W. Burton, *RR* EE-13.

1983e "The 'world' in John's gospel through West African eyes," *TBT* 34.407-413.

1983f "An annotated West African Psalm," *TBT* 34.420-424.

1983g "Strengths and weaknesses of the M.B. Church: As seen by a representative from the United Bible Societies," in: H. Brucks, *Another look at the Mennonite Brethren Church*. Winnipeg, MB.: Canadian conference of the M.B. Church.

1983h "Clean Air or Bad Breath?" *TBT* 34.213-219.

1983i "Developing Moralnets: Twenty-Five Years of Culture Change Among the Chocó," *Missionaries, Anthropologists, and Culture Change*. Studies in Third World Societies, Sept. Publication 25. (Book on shelves)

1984a "Translating the names of precious stones," *TBT* 35.229-233.

1984b Review of *The Moral order: An introduction to the human situation*, by Raoul Naroll, *RR* GG-15.

1984c Review of *Evangiles*, by Andre Chouraqui, *RR* GG-14.

1984d "The names of God: Introduction," *TBT* 35.201.

1984e "The names of God in the Old Testament," *TBT* 35.201-207.

1984f "The names of God in the New Testament," *TBT* 35.208-211

1984g "When you pray. . . ," *Direction* 13(3).33-43.

1984h Review of *Elilim*, by Carlton T. Hodge, *RR* GG-21.

1984i Review of *L'influence de la traduction de la Bible par Martin Luther sur la traduction tcheque de la Bible*, Jiri Elman, *RR* HH-12.

1984j Review of *Quality in translation oder wann ist eine Übersetzung gut?* by Katharina Reiss, *RR* HH-43.

1985a "Witnessing--encouragement in obedience," *MBH* Feb.22 2-4.

1985b "Missionaries: Drivers or spare tires?" *Seeds* March 16-19. Also in: *IRM* "Reflections on mission." LXXV 299.253-260 July 1986.

1985c "Translating the names of God: How to choose the right name in the target language," *TBT* 36-201-207.

1985d "A new look at section headings in West African translations," *TBT* 36.237-241.

1985e "For whom am I translating," *Notes on Translation* 107.9-12. Also in: *TBT* 37.201-204.

1985f "Translating the names of God: How European languages have translated them," *TBT* 36.401-411.

1985g Review of *Tribal Gods or Universal God*, by Kosuke Koyama, *RR* JJ-13.

1985h "Air pur ou mauvaise haleine?" *Cahiers de traduction biblique* 5.3-10.

1986a "Which God Do Missionaries Preach?" *Mss* XIV 1, January 1986.

1986b "The translation of 'holy' in Monkole: Solving a problem," *TBT* 37.222-227.

1986c Review of *Anthropological Insights for Missionaries*, by Paul G. Hiebert, *Mss* 4: 524.

1986d "Who Am I Translating For?" *TBT* 37.201-204.

1986e "Toward contextualization: An analysis of factors motivating or inhibiting syncretism," Paper read at Consultation of Theologians and Anthropologists, Biola University, Apr.14-15, 1986.

1987a "Focus on Translators," *TBT* 38.244-246.

1987b "Culture broker bridges 'vast area of ignorance' with fresh look at god concepts," *MR* May 25. 5.

1987c "Let's make peace with our parents," *MBH* June 12.6-8.

1987d Review of *The Praxis of Suffering: An Interpretation of Liberation and Political Theologies*, by Rebecca S. Chopp, *MF* June 28-29.

1987e "Pour qui dois-je traduire?" *Cahiers de traduction biblique* 8.16-19.

1987f "Demon Possession and Exorcism in Africa, in the New Testament Context and in North America," *Bondage & Deliverance (Exorcism) Consultation*. July 30-Aug.1. Associated Mennonite Biblical Seminaries, Elkhart, Indiana.

1987g Review of *Allegories of the wilderness: Ethics and ambiguity in Kuranko narratives*, by Michael Jackson, *Missionalia* 15(1): 52-53.

1987h "Pastoral, Evangelistic and Missionary Discourse," in *Direction* 16(2).3-10.

1987i Review of *Oral Tradition as History*, by Jan Vansina, *Mss* XV 4, December.

1988a "Demon Possession and Exorcism in Africa, in the New Testament Context and in North America. Or: Toward a Western Scientific Model of Demon Possession and Exorcism," in: *Essays on Spiritual Bondage and Deliverance*. Willard M. Swartley, ed. *Occasional Papers* No. 11.118-145.

1988b Review of *Bible Translation: An Introductory Course in Translation Principles*, and an accompanying Teacher's Manual, by Katharine Barnwell, *TBT* (July 1988): 347-348

1988c "Wann Sitj dee Heeflijchtjeit mett dee Betjierung Fetsaubellt," *Mennonite Mirror*, 18 Oct. 1988.

1988d "Dear Bill," *MBH* 28 Oct. 1988 pp.2-5.

1988e "Strategies for Cross-Cultural Mission: Past/Present and Future," *MF* Dec. 16.4, pp.84-91.

1989a Review of *Ethik des Nord-Süd-Konflikts: Das Globale Machtgefälle Als Theologisches Problem*, by Klaus Nurnberger, *Mss* XVII.3 (July 1989): 361-362.

1989b "A moral basis for mission," *Share*, April-June 1989, pp.6-7.

1990a Review of *Translating the Message: The Missionary Impact on Culture*, by Lamin Sanneh, *Mss* XVIII.2 (April 1990): 229-230.

1990b "Stories From a Bible Translator," *Mandate* 21.3, 1990, pp.31-33.

1991a "Which God Do Missionaries Preach?" in C. Peter Wagner, *Territorial Spirits: Insights on Strategic-Level Spiritual Warfare from Nineteen Christian Leaders*. Chichester, England: Sovereign World Limited, 1991, pp.165-175.

1991b "Need to be aware of culture," letter to Editor in *MBH* 30.12, June 14/1991, p.8.

1991c Review of *Transculturation: The Cultural Factor in Translation and Other Communication Tasks*, by J. Daniel Shaw, *MF* (June 1991): 29.

1991d *Simply Trust Every Day*, The experiences of Johann Enns (in a forced labor camp in the USSR). Translated by Jacob A. Loewen.

1991e "Which God Do Missionaries Preach?" In C. Peter Wagner, *Engaging the Enemy: How to Fight and Defeat Territorial Spirits*. Ventura, CA.: Regal Books, 1991, pp.165-175.

1991f "Several Interpretations" (Letters), *MBH* Dec/6, 1991, pp.12-13.

1992a "Five Centuries of Protestant Christianity in Latin America," *MF* 1 Mar., 1992, pp.4-10.

1992b "What Is Happening in Anthropology?: An Example for Missionaries and Mission Boards." *MF* 3 Sept., 1992, pp.47-50.

1992c Review of *Translation as Mission: Bible Translation in the Modern Missionary Movement*, by William A. Smalley, *Mss* (July 1992): 402-403.

1993a "My Personal Pilgrimage Toward Peace," *ML* Sept/1993, pp.11-14.

1993b "Vignettes from my memories of John A. Harder," *The Harder Family Review*, edited by Leland Harder. 24th Issue, October 1993:10-12.

1994a *I've had a stroke*. Abbotsford, B.C.: For the Abbotsford Stroke Society.

1994b "Russian Mennonites, Property and the Sword," in Calvin Redekop, Victor A. Krahn & Samuel J. Steiner, eds., *Anabaptist/Mennonite Faith and Economics*. New York: University Press of America for Institute of Anabaptist and Mennonite Studies, Conrad Grebel College, Waterloo, Ontario, pp.41-67.

1995a "The Hopi 'Old Testament': A First-Person Essay," *Mss* XXIII. 2, 2 April, 1995.

1996a "The Abuse of Power Among Mennonites in South Russia 1789-1919," *JMS* Vol.14, 1996:17-44. (Co-authored with Wesley J. Prieb.)

1996b Review of *The Faith of the Unbeliever*, by Martin Robinson, *Mss* (July

1996):411-412.

1996c Review of *Anabaptistm: A Dying Candle*, by Walfried Goossen, *MQR* (July 1996):371-373.

1997a *Onze ieashte Missjounsreiz.* Winnipeg, Manitoba: Mennonite Books.

1997b *Only the Sword of the Spirit!* Fresno, CA.: MB Historical Society

1997c "Missionary Reflections on the Anabaptist Concept of the Priesthood of Believers," *MF* Vol. 5, 1997:105-114 (Co-authored with Ray Harms-Wiebe.)

1998a "My Pilgrimage in Mission," *International Bulletin* Vol.22, 2:69-72.

1998b *The Bible in Cross-Cultural Perspective.* Pasadena, CA.: William Carey Library.(Not yet published)

1998c *Educating Tiger: My spiritual and intellectual journey.*

1998d "Toward a Phonemic Alphabet of Plautdietsh," *JMS* Vol 16, 128-146

1998e "P.E. Schellenberg: The Professor Who Became My Friend," *Direction* Vol. 27, 1998:79-83.

1998f "My Personal Pilgrimage Toward Peace," *Alternative Service for Peace in Canada during World War II 1941-1946.* A.J. Klassen, Editor. Abbotsford, B.C.: Mennonite Central Committee, Seniors for Peace.

1999a Review of *A Guide to World Hunger Organizations, Volume II.* Published on line at www.charitycareers by Charity Careers, Aug. 9.

SUBJECT INDEX